Jane Eyre's
American Daughters

Jane Eyre's American Daughters

From *The Wide, Wide World*
to *Anne of Green Gables*
A Study of Marginalized Maidens
And What They Mean

John Seelye

DELAWARE

Newark: University of Delaware Press

Associated University Presses
2010 Eastpark Boulevard
Cranbury, NJ 08512

The paper used in this publication meets the requirements of the American National Standard for Permanence of Paper for Printed Library Materials Z39.48-1984

Library of Congress Cataloging-in-Publication Data

Seelye, John D.
    Jane Eyre's American daughters : from The wide, wide world to Anne of Green Gables : a study of marginalized maidens and what they mean / John Seelye.
        p. cm.
    Includes bibliographical references and index.
    ISBN 0-87413-886-8 (alk. paper)
    1. American fiction—Women authors—History and criticism.
2. Women in literature.   3. Gaskell, Elizabeth Cleghorn, 1810–1865. Life of Charlotte Brontë.   4. Montgomery, L. M. (Lucy Maud), 1874–1942. Anne of Green Gables.   5. Brontë, Charlotte, 1816–1855—Appreciation—North America.   6. Warner, Susan, 1819–1885. Wide, wide world.
7. Brontë, Charlotte, 1816–1855. Jane Eyre.   8. Brontë, Charlotte, 1816–1855—Influence.   9. Canadian fiction—English influences.
10. American fiction—English influences.   11. Women and literature—North America.   12. Marginality, Social, in literature.   I. Title
    PS374.W6S44   2005
    813′.4099287—dc22

                                                                    2004021290

For Leo
With Thanks

Contents

8   CONTENTS

Introduction

As is the mother, so is her daughter.
—The Book of the Prophet

A DISCUSSION OF THE GENESIS OF THIS STUDY, INCLUDING INDEBT-edness to other scholarly and critical authorities, may be found in the Afterword. But for the benefit of intended readers, a few words at the start seem required. Let me say therefore that the pages that follow are concerned with the literary dialectic that began with the publication in 1848 of Charlotte Brontë's *Jane Eyre:* the first part is a discussion of the contexts from which that phenomenally popular romance emerged; the second part is devoted to the main body of the study, being a discussion of a number of novels by American writers that were reactions, directly or indirectly, to *Jane Eyre.*

The popularity of Brontë's novel, along with the attack on it by a minority of Victorians outraged by its presumed impiety and frank dealing with sexual matters, inspired a number of writers in America to create alternative texts aimed at the same audience that had helped make *Jane Eyre* so widely read in the United States—young, primarily female, readers. Brontë was not seeking a youthful readership, indeed the notion of what we now call a young adult audience was not yet in place, but there is no doubt that her novel soon helped create that class of reader.

For one thing, being dependent in part on patterns adapted from the fairy tales that had been the author's favorite reading as a child, the story spoke in whispers as it were to a youthful audience. Chief among those tales was the story of Cinderella, with its marvelous transformations leading to marriage to a prince and the privileged life that rank and wealth can bring, a plot attractive to young women on the threshold of marriage themselves. We may doubt that the youthful readers of *Jane Eyre* were aware of these intertextual matters, yet we may presume that they exerted the power of archetypes drawn from folk sources.

Following the Civil War there was a sudden expansion of an American market for younger readers, signalled by novels of which Louisa May Alcott's *Little Women* (1868) was a pioneering and exemplary instance. I am not concerned here with the reasons for that rapid opening up of a new kind of literature, which have been discussed in a number of studies. I am however concerned with the extent to which Jane Eyre as a plucky yet sentimental heroine was replicated in the girls and young women who figure in books clearly intended for a juvenile readership. As with the adaptation of the Cinderella story to Brontë's gothic frame, the transliteration of the story of Jane Eyre to American versions necessitated some strategic changes to the original, which make up the burden of this study.

Instrumental in this process was Susan Warner's intensely pious *The Wide, Wide World,* which having been published in 1850 was virtually contemporary with *Jane Eyre.* Like Brontë's novel it concerned the travails of an orphaned girl, who, having endured hardships and indignities, eventually falls in love with a wealthy older man, who will marry her when she comes of age. But Warner's novel has a moralistic, sentimental emphasis rather than a gothic, sensational plot, and thereby provided an alternative text to *Jane Eyre.* Though it too was not intentionally pointed to a young readership, Warner's book proved to be popular among that class of readers attracted to Brontë's great romance.

The Wide, Wide World predictably influenced a subsequent generation of writers: Alcott's *Little Women,* the first part of which appeared in 1868, made even more revisions to the basic Cinderella plot, and is as much indebted to Warner as to Brontë. But closest to the pattern in Warner's novel is Martha Finley's *Elsie Dinsmore,* published the same year as Alcott's novel. Finley's book for children and its many sequels were once highly popular but now *Elsie* is a virtual pariah, the book like the child consigned to permanent ignomy for its tedious piety. Yet despite its overwhelming religious emphasis, Finley's novel contains elements we can call perverse, for the subtext is a thematic parable of incest, hints of which we find in *Jane Eyre.*

Chief of the novels discussed in the second part of this study are the following: the aforementioned *The Wide, Wide World, Little Women,* and *Elsie Dinsmore,* followed by three novels of Frances Hodgson Burnett—*Little Lord Fauntleroy, Sara Crewe,* and *The Secret Garden*—then Kate Douglas Wiggin's *Rebecca of Sunnybrook Farm,* Jean Webster's *Daddy-Long-Legs,* Eleanor Porter's *Pollyanna,* and, by way of epilogue, L. M. Montgomery's *Anne of*

Green Gables. Whereas most of the intended readers of this book will undoubtedly be familiar with the Brontës' works, and perhaps with *Little Women*—which has enjoyed a well-deserved renascence of late—I expect that the other texts listed will not have been read by them, not at least in recent years.

Indeed, one motive of this study is to suggest that these are novels deserving serious consideration, that they carry ideological and thematic burdens abstracted from the culture that produced them, and are therefore of more interest than might be expected. They are also—although this is difficult to prove through exposition and explication of texts—quite readable stories still. But they are at this point distinctly marginal, which is to say they are noncanonical texts save for those persons who study children's literature as a scholarly field, much as their heroines—being orphans—are marginalized girls and young women. The novels therefore require a considerable amount of synopsis and quotation in order to convey their meanings. By contrast, *Jane Eyre* is so familiar a story as not to require considerable redaction.

I mention this distinction by way of explaining the obvious difference between the two parts of this study. The first part contains a relatively complex, circuitous argument, by which I hope to explicate on several planes the psychological and sexual implications of Charlotte Brontë's gothic romance. The second part is a much more linear discussion, moving chronologically and sequentially through the novels under discussion. I hope this divided method will be acceptable, and also that my readers will put up with extensive synopsis and quotation for the sake of the larger argument.

In anticipation of that argument, let me say that in *Jane Eyre* we have a special instance of mixed genres, the book being a domestic novel writhing in the embrace of a gothic romance. The heroine passes through several chambers of horror before finally surrendering joyfully to wedded bliss—hardly a traditional gothic finale, at least by the formulae established in America by Charles Brockden Brown and in England by Mary Shelley. Beyond its function as a Victorian fairy tale, *Jane Eyre* is also something of a sentimental fiction, placing considerable stress on the psychological suffering of the heroine, which traditionally promotes an identification of the protagonist with Christ. This Christian association in turn warrants the empowerment of women, which some feminist critics see as the chief function of the genre.

However, it is not womanhood that is empowered by Jane's suffering so much as the specific position of governess, that disjunct and marginalized social role that takes its meaning by occupying an untenable position within a domestic frame—a dysfunction that approximates the traditional stepdaughter role in the Cinderella myth. Henry James may possibly have been inspired by *Jane Eyre* in crafting *The Turn of the Screw,* where if we follow Edmund Wilson's Freudian reading the madwoman in the attic is internalized in the governess herself.

The hapless social position of a governess is seen by Charlotte Brontë as a perverse class phenomenon, where an intelligent young gentlewoman is placed in a privileged environment without privileges, a wealthy family circle in which she is neither servant nor relation. By contrast, James uses it in a traditional gothic plot, with psychological not social implications. In both stories, the gothic element is enhanced by the conventional situation of the governess as a stock figure, which approximates entrapment, thereby promoting horror.

It is the governess's love for the apparently unmarried male employer that is central both to Brontë's novel and to Edmund Wilson's reading of James's novella. It is an aspect of *Jane Eyre* that will be a telltale sign of the influence of Brontë's romance on so much subsequent American fiction. The male romantic interest in many of these novels is, like Rochester, somewhat older than the heroine, and a commanding even mentoring presence, a trope that may be dated back to Jane Austen's *Emma.* Charlotte Brontë read that novel (at the suggestion of one of her own mentors, William Smith Williams) but did not like it and in any event read it after having written *Jane Eyre.* Curiously, Brontë's last, unfinished novel was also called "Emma," toward what end we will never know.

Despite Brontë's negative reaction, we cannot dismiss Jane Austen's influence on the emerging pattern, especially in realistic fiction of the post–Civil War period in America, the author being held in high regard by Howells and Henry James. But what intervened and is so prominently displayed in the figure of Rochester is the Byronic idea, the erotic amalgam of heroic daring and tragic doom that had a hold on the imaginations of romantic writers in America, from James Fenimore Cooper to Harriet Beecher Stowe. As we will see, the figure of Byron gave new meaning to the inherited Cinderella myth as used by Charlotte Brontë. Then too there is the ubiquitous influence of Charles Dickens, for where Austen's heroines are uniformly if often imperfectly blessed with parents, Jane Eyre and most of her American daughters are not, but are examples of those orphans so central to the Victorian version of sentimentality in fiction.

Equally important in determining the dominant position of *Jane Eyre* is the struggle central to American novels aimed at young female readers in which an adolescent woman attempts to gain maturity and ascendancy over the terms of her world, an adversarial bildungsroman often associated with the exercise of creative talents. That is, these heroines at once suggest both Jane Eyre and Charlotte Brontë herself, thanks to Elizabeth Gaskell's biography. Given Gaskell's novelistic talents, the book not coincidentally reads like a work of fiction, domestic at the core and operating within the sentimental mode.

The gothic spirit of *Jane Eyre* does not seem to have appealed to the women writers in America, who provided alternative texts. That is, they borrowed its moral emphasis but eschewed the sensational aspects. During the post–Civil War years the rise of literary realism influenced writers like Louisa May Alcott, for whom gothicism was associated with the wilder aspects of romanticism. These writers also revived the theme of female influence, which waxed and waned during the late eighteenth and early nineteenth centuries, but which plays a defining role in the sentimental version of literary realism in America.

That is, in cloning Jane Eyre as a bright band of young American girls, these authors gentled down the original book—doing to the novel what the shears of fate in the hands of Charlotte Brontë did to Rochester—eliminating gothic and steamily erotic elements and adapting the domestic setting, the sentimental (i.e., Christian) element and the bildungsroman plot to the American scene. Moreover, it can be said that after 1860 Byronism in America was no longer in favor, having as it were gone down with Ahab and his ship or died with Augustus St. Clare.

Realism as in the post–*Uncle Tom* fiction of Harriet Beecher Stowe was gaining the ascendancy, and would fully emerge after 1870, the year Stowe published her defense of Lady Byron. Inspiring outrage in Great Britain, her disclosures of the poet's incestuous affair nonetheless made it impossible to regard the great poet as anything other than perverse in his erotic preferences. Whatever their resemblances to Edward Rochester, the older men with whom young American heroines fall in love in the books under discussion here have no more similarity to Byron than does Silas Lapham.

Jane Eyre's American Daughters

I
Charlotte's Web

The wicked are wicked, no doubt, and they go astray and they fall, and they come by their deserts; but who can tell the mischief which the very virtuous do?

—Thackeray

1

What's That Noise up in the Attic?
Brontë Breathes New Life into Dead Forms

Yes, I am a fatal man, Madame. . . .
To inspire hopeless passion is my destiny.
                                    —Thackeray

I

IN *THE FEMININE FIFTIES* (1940) FRED LEWIS PATTEE RECALLED THAT his mother, who in the late 1840s was "a loom-tender in Lowell," had told him "how 'Jane Erie,' as her companions pronounced it, ran through the mill-girl community like an epidemic" (53). The Lowell women were to mid-nineteenth-century propagandists for the healthful, moral climate engendered by the industrial revolution in America an equivalent to airline stewardesses (a.k.a. flight attendants) of the mid-twentieth century, being drudgery incarnate attractively wrapped. Mill owners built living quarters for them, saw to it they were kept segregated from importuning males, provided libraries and reading rooms, underwrote a journal that published their literary efforts, and in all ways provided an atmosphere in which virtue engendered could take root, in effect a replicated if monstrous parlor.

These mill workers may not have been typical readers, their living conditions creating a dormitory atmosphere, in which fads, like the flu, can spread rapidly, but they certainly represented an intensification of a certain genus of American young womanhood, species New England. Spinsters on a massive scale, tending the thundering looms of Lowell, they lived nunlike lives, praying for a better world and fearing the consequences of becoming maids grown old. They spun romantic dreams as they went about their mechanical and repetitive work. Encouraged to improve their minds and souls by reading uplifting tracts by third-rate hacks, the mill maidens preferred to nourish their fantasy lives with the help

19

of that unique genius, Charlotte Brontë, whose alter ego, Jane Eyre, they took for their own.

Moreover, as an ad hoc family, young women thrown promiscuously together, they identified as well with the entire Brontëan package. As Pattee went on to recount the creation of *Jane Eyre*, "the story . . . fits the setting of the American mid-century as if it were a parable woven for illustration. Three daughters of the manse, marooned on a Yorkshire moor, held in an atmosphere rigidly religious, touching the world only through books that fed their imaginations, and escaping by means of literary creation of a world woven of their dreams and their longings. . . . So it was in dozens of New England homes."

But the mill women did not learn about the Haworth literary factory by reading its most famous production. The source of this information came from Elizabeth Gaskell's *Life of Charlotte Brontë* (1857), a presumed work of nonfiction that slid onto any shelf of domestic novels with effortless ease. We cannot separate the novel from the biography: they are the Chang and Eng of the unique communal world "of dreams and longings" that drew those nameless loom tenders toward their sewing sisters in the Haworth parsonage.

Written with the express purpose of portraying a pious martyr to domestic duty, thereby dispelling the conventional wisdom that the author's virtue had been somehow compromised by the erotic elements in her fiction, Gaskell fabricated from the life of Charlotte Brontë what she never herself created, an equivalent to the heroines of sentimental fiction. After 1857, readers would read *Jane Eyre* through the transforming lens of Gaskell's biography, a book that perfectly suited even as it influenced the sentimental spirit of the Feminine Fifties.

Alexander Cowie, in his magisterial *The Rise of the American Novel* (1951), included a chapter on those scribbling women of the 1850s about which Hawthorne grumbled, whose books were selling where his were not. Given the period in which Cowie himself was writing, the 1940s, his assessments were balanced, yet he was inevitably biased against the sentimentalism of the 1850s, forever alert to elements of nascent hence redemptive realism. In his introductory remarks to the chapter "The Domestic Sentimentalists," Cowie let down his scholarly guard and rendered a parodying formula that he had abstracted from their works, with an emphasis on the elements borrowed from *Jane Eyre*. In this sentimental stereotype, the transition from the abuse of a prepubescent female orphan at the hands of a cruel aunt (Mrs. Reed) to adolescent suffering tempered by the example of a young woman of the evangelical persuasion (Helen Burns/Miss Temple) is capped by the appearance of "a proud, handsome, moody, Rochester-like man aged about thirty who has traveled and sinned (very vaguely) in the Orient" (414).

"If it weren't for Queen Victoria," Cowie continues, "he would try to seduce her, but as it is he is reduced to proposing marriage. To his astonishment she refuses. This sends him darkly off on more travels," leaving the heroine to find work as a teacher or governess. During this period she endures "many trials" and performs "many pious acts," all the while talking "rather briskly about independence for women." The Rochester-like man eventually returns, thoroughly reformed but still very wealthy, and this time his proposal is accepted by the Eyre-like woman, who renounces her notion of "female independence, for she realizes that a woman's greatest glory is wifely submission." The novel ends with everybody "happy in a subdued, Christian sort of way" (415).

The humor of Cowie's parody is derived from exaggeration, and only a few of the novels he subsequently discusses conform to the pattern. Indeed, Nina Baym's discussion of the same works in *Woman's Fiction* (1978) finds little evidence of Brontëan influence, and Gillian Avery in *Behold the Child* (1994) limits the "deep impression" of *Jane Eyre* on American literature to two of Augusta Evans's novels (Baym, 30; Avery, 179). But Cowie's point is surely well taken in one respect, for if the mill women could identify with Brontë's heroine, it was in part because like her they succumbed to the charms of her charismatic if flawed because already married lover. Moreover, as Cowie's description suggests, New Rochester was but Old Byron restyled, much as Lord Byron was himself the virtual incarnation of the charismatic hero-villain of Scott's *Marmion.*

Charlotte Brontë was familiar with Sir Charles Grandison, Samuel Richardson's defender of maidenly virtue and in effect a knight in modern (ca. 1754) dress, and there is something of Grandison also in Rochester, both being blocked from marrying their true loves by a binding earlier commitment. But as his name advertises in bright red neon, Brontë's Rochester was also a modified reincarnation of the notorious Restoration libertine, as well as an updated version of the lustful, loveless Rake of the eighteenth century (and *Clarissa*). Thus Grandison nobly holds back from proposing to Harriet Byron because of a previous engagement to another woman, while Brontë's Rochester, hiding his first wife in the attic, arranges a rigged marriage to Jane, and then when foiled proposes a life lived in luxurious, uxorious sin.

Grandison is in the end freed from having to marry his deranged Italian fiancée on religious grounds, and is able to wed his true love, and it may be said that of that union there sprang Rochester, who is to both Grandison and Byron genetically bound. Between Byron and Rochester we find Zamorna, Charlotte Brontë's youthful projection of her wild romantic dreams, a towering figure inspired by Lord Byron and the Duke of Wellington, and perhaps by her brother and coadjutor, Branwell Brontë. The mill workers of Lowell had been weaned on Scott and nourished by Byron, both the man and his works, and were primed for the Zamorna-derived Rochester, who fit into the emerging pattern like a puzzle piece of the desired shape. Mrs. Gaskell added to this mix a bit of Haworth gossip about a young woman tricked into a bigamous marriage and then deserted with a bastard child, but the literary prototypes prevail.

Nor was Jane Eyre tricked into any kind of marriage, for she is a heroine as necessary to the emerging pattern as she is to Edward Fairfax Rochester, being no lovely and accomplished Harriet Byron or Clarissa Harlow, but a homely little woman with a moral fibre strong as steel. Whether as Clarissa Harlow in England or Charlotte Temple in America, those eighteenth-century damaged hence doomed women have names suggesting harlots, hinting that they are copartners in their own ruination, but Jane Eyre's name has no such connotation. "Miss Eyre," Rochester calls her, suggesting "Misère," thus tagging her as a woman of sorrows, female counterpart to the redemptive Christ. But those spinning women of Lowell came even closer to the truth, for, in pronouncing Jane's surname as "Erie" (i.e., "eerie"), they confirmed that the heroine has a power denied the suffering women of sentimental fiction, a wierdness suited to the gothic mode. Like Hawthorne's Hester Prynne, Jane Eyre is a woman of great psychic strength.

Rather than being seduced then abandoned by her lover, Jane Eyre plays the part of a redeeming woman, a romantic role inconceivable in the rational eighteenth century, where the impossibility of reforming a rake was the basis for novels in the Richardsonian tradition. Long-suffering but finally triumphant, Jane is reunited with her crippled but repentant lover. No "arrangement" for her, no love nest far across the channel, well outside the marriage vows. An orphan at the start of the story, dragged through the narrow, twisting, liminal conduit already set in place by Charles Dickens, she emerges at the end of the process a tough little woman, her very ordinariness a recommendation to her female fans, her great moral strength an inspiration.

As Nina Baym notes in *Woman's Fiction* (1978), it is this independent quality in heroines created along the lines of Jane Eyre that was prized by readers of domestic novels written in America: "The most exciting thing about the heroes of these novels is the intensity of their love for the heroine. This love is a measure of her power, for in a world where women are traditionally assumed to be the playthings of men nothing can be more satisfying than to see the tables turned. . . . The Byronic hero thus is particularly appealing when he becomes a victim precisely because he has victimized so many others" (290). Unlike their eighteenth-century counterparts, these heroines are capable of removing the teeth (as well as other dangerous parts) from the rake.

Jane's holding up under the humiliation she endures at Thornfield Hall provides an admirable model of Christian endurance, and her heart-wrenching refusal of Rochester's proposition validates conventional morality, much as their reunion and marriage and the birth of their child provides not only a happy ending but a boilerplate sanction of the domestic tie. Brontë's many literary allusions promote Jane as a female version of Bunyan's pilgrim, whose journey ends when the gates of paradise are thrown open, and she is domiciled in that new Eden, Ferndale, with the love of her life. She gets it all by waiting, a hyper version of the homely advice dispensed by parents down through the ages: No man pays for what he can get for free.

These domestic and sentimental formulae, however, do not completely explain the unique thrall that *Jane Eyre* had for her readers, a drawing power that none of Charlotte Brontë's other novels enjoyed. The author somehow tapped that great underground river of archetypes, drawn up through her childhood reading of fairy tales and other marvelous matter, including the *Arabian Nights*. Chief of these was the ancient tale that has been defined as the ultimate female wish-fulfillment fable, the story of Cinderella, but beneath the conventional tale of the poor girl who married a prince there may be found a darker parable, keyed by the disparity of ages between Jane and her Byronic lover.

II

That Jane is an updated Cinderella is obvious from the first chapter of the romance, in which Jane Eyre is treated by her guardian—her aunt through marriage to her mother's brother—as by a wicked stepmother. This awful person favors her children over her dead husband's sister's child, then banishes a rebellious Jane by sending her to a terrible orphanage, ruled over by a wicked despot, ogrelike in aspect, where she is protected by an equivalent fairy godmother. In the next stage of her life, Jane finds employment as governess in a grand country house equivalent to a castle, whose owner, Mr. Rochester, is absent from home when she arrives.

When he does return it is as an older, massively masculine presence, gruff and apparently callous to Jane's tender sensibilities. At this point the fairy tale element switches terms, and we for a time are treated to an updated version of the story about the Beauty and the Beast, resolved when the Beast at long last declares his love for the little governess who has adored him virtually from the start. Revealing his tender, loving side, her lover in effect strips off his beastly guise, only to reveal yet another mask, a Prince Charming who is really a clean-shaven Bluebeard, who keeps his wife locked in an attic room.

Alan Dundes (1983) has pointed out that Cinderella in the folk tale recounted by the Grimm brothers is a much more enterprising and inventive person than the passive, long-suffering girl in the Perrault telling of the story. Jane Eyre is also a young woman with a strong will and a temper to match, and yet when in the presence of her master, as she calls him, Jane becomes passive and obedient, even childlike—as Rochester himself is fond of noting. In effect, during their long, drawn-out courtship she assumes the obedient if often tearful because frustrated role of daughter-lover, a complement to the father-lover who holds such a strong hand over her life.

Dundes has proposed an alternative source for Cinderella, derived from a number of folk tales containing common elements, chief of which is a situation in which a king "decides to marry the woman who most resembles his recently deceased wife and that person turns out to be his daughter" (234). The Cinderella connection is found in the version in which the dying queen demands that her husband marry a woman "who can wear her ring," the band being an obvious alternative to the fabulous glass (or golden) slipper.

By evoking the psychological process of "projection," the father-king's lust can be regarded as a mirror reflection of his princess-daughter's desire: "The specific details of how the dying queen insists that the new wife must be just like her would appear to reflect the common fantasy of a girl wishing to literally replace her mother—with respect to being her father's mate. The daughter either looks just like her mother or she is the only one who fits into her mother's wedding ring" (236–37). We need not adhere to the minutiae of Dundes's argument (or condone his split infinitive) to see the extent to which Charlotte Brontë's gothic romance resembles this traditional tale.

Jane Eyre, whose memory is of her mother only, can hardly be thought of as desiring sex with her father. And yet, when the love of her life appears, though not of sufficient age to be thought of as a father substitute, he is cast in an authoritative, quasi-patriarchal role. Much of Rochester's appeal may have been drawn from the Byron myth, for he spent much of his life in profligate adventures on the continent, but it is his maturity and cosmopolitan character that give him such power over Jane, and it is essential to the attraction she feels for her employer.

But then, having accepted her employer's proposal, Jane discovers he is already married, to a mad woman kept imprisoned in a room on the top floor of his mansion. The proposed union would be adulterous—a Victorian equivalent to incest—and like the maiden in some versions of the king-who-loves-his-daughter folk tale, Jane flees, hiding from the man she loves but cannot marry. But as we all know, the story, like most Victorian versions of traditional fairy tales, ends happily, with the marriage between the "king" and the "princess" made possible by the death of the monster in the attic.

Any number of critics have pointed out the presence of the Cinderella story inside *Jane Eyre,* but seldom I think have the parallels to the ancient tale of incestuous desire been emphasized. Admittedly, it does no service to the complexity of *Jane Eyre* to reduce it to a patched-up version of several traditional folk tales. And yet the presence within the story of those elements helps to explain its power over the imaginations of readers, most especially the legion of young women who, like the mill workers in Lowell, were immediately drawn to Brontë's story, which held over them the thrall of archetypes.

The question remains, however, as to the authorial source of Jane's para-incestuous passion, and there have been suggestions that Charlotte herself may have had subconscious feelings for her father, Patrick Brontë, an explanation that frankly is not very convincing, despite the evidence of her filial piety. On the other hand, we know for sure that she was obsessively attracted to Constantin Heger, who taught in his wife's private school in Brussels where Charlotte and her sister Emily worked for a time as student-instructors, and Heger was of an age that closely matches that of Rochester.

Charlotte was invited back to Brussels, *sans* Emily, for a second year as a teacher, but when Madame Heger began to suspect that Professor Heger's protégée was falling in love with her husband, she saw to it that Brontë's connection with her school was ended. Returning to Haworth, Charlotte initiated a correspondence with the man she called "Master," letters begging for a continuation of their friendship, but after a few replies, Heger broke off his end of the epistolary relationship, which Charlotte continued in vain. Correctly blaming Mme. Heger for M. Heger's silence, Charlotte was both hurt and outraged, and all of her novels (save for *Shirley*) in one way or another were encoded responses to the contradictory feelings she entertained toward the Hegers.

The attraction felt by young women for older men may be explained by reference to incestuous myths but there are other explanations, akin to the reasons for the attraction felt by older men (like Rochester) for young women, seldom equated with daughter-love but often with the need to bolster male self-esteem. We may doubt that the crushes female students have on their male teachers is sublimated incest, but much as the teacher who responds is bolstering his sagging ego by the flattering association with a young woman, so she in turn has been raised in her own estimation by the attentions of a man in an authoritative position. He borrows from her youth; she from his authority. What they borrow from each other is power.

In Brontë's case we have a similar instance of a young woman finding in a specific older man a number of desirable qualities, for Heger was an intellectual who was also a masterful teacher. He projected an attentive, friendly presence easily misconstrued as something more than it was, but which certainly filled a vacuum in the psyche of a lonely female student. Perhaps in Heger Charlotte Brontë found as much a father-substitute as a potential lover, for Patrick Brontë was known for his distant and withdrawn ways: away on day-long parish duties, he took his meals in his study, which threw his children even closer together. Thus the absence of a fatherly presence in her life may have produced confusion, to which Heger contributed.

Whatever. But certainly Constantin Heger can be found in several versions in three of Charlotte Brontë's novels, often with a much thinner disguise than that provided by Rochester. And yet it was *Jane Eyre* that had the greatest thrall over Victorian readers, even though *Villette* has been deemed by our own contemporary critics as a superior work of fiction. Perhaps *Jane Eyre* was so popular because of its happy, fairy tale conclusion, perhaps because of the Byronic overtones, perhaps because the author was able to communicate by some subliminal fashion the power of her obsessive love of Heger to young women who shared her need. These are all possibilities but none is an answer, and none moreover explains the powerful influence of Elizabeth Gaskell's biography of Charlotte, where Brontë's feelings toward her Belgian professor are excised from the record.

For when it came to be known, thanks to Gaskell, that Jane and her creator were approximately one and the same—lacking only (in 1857) a real-life Rochester—what resulted was a phenomenon comparable to that modern equivalent of a religious manifestation, the rise of a cult, in which the fiction becomes inextricable from the facts as they were related by her highly selective biographer. Where the story of Jane Eyre is one of romantic triumph, the story of Charlotte Brontë provided a tragic alternative, for whatever the virtues of Arthur Bell Nicholls he was no Edward Fairfax Rochester, and the child he sired was the death not the fulfillment of his bride. Yet coming at the end of a series of slow, fatal declines, whether Emily's stoic, Anne's pious, or Branwell's wretched departure, Charlotte's demise provided a suitable finale, doing her duty as it were to the sentimental mode. Where in her romances she used the sentimental element sparingly, in her life according to Gaskell she exemplified the long-suffering heroines of novels she never wrote.

If Charlotte Brontë qualifies (and who would suggest that she doesn't?) as the leading candidate for literary sainthood in nineteenth-century literary annals, her hagiographer was her friend and fellow novelist. By the end of the 1850s it was impossible to read Charlotte's fiction without viewing it in the light shed by the stained-glass portrait wrought by Elizabeth Gaskell. Moreover, Charlotte Brontë migrated at least in spirit to the American strand, for her romantic muse was far more operative in this country than in Great Britain. The attractions of a romance between a girl barely out of adolescence and an older, cosmopolitan man would endure in America through a half-century and more of novels specifically aimed at a young and presumably female audience.

English readers seem to have been satisfied by the original, and in terms of female authorship the latter half of the century is dominated by George Eliot, who wrote in the great tradition of socially conscious fiction, a genre Brontë attempted in *Shirley* (perhaps under the influence of her friend Elizabeth Gaskell) but without much success. In 1869 there appeared *Lorna Doone,* in spirit closer to Scott's historical romances and *Wuthering Heights* than to Brontë's sentimentalized gothic mode, but we look in vain for evidence of a "school of Charlotte Brontë." Only in the twentieth century, with Daphne du Maurier's *Rebecca* (1938), do we find evidence of influence in Great Britain, and that novel, it has been suggested, owes much to *Vera* (1921) by Countess Mary Annette Russell ("Elizabeth").

But in America, as always, it was different. In the United States Charlotte Brontë was looked to as a muse by the Eyresses of the Age of Sentimentalism, who produced those books cursed by Hawthorne and summed up wryly by Cowie. Her influence moreover would survive the Civil War, and can be found even in novels presumably realistic in their depictions of everyday life, albeit aimed at an audience equivalent to that which tended the Lowell mills. For if Brontë's plot and cast of characters when imported to America quickly declined into a mere commercial formula, on another, higher, if not so easily detectable level, the spirit and form of *Jane Eyre* would be resurrected, undiminished in force and meaning.

By 1870, as realism began its resistless rise, sentimental fiction soon became the thing that was no longer to be. Bret Harte, a pioneering realist whose name is virtually synonymous with local color, owed his sudden fame to "The Luck of Roaring Camp," in which the shedding of sympathetic tears by his readers suggested that realism did not at first make a clean break with the sentimental mode. But as a transitional realist Harte ridiculed *Jane Eyre* in "Miss Mix," one of those parodying *Condensed Novels* that should be better known, not only because they are hilarious but because they reveal Harte's sharp eye for the inherently ridiculous aspects of fiction that took itself too seriously.

Realism, it needs to be said, was not a masculinist scheme to discredit fiction by women: For William Dean Howells we have Sarah Orne Jewett; for Mark Twain we have Mary Wilkens; for Henry James, Junior we have Charlotte Perkins Gilman. Realism was an affirmative action employer, testified to by the presence not only of women writers but of Charles Chesnutt; it was a movement that aimed to put sentimentalism in its place—in the attic, with all the other now useless artifacts of the past, literary coefficients of plaster of paris Rogers Groups. Yet sentimentality, to Christianity so closely allied, never died, but maintained its own humble existence, sticking to the low road of popular fiction, leaving literary realists to hog the high road.

It was a lively ghost that survived the demise of the Sentimental (or Feminine) Years, thanks to a small legion of women novelists who were themselves, like Emily Dickinson, girls in the 1850s, although hardly reclusive in their later years. First among them, in terms of chronology as well as excellence, is Louisa May Alcott, who draws praise from Alexander Cowie and Nina Baym alike, prognostic of her recent revival as an author whose *Little Women* far transcends its modest aims as a work for children. For Alcott in her best-known novel hewed very closely to the Haworth line, yet effected also a number of transformations, resulting in what could be called a realistic sentimentalism, depending on the facts of her own childhood for verisimilitude but drawing also on those occasions from her life that inspired in readers a sympathetic shedding of tears.

Here again, as with those young women in Lowell, it is difficult in assessing the influence of *Jane Eyre* on Alcott to separate Brontë's heroine from the author who created her, not only because of the novel's autobiographical basis but because of the infectious influence of Gaskell's *Life*. It was certainly not difficult for Louisa May to see the similarities between the Brontë ménage at Haworth and the Alcott tribe in Concord. As Fred Pattee pointed out, three daughters, surrounded by a rigidly religious atmosphere, depending on literature to nurture a world of dreams, "so it was in dozens of New England homes," but surely no more so than in the one in Concord.

And yet there is more to the Brontë–Alcott connection than the shared pattern of suffering sisters, for if the sentimental spirit survived by making a bargain with literary realism, so the gothic mode likewise made it past the watershed of the Civil War in America. As we now know, Louisa May Alcott supported her family for a number of years by writing sensational fiction, "Gothics" very much in the mode of Charlotte Brontë's wilder romantic strains, resulting in a doppelganger of creativity, one aspect of the complex influence *Jane Eyre* had upon creative women in America after 1870. But Brontë's romance would also inspire fictions that at least superfically do not at all resemble the original, Alcott's *Little Women* and Burnett's *Secret Garden* among them, yet share with the original a power to enthrall. In time we shall be examining that continuity, but let us start here with the grand original, *Jane Eyre*.

III

As Elaine Showalter has suggested in *A Literature of Their Own* (1977), Charlotte Brontë's famous romance can be seen as a feminist encyclopedia of considerable range and depth. In the opposing shapes of Bertha Mason and Helen Burns, the heroine is presented with antithetical versions of female sexual behavior, extremes that would seem to admit no compromise. Bertha, the sensual Creole, whose name evokes both the Norse earth-goddess and "Frau Bertha," a German folk figure of some ambiguity, is depicted in images inspiring terror and disgust.

She is a personification of passion reduced to its lowest, most extreme form, and belongs in Spenser's parade of vices, being Rage unconfined. An apparently hollow if beautiful mannikin when Rochester at the urging of his father marries her, Bertha turns out to be a vessel of vanity and (it is hinted) gross physical appetites. Succumbing to hereditary madness, she pays a horrible price for her vices, and finally perishes in a fire of her own setting, the flames of which are symbolic of her uncontrollable and destructive passion.

By contrast, Helen Burns, whose given name means "light," is a virtual personification of Christian forebearance: she is simply (and that is the word) a saint, and is one of many versions of the Victorian stereotype, the Angel of the House, type and figure of the sentimental tradition. Self-abnegating and long-suffering, Helen's supreme ecstasy is that of Bernini's Saint Theresa, for whom death is a desired fulfillment. Jane loves and admires Helen, but finds herself unable to follow in her friend's saintly footsteps, no more than she can subsequently permit herself the dubious pleasure of moving without benefit of clergy into Bertha Rochester's bed. The course of action she does determine for herself is something of a middle road, equivalent to the Via Media of the Anglican church. She is a cross between Bunyan's Pilgrim and Goethe's Werther, a romantic imitation of Christ and a victim-heroine (counterpart to the hero-villain), the Suffering Woman.

Given Brontë's upbringing, Winifred Gerin (1967) wonders aloud why there is not more conventional Christian matter in her novels, and the story of Helen Burns's martyrdom at the hands of a purportedly ecclesiastical agency provides a several-layered response. Gerin demonstrates Charlotte's early anguish over the state of her soul, holding herself up against the impossible model provided by Calvinism (thanks to her well-meaning but thinly constituted Aunt Elizabeth Branwell). Charlotte figured as she lamented in letters to her pious friend Ellen Nussey that she was most certainly damned, much as Jane cannot follow the way Helen Burns leads.

Byron himself had to deal with the same anguish, and solved the problem by in effect joining Satan's party, but Charlotte stopped well short of that solution, and while discarding Calvinistic dogma she substituted an equivalent dogged sense of moral correctness. Instead of relying on doctrinal pro- and prescriptions, she forged her own code, a rigid frame that demanded of people the highest level of idealism with actions to suit, of which stoic adherence to duty was the chief virtue, a romantic moral scheme with overtones of chivalric zeal.

There is in the Angria stories composed by Charlotte and Branwell as children not only Byronic but clearly pagan elements, an emphasis on power and wealth, on beautiful and costly raiment, jewelry, and on physical pleasures, in sum the joys of this earth with no thought of the hereafter. It is out of this pagan context that Zamorna emerges, a towering figure of excessive passion. Realizing where the free expression of powerful emotions could lead—Branwell providing a convenient and horrifying example—Brontë in her mature published fiction constructed an alternative world, one in which the suppression of passion was the rule.

It was not so much a matter of absolute self-denial but of forbidding one's self the dubious pleasure of absolute license, clinging in effect to the savior rock of common sense, which loomed large in Charlotte Brontë's consciousness. Clamping the lid down on the pagan exercise of passion, Brontë kept it bubbling in the pot, a savory witch's stew of unrequited desires. Compression is the true source of literary as well as steam power, and the turbulent but essentially formless mass that makes up the Glasstown cycle became in *Jane Eyre* a wickedly effective source of subliminal energy. Rochester retains some elements of Zamorna but he is not Zamorna, no more than he is Harun al-Rashid, with whom he is at one point compared as well.

Nor is he Byron, nor the pluperfect rake from whom his name is derived. He is hardly M. Heger replicated either, but this does not mean that he is not M. Heger in part. Despite the underlayment of autobiography, suggested by the novel's subtitle and first-person narrator, *Jane Eyre* is a highly imaginative construct, made up of sensational materials that transcend not only everyday reality but (so far as her readers' lives were concerned) mere likelihood. As in the intensest of dreams, her romance presents alternating visions of nightmare and wish-fulfillment, as well as close combinations of both, resulting in a mythlike tale of great erotic power.

Like the didactic novels of Richardson and Jane Austen, *Jane Eyre* provides a course of conduct worthy of emulation, but though the book resembles a bildungsroman, in truth Jane's education into reality ends by realizing a dream, the author's post-Angria fantasy that one day M. Heger would come to his senses and call her back to Belgium. As in dreams and fairy tales, Jane's final fate is one that none of her readers (nor Charlotte herself) could ever hope to share. Holding firm to her rigid moral code, as to a spar from a wreck, the heroine is carried by favorable tides to an Ilyria of sudden wealth and power, where she is greeted by the love of her life.

This is the primal stuff of romance, in which closure draws upon the fulfillment of the author's erotic desire rather than any conceivable real-life situation, and in which popularity depends on the universality of the author's fantasy. It is literally a case of *amour propre* (one of Brontë's favorite Francophone phrases) with a plot. Yet it must also be said that at least one Victorian reviewer was quick to censure the book for its depiction of licentiousness as an attractive lure, nor did the reviewer much approve of the freedom of language used by Rochester in relating his wild adventures in Europe, the presumed fruit of which is in plain evidence every day.

That is, as a major weapon in the arsenal of Victorian moral rearmament, *Jane Eyre* seemed to some readers off target, and to the modern eye likewise, if for different reasons, the book appears passing strange. We may, with Ellen Moers in *Literary Women* (1976), see Jane as an expression of the author's suppressed anger, or with Elaine Showalter as an embodiment of "as full and healthy a womanhood as the feminine novelists could have imagined" (124). But the anger is surely perversely channeled, for "the recurring motif in feminine fiction," as Showalter notes in a later place, is an expression of "outright hostility, if not castration wishes, toward men," a repeated "blinding, maiming, or blighting motif. [Thus] Rochester is blinded in the fire at Thornfield and also loses the use of his hand" (150).

If this is an expression of a full and healthy female sexuality, then we seem to have skipped a page. The burning marital bed has recently become a permissable exercise of wifely revenge for years of abuse, but are we to understand that Bertha's pyromania is intended to inspire Brontë's readers to go and do likewise? Although hardly supporting that extreme position, Showalter goes on to explain that Rochester's period of suffering is both positive and projective: "feminine novelists . . . believed that a limited experience of dependency, frustration, and powerlessness—in short, of womanhood—was a healthy and instructive one for a hero," for "in feminine fiction men and women become equals by submitting to mutual limitation, not by allowing each other mutual growth" (150, 124). In other words, Rochester is encouraged to get in touch as we now say with his feminine side, for which purpose he is allowed to retain one hand.

This reading is very close as Gilbert and Gubar (1984) show us to the opinion of Richard Chase, who saw Rochester's invalidism as essential to the process of "domestication," in male animals generally effected by castration (Gilbert and Gubar, 368; cf. Showalter, 152). Whatever the sociopsychological reasons, Rochester like Actaeon discovers that a "symbolic immersion . . . in feminine experience" can result in a painful transformation, akin to the kind of surgical operation once associated with Scandinavian countries. By contrast to this Victorian gelding process, Tania Modleski in *Loving with a Vengeance* (1982) demonstrates the extent to which Brontë's novel provided the plot for Harlequin Romances, modern and highly popular "Gothics." But she observes that contemporary Rochesters are allowed to retain their balls, for contemporary devotées of the Brontëan formula prefer fantasizing about undamaged goods. The bridge over these troubling waters would seem to be *Gone with the Wind,* in which the wounded lover is the emasculate Ashley Wilkes, while Rhett Butler is an updated Byron without the signature limp.

We will be examining Brontë's first novel, *The Professor,* in due time, but it can be said here that as an alternative expression of a full and healthy womanhood (which I am not sure it is), the male protagonist emerges from that story with all his operative parts intact. No, *Jane Eyre* is a special case, in part a pay-back for Heger's continued silence, but also a response to the dangers posed by giving free exercise to the ghost of Zamorna. The wounding of Rochester most certainly allows for a turning of the tables, for having earlier served as the victim of her lover's unusual courting rituals, a kind of verbal pinching of soft places in the soul, Jane at the end is able to torment him playfully concerning her amatory adventures during a prolonged absence at Morton.

But Jane resumes as she began her relationship with Rochester, as his obedient and loyal servant, for the two are finally united not in a husband and wife but patient and nurse relationship, and the news of the birth of their child comes as a shock. For as patient and nurse, they even more strongly evoke father and daughter, less Lear and Cordelia than Oedipus and Antigone—like Jane a woman capable of outspoken speech. I have already mentioned the presumed connection between Rochester and the near-blind and dependent (though hardly "domesticated") Patrick Brontë. In this reading, Jane's lover is a merger of Heger and Patrick the elder, with perhaps something of Patrick the younger, the self-styled Byronic Branwell. The result is surely an incestuous patch-work, one that both validates the dark version of the Cinderella story and approximates Dr. Frankenstein's handiwork.

But these highly tentative (and questionable) psychological matters aside, the final union of Jane with Rochester is a complex mixture of suffering and joy, her emotional misery ended by being joined to a partner who has experienced great physical pain. It is perhaps worth noting that in one version of the incestuous Cin-derella story, the princess desired by her father-king cuts off her hands, thereby making it impossible for any ring to fit any fingers, which as a projective parable suggests a gesture of guilt, in Brontë's version transferred back as it were to the king. But we need no folkloric Freudian explanation for Rochester's mutila-tion: the final tableau vivant places a wounded man in the loving arms of a suffering woman, an uneasy spectacle for the modern reader but one transcendent with Christian symbolism.

Rochester is no more Christ than he is Lord Byron, but he is both as it were, Byron worked through a Christian cookie cutter. But we don't have to evoke the moral grid (built upon the reticu-lations of the Cross) in order to understand what has happened, for Rochester like Oedipus has been blinded because like Oedipus he did not see, and his hand has been taken away to remind him that in attempting to force Jane into marriage he plainly over-reached. Because of these severe exactments, which can operate outside any fairy-tale reference, Rochester is no longer powerful and arrogant. Following the steep pathway of pride he has stum-bled and fallen, a notion as operative for the pagan Greeks as for the Christian English.

In the pages that follow I shall be discussing the steps that lead in Brontë's novel to Jane's assumption of her beloved burden, but it needs to be said here that in *Jane Eyre* as in much British and American literature produced between 1700 and 2000 the rela-tionships between men and women are often perverse in depic-tion. Yet that perversity, which has less to do with Rochester's maiming than with Jane's depth of attraction toward him, first in health but surviving into sickness, seems to have had a powerful draw on the mill girls in Lowell.

Their identification with a woman for whom self-effacement is an act of anger repressed, the sort of thing that today often produces physical evidence of self-laceration—a counterpart to that crazy laughter in the attic that is the expression of anger impounded—contains a mystery never to be solved. I have been suggesting the reasons why so many women readers in the nineteenth century were attracted to *Jane Eyre,* but the question will never be answered to everyone's satisfaction. And from that puzzle there follows the final question, why did so many women writers frame novels in imitation of the erotic situation in Charlotte Brontë's book? There is always the profit motive, which can never be discounted, but it is hardly sufficient to explain how the love of a young woman for an older man survived the transition from romantic to realistic literature, or why it especially flourished in North America.

There is, once again, the archetypal draw, but that is not an explanation that will satisfy all readers. And yet, *Jane Eyre* became in effect a kind of secular scripture, keeping company with other novels with a long reach into the future, like Scott's *Ivanhoe,* Mary Shelley's *Frankenstein,* even, after a decent interval had elapsed, Emily Brontë's *Wuthering Heights.* As secular scripture, these novels found a precedent and often a literal model in fairy tales and the plays of Shakespeare. Such books deserve as Hamlet says about himself careful study, and though our major interest is not so much with *Jane Eyre* as with that book's daughters, to understand a child you had best spend some time examining the parent.

IV

Despite their obvious differences in temperament, which eventually resulted in a coolness between them, William Thackeray sensed the truth about Charlotte Brontë when he noted that "there's a fire and fury raging in that little woman, a rage scorching her heart. . . . She has had a story and a great grief that has gone badly with her" (*Letters,* 3: 12). But in translating that "story" into the relationship between Jane and Rochester, Charlotte altered the facts considerably, whereas in *The Professor* and *Villette,* the Heger affair is plainly visible even while partially concealed, rather like a corpse of a murdered lover that has been hastily covered over with leaves.

Likewise, *Jane Eyre*, as a number of modern commentators have noted, following Thackeray's hint, is an exercise in controlled rage, much as "Eyre" may also be pronounced "Ire," as in Ireland, the place of Patrick Brontë's birth, whose natives have a famously uncertain hold on their tempers. We may doubt that rage was first aroused in Charlotte because of her rejection by Heger: "Angria" after all was the name of the imaginary kingdom she and Branwell dreamt up. But from *The Professor* to *Villette,* her novels virtually seethe with furious resentment over her treatment by Heger and (especially) his wife, indeed were written as literal acts of retribution. "*Je me vengerai*" were the parting words traditionally ascribed to Charlotte Brontë by the Heger family, addressed not to M. but Mme. Here again the testimony of Thackeray is useful: "I think," he wrote to a correspondent, "Miss Brontë is unhappy and that makes her unjust. Novel writers should not be in a passion with their characters..." (*Letters,* 3: 67).

The example of Fred Pattee's mother bears witness to the infectiousness of Brontë's private fantasy, but, as I have already suggested, its power was derived in part from the circumstances of the book's creation, the known facts concerning which were contained in Elizabeth Gaskell's life of the author. Since Gaskell took pains to leave out any suggestion of that sad business with the Belgian professor, the major autobiographical link was missing for many years, a strategic gap which profoundly affected the accepted, public image of the author. In sum, Gaskell was successful in her major aim, which was to rescue the reputation of her friend from attacks on her presumed irreligiousness, but by excising Heger she removed the most vital connection between Brontë's life and her greatest novel.

It is difficult from here to resurrect the Charlotte Brontë who existed before the Heger affair was uncovered. But by removing that illicit if unconsummated connection, Gaskell limited Charlotte's connections with the opposite sex to her brother, her father, and, latterly, to Arthur Nicholls, the curate whom she after much indecision married. These are men with whom her relations were more dutiful than passionate. They are moreover associations that further promoted Charlotte's image as a Victorian saint, a stereotyped Angel in the House, "so patient, silent, and enduring of suffering—so afraid of any unselfish taxing of others," an emphasis that undoubtedly influenced, after 1857, the received idea of *Jane Eyre* (Gaskell, 465).

Few readers had the advantage enjoyed by Thackeray, who having read *Villette* observed condescendingly if truthfully about the author that she was a "poor little woman of genius ... the fiery little eager brave tremulous homely-faced creature! I can read a great deal of her life as I fancy in her book, and see that rather than have fame, rather than any other earthly good or mayhap heavenly one she wants some Tomkins or another to love her and be in love with. ... [H]ere is a genius, a noble heart longing to mate itself and destined to wither away into old maidenhood with no chance to fulfil the burning desire" (*Letters*, 3: 233).

Perhaps the mill girls at Lowell received a similar message subliminally from *Jane Eyre*, whose heroine like Lucy Snow yearns to love and be loved, but the point of the romance is that she does not want love at any price, that despite her great passion for Rochester once she discovers the truth she flees his illicit importunities. The mill women may have been seduced figuratively by Rochester, but in admiring Jane for her restraint in that regard, they soon had the idealized figure of the author portrayed by Gaskell as reinforcement for the heroine's sterling moral conduct. Indeed, it is the tension between temptation and chastity that still provides the book its power, a tension not found in the relationship between the author and the man she loved—she being the aggressor, he the one who failed to succumb. Correspondingly, lacking reference to *l'affaire* Heger, Gaskell's life of Charlotte Brontë lacks any element of romance, while providing plenty of evidence of the hard realities that underlay *Jane Eyre*.

There was at the start Charlotte's experience at Conan Bridge School, which warranted the initiatory episode at Lowood, thereby validating the otherwise Dickensian coloration of that institution and its director. But what would have appeared to Brontë's contemporaries as the strongest tie between the author and her heroine was the sterling sense of duty shared by both, for if Charlotte was an Angel in the House, it was because she is portrayed by Mrs. Gaskell as a female avatar of the Aenean piety. As the oldest and longest surviving child of Patrick Brontë, Charlotte took over the management of his household, assuming duties made even more difficult by poverty and her chronic bouts with illness. Brother Branwell obliged by adding an additional burden, acting out the role of a drunken, degenerate, once-promising-now-doomed ne'er-do-well, by 1857 a familiar Victorian stereotype.

Patrick Brontë likewise did his best for Gaskell the domestic novelist by providing a kind of dreary comic relief, playing the crusty, eccentric, occasionally violent, but essentially well-meaning and almost (but not quite) loveable old *paterfamilias*. Then there was Anne, dying a tubercular, saintly death, of the kind found in countless Sunday school tracts, which allowed for frequent final pronouncements to the tearful survivors gathered round the sickbed to hear them. Emily, by contrast, refused to conform to any literary model, and seems by Gaskell's account to have sulked herself to death. Against this somber backdrop, Charlotte's self-sacrifice and devotion to duty shines like moonglow, illuminating the equally saintly features of Jane Eyre.

"Reader, I married him!" exults the second Mrs. Rochester at the end of her travails, and few of those so addressed could doubt that she had earned the reward. For her labors, Charlotte was given the love of Arthur Nicholls, an equivalent "Tomkins," a courtship in which persistent adoration was the man's part, not hers. It provided her story a tragic not a happy ending, moreover, suggesting that Patrick, who preferred the happy kind, was right in resisting for so long his daughter's marriage to the kindly, devoted, but hardly sensitive and surely lowly curate. Although we may believe Gaskell's assertion that Arthur dearly loved his bride, she cannot prevent us from realizing that he had no understanding of his wife's needs as an artist.

Like Charlotte's father, and in competition with him, her husband insisted that his wants be taken care of before pen was set to paper. And it was Arthur who took Charlotte out in the rain one day to view a neighboring waterfall, a combined display of husbandly and natural power that brought on a bad cold that gave way to the fatal pregnancy for which he was also held responsible, thereby bringing an end to their marriage of nine months and her life. Dying with that unborn, unnamed, unsexed, and probably unwanted child in her womb, Charlotte Brontë comes down to us through the pages of Gaskell's book a Victorian version of immaculate conception, a holy ghost, being a haunting spectre of the life process turned to fatal ends.

Fate thereby brought her story to a suitable period, a quietus of the kind Charlotte as author forbade herself, out of consideration for her father's preferences for positive endings in fiction. It is a conclusion moreover that provides a moral to her story, one that retains even for a modern reader an effective burden of suffering, wherein the life of a woman of genius is warped to the physical requirements of mediocre and insensitive males. Her last words were not, as recorded by Gaskell, those of a literary person but a loving wife, her manner of dying perfectly suited to the traditional role of Suffering Womanhood not the New Woman then emerging.

Jane Eyre of course does not die, but what is chiefly missing from Gaskell's story is the element that provides Brontë's novel its moral crux, the turning away from a powerful temptation in the name of what is right. Gaskell did her best with Charlotte's refusal of Arthur's first proposal, by which she obeyed the paternal behest: "Thus quietly and modestly did she, on whom such hard judgments had been passed by ignorant reviewers, receive [Arthur's] vehement, passionate declaration of love, —thus thoughtfully for her father, and unselfishly for herself, put aside all consideration of how she should reply, excepting as he wished" (Gaskell, 397). But this quiet submission to Patrick's wishes was hardly up to the level of Jane's precipitous flight from Thornfield, nor was Arthur's offer of love (save in Patrick's eyes) an illicit passion but an honorable if overly ardent proposal.

Moreover, the facts in the case of M. Heger when added to the story do not help much. For when Charlotte left Brussels she was not fleeing her teacher's improper advances, quite the reverse, for it was Constantin (with some help from his wife) who was the one in retreat. We may doubt that Charlotte Brontë would ever have maintained an adulterous liaison nor could she have entertained any real expectation that the beloved Master would leave his wife and family for her. Yet the prolonged episode does suggest that for a time at least her fantasy life became entangled in the complex skein of reality, especially once she had returned to Haworth, and in time she would use her literary imagination to fulfil what had become a hopeless dream. Her letters to Professor Heger certainly indicate that she was willing to sustain her unrequited love from a distance, and yet those letters also indicate who was the aggressor, and it wasn't the little professor.

What the effect on her devoted readers would have been had those letters come to light during Charlotte's lifetime or been included in Gaskell's book we can only suppose. But by pouring her passion into Jane's feelings for Rochester, Charlotte vicariously requited through a facsimile of her childhood fantasy-man—Zamorna—her impossible love for the Belgian professor, and though her readers were unaware of the facts, they apparently got the message. Illicit at its inception, the love between Jane and Rochester is made right by the death of his wife, yet as numerous readers have noted, Jane begins her journey to rejoin her lover before she learns of mad Bertha's demise. In sum, he calls and she obeys.

This omission, as we shall see, is a disjunction central to the meaning of the story, but in terms of the relationship of the novel's plot to the facts of the author's life we can see it as the twisted cord binding otherwise disparate parts. To her letters to Heger begging a reply Charlotte received no answer, and her sadness eventually turned to anger over her Master's obvious indifference, a boiling point reached after she saw to it that letters were put directly into the professor's hands, thereby removing Mme. Heger as a possible agent *à couvert*. By contrast, Jane, furious over Rochester's duplicity, goes to great lengths to prevent him from contacting her, yet as soon as the coast is clear a summons comes over the Eyre-waves which she hastens to heed, a discrepancy between fact and fiction that defines the signal difference between real life and romance.

To depend on psychic powers for a critical turn of the plot may seem to some readers a technical weakness, akin to those convenient letters that turn up in Shakespeare's tragedies. But then as Brontë herself pointed out, such things *do* happen, and the electrical message continues to thrill modern readers. Even less likely is the match between Rochester and Jane, the end result of the message and the climax of the plot, for as Mrs. Fairfax points out, the hard fact is, "Gentlemen in his station are not accustomed to marry their governesses" (298).

Still, the happy ending of *Jane Eyre* takes place within the accepted bounds of romantic make-believe, to which we can also add what happens during Jane's absence from Thornfield, the coincidental recovery of her family and the discovery of her inheritance, which puts her on an equal footing with her Master. Once again, this is the stuff of fairy tales and their latter-day equivalents, novels of romance, whereas in real life it usually works out otherwise, much as those who try to realize their Byronic fantasies are doomed to end up, with Branwell and Byron, in a brandy keg.

There were as Gaskell's modern successors have shown us, two Charlotte Brontës, the one who spun passionate fantasies and the one who was a stickler for moral rigor, simply if inadequately defined as "duty." It does seem as though the second Brontë reflected Charlotte's terrified reaction to the possible consequences of remaining the first, which the sad history of her former coadjutor in creating the Glasstown stories had clearly demonstrated long before he graduated to Mrs. Robinson.

The ongoing creation of the Angria cycle was something of a narcotic dream for both Charlotte and her brother, but she seems to have realized that the creative exercise of Byronic fantasies was addictive and painfully withdrew, even as Branwell sank from sight into his own narcissistic self like the House of Usher into its reflecting tarn. It was this combination that provided both the erotic energies and the moral limits found in *Jane Eyre,* where a forbidden but finally a requited because by then a proper passion spins the plot.

2

All the Rage:
Repressed Anger Fuels the Plot

Arms and Hatchments, Resurgam.—Here
is an opportunity for moralizing!
—Thackeray

I

IN A LETTER TO GEORGE LEWES, WHO HAD OBJECTED TO THE USE OF
melodrama in *Jane Eyre*, Charlotte explained that she had written a sensational romance because publishers rejected her first
novel on the grounds that it did not contain sufficient exciting material to hold the reader's interest (Gaskell, 254). Even before
Anne's *Agnes Grey* and Emily's *Wuthering Heights* had been accepted for publication, their sister began writing her great romance. Taking advantage of a month's enforced idleness in Manchester as she waited for her father to recover from the removal
of cataracts, she wrote the first part of the book virtually nonstop.
We can credit some of this speed to the impetus provided by Charlotte's feelings for Professor Heger, but this alone cannot account
for the terrific power projected by the story, so we need to search
elsewhere for the release of elements presumably called up from
deep in the author's consciousness.

In doing so, we should keep in mind that the first part of *Jane
Eyre*, that which was written so swiftly, is chiefly about the heroine's ordeals before and immediately after arriving at Thornfield
Hall. This material was taken from Brontë's recollections of life
(and death) at Cowan Bridge and her brief experience as a governess, expressing anger of quite a different order from that inspired by her Brussels sojourn. Here it is institutions not individuals that drew out her rage, focussing on the inequities that are
reinforced by class and social status. Likewise, it is Charlotte's experience at Cowan Bridge that receives emphasis in Gaskell's bi-

ography, serving as it does as an introduction to the character of the Brontë sisters, whose "wild, strong hearts, and powerful minds, were hidden under an enforced propriety and regularity of demeanour and expression" (59).

As Gaskell saw it, the death of her sister, Maria, who had been "a tender helper and a counselor to them all," passed on the legacy of dutifulness to Charlotte, an inheritance "from the gentle little sufferer so lately dead. . . . This loving assumption of duties beyond her years made her feel considerably older than she really was" (60, 62). During the period of forced maturity following her return to Haworth, Charlotte learned to temper "the thoughtful and dreamy" impressions of a secluded, rural life with "the strong common sense natural to her, and daily called into exercise by the requirements of her practical life. . . . While her imagination received powerful impressions, her excellent understanding had full power to rectify them before her fancies became realities" (70–71). These observations are a key to (and actually may be derived from) the character of Jane Eyre.

It needs to be pointed out that there is a second moral strand to Brontë's fable, which may be indirectly connected to the necessity of maintaining one's chastity. That is, the proper response to angry impulses as to sexual urges is self-control. It is a lesson Jane learns during her extended stay in Lowood, which begins when she lashes out against the horrible Mrs. Reed and her repulsive, bullying son. Her subsequent experience transforms her from a moody, temperamental child to a stoical, silent sufferer, who has learned to stifle resentment and rage. And yet, Brontë passed over Jane's sojourn at Lowood with some haste, limiting her experience to what happened during the first few months of her residence there, equivalent to the real time spent at Conan Bridge by Charlotte and her sisters.

On the one hand, this strategy might be attributed to the author's unwillingness to invent materials beyond the range of her actual experience. On the other, by truncating the account of Jane's stay at Lowood, Brontë missed a grand opportunity to expand on the inequities enforced in a nominally Christian establishment, with the end of inspiring reform. That of course was Dickensian terrain, and not only was Charlotte no Charles Dickens, she may have consciously avoided the risk of comparison. But the net result is that we never do witness the series of events that resulted in the transformation of a tempestuous child to a paragon of self-control and abnegation.

Moreover, nowhere in *Jane Eyre* is it suggested that Helen Burns's death served the transformational purpose attributed by Gaskell to the death of Charlotte's sister, Maria. Rather, it seems to have contributed to the anger seething beneath the governess's polite, compliant manner. Then too, Charlotte herself was never the perfect Christian paragon created by Elizabeth Gaskell, as Gaskell herself discovered upon first opening the letters to M. Heger. In other private writings, especially the so-called Roe Head journal, Brontë on a number of occasions let her beatific smile spread into a secret sneer, nor were the several characters inspired by Mme. Heger a result of Christian forgiveness. Nobody is as nice as the heroine of Gaskell's biography is made out to be.

That Charlotte Brontë was a conflicted personality seems obvious, a woman whose poems and prose are alive with the exercise of passion but who as herself assumed a rigidly moral posture, a repressive suit of armor from which a jet of scalding steam occasionally escaped. In that memorable image of Charlotte scolding the great Thackeray for his lapse of good manners we have a key of sorts to a detectable social imbalance. Rochester may entertain us by playing around with Jane Eyre's tight little frightened little scheme of things, but nobody ever played around with Charlotte Brontë. Gaskell's efforts to confront this dichotomy, as when she repeatedly disassociates Charlotte from the infatuated Jane Eyre, emphasizing the author's moral fiber while insisting that the author was no slave to love, were only possible by ignoring the letters to Heger.

If Brontë's personality was tense with psychic restraint from fear of letting herself go, it took its surface identity from an ambition to become a published author, thereby channeling passion into acceptable forms. Just such a channeling gave a relatively tight construction and considerable moral meaning to *The Professor*, which was not accepted by a publisher where Emily's novel was, with its absolute and for some reviewers deplorable lack of acceptable forms. *The Professor*, having been put into posthumous print, remains a valuable guide to the complexly divided personality of the writer, for though quite different from *Jane Eyre*, it contains materials that would be assimilated into that powerful fable, and serves as a prolegomenon of sorts. The genre was changed but the genius in control remained consistent.

"Novelists," begins the nineteenth chapter of *The Professor*, "should never allow themselves to weary of the study of real life. If they observed this duty conscientiously, they would give us fewer pictures checquered with vivid contrasts of light and shade; they would seldom elevate their heroes and heroines to the heights of rapture—still seldomer sink them to the depths of despair; for if we rarely taste the fulness of joy in this life, we yet more rarely savour the acid bitterness of hopeless anguish" (140). Of course, as Charlotte Brontë noted, perhaps thinking of Branwell, the situation is different if "we have plunged like beasts into sensual indulgence, abused, strained, stimulated, again overstrained, and at last, destroyed our faculties for enjoyment; then, truly, we may find ourselves without support, robbed of hope."

What awaits such persons but the "hideous and polluting recollections of vice, and time brings [them] on to the brink of the grave, and dissolution flings [them] in—a rag eaten through and through with disease, wrung together with pain, stamped into the churchyard sod by the inexorable heel of despair." We must assume that the author meant these strong words, spume-flecked with puritanic zeal, and an author that meant them could hardly have tolerance for the example of Heathcliff, in whose "collapsed mind" there is no place for "God, spirits, religion." It is no secret that Jane was uneasy about the subject matter in Emily's gothic romance.

But it is also worth remembering that after the novel that contained these righteous sentiments found no publisher, and Charlotte Brontë sat down to write a story that would, she took more than one leaf from Emily's book. However, instead of licensing a novel-long display of rage, she was very discrete in the literary use of anger, whether her own—as filtered through her heroine—or the fury associated with melodramatic creations like Heathcliff, which she hid in the attic to be brought down for only occasional display.

Hers was an admirable and hard-won restraint, as Gaskell observed, and promoted the notion that an endless exercise of passion in literature or life is ineffective, whether as a means of achieving one's deepest desires or creating a morally acceptable never mind readable novel. And *Jane Eyre* is therefore a work of art superior to *Wuthering Heights,* as the critical consensus seems to agree. It is, borrowing from Robert Frost, a game of tennis played with a net in which the intervening fabric is the main item, a web woven by the hard-working, self-effacing, Christian spider-lady within.

II

Much has been made, over his subsequent objections, to Arthur Bell Nicholls's remark to his bride, that her last and never finished novel, to be called "Emma," would warrant charges by reviewers that she was repeating herself. This remark, related by Nicholls himself to Thackeray who used it in his introduction to the fragment in 1860, was read at the time as being hostile to Charlotte's ambitions to continue her writing career ("Emma," 241). Not so, claimed Arthur, in 1899: it was a casual observation inspired by the similarity between the situation established in the opening of the projected novel and the situations in other of her works, especially *Jane Eyre* (Gerin, 1967, 554; cf. 500).

Certainly his wife was writing yet another novel that put an emphasis on the anticipated sufferings of a newly created and penniless orphan, and anyone not blinded by an emotional identification with poor, fated Charlotte Nicholls must agree with her husband. We have no idea where Emily Brontë would have gone if indeed she had finished her second novel, but it is fairly clear that her sister had one story to tell, told it over and over, and it was a story with infinite variations inspired by her experiences while residing at Cowan Bridge and at *Chez* Heger in Brussels.

The essential fable of *Wuthering Heights* has been compared to the plot of Scott's *The Black Dwarf,* but if Scott inspired Emily, then Dickens seems to have filled the sails of Charlotte Brontë's imagination, once she shoved off from the Byronic shores of Angria and got beyond the endless rolling waves of unbridled passion. It was, after all, Dickens who created the orphan as a literary type, and who virtually patented the death of a child as a sentimental device. We may credit Charlotte with having added the long-suffering governess to this Victorian cast, but we must in this regard remember that her sister Anne anticipated her with *Agnes Grey.*

What Charlotte Brontë stirred into this mix of suffering souls was an intense emotional elixir, for much as Dickens was moved to fierce indignation by the sufferings of the poor and helpless, Brontë was aroused to anger by injuries done to her sisters and herself. Dickens drew on his own brief period of abandonment to the untender mercies of a blacking factory, Brontë on her miserable short stay in a dank, darksome boarding school, where her beloved sister Maria was virtually bullied to death. Dickens was skilled in using sentimental situations to arouse the indignation of his readers, but it can be said of Brontë, who uses sentimentality sparingly, that her anger was very much her own, sublimated in her novels as in her personality by imposing an iron mask of moral restraint. What happens in Lowood is but a grim threshold to Jane Eyre's ordeal of suffering from an unspoken, unrequited passion, which begins after Rochester returns to Thornfield Hall.

The model for Rochester's mansion has been variously located in Yorkshire, but whatever its architectural equivalent Thornfield was a subtly sublimated version of the *pensionnat* in Brussels. The sufferings of Helen Burns at Lowood were intended to inspire sympathetic Dickensian tears in her readers, but what happens afterward is dry-eyed and darkly conceived, less a literal transcription of *l'affaire* Heger than a highly metaphorical version. In *Villette* Brontë came much closer to the facts of the matter, but because our interest here is with *Jane Eyre*, we need to spend a brief period with *The Professor*, her self-styled "realistic" novel that is in effect an earlier display of ingenious misdirection, a preview of her subsequent and greatly influential novel. "Not that I nursed vengeance," muses the narrator of *The Professor*, clearly speaking here for the author, "but the sense of insult and treachery lived in me like a kindling, though as yet smothered coal" (97).

Like *Jane Eyre*, Brontë's first extended fiction begins with a Dickensian episode, which serves to establish the history and character of the narrator, William Crimsworth, who after his parents' death has received a good education but graduates from college with no expectations. He turns to his wealthy older brother in hopes of employment only to find himself put into a lowly, boring, poorly paid position in his firm. This initial section, which looks forward to the much more detailed awareness in *Shirley* of social inequities brought about by the industrial revolution, is relatively brief. It ends with the appearance of the mysteriously motivated Mr. Hunsden, a wealthy, well-read, cosmopolitan and argumentative gentleman who is an equivalent to those benevolent chaps who show up at critical junctures in Dickens's novels. Like them, Hunsden is in effect a version of fairy godfather, though with an odd but obviously intentional resemblance to Faust's likewise helpful Mephistopheles, with which Brontë finally does nothing.

Hunsden, though free with advice, does not open his wallet, but hectors young Crimsworth into leaving his miserable job for the excellent employment opportunities provided in Brussels (Brussels?), where his good friend Mr. Brown will see to it that William finds a rewarding position, as yet undefined. This turns out to be teaching in a boy's school, hardly a rapid road to wealth, and hard pressed for cash Crimsworth takes on additional work in an adjoining school for girls. This institution is run by an obliquely seductive older woman who makes a play for the young Englishman but who as it turns out is already engaged to the Frenchman who runs the boy's school. Zoraïde Reuter it has been assumed correctly is the first phase of Charlotte's revenge against Mme. Heger.

Mme. Reuter may have been inspired by *la femme* Heger, but her male counterpart, M. Pelet, Crimsworth's other employer, is no Constantin. Crimsworth, in fact, will fill that particular bill himself, his shared teaching responsibilities following the pattern set by the Belgian professor, with results that testify to Brontë's ingenuity in encoding her love for the professor. The young Englishman's anticipation that the girls in his charge will be graceful, filmy angels appealing to his aesthetic side and prettily grateful for his instruction is quickly dispelled by the reality of unruly adolescent Flamandes. But he soon becomes interested in and finally falls in love with Frances Evans Henri, a poor little lace-maker who provides instruction in her craft to the nasty girls at Mme. Reuter's school.

Part English in parentage, Frances is a virtual orphan, and being no older than the girls she teaches, has difficulty in controlling her charges. But she displays a superior skill in her native language, and Crimsworth takes it upon himself to further improve her linguistic abilities, although his motivation is hardly pedagogical. Indeed it verges on pedophilia, so often associated with the relationship between school teachers and their young charges, in recent years without gender limitations, as if bending to the universal pressure of affirmative action.

Frances Henri is Charlotte Brontë in a disguise as easily seen through as the lace she mends, and she rewards her tutor's attention with unmitigated devotion, a loving and obedient even vinelike adhesiveness that is eventually relieved by a certain quality of mischief, lending her a human because somewhat complexified dimension. Through the lace curtain we see a quietly seductive Charlotte who is using her novel as a demonstration to the distant M. Heger of what might have happened had he taken her shy overtures of endless devotion seriously. That she failed to find a publisher must have been doubly disappointing, for her book thereby became yet another intercepted letter.

After circumventing many obstacles placed in their way, Crimsworth and Frances marry, and eventually establish their own school, have a child, save their money—wisely investing it on the advice of Mr. Hunsden, who persists in playing a benevolent "Mephistopheles"—and are able to retire early because of the wealth that results. *Bour* as it were *geoisie*, and terminally boring, made more so by Brontë's virtual abandonment of dialogue for the droning voice of the narrator, always a fatal sign of authorial fatigue.

What gives the first half of the novel its interest is the triangle formed by M. Pelet, Mr. Crimsworth, and Mme. Reuter, which be-

comes a diamond once Frances is worked into the plot and then a
straight line after Pelet and his bride depart for their honeymoon.
That is, as soon as Crimsworth by a display of cold indifference dis-
courages the advances of Mme. Reuter—who is a fascinating blend
of manipulative schemer and openly seductive older woman—so
that she returns humbly to her fiancé, the story becomes a relatively conventional tale of courtship, marriage, etc., etc.

Despite the fancy embroidery work by means of which Charlotte Brontë reworked her experience in Brussels—playing with
points of view and switching roles about, dexterity obvious only to
readers familiar with the facts—*The Professor* is, as the publishers who rejected it observed, lacking in exciting, sensational plot
elements or remarkable, dramatic characters. Resolved to retell
her story in more thrilling terms, and wishing at the same time
to correct what she regarded as her sister's excesses in display-
ing the darker human passions, Brontë set to work on the book
that became *Jane Eyre*. The result was a highly imaginative,
romantic novel in the gothic mode that has ever since rivaled
Wuthering Heights as an example of that genre, there being
nothing published in Victorian England quite like either of the two
books.

In following her sister into the world of gothic romance, Charlotte Brontë in effect reworked the materials of *The Professor*,
telling the story as it were from Frances Henri's point of view and
giving Crimsworth a much different identity, no longer the diffident, sensitive second son of a manufacturing family but a scion
of the landed aristocracy, Edward Fairfax Rochester. And yet, like
The Professor, *Jane Eyre* comes to closure a seemingly conventional story of love and marriage, chief of many of the differences
that distinguish it from *Wuthering Heights*.

III

Ellen Moers's reading of *Jane Eyre* as a sublimated expression of
the author's rage takes as its cue the heroine's outspoken and violent rebellion against John Reed and his arrogant, unfeeling
mother. Certainly, Jane's telling off her aunt and foster-mother is
satisfying for the reader, as if Cinderella had tossed hot ashes into
her stepmother's face. But for Jane it is something else, for although "I smiled to myself and felt elate" for a time, "this fierce
pleasure subsided in me as fast as did the accelerated throb of my
pulses" (46).

By the end of a half-hour, "silence and reflection had shown me the madness of my conduct, and the dreariness of my hated and hating position. Something of vengeance I had tasted for the first time; as aromatic wine it seemed, on swallowing, warm and racy: its after-flavour, metallic and corroding, gave me a sensation as if I had been poisoned" (47). The long-range consequence of getting it off on her aunt will be a stretch in that literal penitentiary, Lowood, where Jane will have plenty of opportunity to consider the high price of her momentary exultation. There may be a temporary ecstasy in releasing one's anger, but the result is an extended period of institutionalized restraint. Control of all passions is the way of wisdom, indeed is the key to survival in a tyrannical world.

Certainly these reflections, though those of a child not yet transformed by extreme hardship and suffering, accord well with the moral drift of the novel. For the implication of Jane's education, her bildungsroman, is that rebellion is folly, submission is wisdom, and although she is unable to emulate Helen Burns's perfect imitation of Christ, Jane with the help of Miss Temple does learn to accept however unhappily the injustice of her humble lot. The reader may cry out in anger over the cruel treatment handed out to the long-suffering heroine, and the author's own fierce indignation is detectable throughout, but Jane herself reluctantly accepts it, and in the end will be rewarded for her patient forebearance. Moreover, by the time Jane arrives at Thornfield Hall, where the great temptation will occur, she is already fully formed, is in fact at the end of the learning process, thanks to her experiences at Lowood, including the guiding example of her mentor, the patient and kindly Maria Temple, that practical not otherworldly Christian.

This is not to say that Charlotte Brontë had changed her mind about her terrible experience at Cowan Bridge. But Jane Eyre is not Charlotte Brontë, and though Lowood is a Dickensian horror, the heroine emerges much the wiser for the experience, reconciled to the necessity of holding her tongue and bowing her will to the stern dictates of necessity. She has at least in the Victorian worldview been strengthened by her suffering, indeed has been prepared by it for what follows in the novel. For what the Thornfield episode provides are two further lessons in the necessity of restraint: Rochester's own history is the first of these, the consequences of which is the child Jane has been hired to teach.

The second, related lesson is found in Bertha Mason, who is released passion personified, bearing witness to Rochester's misguided youth and the consequences of her own sexual appetites. As a Creole she also is a racist amalgam, her sexuality presumably traceable to her exotic lineage, her "black" blood, the miscegenetic flag that traditionally signalled a tragic finale. Where little Adèle is her mother in miniature, a pretty child whose superficial character is a token of Rochester's hitherto wasted life pursuing pleasure, Bertha is a much darker, more powerful witness to the dangers of licentiousness, who must be kept locked away as in a Pandora's box of the passions.

Jane is an admirable (in Victorian terms) young woman, bravely enduring ignomy and shame, drawing strength from her loneliness even as she suffers from it. She is able even as a child to discern between wise and foolish, sinful and virtuous conduct, and will continue to do so when the choice (so often painful) is offered. But she has also learned the lesson of self-control in the face of injustice, which means forebearance when confronted by iniquity. Rochester, likewise, even before Jane returns to him, has accepted his injuries as God's just punishment for his sins: though still high in station, the once proud and fiery gentleman is now himself humbled, grateful for whatever kindnesses he is given. The route of pride and anger is the road to hell, much as Jane's denunciation of her aunt led her directly to the purgatorial Lowood.

In Branwell's painting of his three sisters time's changes have introduced a symbolism unintended by the artist, who originally included himself in the group as the dominant figure, with Charlotte to his left, Emily and Anne to his right. The grouping is primarily chronological, the family according to their respective ages commencing with Charlotte to the far right of the picture. But following the family pairings, Branwell and Charlotte stand together, with Emily and Anne placed opposite. It is easy also to detect a family resemblance in the faces of the paired sisters, while Charlotte bears little resemblance to either of them.

As for Branwell, who inherited his father's sharp features, his likeness has been almost entirely erased, perhaps by Charlotte herself. First replaced by a "great pillar," he now persists as a ghostly shadow, a pale, unfeatured presence further separating Charlotte from her sisters. And if there was a ghost in residence at the Haworth parsonage, it was surely Branwell during his years of slow then rapidly increasing decline. As such he would haunt the works of his sisters, a sympathetic (if appalling) figure in the novels of Anne and Emily, repulsive to an extreme in *Jane Eyre*. It was, noted Gaskell, only by hiking through the "wild and open hills" around Haworth that she "could escape from the Shadow in the house below" (245).

The strongest reflection in his sisters' work of Branwell's decline and fall is in Anne's second novel, *The Tenant of Wildfell Hall,* where Arthur Huntingdon pursues a Branwell-like course of self-destruction through licentious living and drink. His wife marries Arthur with the misguided determination to reform him, and though she is for the most part miserably ineffective, toward the end of the novel—Huntingdon having been reduced through his dissoluteness to complete dependence—she is partially successful in his redemption. Charlotte was unhappy with this portrait, not from any desire to protect Branwell but because, as with Heathcliff, she felt that such types do not belong in serious literature, which should have an uplifting effect on the reader.

Like Huntingdon, Heathcliff (like Branwell) is unredeemable, providing an antithesis to which the addition of Rochester makes a mediating third, for although given Byronic qualities, Rochester has nothing in him of Branwell's self-destructive personality. His profligacy has already been demonstrated to anyone's satisfaction before the story begins, and he seems always in control of himself as well as others until that control is taken away when he is nearly killed during the fire that destroys his great home. One might make a case that Master John Reed is a glimpse of Branwell, being a caricature of weakness and viciousness whose death marks one of the turning points in the plot, but he is a literary convention for the most part, and we see so little of his own degeneration that his role is not significant.

I am not alone in thinking that it is in the unlikely form of Bertha Mason that Branwell chiefly haunts the novel. Her pyromaniacal tendencies are said to have been inspired by Branwell's accidental firing of his bedroom curtains during a drunken spell, and, more important, Branwell like Bertha is associated with scandalous sexuality, although in person he seems to have been the most unlikely sort to get involved in an adulterous liaison. Still, it was his lack of self-control that was Branwell's most disturbing fault, at least so far as Charlotte was concerned.

It was a destructive failure that was all the more poignant and traumatic given the siblings' earlier close relationship dreaming up their Glasstown stories, which were nourished by Branwell's wild genius, now become mere wildness. He was most certainly an object lesson in the dangers of too much indulgence in a fantastic imagination, and those who have had the care of persons no longer in control of themselves can understand how easy it was for Charlotte to translate Branwell into the violent madwoman in the attic who upon occasion breaks free to wreak havoc on the household.

We may allow with Margot Peters (1975) and Rebecca Fraser (1988) that Charlotte's rage was in part the result of seeing in Branwell's hopeless love a mirror image of her feelings for Heger. It was also the result of her being able to distinguish between fact and fiction, at least where her brother was concerned. Branwell moreover had sex with his employer's wife, a weakness of which neither his sister nor her vicarious agent, Jane Eyre, was guilty, and it was the adulterous union that warranted Charlotte's disgust. But then she was never actively pursued, where both Branwell and Jane were, and Jane's strength in denying her employer's overtures cannot be credited to her creator's own history, even though it reflected Brontë's moral values.

Peters and Fraser, in supporting this thesis, quote from a letter Brontë wrote to her editor, William S. Williams, justifying the "shocking" quality of Mrs. Rochester, defending it as only "too natural," a phrase that recalls Edmund's appeal in King Lear to Nature, an abstraction that for Shakespeare and perhaps for Charlotte connoted uncontrolled passion, of which Edmund is the fruit (Peters, 212; Fraser, 263). Bertha's insanity, explained Charlotte, may be termed "moral madness," in which any shred of human goodness disappears to be replaced by a "fiend-nature," with a consequent desire "to exasperate, to molest, to destroy, and preternatural ingenuity and energy are often exercised to that dreadful end."

Charlotte confessed that the proper sentiment inspired by "such degradation" was pity, admittedly absent from her portrait of mad Bertha, which was created chiefly with the intention of inspiring "*horror*." But then she went on to the apparently unrelated observation, which provides the definitive link to Branwell, that "Mrs. Rochester indeed lived a sinful life before she was insane, but sin is itself a species of insanity: the truly good behold and compassionate it as such." Still, we find little compassionating in Charlotte's account of Branwell's "illness," and much outrage and disgust, more evidence that she was not always the perfect model of Christian forebearance portrayed by Elizabeth Gaskell.

Branwell's history of failures, first as an artist then as a railroad clerk, were bad enough, but his adulterous affair was the final straw for Charlotte. The family (and Elizabeth Gaskell) attributed this moral lapse to the predatory advances of Mrs. Robinson, which Branwell was either too weak to withstand or took advantage of in the hopes of improving his fortunes by marrying his in-amorata upon the death of her ailing husband. Either way, Charlotte's indignation was translated into Rochester's attempted seduction of Jane Eyre, protestations of love coupled with visions of a luxurious life to follow, twin temptations that she is successful in refusing by fleeing Thornfield that very night. Branwell by contrast was driven from the Robinson home by an outraged husband, and spent much of his time thereafter in a drunken, narcotic haze, dreaming of the woman and wealth that would be his once Robinson died. When the dream collapsed, so did he, having a psychic structure of sand.

In sum, Branwell did not follow what Charlotte in a letter of 1846 defined as the "right path," but Jane Eyre did, in her case the road leading away from Rochester's mansion. After a terrible journey across the storm-swept heath, it leads her to a snug little house that is the dwelling of two young women who prove to be her cousins, and who, as critics have suggested, are really Emily and Anne together in the Haworth parsonage. Branwell is noticeably no longer at home (his place is taken by the very peculiar but hardly dissolute St. John), having been left back at Thornfield Hall awaiting a fiery fate.

Moral outrage, even in the sincerest breast, is an ambiguous matter, and the fiercest scorn is often aimed at those who give way to the temptations we ourselves fear (hence hate) most. Whatever her motives, though Brontë never had the opportunity to rebuff adulterous advances, we may safely assume that she was quite prepared to do so, and all indications are that her adoration for Heger was a platonic affair, that grew warmer with the safety that distance provides, compounded with the longing that distance makes more acute. Unlike Jane (and Branwell), Charlotte Brontë never had her virtue sorely tempted, but the creation of the mighty Rochester from the inadequate shape of Professor Heger is further testimony to the changing dimensions of Charlotte's obsessive love, an impossible dream translated into an equally impossible fiction.

Her heroine's rejection of Rochester's blandishments, a temptation much greater than anything Heger could have offered, suggests both a testimony to her own moral position should Heger have made a similar proposition (being a Catholic he could hardly have filed for divorce) as well as a pointed comment on her brother's moral weakness. Branwell could have taken the right road but failed to do so, and Jane Eyre in this particular is his reverse image, in both sex and deed, a projection of the severe, moral side of his sister, yet so intimate with Brontë's fantasy life as to be inseparable from her relationship with Branwell, never mind Professor Heger.

Branwell may provide at least a tentative link between Emily Brontë's novel and her sister's response, but equally remarkable is the thing missing from *Jane Eyre* that plays such an important part in *Wuthering Heights* and in the lives of Charlotte and her sisters—the landscape that surrounded the parsonage at Haworth. Elizabeth Gaskell, indeed virtually every biographer who followed her to that inevitable site, devotes considerable space to a delineation of the Yorkshire environment, in terms both of landscape and society. Gaskell remarked of the people of the region that "they are a powerful race both in mind and body, both for good and for evil," from whom "irregularity and fierce lawlessness" may be expected, rather than "pastoral innocence and simplicity. . . . Revenge was handed down from father to son as an hereditary duty" (18–19, 27).

Though Gaskell's intention was obviously to provide the right if anomalous setting for Charlotte Brontë, much of what she says applies explicitly to *Wuthering Heights* rather than to any of Charlotte's works (18, 24). Not only are her novels for the most part what Melville called "inside" narratives, but what happens outside in her stories often occurs in a garden or its equivalent, a romantic, enclosed space that is a green equivalent to an interior setting. As such it provides a perfect setting for the fairy element in *Jane Eyre*.

IV

The fairies are forever departing from the English countryside, a phenomenon equivalent (and perhaps attributable) to the perennial rise of the middling classes. The Brontës' housekeeper, Tabby, credited the disappearance of fairies from Yorkshire to the building of factories, much as six centuries earlier the Wife of Bath blamed it on friaries. Yet like the granite pillars of Stonehenge the belief persists, enduring the ravages of Christianity and capitalism alike, and as recently as the 1920s so staunch a celebrant of rational man as Arthur Conan Doyle was taken in by doctored photographs of little winged people.

The fairy element is an atavistic continuum, a time tunnel through which we can catch a glimpse of a green world, both of ancient and archetypal age. We do not know much about the nature of that world: what survives is fragmentary and diluted thanks to the effects of the well-known monkish sieve. Most certainly the British peasantry was a vehicle of preservation, and the Brontë children like Byron were tutored in this lore by a superstitious peasant woman. Again, there are those frequent references in *Jane Eyre* to conventional fairy tale elements, a sequence intended to lend the novel a further element of the marvelous.

Thus in his jesting, teasing talks with his governess, Rochester repeatedly calls Jane a fairy, an elf, a changeling, while she calls him an ogre, bantering which adds spice to the dialogue and a dominant train of allusive images to the text. The elements of terror and suspense are likewise enhanced by the mystery of the creature kept locked in one of those rooms associated with Bluebeard: characterized as a "vampyre," Bertha Mason is the resident spectre of Thornfield, a succubus as well as incubus, lurking about the beds of Jane and Rochester as if in search of an indecent meal.

The fairy tale mood intensifies during the famous Midsummers Eve scene, a wild-garden interlude in which Jane and Rochester declare their love for each other, a setting borrowed not from Shakespeare's wildwood romances but from the actual garden at the Hegers' *pensionnat* in Brussels. It is in the wild garden at Thornfield that Rochester proposes to Jane, an illicit proposition that in effect converts his courtship to a Comus-like overture, with a suitable wildwood backdrop. But Jane remains ignorant of her true situation until like one of Milton's wandering brothers Richard Mason interrupts the wedding to tell of Rochester's marriage to his sister. Like Milton's Lady, Jane will flee from her intended lover, and in her pell-mell escape from Thornfield she rushes toward the Victorian ideal of womanhood, becoming most Angelic when in flight from the House.

Carried by coach as far as her money will take her, Jane makes her way across the heath on foot, reduced to near starvation and suffering from exposure to the cold, an initiatory passage that prepares her for the snug refuge she finds with the St. John Rivers family, a name connoting baptism and salvation (and perhaps Milton's savior stream as well). In the next section of the novel the fairy furniture disappears, to be replaced by a thoroughly (if often oblique) redemptive parable, dominated by two women called Diana and Mary, names derived from pagan and Christian iconography but both connoting the transcendent power of chastity. As bildungsroman, the novel is closer to the root than to the flower, being more in the spirit of Bunyan and Defoe than Goethe, much as in the use of fairy tale elements it is closer to Spenser and Milton than to Shakespeare.

For *Jane Eyre* at times seems a fictionalized spiritual autobiography in which the heroine operates under the protective aegis of a Calvinist God. Her given name, the female equivalent of "John," means "Grace of God," and the main stations along her road to enlightenment are presided over by persons with quasi-allegorical names, from Helen Burns and Maria Temple of Lowood, to St. John Rivers and his sisters, Mary and Diana, at Morton. But as the example of Bunyan and Defoe warrant, Jane's flight from the pagan fairyland of Thornfield for her Christian trials at Morton does not obviate the marvelous element entirely.

For in the tradition of special providences, Jane's blessedness is demonstrated by the benign circumstances and wonderful coincidences that at first seem to be onerous even fatal hardships. That is, her symbolic three-day ordeal of hunger and cold carries her straight to the window that reveals to Jane the snug, companionable world of the Rivers, a domestic trine who will prove to be her cousins, thereby verifying the elective affinity she feels for them. And as with Oliver Twist's similarly haphazard journey into the bosom of his long-lost family, there is a traditionally romantic recovery operating here as well as a Christian scheme, marvels attesting in both instances to the workings of some supernatural agency, a benign even a loving force. Clearly, Jane is one of the elect, is beloved of God. Thus the pagan elements are eventually absorbed into a Christian parable of suffering and redemption, a key difference between Charlotte's novel and *Wuthering Heights*.

During her stay at Thornfield Jane Eyre goes through the prolonged groveling that is in spiritual autobiography the traditional sign of awakening, being the expression of a profound sense of unworth, not however in terms of the divine will but the whim of her beloved master. Where she finds Rochester's Byronic cynicism attractive, the fanaticism of St. John Rivers, her brother-cousin and namesake, is repellant, and his proposal of marriage is as unacceptable as Rochester's. Where Rochester's illicit expression of love is a cruel burlesque of her feelings toward him, St. John's fanatic commitment to what he conceives to be his sacred mission is a caricature of Jane's own sense of Christian duty. In rejecting his loveless even arrogant proposal she is not necessarily rejecting Christianity as such (as some readers have assumed), for St. John's fanaticism is an extreme and repellant version of faith, a subvert manifestation of personal ambition.

Despite this Christian framework, it is the element of romance that dominates *Jane Eyre,* much as the heroine never stops loving Rochester. Indeed, during her ordeal crossing the moors she prays not for herself but for him, and is reassured by the nighttime display in the heavens that God's is an orderly world and that Rochester will be watched over, little suspecting the rough method of caregiving that will follow. At times during her residence at Morton she seems to be putting on a Hester Prynne mask of Christian humility, to the last (like Charlotte Brontë at Roe Head) disliking her schoolroom chores and the children under her care.

"Show me the path!" she begs of God, but when the summons comes, it is spoken by Rochester. In obeying it, Jane ignores the possibility that Bertha is still alive, but here again coincidence works in her favor, because Bertha is dead. Were she not, the command would never have come, obviously, for to have obeyed it would have been wrong, a situational twist typical of the Calvinist version of a Möbius strip. Thus, when Jane rejoins her beloved Master, the decision to stay with him is now a properly Christian one, his need for her aid a romantic translation of the parable about the Good Samaritan.

That is, as a romance, *Jane Eyre* works in two different yet finally harmonic directions, investing the pagan world of fairies and fate with a thoroughly Protestant élan while modifying the rigors of evangelical Protestantism with a saving grace. There is some unintended irony therefore in a review that grouped *Jane Eyre* with *Wuthering Heights,* denouncing both for an overt display of paganism. To accuse Charlotte of heathenish sentiments because of her attack on pious hypocrites is much like the recent tendency—which may be credited to Sandra Gilbert and Susan Gubar (1984)—to regard mad Bertha as Jane's alter ego, as an expression of the anger that she habitually represses in herself (*The Madwoman in the Attic,* 359–60). In this reading, Bertha's madness is the consequence not the cause of her confinement, a demonstration that in Victorian England a woman who seeks freedom of self-expression will pay a terrible price. Both readings amount to a rigid allegorization that emphasizes one element in a complex plot at the cost of others.

The key scene in this latter connection is the one in which Jane, having become bored by the constricted life at Thornfield, despite the good natured warmth of Mrs. Fairfield and the obedient and diligent if limited performance of her pupil, Adèle, climbs to the roof and looks "afar over sequestered field and hill, and along dim

skyline" (125). She wishes "for a power of vision which might over-
pass that limit; which might reach the busy world, towns, regions
full of life I had heard of but never seen; . . . I desired more of practical experience than I possessed; more of intercourse with my
kind, of acquaintance with variety of character, than was here
within my reach."

When tormented by this restlessness, Jane would pace back
and forth "along the corridor of the third story . . . safe in the silence and solitude of the spot, and allow my mind's eye to dwell on
whatever bright visions rose before it . . . to let my heart be heaved
by the exultant movement, which, while it swelled it in trouble, expanded it with life; and, best of all, to open my inward ear to a tale
that was never ended—a tale my imagination created, and narrated continuously; quickened with all of incident, life, fire, feeling,
that I desired and had not in my actual existence." This pacing as
we know was associated with the process of creation at Haworth,
another imprisoning place, from which escape was only possible
through creativity itself, carrying the Brontë children into romantic realms derived from literature and located in exotic
realms, like Africa.

All human beings, Jane reflects, "must have action," and such
desires if repressed inspire rebellion other than political: "Women
are supposed to be very calm generally: but women feel just as
men feel; they need exercise for their faculties, and a field for their
efforts as much as their brothers do." This restlessness is hardly
satisfied by the domestic round, and if women express their need
for something more than knitting, cooking, sewing, with an occasional interlude at the piano, "it is thoughtless to condemn them,
or laugh at them, if they seek to do more or learn more than cus-
tom has pronounced necessary for their sex" (126). It is in expressing these discontents that Jane anticipates the heroines'
complaints in the domestic novel in America, as defined by Nina
Baym, and it is precisely at this juncture that Jane alludes to the
low sounds of laughter she has learned to credit to Jane Poole, the
"slow ha! ha! which, when first heard, had thrilled me."

Like the snickering of Fedallah from the Pequod's hold, the
laughter has a mocking implication, coming as it does from a
woman under restraints unimagined by Jane. For Bertha also
sought to live free from restrictions placed by society on women,
and as a consequence has gone mad. As Gilbert and Gubar allow,
following Richard Chase, Bertha can be seen, not so much as the
"secret self" of Jane Eyre, her alter ego, but rather as her antithesis, a "monitory" presence (361). In this reading, the mad-

woman serves as an example of the penalty exacted for having expressed the unrestrained passion that is sublimated in the heroine's meditation about women's need for freedom, which reads like a feminist manifesto. It was Jane's soliloquy on the ramparts that seems to have drawn the anger of one reviewer, a woman herself, who faulted Brontë's heroine for her discontent amidst plenty, hers being the sorrows of the well-fed middle class. Both modern readers and the Victorian critic have taken Jane's meditation as the author's own, where if we place it in context we can see that it is a sign that the heroine has not yet finished her education, the next phase of which is about to come.

That improvised novel Jane is composing as she paces back and forth, the vicarious expression of her restlessness, sounds a great deal like the Glasstown books written in partnership with Branwell, being packed with the kinds of "incident, fire, feeling, that I desired and had not in my actual existence." This was the world of Angria that Charlotte Brontë made a conscious decision to turn her back upon, in her first full-length novel opting for what she called "realistic" fiction. It is a Byronic world, much as it is his eternal restlessness that drives Childe Harold on a ceaseless, desperate quest, and it is even more pointedly the world of Branwell, which helps to explain the meaning of mad laughter in a locked room.

Again, Bertha is a personified fury; Jane herself is definably even justifiably angry much of the time, but having been inspired by mad Branwell, Bertha testifies to the dangers of yielding to passion where Jane testifies not only to the virtue of self-control but to the rewards that come of it. The Calvinist system of Election and Grace Abounding did not leave out the element of Free Will, but it was limited to making the right choices: Jane not only benefits from the blessings of Providence but she earns them. At the height of his passion, frustrated by his inability to force Jane into an illicit relationship, Rochester compares her defiant eye to some "'resolute, wild, free thing, defying me, with more than courage—with a stern triumph. Whatever I do with its cage, I cannot get at it—the savage, beautiful creature!'" (357). This creature in a cage is the antithesis to Bertha in her cell, being as Rochester cries, grinding his teeth, "'at once so frail and so indomitable.'"

For it is Jane's body that is the cage, and it acts in accordance with her will not his, obeys the highest moral command not like Bertha the dictates and longings of the flesh. Everything that happens to Jane leads her toward that final reunion with Rochester, when the relationship is sanctified by marriage and then certified by their child. Theirs is a perfection of domestic felicity that, while undoubtedly circumscribed by bounds, no longer inspires in the heroine that restless hunger to experience the whole of life. We certainly hear no more about Jane's wanderlust.

"Reader," says Jane famously, winding up her story, "I married him," and after ten years of married life she knows "what it is to live entirely for and with what I love best on earth" (498, 500). She and "my Edward . . . are happy," their happiness made even more intense by the happiness of her female cousins, who "are both married as well," Diana (read mannish Emily) to a courageous navy captain, Mary (read saintly Anne) to a clergyman, mates that perfectly match their different personalities (501). So everyone will live happily ever after, and is that not how fairy stories are supposed to end?

3

A Man on Horseback:
(Per)Versions of the Masculine

Illuminated with the Author's own candles.
—Thackeray

I

IT IS SURELY NO COINCIDENCE THAT THE EPISODE IN WHICH JANE
Eyre describes her restlessness, in part inspired by the boring
rhythms of her days at Thornfield, is soon followed by the first appearance of the master of the mansion, who not only will add considerable variety to Jane's life but will give new meaning to the
theme of frustrated desires. The meeting occurs out of doors, in the
midst of nature, for Jane is carrying a letter to the nearby village of
Hay, and having delayed her errand to watch the sun set in the
west, she is still walking eastward toward town as the moon rises.

It is then that Rochester appears, announced by a loud clatter-
ing of hooves, a sound that interrupts the hitherto audible rip-
plings of the many region brooks, so quiet has been the evening
air. She compares the interruption to "a picture," in which "the
solid mass of a crag, or the rough boles of a great oak, drawn in
dark and strong in the foreground, efface the aerial distance of
azure hill, sunny horizon, and blended clouds, where tint melts
into tint," an analogy abstracted from William Gilpin's notions of
the picturesque, out of which the solid, great, dark and strong
Rochester will come riding, riding into the story and into her heart
(128). At the start, he is abstracted from the landscape, and
Rochester will prove to be quite a piece of work, a complex figure
of erotic desire associated with the great chestnut tree in the garden at Thornfield.

At first the sound of hooves reminds Jane of a spectre evoked in
the frightening nursery stories of her childhood, "wherein figured

a North-of-England spirit, called a 'Gytrash'; which, in the form of horse, mule, or large dog, haunted solitary ways, and sometimes came upon belated travellers, as this horse was now coming upon me." This is of course a conventional gothic bogie, soon dispelled by reality, yet at the first sight of Rochester's large Newfoundland dog, Jane is forcibly reminded of the Gytrash, the animal being "a lion-like creature with long hair and a huge head" that stares at her as it ran past "with strange pretercanine eyes." The dog, however, is followed by a man on horseback, who, being obviously human, "broke the spell at once," and who in his attempt to pass her on the road, takes a tumble, horse and all.

Once again upright, standing uncertainly because of an injured (Byronic) foot, the man is clearly seen in the moonlight: "enveloped in a riding cloak, fur collared and steel clasped," he is of "middle height, and considerable breadth of chest. He had a dark face, with stern features and a heavy brow; his eyes and gathered eyebrows looked ireful and thwarted just now" (129). Had he been more conventionally handsome, Jane reflects, she might have been struck silent with shyness, "but the frown, the roughness of the traveller set me at my ease" (130).

Having learned that she is the governess at Thornfield, the injured man asks Jane for her help in regaining his mount: "'I must beg of you to come here,'" he requests, and leaning on her shoulder he limps to his horse, then bridle in hand, vaults into the saddle: "'Now,' he said, releasing his under lip from a hard bite, 'just hand me my whip; it lies there under the hedge'" (131). She complies with the request, and he rides on, allowing her to continue her walk to Hay. At this point neither the reader nor Jane realizes that the injured man is her employer, nor has Rochester felt the need to tell his governess who he is.

It is the first step in a series of cat-and-mouse games that he will play with Jane, thereby establishing the teasing terms of what turns out to be a perverse kind of courtship, in which the object of his affections is permitted no inkling of his fond regard. The episode is also prophetic, for having leaned temporarily on Jane, Rochester by the end of the story will be leaning on her a bit more heavily, in both a physical and a psychological sense. Nor should we neglect the implications of that whip he asks Jane to hand him, an icon of control exercised through pain.

Though somewhat resembling Professor Heger in coloration and features, Rochester has a much larger physique and a rougher profile, and it is his sheer size and roughness that comes into play as he bullies Jane. The combination suggests a sexual threat, both frightening and exciting, yet his rough, homely exterior hides a truly loving even tender heart: hidden inside the costume of a Beast is a very human being. Here he can be contrasted to Heathcliff, who though outwardly handsome has a merciless devil inside, and who having courted Isabella through conventional terms of flattery, turns on her cruelly as soon as they are married.

Moreover, for all his outward show of masculinity, Rochester at home is surrounded by females. Though he is the head of the household, all things revolve about the hidden fact of Bertha, who like little Adèle is maintained on the premises because of Rochester's sense of duty—if anything more acute than Jane's. Rochester is a "woman's man," and in this resembles Jane Austen's heroes—Mr. Knightly in particular—a resemblance that is obviously circumstantial and coincidental, knowing Brontë's attitude toward Austen's novels—*Emma* in specific. Moreover, the differences are perhaps more definitive than the similarities: both men are older than the heroines, and both assume a firm superiority, but where Knightly is a rational man of the Enlightenment —and a gentleman farmer to boot—the other is a romantic man of feeling, not otherwise visibly employed. Where Knightly is personified Wisdom, Rochester personifies Passion.

Both are viewed through a perspective in which younger, more "suitable" lovers are seen as imperfect specimens of manhood, having faults hardly recommending them to either the heroine or the reader. But where Emma is offered just the sort of suitor Brontë herself twice turned down, a smug, conceited man of the cloth, Jane's St. John is an exotic, a fanatic enthusiast for carrying Christ into pagan lands, as romantic a figure as a clergyman can become, with a physical beauty that is never given to Austen's alternative suitors.

Brontë was pleased to pass on to her editor, William S. Williams, the man who had urged that she read *Emma,* a letter from a female admirer who formerly had been seeking a Mr. Knightly for her husband, but having read *Villette,* was now looking for "the duplicate of Professor Emanuel, or remain for ever single!" (Gaskell, 405). Most critics have agreed that Paul Emanuel was the penultimate version of Professor Heger, quite a different figure from Rochester, yet we need only recall the testimony of Fred Pattee's mother to understand the popular appeal of Jane Eyre's lover.

Despite these differences, Brontë's novels contain a romantic version of the didacticism that pervades Austen's throughout:

"Passion and Prudence" might well be the title of *Jane Eyre:* "Give rein to your emotions," Brontë seems to be saying, "but never drop the reins." Again, as Gilbert and Gubar point out, the closest eighteenth-century literary parallel would seem to be Fielding's *Pamela,* for Charlotte's story also is of a rake reformed, the antithesis of Anne's *The Tenant of Wildfell Hall* as well as of Emily Brontë's tale of heedless love. Gaskell's biography reinforces the saintly image of Charlotte Brontë by citing a letter from another American clergyman, who writes that "we have in our sacred of sacreds a special shelf, highly adorned, as a place we delight to honour, of novels which we recognize as having had a good influence on character, our character. Foremost is 'Jane Eyre'" (281). We may doubt that *Wuthering Heights* was given a place on that shelf, and yet if *Jane Eyre* is a Victorian parable of a woman who chose the straight and narrow path of virtue, it is, as a number of modern readers have observed, warped throughout with the perverse tensions described by Steven Marcus in *The Other Victorians.*

American ministers and mill girls might place the book in their inner sanctums, but like Lord Petre's altar *Jane Eyre* as a sacred object has an erotic even gargoylish look when examined closely. Given Charlotte Brontë's conflicted motives, her stiff morality erected to protect herself from falling back into fantasies of passion, her intense religious idealism that never seems to have had a conventionally pious expression, and her frustrated love for Professor Heger that found release by writing novels that obsessively fulfilled it, we might well expect to find a few tangled threads in the weave.

But the closer we look the more tangles we detect, until what seemed to most of Charlotte Brontë's contemporaries (with some help from her friend Elizabeth Gaskell) an admirable Christian fable turns out to be a subliminal expression of psychic disarray. It is a kind of pornography, not the obvious delineation of perversity described by Marcus, but an oblique and presumably unconscious expression of desires which when detected appall. We have already detected shadow shapes derived from the dark version of "Cinderella," but there are other equally alarming spectres yet to be revealed. In modern terms, Charlotte maintained a Web site best closed off to minors, those young women who made up a large part of her audience at the start, a few of whom would be the writers of the books intended for the next generation of adolescent readers, writers who would set about to establish alternative sites.

II

In writing *Jane Eyre*, Brontë, even while claiming to be presenting the "truth," set forth virtue in a pattern that while championing the ideal of duty did so in a way that when closely examined
proves ambivalent even repellant. In drawing on her fantasy life
to lend excitement to her narrative she revealed more than she or
her readers knew about herself and, finally, about themselves as
well. Certainly there is sufficient drama and suspense in Brontë's
christianized fairy tale to explain its popularity, but when a book
has the overwhelming generational impact of *Jane Eyre*, we are
well advised to look for the textual equivalent of a voltaic pile. In
Brontë's case it is not a matter of intentional ambiguity but of
something equally oblique, being a deeply private perverseness
that haunts the book throughout.

Let me give emphasis to what is to come by returning to *The
Professor*, which as I have said seems a thoroughly conventional
story of love conquering all. I say "seems," because it is not entirely conventional. With her odd blend of steadfast devotion and
mischievous rebellion, Frances Evans Henri has a certain interest and originality that carries us through the otherwise predictable story. Once she and Crimsworth are married, she is both
authoritative in her role as teacher to others and seductively submissive as a lover, wife, and continuing student.

An independent professional at work, hence a preview of the
"new woman," when at home Frances inevitably submits to the
judgment and rule of her husband, acting out the conventional
role of House Angel. She persists even after marriage in calling
him "Monsieur," a title suggesting the power invested in the male
side of the relationship, even more emphasized by her other affectionate name, "Master," both being the titles with which Charlotte habitually addressed her former teacher in letters to the distant and unresponding Heger.

This seems a good time to introduce to our discussion the example provided by a book first published in 1835 as *Goethes
Briefwechsel mit ein Kinde*, correspondence purportedly between the great German writer-philosopher and "Bettina," a.k.a.
Elizabeth Brentano, Countess von Arnim. The book had quite a
vogue during the mid-nineteenth century, obviously borrowing
from Goethe's fame, but with considerable interest of its own,
given the correspondence's romantic character. While enrolled at
the *pensionnat* in Brussels, Charlotte became modestly profi-
cient in the German language, and whether or not she actually

read the original, it seems likely that she knew of the *Briefwech-sel,* the origins and contents of which have a familiar ring.

According to the *Britannica* (11th edition), Bettina in 1807, aged twenty-two and hardly a *Kinde,* "made at Weimar the acquain-tance of Goethe, for whom she entertained a violent passion, which the poet, although entering into correspondence with her, did not requite, but only regarded as a harmless fancy. Their friendship came to an abrupt end in 1811, owing to 'Bettina's' in-solent behavior to Goethe's wife" (entry under "Arnim, Elizabeth Von"). This capsule description could as easily be applied to Brontë's relationship with M. Heger, even to the final note re-garding Goethe's wife. "Dear master," was Bettina's occasional form of address, but "Dearest Goethe" was the usual, and she ap-parently anchored the relationship by forming an affectionate bond through an exchange of letters with Goethe's mother, the surest way to many a man's heart when his stomach is not read-ily available.

Bettina, judging from her side of the correspondence, seems to have been an egocentric young person, perhaps the type neces-sary to repeatedly pledge her love while getting back the blandest expressions of avuncular affection: "As long as I have anything to tell you, so long I firmly believe thy spirit is fixed upon me," she writes early in the relationship, "as upon so *many* enigmas of Na-ture; thus, I believe each being to be such an enigma, and that it is the office of love between friends to solve the enigma; so that each one may become acquainted with his more secret nature, *through* and *in* his friend. Yes, dearest, this makes me happy, that my life gradually develops itself through thee; therefore would I not be *counterfeit;* rather suffer all my faults and weaknesses to be known to thee, than give thee a wrong notion of myself; because *then* thy love would not be busy with *me,* but with a false image, which I had inserted instead of my own" (Arnim, 151). Bettina labored hard not to be enigmatic, promoting herself as a child of nature, with intellectual interests withal, but Goethe remained something of a sphinx. Nor was he as eager or as regular a corre-spondent as Bettina desired, and she frequently complained about delays in getting a response to her voluble self-revelations, and when Goethe's replies came, they were often quite brief.

There was of course no extended reciprocal correspondence from Heger, but the passion Charlotte felt for her Belgian profes-sor and her contempt for Mme. Heger certainly fit the Bettina pattern. More important, whether or not she was aware of the framing circumstances, Brontë would have regarded the Bettina/

Goethe correspondence as an ideal to imitate. Her surviving letters to Heger obviously yearn for the intimacy Goethe's admirer enjoyed, for it is clear that Bettina felt free to address Goethe in both loving and equal terms. This would have been for Brontë a realized dream, the denial of which has enriched our literature far more than has Bettina's presumed correspondence. Certainly the model was apt—the eager, passionate student, the patient, kindly mentor—but Goethe's *Correspondence with a Child* was as it were printed on paper with two sides, for if Brontë knew the book, so we may well imagine did Mme. Heger, who had no wish to find herself in Frau Goethe's shoes.

Well, a pound of conjecture is worth an ounce of fact, and the fact is that the Brontë-Heger correspondence was brief but the consequences long. In any event, Charlotte was never in Bettina's privileged position, and her letters are for the most part supplicating and piteous, desperate in their expressions of longing for continued contact, and humble in their repeated entreaties for a response. What the actual relationship was while Brontë was still in Brussels we cannot know, but unless *The Professor* like *Jane Eyre* is entirely fantastical, which seems unlikely given Brontë's declared fealty to "truth," it probably gives us at least a slight hint of how things went as well as a strong indication regarding the way in which the author would have liked them to have gone. That is, we can trust Brontë's fiction about as far as we can trust Bettina's correspondence.

From the start of their relationship as Master and Student, Crimsworth takes a stern, commanding posture, "allowing her to stand deferentially at my side; for I esteemed it wise and right in her case to enforce strictly all forms ordinarily in use between master and pupil; the rather because I perceived that in proportion as my manner grew austere and magisterial, hers became easy and self-possessed—an odd contradiction, doubtless, to the ordinary effect in such cases" (121). Odd seems the right word, and getting odder: On their first meeting as teacher and student, Crimsworth reprimands the shy, terrified Frances for being late to class and thereafter insists that she speak only English in his presence, "punishing" and "chastising" her for failures to do so. The specifics of these disciplinary measures are never given, and the story does not have those kink aids favored by the British—whips, paddles, rods, canes, birch twigs, thongs, straps, cricket bats, hearthbrooms, fanbelts, or whatever blooms in the punishing hand—but we can hear the smacks, cracks, and adoring cries for eventual mercy in the next room as it were.

"'Come here,'" commands Crimsworth early on in their relationship, then, when Frances hesitates, "'Step up,' I said, speaking with decision. It is the only way of dealing with diffident, easily embarrassed characters, and with some slight manual aid I presently got her placed just where I wanted her to be. . . . I knew what I was doing would be considered a very strange thing, and, what was more, I did not care. Frances knew it also, and, I fear, by an appearance of agitation and trembling, that she cared much. I drew from my pocket the rolled-up devoir" (118-19). He does not do with the rolled-up devoir what we might expect, but he does criticize the composition for its faultiness, assuming a stern and authoritative air, which "kindles" a responsive fire in his student: "Her depression beamed as a cloud might behind which the sun is burning."

Upon Frances's first lapse back into speaking her native French, Crimsworth notes that were she "a child, I should certainly devise some slight punishment," and in effect, though Frances is nineteen, he treats her like a child, subjecting her to an informal catechism regarding her personal history, scolding her for her faults, real and imaginary, and purposely withholding praise for her devoirs until the precisely right psychological moment, postures to which she readily adapts her passive responses. Frances literally blossoms under this regimen, not only psychologically but physically: "That look of wan emaciation which anxiety or low spirits often communicates to a thoughtful, thin face, rather long than round, having vanished from hers; a clearness of skin almost bloom, and a plumpness almost embonpoint, softened the decided lines of her features. Her figure shared in this beneficial change; it became rounded . . . in contours . . . compact, elegant, flexible— the exquisite turning of waist, wrist, hand, and ankle satisfied completely my notions of symmetry" (130). It is not difficult to see in this newly "wakened to life" maiden a reasonable approximation to Galatea, shaped by the discipline of her Master, the approximate Pygmalion who has whipped her into the desired and desirable shape: "I watched this change much as a gardener watches the growth of a precious plant" (131).

Though obviously attracted sexually to his pupil, Crimsworth several times insists that Frances is not in any conventional sense beautiful, a point Charlotte Brontë as well as many others made about herself. Frances's charm is found in her personality, early defined as a combination of "perseverance and a sense of duty," but later emerging as something much more attractive. There is a creative brilliance found in her compositions ("devoirs," as they are traditionally called, with a dutifully pious implication), and her capacity for happiness is revealed in her eyes, "bright hazel . . . irids large and full, screened with long lashes; and pupils instinct with fire" (114, 130). As we know, and as Charlotte Brontë realized, her eyes were the most commanding feature in an otherwise commonplace, undistinguished face. It was Jane Eyre's eye, we will remember, that Rochester compared to a defiant if caged wild creature.

Realizing what is going on between Crimsworth, still the object of her affections, and Frances, the jealous Mme. Reuter discharges the poor little lace-maker on a specious pretext. Crimsworth searches for her throughout Brussels before impulsively entering the Protestant cemetery, where the teacher and his favorite pupil are reunited over the fresh grave of Frances's aunt, her only surviving relation. His passion inspired by "the light of Frances Evans' clear hazel eye," Crimsworth now acknowledges to the reader (but not to Frances) that he is in love.

Her eyes may have him, but Crimsworth is also aroused by the sight of Frances standing by her aunt's grave, now entirely an orphan, "penniless and parentless." Such an arrangement would be "for a sensualist charmless, for me a treasure—my best object of sympathy on earth, thinking such thoughts as I thought, feeling such feelings as I felt; my ideal of the shrine in which to seal my stores of love; personification of discretion and forethought, of diligence and perseverance, of self-denial and self-control,—those guardians, those trusty keepers of the gift I longed to confer on her" (149).

Let us remember that the narrator is rendering a self-portrait here, that in Crimsworth's rhapsodic description of Frances, Charlotte Brontë is summing up what she regarded as her virtues, qualifications for the affection she had hoped to inspire in Professor Heger. Professor Crimsworth is Heger's stand-in, being made to mouth the words Brontë longed to hear. As for Frances, raising her eyes to his, not fearing "to look straight into mine," it is her cry of recognition that binds the two into one: "'Mon maitre! mon maitre!'" She takes him to her simple but clean and tidy apartment, a Quakerish aesthetics reflected also in her plain black dress and white collar, divested of any ornament— "perfection of fit, proportion of form, grace of carriage, agreeably supplied their place"—precisely the simple *couteur* favored by Charlotte Brontë (154).

Now almost overwhelmed by the emotion of love—"the intelligence of her face seemed beauty to me, and I dwelt on it accordingly"—Crimsworth-Heger brings himself under control by bring-

ing Frances-Charlotte under control: "Recollecting the composing effect which an authoritative tone and manner and had ever
been wont to produce on her," he orders his love to fetch an "English book," which turns out to be *Paradise Lost.* Secure in their
new Eden, Frances reads aloud while William listens, and though
delighting as always in the silvery sound of her voice, he does not
hesitate to find "fault with an intonation, a pause, or an emphasis,"
and the rules of their courtship prove to be the decorum of the
classroom extended into a private sphere (155).

Having already resigned from Mme. Reuter's institution, Crimsworth now quits his position in the boy's school, and finds new employment as a bona fide "Professor" with much greater pay. He
meanwhile stays away from Frances until he has saved enough
money to warrant a proposal of marriage. During this interval,
Hunsden reappears with news from home: Crimsworth's brother
Edward is a bankrupt, his wife has left him, and his possessions
have been sold at auction, including a portrait of his and William's
mother.

This painting has long been cherished by her orphaned son and,
as it turns out, had been secretly bought by Hunsworth, who later
will send it to him. Unpacking a mysterious box delivered to his
residence, Crimsworth pulls out the beloved visage, "a pale, pen-
sive-looking female face, shadowed with soft dark hair, almost
blending with the equally dark clouds; large solemn eyes look re-
flectively into mine; a thin cheek rested on a delicate little hand.
. . . A listener (had there been one) might have heard me, after ten
minutes' silent gazing, utter the word 'Mother!'" (186).

The sentimental incident is creakingly contrived, for William's
cold-hearted brother quickly regains his wealth (and his wife), and
the bankruptcy is a rigged occasion for the younger son's recovery of his dead mother's image. Her face not a little resembles that
of his love, being chiefly characterized by "the intelligence, the
sweetness, and—alas! the sadness also of those fine grey eyes."
Charlotte Brontë was only three when her mother died, and the
likeness most familiar to her of Maria Branwell was a portrait of
a sweet-faced, sad-eyed girl of sixteen, so at this point the author
identifies herself with Crimsworth, toward what end it is not clear.

The cry of "Mother!" comes at a critical juncture in *Jane Eyre,*
but here it seems chiefly introduced for Dickensian reasons, attesting to Crimsworth's own filial piety, which he shares with
Oliver Twist, who has never known his mother but will hurl himself recklessly at a bully who has insulted her sacred name. The
narrator has had few previous occasions to remember his mother's

portrait, seen early in the novel, and sentimentality all aside, perhaps it is here reintroduced to suggest her resemblance to Frances, but the episode is forced and artificial. Still, to the extent that Crimsworth sees Frances Henri as a duplicate of his mother, an incestuous motive cannot be ruled out, a reminder once again of the dark version of the Cinderella myth.

Certainly Frances will never assume a maternal pose where her husband is concerned, but bends over forward to remain the obedient child. On their next encounter, when Crimsworth takes it upon himself to resume his courtship by visiting her apartment unannounced, Frances is heard in another room recited a poem of her own composition, of which the key stanzas are the following:

> Obedience was no effort soon,
>   And labour was no pain;
> If tired, a word, a glance alone
>   Would give me strength again.
>
> From others of the studious band,
>   Ere long he singled me;
> But only by more close demand,
>   And sterner urgency.

(192)

In the interview that follows, Crimsworth finds another poem by Frances which extends these stanzas into a long exercise that is clearly inspired by her subservient, adoring attitude toward her teacher. Moreover, the poem provides a very close link to *l'affaire* Heger, having been independently composed by Charlotte Brontë then inserted into the novel.

The narrator of the poem is a young woman called "Jane," who has been sent into the garden by her teacher for an enforced day of rest, but "when my master's voice I heard / Call, from the window, 'Jane!'/ I entered, joyful, at the word, / The busy house again" (194). The call anticipates Rochester's long-distance summons to Jane Eyre, but the context is clearly derived from *l'affaire* Heger:

> He, in the hall, paced up and down;
>   He paused as I passed by;
> His forehead stern relaxed its frown;
>   He raised his deep-set eye.
>
> "Not quite so pale," he murmered low;
>   "Now, Jane, go rest awhile."

And as I smiled, his smoothened brow
  Returned as glad a smile.

My perfect health restored, he took
  His mien austere again;
And, as before, he would not brook
  The slightest fault from Jane.

                               (194)

The poem ends with "Jane" having to leave the stern but tender care of her Master, who, holding her in his arms, wonders aloud why they are being parted, but then, asking God to watch over his "foster child," the Master releases her, with the reassuring words that when Jane is "deceived, repulsed, opprest," she is to "come home to me again!" (196).

At this point we have a complex knot tying together the relationship between Charlotte and Professor Heger (as she conceived it) and that between Frances and Crimsworth, even while anticipating the much more complex attraction between Jane Eyre and Rochester. In *The Professor* (a title not enjoyed by the narrator until rather late in the narrative: "The Master" would be much more appropriate), the song serves to reinforce the erotic basis of the student-teacher relationship. Having read Frances's poem and recognizing its message, Crimsworth impulsively pulls her "on my knee, placed there with sharpness and decision, and retained with exceeding tenacity. 'Monsieur!' cried Frances," the cry expressed by how many maidens and servant maids in literature written by and enjoyed by those "other" Victorians, and the single cry of surprise and protest is followed by the silence of obedience to his desire.

"After all," reasons Crimsworth, "she was only a little nearer than she had ever been before to one she habitually respected and trusted" (197). And so, with this one gesture, Crimsworth converts the terms of the master-student relationship to, what? Master and Mastered? He demands to know whether Frances loves him, and after a considerable conversation, much of it in the forbidden French language, Frances admits that she is willing to live forever with her dear Master, "as stirless in her happiness as a mouse in its terror" (199).

As a hard-working wife, Frances will remain "docile as a well-trained child . . . a curious mixture of tractability and firmness," meaning tractable when with her husband, firm while with her students. Ten years pass, and Frances becomes "a stately and elegant woman . . . Madame the directress" of the school she runs, but when the students leave at the end of the day, she becomes once again Crimsworth's pupil, for it was "her pleasure, her joy to make me still the master in all things" (223). Thus every evening, as Crimsworth returns home from his college, "the lady directress vanished from before my eyes, and Frances Henri, my own little lace-mender, was magically restored to my arms." And as before, "talk French she would, and many a punishment she has had for her wilfulness. I fear the choice of chastisement must have been injudicious, for instead of correcting the fault, it seemed to encourage its renewal."

The relationship after ten years with her husband has become so intimate that for Frances "topics of conversation could no more be wanting with him than subjects for communion with her own heart." Yet she was capable also of expressing "a wild and witty wickedness that made a perfect white demon of her while it lasted." But when "I used to turn upon her with my old decision, and arrest bodily the sprite that teased me . . . no sooner had I grasped hand or arm than the elf was gone; the provocative smile quenched in the expressive brown eyes, and a ray of gentle homage shone under the lids in its place. I had seized a mere vexing fairy, and found a submissive and supplicating little mortal woman in my arms" (224).

In continuing to improve his wife's understanding of English, Crimsworth uses the poems of Wordsworth as punishment for real or imagined faults, for "she had a difficulty in comprehending his deep, serene, and sober mind; his language, too, was not facile to her; she had to ask questions, to sue for explanations, to be like a child and a novice, and to acknowledge me as her senior and director. Her instinct instantly penetrated and possessed the meaning of more ardent and imaginative writers. Byron excited her; Scott she loved; Wordsworth only she puzzled at, wondered over, and hesitated to pronounce an opinion upon" (224).

And so it was with Wordsworth that Frances was punished, as across the years the still surviving author of the *Lyrical Ballads* (1798) reached a withered hand out toward the author of *Poems and Ballads* (1866). Swinburne was only ten years old at the time but was already receiving the formative impressions that would give punishment a permanent place in that so very English literature kept hidden from public view until brought pale and blinking into the light by Steven Marcus (224). "Victor" is the name the Crimsworths give their child, "pale and spare, with large eyes, as dark as those of Frances," a boy with "a susceptibility to pleasurable sensations almost too keen, for it amounts to enthusiasm" (232–33). Or call the child Victoria, after the reigning queen—whatever.

III

The orphan, whether Oliver Twist or Frances Henri, is a peculiar Victorian construct used to emphasize the horrors of being separated from the orderly comforts of middle-class society, a figure of helplessness, lacking the power to resist whatever outrages that are visited upon it. In Dickens's stories such waifs are often, as in the case of Oliver, restored to domestic felicity, and even Little Nell finds a haven before dying. But during their long exile they gain terrific power as Jane Tompkins suggests from their suffering, drawing our attention and our sympathy and inspiring our outrage over the purposeful or unintentional cruelties visited upon them.

A similarly abandoned and despairing figure is at the center of the novel Charlotte Brontë began before she died, in which as her husband observed correctly she was beginning to repeat herself. So obsessive was this figure that, despite the tight and supportive sibling circle with which she herself was surrounded, Charlotte would seem to have been drawn to it for other reasons than its proven popularity in stories by Dickens. It appears to have been a psychological projection —much as she self-cast herself as orphans in both *The Professor* and *Jane Eyre*—and as such was a working-out in her fiction the terms of her fantasies. Her Cinderellas do not dream of finding a prince but a master, a stern figure of authority, and that this imagined lover exercises control matching overzealous parental rigor seems clear, hinting at the dark, alternative version of the myth.

The repeated pattern is strengthened further by the opening chapters of *Villette*, Brontë's third autobiographical novel derived from the Brussels situation. There, a doll-like "creature," Paulina Home, is left by her widowed father in the home of distant relations, to be cared for while he travels for his health—a journey that will be, it is implied, of considerable duration. This is a situation anticipating the opening pages of the unfinished "Emma," and Paulina is a reminder of Jane Eyre as well, for she is frequently compared to an elf or changeling, and though quite small she has the manner of an adult. She is made much of by the young son of the household, Graham Bretton, "a handsome, faithless-looking youth of sixteen," who carries on a mock flirtation with "Polly" and finally succeeds in earning the little girl's trust and love but only to hurt her. (That Paulina seems to have been modelled upon a little girl named Fanny Whipp need not detain us overlong.)

Graham is not bad at heart, only (like Branwell) "spoiled and whimsical," but he thoughtlessly plays with Paulina as with a pet, having no regard for the depths of her response. Having wooed her away from her absent father, whom she adored, Graham becomes bored with the game and ignores the little girl. When Paulina at last departs to rejoin her father, she is abject at having to leave the boy whom she now loves with a slavish devotion, but Graham for his part is thoughtlessly indifferent to her fate:

> "Polly going? What a pity! Dear little Mousie, I shall be sorry to lose her: she must come to us again, mamma."
> And hastily swallowing his tea, he took a candle and a small table to himself and his books, and was soon buried in study.
> "Little Mousie" crept to his side, and lay down on the carpet at his feet, her face to the floor; mute and motionless she kept that post and position till bedtime. Once I saw Graham—wholly unconscious of her proximity—push her with his restless foot. She receded an inch or two. A minute after one little hand stole out from beneath her face, to which it had been pressed, and softly caressed the heedless foot. When summoned by her nurse she rose and departed very obediently, having bid us all a subdued good night. (90)

The story will end happily for Paulina, who becomes (like Jane Eyre) a wealthy heiress and eventually marries Graham. But the episode has for the modern reader perverse connotations, particularly the child's stroking the boy's offending foot. Like the use of sadomasochistic postures in *The Professor*, Paulina's adoring position is a peculiar statement about the nature of love, in which the woman experiences what is essentially an abasement of self while the man expresses himself by a detached, even indifferent participation in the process.

Along with the changeling-waif theme, the nature of the early relationship between Paulina and Graham acts as a gloss on *Jane Eyre*. There is, first of all, the disparity of ages between Jane and Rochester, but more important is the selfsame abasement, the worshipful, doglike attitude of the heroine toward her "master," brought forward from *The Professor* and repeated in *Villette*. Both little Paulina (the name means "small and gentle") and demure Frances Henri engage in sprightly banter with the men in their lives, and the dialogues between Rochester and his diminutive governess are deservedly famous, being a Victorian version of the verbal sparring between Beatrice and Benedict.

But it is a game over which Rochester remains, like Graham and Crimsworth, very much in control, and he uses it as a means of tormenting Jane, holding out then withdrawing his affection, pretending that he is in love with and planning to marry the beautiful but arrogant Blanche Ingram, when that is far from his true intention. He is, as we find out, simply testing Jane, but it is a long, drawn-out tease that like tickling can approximate torture. We may accept in Austen's *Emma* the verbal chastisement of the heroine at the hands of Mr. Knightly as essential to her reformation, a sudden drawing back the curtain to reveal the arrogant silliness of Emma's scenario for her little protégée, Harriet Smith. But the humiliation of Jane by Rochester goes on and on, without any corrective function, being punishment without a crime. For Jane unlike Austen's Emma is as humble as plain pie in her conduct, and "deserves" nothing but understanding and love.

Though reaching beyond her station in dreaming of marriage to her employer, Jane herself recognizes the fatuity of her dream, which turns out in the end not to be fatuous at all. We learn, likewise, that Rochester's callous manner is the result of his previous experience with women, but that is just the point: Jane, as the victim of his cynicism toward women, does not suffer for the sake of herself, but for him, for Rochester's improvement, his redemption. And the blade behind the point is that she obviously enjoys it. In the parlance of Victorian subterranean fiction, she kisses the rod much as Paulina strokes the foot.

The resemblances between Jane Eyre's sufferings and the tortures inflicted on women in sadomasochistic literature of the Victorian period have been pointed out by Elaine Showalter, and as the earlier examples of similar behavior and response in *The Professor* suggest, it seems to have been a pattern triggered whenever Charlotte Brontë used her blighted love for Heger as a basis for fiction. Commencing with the actual physical pain inflicted by John Reed at Gateshead and proceeding to the psychological suffering she experiences because of the over-rigorous regimen at Lowood Institute, Jane is subjected to abuse in a series of "houses" that could, with strategic revision, amount to a Victorian "Story of O."

But unlike a bone-deep masochist, the narrator is clearly outraged by her treatment at Gateshead and does not suffer the humiliations at Lowood gladly. It is only after she has reached Thornfield that her outrage is set aside for a resigned submission to the rules of the game established by Rochester, a more subtle (and sexual) version of the tyranny she experienced elsewhere. This is a signal difference, for if Jane does not object to her treatment in the hands of her "master," it is because she adores him, and submits to his catlike toying and teasing, his perpetual playing upon the fact of his absolute authority over the little governess in terms with sadomasochistic overtones:

> "Miss Eyre, draw your chair still a little further forward: you are yet too far back; I cannot see you without disturbing my position in this comfortable chair, which I have no mind to do."
> I did as I was bid, though I would much rather have remained somewhat in the shade: but Mr. Rochester had such a direct way of giving orders, it seemed a matter of course to obey him promptly. (149)

The male dominance and female submission displayed here should remind us of the pedagogical tactics used by Crimsworth-Heger in *The Professor,* but this time as seen by the victim-student not the teacher. More remarkably, however, both can be compared with the similar but much more violent scene beween Jane and John Reed at Gateshead, when the bullying son of her aunt orders her "'to come here,'" precisely the first command given by Crimsworth to Frances and with a bullying positioning that looks forward to the interview between Jane and Mr. Rochester:

> [S]eating himself in an arm-chair, he intimated by a gesture that I was to approach and stand before him. . . . Habitually obedient to John, I came up to his chair: he spent some three minutes in thrusting out his tongue at me as far as he could without damaging the roots; I knew he would soon strike, and while dreading the blow, I mused on the disgusting and ugly appearance of him who would presently deal it. I wonder if he read that notion in my face; for, all at once, without speaking, he struck suddenly and strongly. I tottered, and on regaining my equilibrium retired back a step or two from his chair. (16)

There are great differences, in motive and appearance, between this episode and those involving Crimsworth and Frances or Rochester and Jane, including the phallic display suggested by the protruding, invasive tongue, yet in all three episodes the female response to male commands is the same, a subservient, obedient posture, a placing of their bodies at set commands in a position adjusted to the male's preference. Even the cold, unattractive (though physically beautiful) St. John Rivers is able to evoke a similar response from Jane, exerting so great a degree of control that she realizes he has the power to kill her by demanding more of her than she can possibly perform. I don't think it is overreading to translate these terms as figurative rape.

Again and again, Jane tells us that she will do anything for her male "masters" that does not violate her sense of moral correctness. Thus she is able to escape from Rivers because he insists on a marriage without love, much as she earlier fled from Rochester when he proposed love without marriage. But so long as the demands seem rightful, she is bound as if under some "awful charm" to obey them, as when with the cold St. John "I fell under a freezing spell. When he said 'go' I went! 'come', I came; 'do this', I did it. But I did not love my servitude" (447, 443).

With Rochester, however, she does love her servitude, as Jane herself makes perfectly clear in a moment of crisis, when Rochester has just discovered that Bertha's brother has come to Thornfield, a threat to his plans for taking Jane as his "bride":

> "Jane, I've got a blow; —I've got a blow, Jane!" He staggered.
> "Oh—lean on me, sir."
> "Jane, you offered me your shoulder once before; let me have it now."
> "Yes, sir, yes; and my arm."
> He sat down, and made me sit beside him. Holding my hand in both his own, he chafed it; gazing on me, at the same time, with the most troubled and dreary look.
> "My little friend!" said he, "I wish I were in a quiet island with only you; and trouble, and danger, and hideous recollections removed from me."
> "Can I help you sir? —I'd give my life to serve you." (229)

The mention of the idyllic island is a whisper derived from Byron's poem of that title, but it is also essential to Rochester's manipulation of the little governess, much as the physical leaning on her is less an expression of dependency than of putting on her the full weight of his authority, the pressure by means of which he habitually expresses his needs.

As always, Jane is ready and willing to place her body where it is most wanted, for if the motto of Helen Burns, the perfect Christian maiden, is *"Resurgam,"* Jane Eyre's secret slogan seems to be *"Serviam,"* for if Helen is Mary, then Jane is Martha. True, her subservience is not always associated with men. There is the guidance of the authoritative Maria Temple at Lowood and at Moor House Jane is under the tutelage of Diana Rivers. Yet these being feminine are relatively gentle influences, being of the mentoring not the hectoring kind, providing models for emulation not dictatorial figures demanding complete surrender of self.

Gilbert and Gubar point out that the rhythm of Brontë's plots may be summed up as enclosure and flight, but this, given the author's indebtedness to Scott, is but a variation on the formula of pursuit, capture, and escape that characterizes his adventure stories. Scott's protagonists in his historical adventure-romances are invariably male and though the hero of the Waverley Novels is more often than not Hamlet-like and indecisive (traditionally regarded as feminine qualities), he is given opportunities for action denied his female counterpart in *Jane Eyre*.

In point of fact, Jane flees only once: her departure from Gateshead is at the behest of her Aunt Reed; she leaves Lowood following the end of her formal education. She does, as we have seen, entertain romantic notions of travel to exotic places—again, the old Byronic mood—but when Byron comes to her, as it were, she finds sufficient excitement at Thornfield Hall to stay on. However, she remains only until her imagined Byron turns out to be too real a Byron, his intriguing mysteriousness congealing as his marriage to Bertha Mason. It is then that her enclosure becomes intolerable and she flees, but if her sanctuary turns into yet another trap (one more of Scott's formulaic tricks), the scheme hatched for her by St. John Rivers, it can be said that she does not so much flee Morton as return headlong to Thornfield, there to remain.

Jane's only real flight then is from Thornfield, inspired first by the horror of Rochester's revelation, second by his alternative scheme to lawful marriage. Jane's master attempts once again to assert his authority, insisting that their illicit relationship would be equivalent to marriage, but Jane realizes that if she succumbs to his will this time she would be exchanging virtuous servitude for something loathsome: "It would not," protests Rochester, "be wicked to love me." "It would be to obey you," responds Jane (355). She of course does love him, that is never in doubt, but moral considerations are the highest on Brontë's non-Platonic ladder: "conscience, turned tyrant, held passion by the throat," and obeying the old Miltonic abstraction, right reason, she sets out for the world beyond the horizon, no longer a territory of freedom but of "drear flight and homeless wandering" (335, 360).

Later, in the enforced quietude of the schoolroom at Morton, Jane permits herself a Hamlet- (and Waverley-) like soliloquy, in which she weighs the alternatives that had confronted her back at Thornfield, a monologue that reveals her undiminished love for

Rochester but also her undiminished fealty to moral conduct at the highest, self-sacrificing plane:

> Let me ask myself one question—Which is better? —To have surrendered to temptation; listened to passion; made no painful effort—no struggle;—but to have sunk down in the silken snare; fallen asleep on the flowers covering it; wakened in a southern clime, amongst the luxuries of a pleasure-villa: to have been now living in France, Mr. Rochester's mistress; delirious with his love half my time—for he would–oh, yes he would have loved me well for a while. He *did* love me—no one will ever love me so again. I shall never more know the sweet homage given to beauty, youth, and grace—for never to any one else shall I seem to possess these charms. He was fond and proud of me—it is what no man besides will ever be. —But where am I wandering, and what am I saying; and above all, feeling? Whether is it better, I ask, to be a slave in a fool's paradise at Marseilles—fevered with delusive bliss one hour—suffocating with the bitterest tears of remorse and shame the next—or to be a village schoolmistress, free and honest, in a breezy mountain nook in the healthy heart of England? (401)

This passage is a marvelous tour de force, being one of the longest leading questions in English literature. It is, moreover, squarely within the Waverley tradition of internalized moral debate, and predictably it is the virtuous alternative that wins the argument.

Weeping with Jane, her readers could not but agree with her decision even while sympathizing with her indecision—expressed by those many parenthetical dashes—for any doubt is resolved by Jane's insistence that however pleasant her life might have been in the south of France, a man not bound by the marriage vow is not a husband but a lover and may at any time depart: "He would have loved me well *for a while*." Thackeray, in intuiting that Charlotte Brontë was suffering from the pain of having been disappointed in love, quoted Tennyson's familiar line, "'Tis better to have loved & lost than never to have loved at all" (*Letters*, 3: 12). But through Jane Eyre Brontë seems to be posing an alternative question: "Is it better to have loved and lost your virtue than never to have loved at all?"

There can be only one answer, and Jane provides it: "Yes," she declares, "I feel now that I was right when I adhered to principle and law, and scorned and crushed the insane promptings of a frenzied moment. God directed me to a correct choice: I thank His providence for the guidance!" This assertion would seem to have been overlooked by those reviewers who faulted *Jane Eyre* for its immorality, and yet Jane having thanked God for deliverance turns to weeping "for the doom which had reft me from adhesion to my master: for him I was no more to see; for the desperate grief and fatal fury—consequences of my departure—which might now, perhaps, be dragging him from the path of right, too far to leave hope of ultimate restoration thither" (403). Divine providence may have been responsible for saving Jane from the snare and delusion of sexual passion, but pagan "doom" has removed her as Rochester's chief moral prop.

She loves him but he *needs* her, and it is that call to further service that will put wings to her feet when it comes, Jane being heedless now of moral considerations because still ignorant of Bertha's death. Whether Brontë realized it or not, her heroine surrenders like Heathcliff and Cathy to a pagan because forbidden love. True, as I have earlier maintained, she is being guided by providence, for Bertha is dead and the block to marriage has been removed, but Jane does not know that, and acts from love without regard to the morality of her impulse.

But prior to receiving Rochester's message, Jane suffers the consequences of her virtuous flight, and very nearly makes a tragic mistake herself when her loneliness is assuaged by St. John Rivers's hyper-virtuous attentions. But once again Jane makes the "right" decision, a decision moreover that frees her to obey Rochester's summons, and to enter a marriage in which her role thenceforth will be that sustaining prop her body provided at their first meeting. Like *The Professor, Jane Eyre* is a long letter to the unheeding Heger, in which for his edification she refuses an overture that was never made, assuring him that if he had indeed proposed an illicit affair, something beyond an intense but nonetheless Platonic correspondence, she would have instantly cut him off. Yet in the end Brontë repeats the message sent in the poem composed by Frances Henri: if he calls her she will come.

We may pick apart the strands of Brontë's conflicted protestation, her complex response to a temptation never offered, but we cannot separate the author from her fictional self-creation. Thus Jane's consummation of Charlotte's fantasy is Branwell's hoped-for conclusion of his affair with Mrs. Robinson, the futility of which aroused his sister's fury and disgust, which is not the paradox it might seem to be. When Charles Kingsley congratulated Elizabeth Gaskell for having produced in her life of Charlotte Brontë "the picture of a valiant woman made perfect by suffering," he was describing as well Charlotte's most famous novel, but it would be *Villette* that would most perfectly realize a woman's suffering and self-denial, in the last of those three long love letters to Professor Heger (Gaskell, Elizabeth Jay introduction, xxix). Instead of ending in marriage, the novel closes with the virtual because presumed death of Lucy's lover and with her consequent fate presiding as an old maid teacher in the tiny schoolhouse provided for her by the man she has redeemed through her love but then lost not to another but to fated circumstances.

Her publishers backed her father's wish that Charlotte would give *Villette* an unequivocally happy ending. Her refusal to do more than merely soften the original conclusion undoubtedly contributed to the artistic heft of a novel that leaves the reader without any final consolation, ambiguity that recommends it over the sentimental finale of *Jane Eyre*. In *Villette* the heroine does love and lose but like Jane retains an enforced virtue, giving meaning to the repeated allusions to female monasticism found in the novel. For these reasons, most critics have from its publication felt that her last was Brontë's greatest work, but it was *Jane Eyre*, popular in its own day and popular still, that had a significant impact on writers who were for the most part young girls able to empathize with the heroine. Lucy Snowe's fate was realistic, at least within the terms of Victorian mores, but Jane's was preferable, because after an extended period of self-sacrificial suffering there came that perfection of realized love, a marriage. Brides of Christ may not fret behind their convent walls, but the dreams of mill girls tending the thundering looms of Lowell were not fantasies of becoming New England nuns.

IV

I want to end this consideration of *Jane Eyre* with a discussion of a sequence of images that is equivalent to the figure of a nun that haunts the pages of *Villette*, for if Jane is a prototypical suffering woman, her status is enhanced by a recurring dream of a crying infant, which a servant woman tells her is premonitory of dire events. Again, given the tangled web binding Jane to Charlotte Brontë, the dream certainly has dire implications, but in the novel it is used for mostly atmospheric effects. Like Lockwood's dream of a screaming child in *Wuthering Heights,* the "baby-phantom" enhances the gothic element, even while validating what is essentially a domestic fiction ending with marriage and the birth of a child. That Jane is often carrying the child in her dream is symbolic in a Freudian sense surely, for to "carry" or "bear" are verbs teeming (is there a better word?) with significance for women.

In terms of fictional technique the baby-phantom is integral to the fate of the heroine and is associated with her fears of losing Rochester: "I was following the windings of an unknown road; total obscurity environed me; rain pelted me; I was burdened with the charge of a little child: a very small creature, too young and feeble to walk, and which shivered in my cold arms, and wailed piteously in my ear" (315). The dream reveals a curious ambivalence toward the dependency of infancy, the helplessness and weakness that Jane displays when in the company of Rochester, which we might explain as a conflicted response by a child woman to the child forced by some mysterious agency into her arms. Charlotte Brontë is on record as not being fond of children, and her terrible death brought on by continuous, unrelenting morning sickness has been interpreted by modern psychologists as a violent rejection of her pregnancy.

But that of course is the author's nightmare, not Jane Eyre's, for in the novel the wailing, burdensome child is an impediment to Jane's pursuit of her master, who in the dream "withdrew farther and farther every moment," and the nightmare of futile pursuit is succeeded by another, similar dream, set against a ruined Thornfield Hall: "Wrapped up in a shawl, I still carried the unknown little child: I might not lay it down anywhere, however tired were my arms—however much its weight impeded my progress, I must retain it . . . [though] the child clung round my neck in terror, and almost strangled me" (316). Within the context of the novel, the crying, barrier child is a dream echo of Bertha Mason's inarticulate complaints, for Jane awakens from the dream to the horror of her first confrontation with the madwoman of Thornfield Hall, with her bloated, purple face, "lips swelled and dark, the brow furrowed, the black eyebrows widely raised over the bloodshot eyes" (317). This could, with some critical license, be seen as the face of a furious infant, albeit set in a Goyaesque frame.

The interplay between the dream of the burdensome "baby-phantom," with the apparition-like Bertha, is central to the plot, for both hold Jane back from her desired goal of union with Rochester. The baby therefore would seem to be not prognostic of the fruit of that union but a hindrance to it, although it is interesting that a contemporary "Dream-Book" says "For a maiden to dream she is with child denotes that some man will make an attempt to rob her of her chastity, and that if she resists, she will marry and be very happy" (*The Complete Fortune-Teller and*

Dream-Book [New York, 1829]). Whether or not Brontë availed herself of this or a comparable authority, certainly Jane's dream of being "with child" works out exactly to formula, though given the immediate context, it validates a servant-woman's pronouncement that to dream of a child is a "presentiment" of trouble (248).

The wailing infant, moreover, is a variation on the abandoned waif theme in *Jane Eyre,* of which the heroine is the chief representative, and it is the same servant who sings the "poor orphan child" ballad who is the one that interprets Jane's dream as foretelling dire events. The "baby-phantom" takes on a different, less hostile shape the night before Jane is to be tricked into marriage to Rochester: Lying sleepless with "little Adèle" in her arms, Jane "watched the slumber of childhood—so tranquil, so passionless, so innocent—and waited for the coming day. . . . I remember Adèle clung to me as I left her: I remember I kissed her as I loosened her little hands from my neck; and I cried over her with strange emotion, and quitted her because I feared my sobs would break her still sound repose. She seemed the emblem of my past life, and he I was now to array myself to meet, the dread, but adored, type of my unknown future day" (320).

Jane, not knowing of the trick that is about to be played on her, weeps over the innocence she will surrender within what she assumes will be the lawful bonds of matrimony. That is, she is soon to submit to the desires of the man she both adores and dreads, who has in his persistent prenuptial teasing "threatened awful vengeance for my present [coy] conduct at some period fast coming" (307). Such a threat does not suggest a loving consummation of vows; it suggests the rape that Rochester's hoax would permit. In plain fact Adèle is less a symbol of innocence than a token of Rochester's past life, that amoral path of erotic conquests of which the little girl is a visible result. Jane would seem to be next in the sequence, validating the early allusion to Bluebeard's castle.

Having discovered Rochester's perfidy, Jane describes her feelings in terms once again of the ailing infant: she had arisen that morning "an ardent, expectant woman—almost a bride," but now her love for Rochester lies shivering "in my heart, like a suffering child in a cold cradle; sickness and anguish had seized it" (330–31). This repeated pattern might possibly be attributed to careful, thought-out sequencing, but it seems most likely to have been the fruit of the author's subconscious, the source of the archetypal power of the novel throughout, its absorption of pagan themes that threaten ever and again to break through the Christian overlay.

Another, earlier, and perhaps most startling of these infantine images is inspired by Jane's premature but prophetic apprehensions that she entertains while returning to Thornfield from Gateshead, where she has witnessed the death of Aunt Reed. Repentant, her dying relative produces a letter sent long ago from Jane's paternal uncle in Madeira promising his niece a life of wealth and ease if she will join him, but which Aunt Reed has kept hidden, one more consquence of Jane's having given free expression to her rage and resentment. John Reed has also died, and the episode cuts Jane free of her past, a rebirth of sorts coming nine years as she reckons after she left Gateshead (at age nine) for Lowood. But in her dream the gates to Thornfield are closed by Blanche Ingram, who "pointed me out another road," while Rochester looks on "with his arms folded—smiling sardonically, as it seemed, at both her and me" (273).

Terrified by the dream, Jane hastens back to Thornfield, urged on by an inner voice bidding speed in the face of the certainty that she will lose Rochester to Blanche: "'Hasten! hasten! be with him while you may: but a few more days or weeks at most, and you are parted with him forever!' And then I strangled a new-born agony, —a deformed thing which I could not persuade myself to own and rear—and hurried on" (279). It is this kind of imagery that made Brontë's Victorian readers uneasy, and which is troubling to the modern reader too, if for different reasons.

The persistent presence of these misbegotten, unwanted babies outweighs the unseen infant Jane will finally present to Rochester as the fruit of their long deferred passion: Whether as a symbol of erotic impediment, of lost childhood (read virginity), of blighted love, or of fears of abandonment, the burdensome, suffering child in *Jane Eyre* is clearly a projection of the suffering, burdened woman that her readers would find apotheosized in Gaskell's biography. Given Charlotte Brontë's manner of dying, nine months after her marriage, it is an irony with a scalpel-like edge.

In terms of Victorian ideology it may be said that for the suffering woman to die in childbirth is a capstone to her perfection, indeed it is often across that fatal threshold that literary orphans are thrust onto the rough, perilous road of life. Jane like Oliver Twist is born an orphan, and Oliver like Jane keeps sacred the memory of his lost mother. Though he never knew her, Oliver is driven into a fury when her virtue is questioned, and in time will regain his birthright, much as Jane will regain hers. If the orphan is a powerful Victorian archetype so it can be said is the mother who died in bringing the homeless child forth.

While suffering the traumatic terrors of the red-room at Gateshead, which little Jane believes is haunted by the spirit of her dead uncle, her fears are apparently realized when "a light gleamed on the wall," then "glided up to the ceiling and quivered over my head" (24). But as a ghost this mysterious light is another gothic bogie, for a mature Jane in recalling the incident "can now conjecture readily that this streak of light was, in all likelihood, a gleam from a lantern carried by some one across the lawn." By contrast, there is the apparition that appears to her much later in her life, after Rochester has pled with her to remain with him as his mistress: this comes during a dream that places Jane back in the red-room at Gateshead, a dream in which the trembling light on the ceiling takes on much more positive connotations:

> I lifted up my head to look: the roof resolved to clouds, high and dim; the gleam was such as the moon imparts to vapours, she is about to sever. I watched her come—watched with the strangest anticipation; as though some word of doom were to be written on her disk. She broke forth as never moon yet burst from cloud: a hand first penetrated the sable folds and waved them away; then, not a moon but a white human form shone in the azure, inclining a glorious brow earthward. It gazed and gazed on me. It spoke to my spirit; immeasurably distant was the tone, yet so near, it whispered in my heart—
> "My daughter, flee temptation!"
> "Mother, I will." (358)

Where before, in the red-room, Jane had feared her mother's brother's ghost would be roused to wrath over her aunt's cruel treatment of her, in this dream the apparition is her mother's ghost, gazing on her with solicitous care, a female bond intensified by the association with the moon. It is of course pointedly a dream, but for Jane Eyre and presumably for Charlotte Brontë dream visions are prophetic, classed as supernatural phenomena. Like the dream child, moreover, the dream spirit is an apparition standing between Jane and Rochester. But where the wailing infant is an ambivalent symbol, as a guardian angel the maternal spirit asserts a protective aegis against the world of men. In this dream as in the red-room horror, it is Jane who is the suffering child.

Notably, when the supernatural evinces itself outside the world of dreams, it is as a message from Rochester, and it is a message that counters the instructions delivered by the maternal spectre in Jane's dream. When pressured by St. John Rivers to marry him, Jane "sincerely, fervently longed to do what was right," but when she "entreats of Heaven" that the true way be shown her, the answer comes not from her mother but from her lover (466). True, she later discovers that Rochester's summons came to her when he was himself asking of God, "at once in anguish and humility, if I had not been long enough desolate, afflicted, tormented; and might not soon taste bliss and peace once more" (496). But in the wholly male trinity made up of Rochester, St. John Rivers, and God, there is no room left for that maternal ghost.

It is this sort of thing that recommended *Jane Eyre* to the American minister, for it is God and Rochester, finally, who make the way straight for Jane back to Thornfield, overruling the dictates of the overbearingly and falsely pious St. John. It is Rochester not St. John who delivers the concluding homily concerning the works of "the beneficent God of this earth," who "sees not as man sees, but far clearer: judges not as man judges, but far more wisely" (495). It is Rochester who humbly thanks God for Jane's return, while Jane, for her part, "kept these things" to herself, and "pondered them in my heart" (497). We are therefore to conclude that Rochester has been ordained by his suffering to speak of such matters, in contrast to St. John the institutionally sanctioned divine, who uses God to empower his proud purposes. We must assume that the "American divine" was a Unitarian.

"My Master," the book concludes, "has forwarned me. Daily he announces more distinctly, —'Surely I come quickly!' and hourly I more eagerly respond, —'Amen; even so come, Lord Jesus!'" (502). This is the final message delivered to Jane by St. John, who anticipates a martyr's death in the blessed service of *his* master, but the missionary's way, as Jane has told us, is different from her own. Rochester may pray to his cruel but just God, Rivers may await the ultimate call from his marble Christ, but Jane in answering the psychic summons of Rochester has found herself in her husband.

Ferndean Manor is heaven enough for Jane Eyre, where in tending to her even more dear because crippled Edward's needs she experiences "a pleasure in my services most full, most exquisite, even though sad" (500). It is finally in service to Eros that Jane finds salvation, in celebration of which Charlotte Brontë built her gothic temple with its soaring towers pointing toward heaven and its many grinning gargoyles that are only detected by drawing so close to the structure that the details speak for the whole.

II
Sleeping and Other Beauties

Who asks for me . . .
must lay his heart out for my bed and board.
—Robert Lowell

4

A Sentimental Education:
Susan Warner's *The Wide, Wide World*
and the Christian Crux

Art thou gone, yes thou art gone, alas!
—E. Grangerford

I

We know that Charlotte Brontë was shocked by Elizabeth Rigby's negative review of *Jane Eyre,* which appeared in the influential *Quarterly Review,* a notice overflowing with hostility even outrage that not only devastated the author but baffled her as well. She felt that her book and her intentions had been completely misunderstood by the reviewer, who attacked the novel for its irreligious qualities, shaking a long Victorian digit at the heroine for her lack of gratitude toward persons who were her benefactors. "It pleased God to make her an orphan, friendless, and penniless—yet she thanks nobody, and least of all Him, for the food and raiment, the friends, companions, and instructors of her helpless youth—for the care and education vouchsafed to her till she was capable in mind as fitted in years to provide for herself" (Gates: *Critical Essays,* 139).

In this pluperfect expression of self-righteous indignation Rigby sounds like a character out of Dickens, leveling a ferule at any miserable little foundling who thinks that one bowl of thin gruel is not sufficient for a meal. Indeed, most of the charges she aims at *Jane Eyre* could be aimed as well at the "orphan" novels of Charles Dickens—not a coincidental matter—for it must be said of both Oliver Twist and David Copperfield that they share with Jane Eyre a sense that what they are offered by way of food and raiment, never mind care and education, falls "far short" of what they deserve from the hands of public or private charities.

Ignoring these parallels, Rigby regarded Jane's chief sin as that summit of vice, pride, evidenced by her total lack of humility. The novel is "pre-emininently an anti-Christian composition," a subversive writing that throughout is aimed "against the comforts of the rich and against the privations of the poor," in plain fact "a murmuring against God's appointment" of class distinctions (140). This kind of thing should not be tolerated in a well-organized, divinely ordered world, nor should we allow in works of fiction "a proud and perpetual assertion of the rights of man, for which we find no authority either in God's word or in God's providence."

Elizabeth Rigby, in short, wrote from an entrenched establishmentarian position, railing against "that pervading tone of ungodly discontent which is at once the most prominent and the most subtle evil which the law and the pulpit, which all civilized society in fact has at the present day to contend with." It is this unwarranted discontent that has resulted in "Chartism and rebellion" in England and has "overthrown authority and violated every code human and divine abroad." The year, we must not forget, was 1848, and had Elizabeth Rigby been writing a century later, Godless Communism would also have been laid at the feet of Currer Bell. Rigby's zealous censoriness has provided modern studies of *Jane Eyre* with a useful stalking horse, and few critics have missed the opportunity to fling a dart or two at such an opportune target of officious Victorian smugness, preening itself for its patriotism and piety while walking in the narrow Pharisaical pathway of Pauline moral rigor—hypocrisy personified.

Rigby was not alone in leveling charges of irreligiousness at *Jane Eyre,* and her point about disestablishmentarianism may be well taken even if it was overstated: There is indignation and outrage seething beneath the surface of the novel, occasionally erupting in rage against oppressors of the poor and friendless. In Charlotte Brontë's created world as in Dickens's, whether figured as the hilariously sinister beadle Mr. Bumble or the cruelly pious Mr. Brocklehurst, institutionalized Christianity does not unfold like a glorious banner but rather sits with crushing weight on the dispossessed of the world. If *Jane Eyre* was popular among the mill girls in Lowell in part because of the Byronic figure of Rochester, Brontë's democratic assertion of the inherent rights of humankind to a square meal, stout shoes, and a warm overcoat surely helped the book find a sympathetic audience in milltown Massachusetts.

But we can also understand Brontë's bewilderment regarding Rigby's hostility, for if Jane is indignant over the harsh treatment accorded orphans at Lowood, then it is because of the obvious disparity between the presumed Christianity of its director and the harsh perversion of the Gospels that established the rules and regimen of the school. It is clearly the kind of charity that lacks *caritas*. Jane herself may never attain the absolute selflessness of a Helen Burns, but she rails against the unChristian treatment accorded that paragon of virtue, who remains perfectly submissive to unjust treatment until she virtually dies from an excess of humility.

And yet, until Elizabeth Gaskell set the record straight regarding the pious humility of the author, her works provided plenty of evidence to the contrary. Indeed, if we prize those novels today it is because they are relatively free of Christian cant. We approve Brontë's attack on establishmentarian injustice and her assertion of individual rights, precisely the qualities for which we value the novels of Dickens. But for some of her contemporaries, Charlotte Brontë was guilty of incorrect thinking, nor were all such willing to limit themselves to hostile reviews. On an island in the middle of the Hudson River, just across from the academy at West Point, a young woman was by 1848 at work on a novel that would serve in effect as a response to *Jane Eyre,* a book that went on to enjoy a popularity that for a time rivaled that of the original.

In his biography of Susan and Anna Warner, Edward Foster tells us that, according to her sister, Warner began writing *The Wide, Wide World* in the winter of 1847, well ahead of the publication of *Jane Eyre* in October of that year (Foster, 34). But Anna also testified that the novel took a year and a half to write, so that the process of composition bracketed the birth of Brontë's prodigy, allowing for at least a marginal anxiety of influence. But whether or not Warner was reacting to the perceived sins of *Jane Eyre,* the outcome remains the same, for her best-selling novel can be read as a counterpart to Charlotte Brontë's equally popular but insufficiently pious book.

The Wide, Wide World is, first of all, a domestic fiction not a gothic romance; there is no sardonic, sexy Byronic figure lurking about the mansion, no mysterious sounds coming from a locked room in the attic, no sinister secrets worth mentioning at all. Instead, we have as Jane Tompkins has told us a fiction that takes its being not from fairy stories but from the tractarian literature of the day, a story rife with evangelical piety. Warner's novel enforced a worldview not much different from that of the Reverend Brocklehurst, who felt that the happiest future possible for a young girl was an early death, which coming to a certifiable virgin guaranteed a rapid passage to heaven. Even Dickens, who hardly had any sympathy with conventional evangelical rigor, in his story of Little Nell created a child so innocent in character as to guarantee an instant passage to heaven, where she is pictured at the last in the company of her fellow angels.

Following Dickens's example, as in much of the pious, sentimental fiction that gave the 1850s in America its alternative literary track, the Church as an institution plays no important role in Warner's novel, though a young theological student does emerge as the romantic interest. The vehicles of piety are chiefly women operating outside of ordination, for whom the Bible is a self-sufficient text not needing clerical interpretation. They act as agents of pious influence, a concept that, as Ann Douglas has demonstrated, is a hallmark of the feminization process, which puts a premium on women as examples of Christian idealism, a notion clearly derived from the Victorian version of chivalric behavior. In that frame, men serve as stalwart, great-hearted guardians of women, women as agents of goodness, evinced through acts of charity and self-sacrifice, thereby serving as relatively passive witnesses to the beauty of Christ's own example.

Following the lead of Nina Baym, Jane Tompkins insists in *Sensational Designs* (1985) that Warner's novel is a parable of power, of the kind women borrow from a deep engagement with the gospel spirit, specifically by an intimate identification with Christ, the essential dimension of sentimental literature (162–63; cf. Baym, 144–45). Succor is found not in church (which the heroine does not attend) but in parlors and pastures wild, suggesting a strong antinomian undercurrent, the rebellion against ordained authority that got Anne Hutchinson into trouble in seventeenth-century Boston. By 1850, such rebellion was identified with the emergence of the New Woman and the outrage of Nathaniel Hawthorne, for whom Margaret Fuller was Hutchinson Redevivus.

As in *The Scarlet Letter,* a minister does play a significant role in *The Wide, Wide World,* but not until the novel has run half its course, and as in Hawthorne's novel there is seduction at work, but without an overtly sexual dimension. Ellen Montgomery, unlike Hester Prynne, does not get pregnant; instead she gets filled with the spirit of Christ, an immaculate conception of sorts. Indeed, the story ends with Ellen on the verge of adolescence, just short of sexual awakening, closure that guarantees her virginal status, the which, combined with her coming to Christ, provides an American analogue to that nun who haunts Charlotte Brontë's fiction. But for Warner it is not the unwilled isolation of a woman denied the marriage bond (the author's own fate), but a signification of the power that comes to heroines of sentimental fiction who are absorbed into the body of the Savior.

II

"Need we," wrote Nina Baym in 1978, "say something in defense of tears?" (144). Well, no longer surely, Baym being the first of a number of feminist critics who regarded the sentimental novel as a serious art form essential to the workings of the female muse in America at mid-century. "Women do cry," Baym went on to declare, "and it is realism in our authors to show it." Yet a sufficiency of any emotional display would seem enough for the literary occasion, and as Alexander Cowie observed of *The Wide,Wide World,* Ellen Montgomery's lacrymose spells are so frequent as to invite ridicule. When in 1885 William Dean Howells wished to reinforce his notion of literary realism in *The Rise of Silas Lapham* by attacking the sentimental tradition, he invented a novel entitled "Tears, Idle Tears," an obvious borrowing from Tennyson but targeting also the convention set flowing by Susan Warner.

Cowie was writing from the (dis)advantage point of 1950, when critical standards were still operating under the influence of the kind of realism promoted by William Dean Howells and Mark Twain, who attacked head-on the sentimental tradition as a factitious celebration of the ludicrously bathetic. In 1950, also, in an introductory chapter to her study of three women writers of the Victorian era, Marghanita Laski despaired of gaining sympathy for her subject at a time when critics invariably "when confronted with sentiment reach for their guns," a telling figure of speech (12). Nina Baym published her study of novels "by and about women in America" nearly thirty years later, establishing a vast divide of sensibility at least in critical terms. Of course, sentimentality never really died, as Charlie Chaplin and his orphan waifs and little flower girls and the prolonged sufferings of Stella Dallas should prove, but we can from this vantage point make a few useful distinctions.

Much has been written over the past twenty years about sentimentality, an expanding parameter made complex by the jargon of literary theory, but nothing has discountenanced Baym's remark that grief in sentimental fiction of the Victorian era is not the only occasion for the shedding of tears, anger and frustration being vented likewise. As Baym notes, it is a false emphasis to associate sentimentality with feminine tenderness: "One might theorize that the frequency of tears in a woman's fiction is proportional less to the amount of tenderness and sensibility that imbues it, than to the amount of rage and frustration that it carries" (144). Such a pronouncement brings *Jane Eyre* quickly to mind, as does Jane Tompkins's remark, anent *The Wide, Wide World,* that "[a]nger and indignation—no matter what the cause—are a disease," impieties that must be cured, not by expressing such emotions with tears but by losing oneself in Christ (177).

Baym may be correct in regarding the shedding of tears as "therapy," the suppression of intense emotions being unhealthy even at times fatal, but hers is a post-Freudian opinion given increased strength by the mood of the 1970s, which licensed the notion that primal release was a necessary step toward getting in touch with one's inner self. That was not the opinion of Charlotte Brontë, as we have seen, nor of Susan Warner either, as we shall soon see. For these two writers, despite a world of differences between them, giving vent to emotions is a weakness; strength is identified with a conscious restraint of the passions, which gives interest to the whole. Lacrimation may be a characteristic of sentimental fiction, but it is accounted no virtue by the very terms of the genre. The assumption has been that Ellen's tears are bids by Warner for the readers' sympathies, but a careful reading of the text suggests otherwise.

In effect, as Jane Tompkins insists and as Ellen's mother begs, not only is weeping wrong because it is self-indulgent, weeping is harmful to others because it upsets them. Ellen needs, in the words of Jane Eyre's Aunt Reed, "to acquire a more sociable and childlike disposition, a more attractive and sprightly manner— something lighter, franker, more natural," something, in short, less self-indulgently sorrowful (Brontë, 13). Where Jane must learn to stifle her rage, Ellen must learn to become less sad, to abandon passionate human feelings for that peace that passeth understanding. Indeed, the burden of her bildungsroman is devoted to repeated episodes of *lacrimae interruptae,* which if designed to draw upon the readers' sympathy, inspiring empathic tears, were intended also as an approximate prophylaxis.

Both Baym and Tompkins pay close attention to the opening pages of Warner's novel, which begins as Ellen Montgomery sits in her mother's parlor late one afternoon staring out at a rainy New York street, where carriages and passersby fill the scene. With the arrival of the old lamplighter and early evening, Ellen turns to the elaborate ceremony of preparing tea for her ailing, much beloved mother. Baym praises the long descriptive street scene, a tour de force of photographic verisimilitude, a tightly controlled realism that contrasts sharply with the kind of overblown diction one expects from a sentimental writer.

Not incidentally, the episode seems to have been inspired by a similar scene that occurs early on in *The Old Curiosity Shop*, in which Little Nell, that prototypical long-suffering orphan girl, sits looking out a window from the safety of her grandfather's shop at a busy London street as dusk gathers. There, the scene emphasizes the very thin line separating Nell from the callous even dangerous world into which she is so shortly to be thrust thanks to the machinations of the evil Quilp. In Warner's novel, the view from the window provides a dramatic backdrop that will enhance the discussion that follows between Ellen and her mother regarding the difficulties that lie ahead.

For Tompkins, the description of the street scene is less important than the frame situation, for Ellen's position, as she sits silently by the window, a silence requested by her ailing mother, is one of "entrapment," an equivalent to the "enclosure" device associated by Gilbert and Gubar (1984) with *Jane Eyre* (338–39). The vividness of the scene outside is not merely an exercise in verisimilitude but a means of "drawing the reader into its own circuit of attention," so that the reader, "forced into the dark parlor with Ellen . . . has to pay attention to what Ellen pays attention to" (Tompkins, 174). Well, in a word, yes, but this self-evident proposition is a key to Tompkins's argument, which insists that the suffering of the heroine is a catharsis by means of which the reader by sharing it empathically empowers the sufferer.

Tompkins more than Baym emphasizes the ceremony of making tea, which Warner describes in minute detail, a ritual of communion that signals "the opening of the heart in an atmosphere of closeness, security, and love" (170). The sacramental sharing of tea and sympathy promotes an intimacy between invalid mother and loving daughter that is soon to be ruptured by the mother's announcement that she will be leaving the country in hopes of finding a cure in Europe and that Ellen cannot, because of her father's financial losses, go along. This announcement not only disrupts the ritual moment but signals the first shedding of tears by Ellen, grief her mother finds so painful that she orders her daughter to cease weeping because it will adversely affect her own fragile health. "If you cry, then I will die," is the unspoken prepositional phrase, which compounds Ellen's grief by adding a burden of guilt, the weight of which is intended to seal off the flow of water.

Tompkins does not mention this latter incident, preferring instead to regard the tea ceremony as an intense, sharing experience, a female moment akin to the male bonding that comes from "squeezing case aboard a whaling ship," being a "reaction against pain and bondage, and a means of salvation and grace" (170). The mother, while repeatedly citing scripture and urging her daughter to accept Christ as her savior (Ellen for much of the novel will remain hard of heart, despite—indeed because of—her devotion to her mother), once again represses her daughter's grief by pleading her own well-being. Likewise, the trip to Europe is in quest of Mrs. Montgomery's own health, while Ellen will be sent off to the farm of her father's half-sister, located far up the Hudson River, with a vague hope that the experience will somehow be good for her.

We are made to feel very sorry for Ellen but not terribly sorry for Ellen's mother, who is using her illness to repress her daughter's natural feelings of grief, yet this will be the first in a long series of lessons in which Ellen will learn that grief is a selfish emotion, that sorrow can only be turned to good use by carrying it to Christ. Ironically, if Warner's is an *echt* sentimental novel, it not only explicitly disapproves of novel reading but can be read as a *tractatus* against tears. "Please don't cry," is an echoing refrain throughout the novel, which in reverse reads "Crying doesn't please." In sum, weep and you weep alone. Critics like Alexander Cowie who have faulted the novel for its too plentiful shedding of tears—and they have followed the lead of the book's contemporary reviewers—seem to have missed the point of all that salt water.

We may add to this sequence the first scene in *Jane Eyre*, which also involves a window view but in a completely different context, not an urban scene abstracted from Dickens but that wild natural prospect associated with gothic fiction. Rather than enjoying the loving company of her mother, Jane has been sent out of the drawing room by her Aunt Reed, exiled from the rest of the family for having somehow violated the norms established for "contented, happy, little children," a fault otherwise not specified (13). Taking with her a favorite book, Jane climbs into a window seat, and draws a heavy red drape around her so as to enforce her privacy, where she can enjoy a comfortable solitude: "I was shrined in double retirement." Through the "clear panes of glass," that protect but do not separate her "from the drear November day," she views the wintry scene: "Afar, it offered a pale blank of mist and cloud; near, a scene of wet lawn and storm-beat shrub, with ceaseless rain sweeping away wildly before a long and lamentable blast" (14).

In contrast to Warner's matter-of-fact description, this is the heightened language one associates with romantic not sentimental literature. Bereft of the passers-by that populate Ellen's (and Nell's) vista, it is a scene that enhances the book Jane has taken with her, Bewick's *History of British Birds,* which she prizes not for its prose but for its fanciful landscape illustrations, inspiring Jane's Poesque vision of a desolate ocean-wracked coast, with a "cold and ghastly moon glancing through bars of cloud at a wreck just sinking" (15). Happy with her wild, enchanted visions inspired by Bewick, Jane is rudely interrupted in her sanctuary by the loathsome John Reed, who begins the taunting that will result in Jane's violent response and Aunt Reed's command that the rebellious girl be taken to the red-room. That is, where Ellen turns from her silent, obedient vigil to making tea for her adored mother, Jane is yanked abruptly from her gothic dreams into what becomes a gothic nightmare. It is an action initiated by John Reed's unwarranted intrusion and culminates in Aunt Reed's unjust order that Jane's comfortable exile in the womblike red-draped window seat be ended by banishing her to the tomblike red-room.

And yet, as I have just suggested, the loving moment between Ellen Montgomery and her mother soon enough turns into an extremely painful episode, in which Ellen's expression of grief over the prospect of being separated from her mother is stifled at the urging of the very object of her affections. Despite signal differences, both of these introductory episodes center on the theme common to *Jane Eyre* and *The Wide, Wide World,* namely, the necessity of keeping passions under control. It is a theme reinforced by Jane's imprisonment in the red-room and her being sent off to Lowood, while Ellen's education in self-control will be continued during her subsequent exile to an equivalent Lowood, the strict, unloving regimen at her Aunt Fortune Emerson's farm.

Once again, there is no gothicism in *The Wide, Wide World,* and the careful realism of the opening description extends through much of the narrative, which renders in detail the minutiae of life in rural northeastern United States at mid-century. The book is a pioneering instance of local color writing, as many critics, following Nina Baym, have recognized. On the other hand, there is also a preponderance of pious material, that tractarian emphasis on finding oneself in Jesus, on accepting humility as the perfection of virtue, on gratefully obeying the instructions of persons superior in age, moral rectitude, and ecclesiastical sanctity, precisely the elements Elizabeth Rigby found missing from *Jane Eyre*. Given its strong autobiographical element, we cannot regard *The Wide, Wide World* as a self-conscious imitation of Brontë's novel, but it most certainly reads like a shadow text, even if, following Edward H. Foster in *Susan and Anna Warner*, we admit the intervening influence of Catharine Sedgwick's *A New England Tale* (1822).

Like her heroine, Susan Warner as a child lost her mother and on the threshold of her young adulthood Susan's father lost his fortune, so that the family was exiled from a luxurious life in New York City to straitened circumstances in an old farmhouse on Constitution Island in the Hudson River. Susan's father (like Ellen's) became involved in costly lawsuits, continued to make unwise investments, and was chiefly supported by the labors of his daughters, who turned to writing novels with the hope of restoring the family's prosperity. On the other hand, all evidence suggests that Susan was never the paragon of self-sacrificing humility that Ellen strives to become, but was spoiled and self-centered even in the midst of poverty, shamelessly using her younger sister, Anne, as a personal servant and emotional foil.

Thus the bildungsroman aspect of *The Wide, Wide World*, the main thrust of a plot in which, as even contemporary readers noticed, very little actually happens, was chiefly a fiction, and as a fiction, it acted to remedy the presumed faults of that other bestselling novel about the suffering and redemption of an orphan, *Jane Eyre*. Notably, where Brontë's Cinderella in the end gets her aging, somewhat damaged Prince, thereby vicariously fulfilling the author's devout wish, Warner's is left a few steps short of the altar. At a later time, she wrote an additional chapter in which her heroine marries the man for whom she has been prepared by her education to serve, perhaps in response to popular demand, but in the original she keeps Ellen back from marriage, a convert to Christ who remains chaste—remains, in effect, a nun.

The monastic figure that flits through Charlotte Brontë's *Villette* is a spectre with meaning for an author who for much of her adult life despaired of ever marrying the man she loved. Likewise, for a pious spinster like Susan Warner a certain validation of celibacy was warranted. Yet it is a theme that runs counter to the traditional emphasis of woman's fiction, as defined by Nina Baym, which is on marriage and family, a situation centered by a maternal not a virginal figure. There are several maternal figures that serve as mentors for Ellen Montgomery—Mothers superior, as it were—but they are uniform in pointing her toward finding herself in Christ.

This maternal mentoring sequence provides a parallel to Ellen's loss of connection to her absent mother, reduced to writing unanswered letters begging for response, a vacancy her mentors strive to fill with the surrogate love to be found in Christ. Jane Tompkins has pointed out the obvious symbolism of the episode in which Ellen's mother, on the eve of her departure for Europe, sells her own mother's ring so as to buy her daughter a Bible. While acknowledging that the act "symbolizes the tacit system of solidarity that exists among women" in sentimental novels, we can also note that the sale of the ring leads to a curious literary moment, in which the selection of a Bible proper to the occasion amounts to a pious version of consumerism (163).

The gift of a Bible in sentimental literature, notes Tompkins, "is invested with supernatural power because it testifies to the reality of the spiritual order where women hold dominion over everything by virtue of their submission on earth," but to this complex abstraction we can add a material dimension: Like Goldilocks, Ellen lights first upon a Bible that is too big to be practical, then upon one that is too small, before with her mother's help she finds one of exactly the right size. The Bible, in part because of the passages of Scripture inscribed by her mother on the fly leaf, will serve as a continuing reminder to Ellen not only of her missing parent but of her mother's urging that she find herself in Christ, yet much is made of its "moderate size and sufficiently large type," set off by a handsome red binding (31).

There are that is to say utilitarian and aesthetic considerations underlying this spiritual gift, and the choice of a Bible is followed by two more practical, attractive gifts, both found in "a large fancy store," so filled with "beautiful things" that it reminds Ellen of "fairy-land" (32). Here, as Ellen strolls about the enchanted world of beautiful things, her mother selects "a neat little japanned [sewing-]box, perfectly plain but well supplied with everything a child could want in that line" (32). Next, taking Ellen in tow, Mrs. Montgomery buys her a little portable writing desk, the prospect of which sends her daughter into a paroxysm of ecstacy: "I can't thank you, mama; I haven't any words to do it. I think I shall go crazy." Here again Mrs. Montgomery stresses both the pious and the practical, for she wishes her daughter in her absence "to be always neat, and tidy, and industrious; depending upon others as little as possible; and careful to improve yourself by every means, and especially by writing to me. I will leave you no excuse, Ellen, for failing in any of these duties" (31–32).

Tompkins ignores this other symbolic object that Ellen's mother uses the ring money to buy, yet the act of writing, along with the inscribed scripture, provides a double filial link. The correspondence proves to be largely a one-sided effort, for Ellen's letters to her mother remain for the most part mysteriously unanswered. But the notion that the desk and its little compartments filled with many kinds of stationery is a gift of love as well as a relic of Ellen's former life of comfort, has a multiple dimensionality. In fact, it contains a dimension entirely outside the perimeters but hardly the parameters of *The Wide, Wide World*.

Susan Warner in 1848 could not have known of Charlotte Brontë's equivalent one-sided correspondence with her beloved teacher in Belgium, but much as *Jane Eyre* was a logical and emotional outgrowth of that frustrated correspondence, so the initial giving of the gift of the little escritoire in *The Wide, Wide World* serves to empower writing as an act of love. It enforces the filial devotion that will in time be transferred from Ellen's mother to a series of other persons and finally to the desired and long-deferred object of her greatest love, Jesus Christ. Warner was eight when she lost her own mother, Ellen's age at the start of the novel, and there is in this complex symbol of an unanswered correspondence a suggestion that she felt betrayed by her mother's departure.

The failure of Ellen's mother to respond, which the reader understands is a signal that her health has continued to weaken, is inexplicable to the little girl, who has not been told of the seriousness of her mother's illness. It increases the pain of her existence on the farm of the appropriately named "Miss Fortune," for her mean-spirited aunt contributes to her anguish, torturing Ellen by holding back the few letters her mother sends. Even worse, she conceals her mother's deathbed letter as punishment for what she conceives to be Ellen's proudful airs, an echo of Aunt Reed's concealment of the letter from Jane's wealthy uncle.

We may take at face value Susan Warner's claim that she wrote *The Wide, Wide World* solely in the hope of improving the family finances, but that was also Charlotte Brontë's aim in writing *Jane Eyre*, yet both novels reveal considerable investments of self, and both put a premium, explicitly or implicitly, on writing as an act of love. That is, what is explicit in Warner's novel is implicit in Brontë's, for Rochester's cruel little game of hinting at yet withholding his love was in part inspired by Heger's failure to respond to letters begging that the friendship begun in Brussels continue.

What *The Wide, Wide World* also shares with *Jane Eyre*, authenticating Warner's as a domestic novel, is an emphasis on home as a sanctuary of love. Here again Jane Tompkins hits the right emphasis: Women carry the burden (and the burdens) of domestic fiction and in the ongoing battle "to conquer one's own soul" they "possess a territory of their own . . . the home, which operates in these novels as the basis of a religious faith that has unmistakably worldly dimensions. The religion of the home does not situate heaven in the afterlife, but locates it in the here and now, offering its disciples the experience of domestic bliss" (165–66). According to Baym, however, the woman's novel in America during the 1850s often portrayed the home as a battleground between the sexes but no such generality can apply to *The Wide, Wide World*.

We have again a parallel provided by *Jane Eyre*, in which the cottage at Morton is a citadel of sanctity and love, but not every house is a home, and the place ruled over by Miss Fortune with an iron hand is very low on contentment never mind sanctity and bliss. It is elsewhere that Ellen finds happiness, in a nearby parsonage where lives the Humphreys family, who will be instrumental in her pilgrimage toward salvation. And a pilgrimage it is, for Warner like Charlotte Brontë enfolds Bunyan's great book into her own as an intertextual staff to help Ellen on her way toward the Celestial City, though by the end of the book she has only reached the House Beautiful, identified with the Humphreys parsonage.

Both Jane Eyre and Ellen Montgomery are orphans who like Oliver Twist are searching for a loving home, and like Oliver they both are successful, for Jane finds herself in Rochester at Ferndale and Ellen finds herself in Christ, who is everywhere—even, as she ultimately discovers, in Scotland. Home, as the old adage has it, is where the heart is, or, as Robert Frost puts it, where they have to take you in. Home is also, as Tompkins defines it, a woman's place, and although women are not quite the exclusive vehicles of God's will in *The Wide, Wide World* as Tompkins implies, they are certainly much more central to Ellen's progress than they are to Jane Eyre's.

Jane in fact is very much a man's woman, much as Rochester is a woman's man. Once she has entered Thornfield, her destiny is in her own hands (another offense that grated the hard-line piety of such as Elizabeth Rigby), and is centered on the figure of Rochester. Only latterly do Mary and Diana, her cousins, enter the picture as mentors, with St. John Rivers providing an anti-

Rochester (even perhaps an anti-Christ). By contrast, Ellen's well-being is for most of the book in the hands of mentoring women who like handmaidens are preparing the girl not only for union with Christ but ultimately for union with one of Christ's ministers here on earth.

III

Although Bunyan's *Pilgrim's Progress* may have been in the forefront of Warner's imagination as she structured her heroine's troubled passageway toward salvation, there are elements as well of *Robinson Crusoe*, a book that was an inevitable text in any Victorian home. Stranded on their own island in the Hudson, their father often absent, the Warner sisters must have felt at times like female Crusoes, and their first joint effort to earn income was a children's game called "Robinson Crusoe's Farmyard." Certainly Ellen's exile to her aunt's farm results in a Crusoe-like education in both the hard and the practical facts of life, from the right clothing to wear while strolling through a swamp to the way in which butter is made and pork butchered and preserved. And the title of the novel evokes the well-known line from Coleridge's *Rhyme of the Ancient Mariner* (another parable of penitential regeneration by isolation) about being "alone on a wide, wide sea."

As Jane Tompkins has pointed out, Ellen may often feel alone and abandoned to her fate, but in truth she is helped along to salvation by a sequence of kindly persons who lend a benevolent presence to the narrative, equivalent to fairy godmothers and -fathers and to the warm-hearted people who appear at critical moments in Dickens's novels but are quite scarce in the fiction of Charlotte Brontë. The first of these Dickensian types shows up while Ellen is still in the city, and intervenes on her behalf when the little girl visits a large department store so as to purchase some merino fabric for a warm coat and dress, her mother being too ill for the venture and her father (as always) too busy. Confronted by a rude, uncooperative clerk, Ellen is helped by "an old gentleman" who has noticed her distress, and who will in the days before her mother departs prove to be "a dear old gentleman," supplying the Montgomery home with delicacies for their table. He also sees to it that the clerk is fired for his attitude, an act that will have future implications.

The second benevolent person is also a man and a stranger, whom Ellen meets on the boat carrying her up the Hudson toward her Aunt Fortune's farm. The parting with her mother has been calculatingly sudden, thanks to her father's dislike for unpleasant scenes—"she was a child of very high spirit and violent passions, untamed at all by sorrow's discipline" (63). Having literally torn Ellen from her mother's arms, Captain Montgomery puts his daughter in the care of the wife of a well-placed friend who happens to be traveling by steamboat and then by stagecoach to the town of Thirwall, where Ellen is to meet her Aunt Fortune. But Mrs. Dunscombe and her daughter Margaret prove to be terrible snobs, who object to taking charge of a very unhappy little girl dressed in what they regard as unsuitable which is to say unfashionable attire.

Overhearing their insulting opinion, Ellen seeks a private place on the crowded boat, "her heart . . . almost bursting with passion and pain," where she can give vent to the "pent-up tempest," which breaks forth with such "a fury that racked her little frame from head to foot; and the more because she strove to stifle every sound of it as much as possible. . . . And through it all, how constantly in her heart the poor child was reaching forth longing arms toward her far-off mother, and calling in secret on her beloved name. 'Oh, mamma! mamma!' was repeated numberless times" (67).

In the midst of her grief, Ellen is consoled by a gentleman who first asks the cause of her distress and then, his kind question having released "the floodgates of Ellen's heart," takes her with him "to a retired part of the deck where they were comparatively free from other people's eyes and ears; then taking her in his arms he endeavoured by many kind and soothing words to stay the torrent of her grief" (69). Modern readers may feel some discomfort in this sudden intimacy between a middle-aged man and a little girl, but should be reassured by Warner's description of the stranger, whose eyes are filled with a "look of kindness," and whose "whole countenance" is one of "gentleness and grave truthfulness."

This charitable gentleman suggests a personification of Christ himself, and it is not long before he leads Ellen out of her grief into a tractarian dialogue, in which he makes the point that "the God of love . . . does not trouble us willingly," for if the Lord makes us suffer it is always for a good purpose. What follows is essential to the logic of much that will happen subsequently to Ellen Montgomery, and may to a modern reader seem cruel and unfeeling but not to persons of an equivalent evangelical temper:

> "Sometimes [Christ] sees that if he lets them alone, his children will love some dear thing on the earth better than himself, and he knows

they will not be happy if they do so; and then, because he loves them, he takes it away,—perhaps it is a dear mother, or a dear daughter,—or else he hinders their enjoyment of it; that they may remember him, and give their whole hearts, that he may bless them. Are you one of his children, Ellen?"

"No sir," said Ellen, with swimming eyes, but cast down to the ground.

"How do you know that you are not?"

"Because I do not love the Saviour."

"Do you not love him, Ellen?"

"I am afraid not, sir."

"Why are you afraid not? what makes you think so?"

"Mama said I could not love him at all if I did not love him best; and oh, sir," said Ellen weeping, "I do love mamma a great deal better."

"You love your mother better than you do the Saviour?"

"Oh, yes, sir," said Ellen; "how can I help it?"

"Then if he had left you your mother, Ellen, you would never have cared or thought about him?"

Ellen was silent.

"Is it so?—would you, do you think?"

"I don't know, sir," said Ellen, weeping again,—oh, sir, how can I help it?"

"Then, Ellen, can you not see the love of your Heavenly Father in this trial? He saw that his little child was in danger of forgetting him, and he loved you, Ellen; and so he has taken your dear mother, and sent you away where you will have no one to look to but him; and now he says to you, 'My daughter, give me thy heart.'—Will you do it, Ellen?" (69–70)

At this point in her pilgrimage, Ellen can make no such promise, indeed she admits to the gentleman that her mother has told her she has a heart hardened against Christ. In response the gentleman urges her to pray to Jesus, and goes on to mount a lengthy argument in which he suggests that Ellen should love Christ for the very same reasons that she loves her mother, ending once again with the proposition that he has taken "away your dear mother for the very purpose that he may draw you gently to himself and fold you in his arms, as he has promised to do with his lambs" (73).

Ellen of the hard heart remains unconvinced by this higher logic, but it is an argument that will be repeated over and over during the course of the novel, for every time Ellen loses someone dear to her, the loss is attributed to Christ's desire that she love no one other than himself. In short, tough love on the divine plan, but then, to the evangelical turn of mind, Christ's love is a kind of transcendent selfishness, drawing all things to him at whatever human cost, and considering the alternatives being weighed in the balance, the pain that Ellen is feeling is undeniably for her own good: "Come to Jesus," urges the kindly stranger: "Do not fancy he is away up in heaven out of reach of hearing—he is here, close to you, and knows every wish and throb of your heart" (74). Notably, there is nothing here of the traditional evangelical reference to the motions of grace, but rather an appeal to the stern humanity of Christ.

With further consolations of this sharp-edged sort, the kindly gentleman remains by Ellen's side for the rest of the voyage, reading to her from his Bible and giving her a little hymnal as a parting gift when Ellen leaves the boat, where she is once again turned over to the callous Dunscombs. It would be easy enough to draw conclusions hostile to evangelical Christianity from this episode, but the dialogue with the kindly gentleman follows lines already established by the conversations between Ellen and her mother.

From the opening chapter of the novel, the chief goal is to bring Ellen to Christ, to which all other matters are secondary. Though modern readers may find the other matters the chief reason for sticking with the text, such readers clearly have not found themselves in the Lord. To such unbelievers, the pressures put on the sad little girl by the friendly gentleman seem intolerably insensitive, a kind of pious brainwashing in which the empty place left by Ellen's mother is to be filled by Jesus Christ, a process kin to that transfer of affections associated with the grief of loss acknowledged by psychologists.

But if some modern readers may be repelled by this emphasis, which represses Ellen's individuality in order to make her conform to a doctrinal ideology, it would have made Victorian readers like Elizabeth Rigby very happy indeed. It provides *The Wide, Wide World* precisely that element missing from *Jane Eyre*, namely, the reduction of a passionate little girl to a humble servant of Christ, indeed of service to anyone who claims to represent Christ here on this earth. She eventually learns the identity of the kindly gentleman, but is never reunited with him in any meaningful way. Instead, Ellen goes on to meet other, subsequent pious mentors, the most of whom, as Tompkins notes, are women.

Yet it is a man who at the start of things gets Ellen's mind turning in the right direction, if reluctantly and with a great shedding of painful tears, much as it will be a man who is there at the end, to receive into his care the final, finished, humble, and pious product. In place of the cruel and bullying Reverend Brocklehurst, we have at the initial stage of Ellen's pilgrimage a kindly Christian gentleman, but in effect the logic of both pious persons is the same: human emotions are nothing in the face of divine love, indeed suffering is the truest path to salvation. And salvation finally is the thing, the Alpha and Omega of the evangelical, tractarian movement which lends *The Wide,Wide World* its dominant purpose and motivating impulse.

There is moreover another man who becomes important to Ellen's life, not a vehicle of the gospel but a kindly, low-placed human being, a farmhand who works for her aunt and who is called upon to carry the girl in an ox-cart to Fortune Emerson's farm, her aunt having failed to meet her when she is left off in the town of Thirlwell by the Dunscombs. Mr. Van Brunt is a representative of the working class, and has the common man's warm heart and kindly disposition. More important, like the benevolent gentleman Ellen encountered in the department store, Brahm Van Brunt is straight out of Dickens, Dutch in descent but Yankee in terms of local coloration and second cousin to the equally rough-surfaced but kindly Barkis in *David Copperfield.*

The charitable warmth with which Ellen is welcomed by Mr. Van Brunt contrasts not only with the reluctant company of the Dunscombes but with the reception given the little girl by her Aunt Fortune, who as Tompkins suggests will act the part of the wicked stepmother in Warner's version of the Cinderella story. Hers is truly a cold comfort farm, and though a citadel of the Protestant ethic it leaves little room for Christian charity never mind simple human affection. Ellen's first sight of the farmhouse is at night, and as she enters through the door to which she is directed by Mr. Van Brunt it is directly into the heart of the house, the kitchen.

The room is described as "good-sized" and "cheerful-looking," with a fire in the great fireplace, white walls tinted yellow from the flames, and a table set for supper (99). "With its snow-white tablecloth and shining furniture," the table "looked very comfortable indeed," exactly the kind of sanctuary Tompkins associates with the sentimental novel. Indeed, much of the subsequent action will take place in Miss Fortune's kitchen, but its look of comfort proves to be an illusion.

The only person in the room is an old woman, who sits by the fire with her back to Ellen. The girl wonders if this is her aunt, but then a moment later Miss Fortune Emerson steps through a door, struck with surprise at the sight of the strange child.

As it turns out, she had no warning that her step-niece was to arrive that day. Ellen's father had (typically) failed to notify his half-sister of Ellen's scheduled arrival, which, along with his failure to pay back money borrowed from his sister, will be held by

Aunt Fortune against the little girl. Things get off on the wrong foot from the start, and though as the description of her kitchen reveals Fortune Emerson is a fine housekeeper, she is also a single woman with the care of her elderly mother—the old woman by the fire—and the management of a farm on her hands. The unbidden guest is about as welcome as a stray cat.

Given supper, Ellen is shown to her bed, but the gruff treatment at the hands of her aunt brings her to tears once again, and when she awakes the next morning, it is to discover that the room she is to occupy is hardly up to her notion of style, the woodwork being "paintless and rough," though temporarily "gilded" by the bright morning sun (101). "Ellen was not much pleased with the result of her survey. The room was good-sized, and perfectly neat and clean," but there was no carpet on the floor, and the bare boards were uncomfortable looking.

The rest of the room followed suit, with no furniture save an inadequate dressing table, two chairs, and Ellen's cot. No pitcher and basin is provided, and Ellen finds that she must go outside to an open spout if she wishes to wash her face and hands. Breakfast is a simple affair, coarse and plentiful, being slices of pork fried up with a kind of pancake, and Ellen as well as the reader is impressed with the fact that the world she has entered bears no resemblance to the one she left behind. There will be no tea and toast and precious little sympathy served up in Miss Fortune's kitchen.

For a time, Ellen's aunt leaves her to her own devices, but soon the girl is assigned her share of domestic chores, starting with making up her own bed, a duty she finds not to her liking. Sympathy, mostly silent, is supplied by Mr. Van Brunt, who takes his meals with his employer although he spends his nights at home with his elderly mother. Ellen obeys her own mother's wish, and writes regular letters, recounting her adventures and putting the best slant on matters, and though she admits she is not terribly fond of Aunt Fortune, she declares she will do her best to please the woman in whose charge she has been placed.

Ellen is anxious to continue her education, being ambitious to learn French and Italian among other genteel subjects, but learns there is no school nearby, another reversal of expectations that puts still more distance between aunt and niece. Some problematic diversion is provided by Nancy Vawse, an older girl described by her aunt as "no good," yet who serves as Ellen's guide about the countryside. Though wild and inclined to mischief, Nancy provides companionship, a commodity the lonely little girl finds is in very short supply thereabouts.

On one of these excursions Ellen falls into a brook, and is taken by Nancy to the Van Brunt home where she is dried out and fussed over by Brahm and his mother, who shares her son's affection for the little girl. Ellen finds a certain happiness in helping Van Brunt around the farm, especially in milking the cows, a chore she keeps secret from her aunt, who did not authorize it. Her relationship with Miss Fortune becomes increasingly strained, and though Ellen does her best to act respectful and pleasant, her aunt continues her harsh and punitive ways, and when Ellen discovers she has actually opened and read a long-awaited letter to her from her mother, the little girl explodes in rage, tossing the letter down unread and dashing from the house.

Heedless in her anger as to where she is heading, Ellen finds herself on "a most lovely wild wood-way path," which leads up a mountainside, and which takes her to a kind of natural sanctuary: "Carpeted with moss, and furnished with fallen stones and pieces of rock, this was a fine resting-place for the wayfarer, or loitering place for the lover of nature" (147). Ellen takes a seat on one of the rocks, and looks "sadly and wearily" at the magnificent vista opening before her, and though at first she is untouched by "the picturesque effect of all this, yet the sweet influences of nature reached her, and softened while they increased her sorrow" (148). Nature, in short, supplies a vision of beauty but provides inadequate consolation.

Overcome by the thought of how far away over the distant hills her mother is, Ellen begins to weep violently—"When once fairly excited, Ellen's passions were always extreme"—and alone in her refuge she is "wrought up to the last pitch of grief and passion," sobbing aloud "and even screamed for almost the first time in her life" (148). As on the steamboat, her grief attracts the attention of a kind stranger, this time a young woman, who addresses her in a voice the sweetness of which is matched by her face: "What is the matter, my child?" But the expression of sympathy as on the steamboat only increases Ellen's grief, as she cradles her head in "the bosom of a better friend than the cold earth" (149).

In response to Ellen's despairing declaration that "[n]obody in this world can help me," the lady tells her that "[t]here's one in heaven that can. . . . Have you asked *his* help, Ellen?" (150). The young woman we eventually learn is Alice Humphreys, the daughter of a local minister and the sister of a divinity student. She picks up the thread left by the kindly gentleman on the steamboat, her Christian solace giving a spiritual aura to the beautiful natural setting. They pray together and Ellen resolves to try even harder "to be a Christian."

Strengthened by the loving care projected from the pious Alice, Ellen returns to "the path of duty," which takes her back to Miss Fortune and the farm (156). Matters, however, continue to grow worse between Ellen and her aunt, for the girl resents the woman's attempts to control her and Fortune regards her niece's resentment as rebellion. Try as she might, Ellen cannot keep a lid on her passions, and after another violent confrontation with her aunt, sparked by an unkind remark made about Ellen's mother, she seeks out Alice Humphreys for comfort and advice, the first of many visits resulting in a relationship that her aunt resents.

The Humphreys home is a large white house virtually enclosed by "the trees of the wood" with which it is surrounded, a sanctuary in the midst of nature and an equivalent to the lovely place Ellen found on the mountainside where she first met Alice. They meet now in Alice's sitting room, which is set with windows providing views of the natural world; its counterpart is Alice's bedroom, an immaculate chamber painted white set off with curtains of white dimity, and a table covered with pure white muslin on which sits a vase of flowers. It is a room that provides a sharp contrast with the uncouth quarters assigned Ellen by her aunt, and is amply furnished with books, which Alice describes as her "greatest treasure" (164).

In this pure, monastic space the two engage in another dialogue concerning Ellen's unsuccessful attempts to lead a Christian life, which the little girl admits has been hampered by her dislike of her aunt. She feels that Miss Fortune had "no right to talk as she does about mamma," nor any right to strike Ellen by way of rebuke (165). But Alice gives her little comfort: instead she points out Ellen's fault in the matter, and advises her to apologize to her aunt; there then follows more talk of a similar kind, bearing on forgiveness and the strength to be found by relying on Jesus in times of need, advice that is always forthcoming in Ellen's subsequent conversations with the kindly, loving young woman. Clearly, Alice picks up the maternal role, never assumed by Aunt Fortune, and attempts by example and precept to lead Ellen to Christ. But as an instance of feminine influence, a concept essential to the sentimental mode, Alice it must be said is largely ineffective: Ellen comes to love and admire her dear friend, but she loves her real mother even more, who remains between her and salvation.

We have moved far away from the world of *Jane Eyre,* where Christianity plays virtually no role after the opening chapters until Jane flees to Morton, yet the central issue, the control of passion, remains the same. Again, "good" in pious Victorian minds brings with it sanctions of behavior that in this post-Freudian age strike us repeatedly as bad in execution. So long as Ellen's mentor is that anthropomorphized Sunday school lesson, Alice Humphreys, we can find little fault with the methodology of instruction, whatever we may feel about its qualities as literature. But once Alice's long absent brother, John, appears, it is with footfalls reminiscent of the sounds made by the riding boots of Edward Rochester.

5

Painful Matters: The Wide, Wide Underworld in Warner's Book and Its Sequel, *Elsie Dinsmore*

To resist him that is set in authority is evil.
—Adolph Erman

I

Jane Tompkins, in her afterword to Warner's novel, notes of sentimental fiction that "their heroines rarely get beyond the confines of a private space—the kitchen, the parlor, the upstairs chamber," and while this is certainly true of Jane Eyre, we find Ellen Montgomery forever fleeing the Emerson house for an Emersonian garden, whether the barnyard where she enjoys the company and conversation of Brahm Van Brunt or the natural world beyond the farm fence (594). The typical heroine of woman's fiction as defined by Nina Baym spends much of her time in domestic captivity, held by the bond of marriage, but being still a child Ellen is not yet married, and so her bildungsroman in traditional form involves a considerable amount of physical movement.

Moreover, as the novel develops Ellen moves (or is led) from one symbolic center to another, in effect a passage toward increasingly benevolent surroundings but not to a conventional domestic zone of familial contentment. It is after all on a mountainside that she first meets Alice Humphreys, her spiritual guide and friend, the female Christ in the garden. And the female Thoreau in the frame is old Mrs. Vawse, Nancy's grandmother, to whose home Ellen is led by Alice, a remote sanctuary on the top of the same mountain where the two first met: there like Thoreau Mrs. Vawse lives content in her solitude, sustained however not by the Vedas but by the Gospels.

The putative reason for the pilgrimage up the rough mountain path by Ellen and Alice is to employ the Swiss-born woman as an instructor in the correct pronunciation of French, which Ellen and her mentor intend to study. But Mrs. Vawse has much more to teach than her native language, for she is a version of female Crusoe, having mastered her microcosm with the aid of industry and the consolations of the Bible. In Alice's description, Mrs. Vawse had "'been tossed from trouble to trouble;—a perfect sea of troubles;—now she is left like a wreck upon this mountain top. A fine wreck she is!'" (172). Mrs. Vawse is Warner's counterpoint to Bertha Rochester, an isolated woman set apart from society, not however because she is insane but because that is her personal choice, to live alone on her mountaintop—which reminds her of her native Switzerland—a setting traditionally associated with personal freedom.

She is in fact an abstraction of Susan Warner's ideal state, as Nina Baym defines it in *Woman's Fiction,* the freedom of "being left alone, protected and comfortable, to pursue one's own interests," for Warner's notion of "independence was intransigently self-centered" (150). According to Jane Tompkins, in *Sensational Designs,* "Mrs. Vawse is the most completely happy and fulfilled person in the novel because economically, socially, and emotionally she is the most independent" (167). She is a benign spirit, a demonstration of the peace that comes with complete self-control, and her isolation on the mountaintop acts like Wallace Stevens's jug, giving a centripetal order to the world about her.

The interior of Mrs. Vawse's mountain cottage is a severe version of those domestic spaces central to the sentimental tradition, containing a single room that combines both kitchen and bedroom kept in immaculate condition: "[N]othing was to be seen here that did not agree with a very comfortable face of the whole. It looked as if one might be happy there; it looked as if somebody was happy there; and a glance at the old lady of the house would not alter the opinion" (190). If Mrs. Vawse is happy in her "little house on the rock," it is not only because the mountain reminds her of "my Alps" at home: the rock on which her house was built is also the rock of faith on which Christ proposed to build his church. When Mrs. Vawse tells Ellen that she is "never alone," it is a Christian version of Thoreau's recipe for companionship in his hermitage at Walden Pond, which depended not on people but on the constant presence of the natural world (193). Her mountaintop home makes her happy with her lowly condition on earth, but it is also a gatehouse to "my home in heaven," where "my Saviour is preparing a place for me" (189).

On their way back down the mountain, Alice and Ellen are caught in a sudden snowstorm and become lost, a perilous situation from which they are rescued providentially by Brahm Van Brunt, who happened to leave his house to check his horse and the light of his lantern caught the attention of the two girls, who otherwise would have perished only a short distance from succor. The two spend the night with the Van Brunts, whose home is "a perfect storehouse of comfort," and the next morning there occurs another of those interludes that strengthens the female bond, repeating with small variations the interview with Mrs. Vawse.

An alternative to the pious, somewhat ascetic woman on the mountain, Mrs.Van Brunt is a fountain of domestic generosity: "Kindness and hospitality always kept Mrs. Van Brunt in full flow" (205). Alice and Ellen "went away full of a kind feeling for every one and much love to each other. This was true of them before; but their late troubles had drawn them closer together and given them fresh occasion to value their friends." As for Alice, she "exerted herself and applied what was wanting everywhere, like the transparent glazing which painters use to spread over the dead colour of their pictures; unknown, it was she gave life and harmony to the whole."

For a time after her visit to Mrs. Vawse Ellen is confined to her bedroom, for the ordeal on the mountain brings on a spell of illness, during which she is cared for industriously but without compassion by her aunt, tormented by the mischievous Nancy Vawse, and visited and comforted by Brahm and Alice. This last is the most important visitor, for the pious, beautiful young woman is gradually taking the place of Ellen's missing mother: "Alice presently rose, sat down in the rocking chair, and took Ellen in her lap; and Ellen rested her head on her bosom as she had been wont to do of old times on her mother's" (219).

The maternal connection is strengthened when Alice produces a long-delayed letter from Ellen's beloved parent, not only because of what the letter means to the little girl in the sickbed, but because Alice herself had earlier lost her mother to death, so that "we are both motherless, for the present at least. . . . I think God has brought us together to be a comfort to each other. . . . You shall be my little sister and I will be your elder sister, and my home shall be your home as well" (224). The strengthened bond in no way diminishes Alice's role as mentor, and she constantly reminds her "sister" of her Christian duty: "You cannot love Christ without loving to please him," which translates into "the faithful, patient, self-denying performance of every duty as it comes to hand" (243, 239).

Although her life with Miss Fortune is enlivened by the excitement generated by a rural harvest bee, in which the neighbors gather to help pare apples and stuff sausage for winter supplies, Ellen finds herself more and more with the Humphreys. She is drawn in as well by the upper-class social life of the Marshmans, a hospitable family the husband of which as it turns out is the brother of the kindly gentleman Ellen met on the steamboat. We may regret that one result of this change of scene is to diminish the element of local color, but as Warner notes by way of introducing the events of a typical day on the farm, "the history of one day may serve for the history of all those weeks" (362). This is always a problem for the writer who seeks to promote a realistic account of everyday rural matters, and for the sake of the narrative as well as herself, Ellen must not remain forever down on the farm. Moreover, her move to more sophisticated and social surroundings is accompanied by leaving a circle of predominantly female mentors for one influential male, perhaps the most significant transition in the novel.

II

The shift of gender emphasis as well as an addition to Ellen's ever widening (and elevated) social circle occurs with the return of Alice's brother John, who has come home for the Christmas holidays from divinity school, and whose handsome features and dark eyes prove a magnet for the little girl. Mr. John as she calls him reinforces the efforts of Alice to bring Ellen to Christ, indeed by this point in the story it is difficult to determine what is holding the child back, given the preponderance of piety with which she is surrounded. But then Ellen's conversion is the point of the plot, and her hard heart must endure for a while longer, as always paired with her love for her missing mother.

John and Alice share a sibling intimacy that, expressed by frequent hugging and kissing, seems to a modern reader as bordering on incest, but this is not Roderick and Madeline Usher. Their love is reinforced by its purity and piety, forming a tight little circle to which Ellen is admitted as a third, adoptive family member, becoming their little "sister." At the Marshmans she meets another child, the lively Ellen Chauncey, a further attraction drawing Ellen Montgomery away from Miss Fortune's farm. (Why Warner elected to name these two girls Ellen is another puzzle of nomenclature; perhaps the implication is that they are alter egos, but the effect is to cause confusion in the reader.)

During the holidays John increasingly monopolizes Ellen's time, and it is not difficult to recognize the erotic underpinnings of the second "brother-sister" relationship. John takes a stern, authoritarian line, in contrast to his sister's loving lectures, at one point commanding Ellen to join him in the library, where he sets her to work mastering the art of drawing, overriding Ellen's preference to be doing other things. John disapproves of Ellen's reading mere fiction and gives his disciple historical and moral texts, including Weems's (misspelled "Wiems") *Life of Washington.* So great becomes his control over the girl that Ellen declares he knows "every thing I am thinking about," and she also learns that Mr. John is no milk-toast Christian, for when roused to anger he has, as a friend attests, "strength enough for twice his bone and muscle" (317–18).

With these consolations and interests, Ellen begins to find her days on the farm more pleasant, and though the continuing silence from her mother, despite Ellen's written "supplications for letters," brings her pain, she finds the stern discipline of Mr. John a solace of sorts. But then, as quickly as he appeared, her young master is gone, having returned to his divinity studies. The following September brings the crushing news, withheld by her aunt but revealed accidentally by a gossiping neighbor, that her mother has died. The sudden shock leaves poor Ellen devastated, a depth of grief that cannot find relief in tears, and though the girl of sorrows seeks refuge at the Humphreys', Alice seems powerless to bring her comfort.

During her extended stay with Alice, Ellen comes to find solace in her Bible: "She loved to read about Christ,—all he said and did; all his kindness to his people and tender care of them. . . . She began to cling more to that one unchangeable friend from whose love neither life nor death can sever those that believe in him" (347). Grievous as it is, the loss of her parent impels Ellen to turn to Christ for companionship and comfort, much as her mother, while still alive but absent, kept Ellen from union with her savior—precisely the point made by those who tried to solace her. But she continues to remain withdrawn and pale, and it is only with the return of Mr. John for the New Year's holiday that she begins to come out of herself. At his urging, she confesses that rather than loving Christ less for having brought her such sorrow, she loves him, as she sobs out the word, *"more."*

Where Ellen has refused to speak to Alice about her mother's death, John draws her out, consoling her with the thought that all that Christ does is "done in love, and shall work good for you; and if we often cannot see how, it is because we are weak and foolish, and can see but a very little way" (349). John is able to bring about the cure that Alice had striven to effect in vain, but in plain fact Ellen is finally able to come to Christ because her mother no longer stands in the way. Indeed as John suggests, "she is with him—she has reached that bright home where there is no more sin, nor sorrow, nor death," to which Ellen adds the all-important "Nor parting either" (348). If Ellen's heart is no longer hard, it is because she can now look forward to rejoining her mother forever, indeed understands that if her mother is now in Christ, that is where she also belongs.

We may from our perspective wonder about the meaningfulness of Ellen's awakening. She has not foresworn her love for her mother, but now, in a Protestant version of the Platonic ladder, regards it as the lamp lighting the way up the stairway to paradise. It is a situation equivalent to Jane Eyre's setting aside her moral objection to union with Rochester at precisely the moment when that moral objection no longer applies. The death of her beloved's wife removes the obstacle to her own happiness, a union not with Christ but with Rochester, that secular savior.

All of the sermonizing, by the gentleman on the boat, by Alice and John Humphreys, has had little effect on bringing the little girl to Christ, and if we are to follow their logic, then it was Christ himself who brought about Ellen's salvation, by calling her mother away. This is an antinomian process, in which salvation is a matter for individuals to gain by themselves; but it is also an authoritarian view of the savior, which would seem to leave little room for the exercise of free will. As we shall see, it is a role that will be assumed by Mr. John, the minister-in-training who pointed the way through a door already opened by the death of Ellen's mother.

John Humphreys resumes his role as tutor, and it is at this critical point that he gives Ellen a copy of *Pilgrim's Progress* which he has carefully annotated for her enlightenment, a book that is to be her companion, guide, and solace during his future absences, in effect replacing her mother's Bible. John's influence continues to operate once he has left: "[H]is will seemed to carry all before it, present or absent," and Ellen continues to recover, and she keeps up with her studies, being "untiring in her efforts to do whatever he had wished her, and was springing forward, Alice said, in her improvement" (353).

The obvious parallel here is with Brontë's *The Professor*—a novel Warner could hardly have known about in 1848—for Mr. John as Ellen's stern yet loving mentor plays a role like that performed by Crimsworth in his relationship with Frances. And eventually Ellen's tutor like Frances's will hold out the promise of becoming a suitor, having helped her attain a state of perfect Christian humility and submission to his will. Both mentors, in effect, shape their disciples to fit an ideal pattern, thereby illustrating the Pygmalion/Galatea perplex.

It is this relationship that reminds Jane Tompkins, in her "Afterword" to Warner's *Novel*, of *The Story of O*, "another education in submission in which the heroine undergoes ever more painful forms of self-effacement," which we have also seen operating as an analogue to the disciplining of Frances by her professor-lover (Warner, 599). For Tompkins, Warner's version of "the basic pornographic situation . . . the novel's dramatization of domination and submission . . . is sexualized from the start," but it is with the entrance on the stage of Mr. John that sexuality takes a gendered turn, with clear if unintended parallels to the situation in *The Professor*. And any echoes of that book, prior to its posthumous publication, inevitably resonate with equivalent themes in *Jane Eyre*.

Moreover, if we turn to the Morton episode in *Jane Eyre* we can establish another counterpoint parallel with that novel, for Mr. John in his move to exercise complete control over a girl he will think of finally as his future wife may be compared to the relationship between St. John Rivers and his cousin Jane. St. John the evangelist promotes a line not much different from that of Mr. John the divinity student, calling on Jane to submit to the will of Christ, which soon becomes inseparable from the will of St. John Rivers.

But where Jane Eyre, independent as ever, escapes the dominance of St. John at the last possible moment, Ellen Montgomery is clearly willing to make herself over into the desired pattern of humble submission, which is Jane's posture when in the presence of Rochester. Beyond matters of intention, this difference is a key to the essential disparity between two novels that in so many ways resemble one another. In effect, Ellen is willing to marry the man that Jane rejects, identifying Mr. John's stern, unbending will with the will of God, where Jane regards St. John's iron soul as another perversion of the Christian ideal, and returns willingly to Rochester's pagan world. Here again, Elizabeth Rigby would have approved of Ellen's attitude, much as she disapproved of Jane's.

The sexual implication of John Humphreys' domination over Ellen does not have the sadistic overtones of the relationship in *The Professor,* but there is some indirect matters that promote a similar off-coloration. Ellen is given a pony by the generous Mr. Marshman, and during the discussion of what name to give her new pet, she learns that Mr. John has a stern hand with horses as well as with his protégée, this time one that holds a whip: "Do you remember, Alice," asks Sophia Chauncey, Ellen's older sister, "the chastising he gave that fine black horse of ours we called the 'Black Prince'?—a beautiful creature he was,—more than a year ago?" (376).

When Ellen asks why John whipped the horse, Alice explains that "it sometimes is necessary to do such things. You do not suppose John would do it cruelly or unnecessarily?" John, like her version of Christ, always causes pain for a good reason: "The horse was resolved to have his own way and not do what his rider required of him; it was necessary that either the horse or the man should give up; and as John has no fancy for giving up, he carried his point,—partly by management, partly, I confess, by a judicious use of the whip and spur; but there was no such furious flagellation as Sophia seems to mean" (377). And yet Sophia sticks to her story, and advises Ellen "not to trust your pony to Mr. John; he will have no mercy on him." There is never a question of the girl being whipped by her loving master; his "chastisement" is always psychological, but like Crimsworth's in *The Professor* it is always exercised with the intention of forcing submission to his will.

At a later point in the novel there is an episode of openly physical sadism that directly involves Ellen, who has ridden to town on her beloved pony, Brownie, to fetch a doctor for Brahm Van Brunt, who has broken his leg in a fall. On her return, she has an encounter with the man who had caused her so much trouble in the New York department store, Mr. Saunders, who has seen her earlier in the day in the Thirlwall post office and is waiting for her on the road. Thanks to the intercession of the kind old gentleman Saunders had been fired from his clerkship, and "Ellen and the old gentleman had lived in his memory as objects of the deepest spite" (400).

Following Ellen and her pony, Saunders cuts a sapling for a switch ("don't that look like a whip?"), and begins to torment Brownie, who had never received anything but the kindest treatment, threatening to "make him leap over a rail," though as Ellen pleads she has not learned "to leap yet" (397). As the pony begins to dance about, his rider is in danger of falling off, and she begs

Saunders to desist but to no avail: "For some time he amused himself with this game, the horse growing more and more irritated. At length a smart stroke of the whip upon his haunches made Brownie spring in a way that brought Ellen's heart into her mouth, and almost threw her off. 'Oh don't!' cried Ellen, 'poor Brownie!— How can you! Oh, please let us go! please let us go!'" (398).

But Saunders persists in exacting his revenge, for it is not the pony he seeks to hurt but Ellen, not by causing her to fall but by tormenting her through the pain being felt by her beloved Brownie. Saunders demands that Ellen dismount, so that he can have a free hand with his switch, threatening "If he hasn't been used to a whip he'll know pretty well what it means by the time I have done with him; and then you may go home as fast as you can" (399). But Ellen clings in desperation to her pony, and in the nick of time John Humphreys appears, having by a fortunate coincidence an errand in Thirlwall.

Dismounting from Black Prince, John takes matters literally into his own hands: ordering Ellen to ride on he has a brief exchange with Sanders before seizing him "by the collar, and hurl[ing] him quite over into the gully at the side of the road, where he lay at full length without stirring" (401). Regaining his saddle, John joins Ellen, who is overcome with shock and grief: "'Oh, how could he! how could he!' said poor Ellen;—'how could he do so!—it was very hard!' An involuntary touch of the spurs made John's horse start." The analogy between the sadistic Saunders and the masterful John Humphreys is here given a syntactical link.

"How beautiful he is!" exclaims Ellen in admiring the Black Prince: "'Is he good?' 'I hope so,' said John smiling;—if he is not I shall be at the pains to make him so'" (402). Soon after, John begins to give Ellen riding lessons, teaching her to leap over a bar (in effect making good Saunders's threat) and to ride without stirrups or reins, and though Ellen "trembled very much at the beginning," she discovered that "her teacher was careful and gentle, but determined; and whatever he said she did, tremble or no tremble; and in general loved her riding lessons dearly" (410). The drawing lessons also continue, in which Mr. John exercises the same stern authority, and for her part, Ellen becomes something of an evangelist herself. She seeks to bring Brahm Van Brunt to Christ, using not the Bible but her beloved annotated copy of *Pilgrim's Progress*, and Ellen's increased devotion to "religion and discipline" result in an increasing "sweetness of temper" not unlike that of Alice Humphreys, the woman whom Ellen increasingly resembles.

Ellen's intimacy with her adoptive brother and sister is increased when Brahm Van Brunt takes Aunt Fortune for his wife, his old mother having died and thereby set him (and Ellen) at liberty. Soon thereafter Alice herself begins to fade away, that long, pathetic, and aphorism-laden process associated with consumption so essential to Victorian sentimentalism, further cementing the association with Ellen's mother: "The bright spots of colour in Alice's face were just like what her mother's cheeks used to wear in her last illness" (427). This crisis warrants another lengthy stay by Ellen at the parsonage, where "at Alice's wish she immediately took up her quarters . . . to leave her no more" (430). Alice also orders Ellen to take her place when she dies, to live on in the parsonage "and take care of those I leave behind . . . and they will take care of you" (432).

There follows the inevitable death scene, another chapter taken from Dickens, with Alice in bed surrounded by her family and friends, awaiting the return of her beloved brother, John, who arrives at the critical moment: "'Are you happy, Alice?' whispered her brother. 'Perfectly. This was all I wanted. Kiss me, dear John'" (440). He kisses his sister, "again and again," his tears falling on her cheek, as Alice, her last wish having been granted, slips quietly away: "*Alice* was gone; but the departing spirit had left a ray of brightness on its earthly house; there was a half smile on the sweet face, of most entire peace and satisfaction" (441).

Kissing his sister one last time, John leaves the death room, as does Ellen, who climbs the mountain path to the place where she first met Alice. She stands alone, looking through her tears "over the beautiful landscape. Never more beautiful than then," made so by its associations with her dead "sister" (442). From far off she hears the tolling of the church bell for Alice, and breaks into sobs when the last of the twenty-four strokes, one for each of Alice's years, dies on her ears:

> Just then a voice close beside her said low, as if the speaker might not trust its higher tones,—"I will lift up mine eyes unto the hills, from whence cometh my help!"
>
> How differently that sound struck upon Ellen's ear! With an indescribable air of mingled tenderness, weariness, and sorrow, she slowly rose from her seat and put both her arms round the speaker's neck. Neither said a word; but to Ellen the arm that held her was more than all words; it was the dividing line between her and the world,—on this side everything, on that side nothing.
>
> No word was spoken for many minutes.
>
> "My dear Ellen," said her brother softly,—"how came you here?"

"I don't know," whispered Ellen,—"there was nobody there—I couldn't stay in the house."

"Shall we go home now?"

"Oh, yes—whenever you please." (443)

Here again is a moment recalling *The Professor,* specifically the scene in which Crimsworth finally realizes that he loves Frances when he finds her at the grave of her aunt, again not a matter of influence but rather of elective affinity, echoes of a symbolic language typical of the Victorian version of sentimentality.

Moreover, John consoles Ellen on the very spot where the grieving girl first met Alice, and is drawn to her by some mystical force equivalent to that which summoned Jane to the wounded Rochester's side, a mystery objectified in their joint memory and love of the dead Alice. The saintly maiden has lived and died that they might come together, here as adoptive brother and sister, eventually (it is hinted at the final curtain) as husband and wife. These may once again be coincidental correspondences, but they serve to define the similarities and differences between the two equally popular novels. Hardly proof of influence, they remain suggestive.

But Warner's emphasis is not Brontë's in *The Professor:* before returning to the parsonage, John Humphreys delivers the necessary pious and by now familiar injunction that they both "try to love our God better," now that there is less "we have left to love in this world;—that is his meaning—let sorrow but bring us closer to him. Dear Alice is well—she is well,—and if we are made to suffer, we know and we love the hand that has done it,—do we not Ellie?" After a few more consoling remarks of this hard-edged kind, John again asks, "'Shall we go home, Ellie?'... and looking for a moment at the tokens of watching and grief and care in her countenance, he gently kissed the pale little face, adding a word of endearment which almost broke Ellen's heart again. Then taking her hand they went down the mountain together" (444).

III

The novel does not (though it perhaps should) end here, for Ellen's Bunyanesque pilgrimage is as yet incomplete: following Alice's death she travels to Scotland, unwillingly obeying her dying mother's wish that she live with the Lindsays, Mrs. Montgomery's wealthy mother and her two children. Ellen's aunt and uncle (a

widow and a widower) are both single and childless, and her uncle quickly develops a great fondness for Ellen, expressed through
an intense possessiveness: "You are my own child now,—you
are my little daughter. . . . You belong to me entirely, and I belong
to you;—my own little daughter!" (504). Already having been
"adopted" by the Humphreys family, Ellen is bothered by this new
relationship, which grows even more troublesome as tensions
develop, not only because of the British scorn for the "Yankees"
who inhabit their former colonies but, more important, because
of the conflict between Ellen's strict piety and the easy morality of
the Lindsay home.

Mr. Lindsay demands that his patriotic niece forgo her
birthright, that she think of herself as English not American, and
that she regard him as her father not her uncle, for "you are my
own little daughter, and must do precisely what I tell you" (510).
Though her uncle's affection is pleasing to Ellen, she is troubled
by his possessive, authoritarian manner. The relationship becomes a conflict when Mr. Lindsay insists that his niece take a
glass of wine, which violates her moral principles, but her uncle
demanding as her "father" that he be obeyed, Ellen has no choice
and drinks the wine (517–18).

Her uncle continues to tighten the reins, insisting that he will
"have only obedience . . . without either answering or argument-
ing," and Ellen does her best not to displease him. She also struggles to please her equally demanding grandmother, finding that
humility in the face of authoritarianism is necessary for the relationship to remain on loving terms (527). As a result, "she was petted and fondled as a darling possession—a dear plaything—a
thing to be cared for, taught, governed, disposed of, with the greatest affection and delight," and Warner's loaded diction is telling:
The authority and love of Mr. Lindsay and his family, which per-
sistently attempts to discourage Ellen's piety, is no substitute for
Mr. John's, which was both "a higher style of kindness, that entered into all her innermost feelings and wants; and . . . a higher
style of authority too, that reached where theirs could never attain; an authority . . . sure to be exerted on the side of what was
right" (538–39).

Though life with the Lindsays goes "smoothly," it is a slow slide
into a way of life alien to Ellen's experience and offensive to her
strict Christian faith. Matters grow worse when Mr. Lindsay con-
fiscates her beloved copy of *Pilgrim's Progress,* in effect cutting
the only cord that still attaches Ellen to Mr. John, who has not written to her since she left America. Angry words are exchanged, af-

ter which there is a battle in Ellen's mind between "reason and conscience," for her conscience maintains that she owes her "father" an apology for having argued with him, while reason tells her that she has done nothing wrong (553). Through all of these conflicts she longs for word from Mr. John, but as earlier with her dying mother, no letter comes in response to her own.

Here again we have what can only be called an uncanny parallel with the facts of Charlotte Brontë's life, but with a signal difference that merges with the ending of *Jane Eyre:* The climactic moment occurs on New Year's Eve (apparently the family does not keep Christmas), which the wealthy, self-indulgent Lindsays celebrate in grand style, insisting that Ellen be dressed in fancy clothes, and that she also put on a happy face for their friends. But then, at the height of the festivities, Mr. John appears, literally forcing his way into the gathering, and having taken Ellen into his arms, he takes her to her room.

There he comforts the tearful young woman by assuring her of his undying affection, hinting that when she has come of age, they will never again be separated. Until then, however, Ellen must remain with her relations, in accordance with the wishes of her dead mother. In a subsequent interview with the hitherto inhospitable Lindsays, Mr. John makes it perfectly clear that he and his father have their rights to Ellen as well, an argument put forward in straightforward terms but so politely that the Lindsays cannot but acknowledge the Humphreys' priority.

Her Scottish relations end up quite fond of Mr. John, and allow Ellen to "keep up a regular and full correspondence" with the man she loves. As Warner reassures her readers in a final paragraph, a few years "of Scottish discipline wrought her no ill," but made a better Christian of Ellen, until, with "unspeakable joy, she went back to spend her life with the friends and guardians she best loved" (569). This return and her marriage to John Humphreys is the substance of an additional chapter Warner subsequently wrote but never published, and in the novel Ellen is left waiting not at but a few feet short of the altar, setting a pattern that will endure through a number of novels written for girls and young women, and a significant departure from the tradition established by the romances of Charlotte Brontë.

But that departure is precisely the point: it is difficult not to regard Mr. John as a consciously wrought blend of St. John and Rochester, his appearing in Edinburgh at precisely the right moment, like his showing up on the mountain following Alice's death, being equivalent to the mysterious message Jane obeys from her beloved, which helps preserve her from the hypnotic influence of St. John, who like Mr. John is an intensely pious avatar of the Pauline spirit. Again, the point is less to bring Ellen to Mr. John than to Christ, so that the ending, just this side of the altar, reinforces the pious emphasis at the cost of the romantic element. There may be a question regarding the extent to which Warner was responding to Brontë's novel, but the echoes are certainly suggestive.

We know that in April 1848 in a letter home to her sister, Anna, Warner wrote that a friend, who had been reading Brontë's novel, "says I am so much like [Jane Eyre], and wanted to know if you did not think so. I did not tell her that *I* thought so, but I do, as you know" (Foster, 121). Edward Halsey Foster, who quotes this in a footnote to his biography of the Warner sisters, remarks that there is very little similarity between Brontë's heroine and Ellen Montgomery, and if there was any influence, that it "was distant and weak."

But that of course is just the argument I have made here, that there is very little in common between the two novels save for the Cinderella theme. Warner's novel is a heavily Christianized parable, a classic example of domestic, sentimental fiction in which the heroine bows her will to that of God, whereas Brontë's is a gothic romance with so great an emphasis on the heroine's self-determined actions as to be taken by some readers as a pagan exercise. Yet both novels emphasize the lesson of self-control, mastered by Jane Eyre and taught Ellen by a series of mentors. Warner may, as her sister attested, have started writing her own novel in 1847, at a time when there could have been no possibility of influence by *Jane Eyre*, but this does not rule out the possibility of subsequent indebtedness, given that Warner's novel was at least a year in the writing.

In *Behold the Child*, Gillian Avery agrees with Edward Foster that there are numerous parallels between *The Wide, Wide World* and Sedgwick's *A New England Tale*, which she regards as the literary progenitor of the mean-old-maid-and-suffering-orphan-girl trope in America (179). At the same time, it is notable that John Humphreys, who seems in so many ways a calculatedly favorable revision of St. John Rivers—hence a corrective to the figure of Rochester—is not introduced to the plot until it is well under way. Early on, as we have seen, it is Alice Humphreys who is the dominant influence on Ellen, a situation that is obviously operating under the influence not of Brontë or Byron but Dickens, as filtered through the tractarian literature of evangelism. That Alice Humphreys has an absent brother is alluded to, but it is not until half-way into the novel that Mr. John appears, allowing time for Warner to have read and been inspired to "correct" *Jane Eyre.*

With its episodic structure, Warner's novel has no predictable ending worked into the set of circumstances and characters at the beginning, and there is no reason why, having belatedly read a novel with whose heroine she closely identified, she could not have brought her own heroine to a promised union that in her mind rectified what she (along with Elizabeth Rigby) would have regarded as the wrong direction taken by *Jane Eyre.* Again, as Nina Baym maintains, most of the female writers of the period were concerned with the plight not of single girls but of married women, troubled wives who had made wrong choices or who were forced by circumstances into wretched situations, from which those with sufficiently strong characters were able to extricate themselves. Circumstances might be strained, characters exaggerated, scenes overdone, but these women were writing "realistic" not romantic novels.

Thus, if we go back to Cowie's amusing redaction of works produced by the "Domestic Sentimentalists" we find that only four novels fit the elements of his parody: *The Wide, Wide World,* Maria Cummins's *The Lamplighter* (1854), and Augusta Jane Evans Wilson's *Beulah* (1859) and *St. Elmo* (1867). This last novel Cowie regards as a virtual "synthesis of all the sure-fire tricks of the lady novelists" to date, and Baym sees it as a threshold to "the transformation of woman's fiction into girl's fiction" (Cowie, 432; Baym, 296). Significantly, it is only Warner's novel that promises the heroine marriage with an older, authoritarian male; the others deal with handsome prospects of a suitable age for suitors, whatever their Byronic proclivities. And it is that singular dimension, typical of Charlotte Brontë's romances, that will hold steady through the other novels we shall be discussing.

Certainly Warner had her own reasons for creating John Humphreys, the most important of a wide range of admirable older men in her novel, all of whom have qualities contradistinct from those of her father. Henry Warner may have been a conventionally pious man, but his easy way with money, even after losing his fortune, indicates a weak and impulsive character. Notably, Ellen's father, Captain Montgomery, is like Warner engaged in a lawsuit connected with his own financial problems, and his portrait is to say the least a harsh caricature of a callous, conceited, and socially ambitious man.

By contrast, we have in Mr. Marshman a Dickensian mix of generosity and kindliness, and Mr. Humphreys is likewise a positive presence, as is Brahm Van Brunt on a lower social level. These are all obvious father figures, dispensing gifts, affection, and good advice at every turn, and although John Humphreys likewise assumes a parental position, being a stern authoritarian but a loving presence as well, he is well short of middle age. Once again, he is an uncanny replication of William Crimsworth, as well as a more human version of St. John Rivers.

That *The Wide, Wide World* is yet another retelling of the Cinderella story seems too obvious for discussion, that being the common fable underlying virtually all fictions about orphan girls who eventually are redeemed to a well-placed position in polite society. But as we have earlier seen, when the redemptive prince has a fatherly profile, then it is the darker version of the Cinderella myth that needs to be considered. Still, as with Brontë's use of older, mature lovers, we are talking here about the possibility of substitutes for inadequate or missing fathers not projective, fantasized facsimiles of either Patrick Brontë or Henry Warner. Incest is not the theme, but rather a deep-seated need to express an infantine dependency, to remain forever a submissive if supportive and caring child, for reasons perhaps beyond conjecture.

But when we consider the influence of *Jane Eyre* on books yet to be discussed, even when filtered through the pious alternative provided by *The Wide, Wide World,* we will find much more problematic uses of older lovers, in which suggestions of incestuous feelings become much stronger. Most of the books in question continue to rely on the Cinderella story, even when parents are still very much alive, for a child need not be without parents to feel like an orphan nor lack a father to search for one elsewhere.

That older men can be attractive as romantic lovers was a lesson made clear by the popularity of both *Jane Eyre* and *The Wide, Wide World,* a lesson not ignored by younger writers. God knows that Emily Dickinson had her notional and occasionally real-life Rochesters, expressing passions in her poems that would have given Elizabeth Rigby a conniption had she been alive and able to decode the cipher. And in at least one instance, as we shall soon see, a father-lover as in that dark version of the Cinderella story was not compensation for an inadequate parent but papa himself.

IV

Augusta Jane Evans's *St. Elmo*—as Cowie, Baym, and Avery concur—is a quintessential instance of an American novel that is perversely dependent on the plot of *Jane Eyre*. The story is about Edna Earl, a pious orphan who spurns the advances of her dissolute stepbrother (for whom the novel is named), becomes a successful author of pious novels, and eventually inspires St. Elmo's conversion to Christianity, thereby enabling her to marry the man she has always loved. It differs from Brontë's romance in two strategic ways: first, it is an intensely sentimental novel; and second, it is one in which the heroine finally is in love with and marries a man of her own age. Unlike Warner's book, it is the orphan who exerts influence over her wayward lover, clearly in imitation of *Jane Eyre*, but with the kind of changes that would have been approved by Brontë's Victorian critics, the reform having taken place under the aegis of Christianity.

In 1868, the year after *St. Elmo* appeared and almost twenty years after *The Wide, Wide World*, two books were published that were obviously aimed at a young, female readership, both derived in part from Warner's story about the sufferings of a poor orphan child but quite different from Augusta Evans's Christian parable. Neither of the stories had an orphan heroine, and in most respects the two were quite different, yet each sold so well as to warrant a number of sequels. The first of these was Louisa May Alcott's *Little Women;* the other was Martha Finley's *Elsie Dinsmore*. It was the publication of these two novels that, according to Nina Baym, signaled the epochal shift in popular fiction from an adult to a juvenile audience.

The March family saga would be continued through several more volumes; the sorrows of Elsie would warrant a series of twenty, the popularity of which is a puzzle to modern readers: "A doctorate in psychology," note Kunitz and Haycraft in *American Authors, 1600–1900* (1938), "might be earned by a thesis on the Elsie books. It is difficult to understand how even Victorian children could be persuaded to swallow this compound of sentimentality and masochism, and clamor for more. . . . Obedience, piety, and smugness are the key notes . . . and Elsie, eternally 'bursting into tears,' would seem to a present-day child what she is, a nauseous little prig." There is no need here to discuss Finley's book at length, as it is tangential to *Jane Eyre* at best, but the description by Kunitz and Haycraft suggests its debt to Warner's novel, and it thereby deserves some consideration, if only to point up the different emphases in Alcott's book as well as to suggest the unintentional mischief that a book like Warner's could do.

Elsie Dinsmore, like so many heroines of sentimental novels, lost her mother when she was still an infant, and she is the only child of a father who has for many years been living abroad. She has grown up a virtual foster child in a strangely constituted family, for Mr. Dinsmore, her grandfather, remarried soon after the death of his first wife, and the second Mrs. Dinsmore not only dislikes his son by the first marriage—Elsie's father—but plays wicked stepgrandmother to little Elsie. Several of the elder Mr. Dinsmore's children are near the girl's own age, even though they are Elsie's aunts and uncles, and take on roles reminiscent of the Reed family in *Jane Eyre*. Which is to say that Finley like Brontë and Warner is indebted to the Cinderella archetype.

"Uncle" Arthur is a ten-year-old bully and a sneak, constantly tormenting Elsie, who like Ellen is eight. The youngest child, little Enna, is a spoiled brat, forever getting her own way, even when it means a violation of Elsie's rightful wishes. The pious, sweet little girl strives through all these persecutions to control her temper, efforts in which, like Ellen Montgomery, she is not always successful, and like Ellen's her lovely eyes are ready conduits of salt water. The "mischievous" Arthur is her chief tormentor, but little Enna contributes as much if not more to Elsie's miserable existence, always being backed in her selfishness by Mrs. Dinsmore.

Into this complicated quasi-sibling situation comes the younger Mr. Dinsmore, whose announced arrival has been looked forward to with tearful eagerness by little Elsie, but her father is an insensitive martinet who demands absolute obedience by his daughter to his every order: "You *must* remember my commands; and if your memory is . . . poor I shall find means to strengthen it" (Finley, 101). Horace Dinsmore is the chief sadist alluded to by Kunitz and Haycraft, and it is the adoring Elsie who fills the masochist's ever-tight shoes, for in this version of the Cinderella myth the slippers put on the heroine's feet are a size too small, though deemed by Horace Dinsmore a perfect fit. Finley explains that Dinsmore has never experienced the responsibilities of fatherhood, and he tends in all matters to overreact, unnecessarily punishing his daughter for what are minor often mistaken offenses, then later smothering her with affection and gifts.

As this two-faced behavior suggests, Horace Dinsmore may somewhat resemble Warner's Mr. John, but he contains a character flaw apparently derived from Ellen Montgomery's uncle Lindsay. He is selfishly possessive of little Elsie, insisting that she obey his orders without question: "All you have to do," he tells Elsie, "is to obey, and you need never ask me why, when I give you an order" (94). Like Mr. Lindsay, also, Mr. Dinsmore is an imperfect Christian, paying "outward respect to the forms of religion," and though strict in his notions of morality, "cared nothing for the vital power of godliness" (61).

Therefore Mr. Dinsmore's commands like Mr. Lindsay's occasionally conflict with his daughter's piety, for unlike Ellen Montgomery, little Elsie has long since accepted Jesus as her savior, a love she openly places above that of her father, even while protesting that she loves her papa very much: "You know He loves me even better than you do," Elsie explains, "'and I must love Him best of all; but there is no one else that I love half so much as I love you, my own dear, dear, precious father" (280). Where Ellen's acceptance of Christ was blocked by love for her mother, Elsie's love of her father is less than her love of the Savior, and Horace Dinsmore's haughty pride is offended by this preference, adding more fuel to his fiery southern temper: "Can it be *possible* that you love any one else better than you love me?" (281).

Never having known her mother, Elsie has become a pious Christian because of the influence of her black mammy, Aunt Chloe, and through her constant reading in her Bible, but as with so many children in the sentimental bildungsroman, her favorite work of fiction is *Pilgrim's Progress*. Elsie's greatest grief (of many) is that her father has not taken Jesus as his savior, but her attempts to convert him are unsuccessful, for Horace "looked upon Christians as hypocrites and deceivers" (61).It is unfair to regard Elsie as a "nauseous little prig," but her piety does get on Horace's nerves, for he regards it as "notional" and not worth heeding, whereas for the author Elsie's stubborn love of Christ is the main point of the book.

Martha Farquarson Finley was Ohio born (1828), and as an adult lived and worked in Philadelphia and New York City, where she taught school and wrote Sunday school literature for the Presbyterian church until her writing became such a profitable occupation that she quit teaching entirely. Her output soon became voluminous: in 1868, the first of the *Elsie* series appeared, along with four more books, *Grandma Foster's Sunbeam, The Little Helper, Loitering Linus,* and *Milly; or the Little Girl who Tried to Help Others and to do them Good,* the sort of thing that inspired fierce laughter in Mark Twain.

Given her background, Finley's pious emphasis in the story of Elsie is understandable. But it is something of a mystery why, given her northern background, Finley chose to set the action in Roseland, a southern plantation, during the antebellum period. Though the chronology is vague, Chloe and the other house servants are obviously slaves, subject to flogging by an overseer when accused even by children of theft. Abolition as an issue was hardly in the forefront of the public's attention in 1868, but the regional basis of the antislavery controversy long endured, and for Finley (as for Mark Twain) it obviously survived the northern victory. The Dinsmores are a spoiled, fractious lot, clearly derived from the caricatures of southern aristocrats found in *Uncle Tom's Cabin*, from whose little Eva the angelic Elsie seems at least in part derived, much as Aunt Chloe is Tom's pious counterpart.

That is, the Dinsmore family is the dubious fruit of the slavery system, accustomed to having their every whim obeyed, but regional balance is achieved by the equally dictatorial Miss Day, the governess who acts as the Dinsmore children's school mistress, and who, recognizing that she can have a free (and hard) hand with little Elsie, takes pleasure in making the girl's life miserable. For Miss Day is pointedly from "the North," and though Findley's broad regional reach may also have been borrowed from Stowe's great book, it is used for different ends.

Southern decadence and northern rigidity are focussed not on a great geopolitical controversy but on the unhappy little girl. Also from the north is Rose Allison, an intensely religious young friend of the family who has come south for her health, and who at the start of the novel establishes a pious bond with little Elsie, whose angelic character she appreciates. But Rose after a time returns home, and though the two are supposed to carry on a correspondence, this idea is abandoned, apparently by the author, soon after she leaves.

Rose is comparable to Alice Humphreys, though she does not die in the course of the novel, but rather is simply forgotten, as is Miss Day, who heads back to the north on vacation and seems never to have returned. Where the governess is a stereotypical mean old maid, Rose is the pious virgin, an admirable model for Elsie, but after she leaves there is no one of her own sex to comfort or defend the child, save for Aunt Chloe, whose humble station prevents her from speaking out. Aunt Adelaide, who appears to be about Horace's age, is sympathetic to the plight of her little niece, and accuses her brother of "taking pleasure in thwarting" his child, but Adelaide is not an active Christian and her objections are half-hearted (107). Moreover, any attempts by his sister to interfere with Horace's notion of morality, which includes matters of diet (no nice hot rolls and butter for his daughter), are bound to inflame his authoritarian temper, making matters even worse for Elsie.

In one often-cited episode, Elsie's father, angered over her refusal to play the piano on the sabbath and sing for the amusement of his guests, orders his daughter to remain seated on the piano bench until she is willing to obey him; after many hours, Elsie faints dead away, injuring herself in the fall. "But at length the soft eyes unclosed, and gazing with a troubled look into his face, bent so anxiously over her, she asked, 'Dear papa, are you angry with me?'" (246). If suffering as Jane Tompkins suggests is the empowering feature of sentimental fiction, then *Elsie Dinsmore* together with its many sequels must be accounted a voltaic pile, discharging the highest redemptive power of all the books under consideration here.

As literature, however, Finley's pious effort has nothing to redeem it, and is deservedly neglected, even by Jane Tompkins. Yet it is worth some attention here, if only for the mystery of its popularity, and because the father figure is a real father, whose motives, though obviously wrong-headed, are the expression of a parent who claims to be acting from both duty and love. But the question to be asked is what kind of love are we talking about, for much is made of Elsie's resemblance to her dead mother, whose image she carries in a locket hung round her neck: "She was very beautiful, with a sweet, gentle, winning countenance, the same soft hazel eyes and golden brown curls that the little Elsie possessed; the same regular features, pure complexion, and sweet smile" (21).

At a critical juncture in the plot, as Horace has begun to realize the extent of his daughter's love for him, which inspires affection in his own heart, he accidentally opens the locket and is confronted by the similarity between his dead wife and his living daughter: "Yes, she is very like—the same features, the same expression, complexion, hair and all—[she] will be the very counterpart of her—if she lives" (207). This forboding note hints that Elsie like her mother is doomed to an early death, that with her thoughts constantly on Christ in heaven she is destined to leave her father for the one she loves the most.

"Ah me!" Horace exclaims to his daughter, "You seem almost too good and pure for earth. But oh, God forbid that you should be taken from me to that place where I can see that your heart is even now. How desolate I should be!" (288). This is the Little Eva theme, associated also with the early deaths of Little Nell and Helen Burns, Angels of the House whose true dwelling is in heaven. Unlike these sentimental sacrifices Elsie will be spared so she may suffer through all those sequels, the victim of her father's perverse, possessive love, as an object "to keep, to love, and to look at," and, when necessary, to punish (278).

We can add yet another motive here for Mr. Dinsmore's behavior, for here is his adored wife in miniature, a mini-Elsie as it were, much as it is a miniature of her mother that his daughter wears around her neck. Horace's severe handling of the live little replica of his dead Elsie can be seen as a subconscious blocking of what, in a more sophisticated fiction, might be interpreted as incestuous feelings. Such a reading would necessarily evoke the dark version of the Cinderella story, in which parental love becomes lust. Certainly in treating his daughter as an object to be possessed, Horace Dinsmore acts the part of a most unnatural father, and Elsie's adoration is always expressed in intensely physical terms: placing herself on his knees to be hugged and kissed seems the *sine qua non* of her existence.

Horace's strange notions of parenting may be attributed to his own father, who is hardly an exemplary model, being a temperamental and arbitrary authoritarian, whose belief in the efficacy of corporal punishment is frequently expressed: "If you do her *justice,* you will whip her well" (221). In attempting to exert his own parental authority, Dinsmore the son does so in a manner that borders on sadism, punishing his daughter severely for very minor infractions of the rules with which he constantly surrounds her. If a heroine's enclosure and fear of bodily harm define the gothic novel, then *Elsie Dinsmore* in all respects meets the requirements.

Despite all the talk about whipping, Elsie's punishment is more often than not expulsion from the presence of her father, usually being sent to bed with nothing for supper but bread and water, that harsh sacrament shared by so many long-suffering children in Victorian fiction. Expulsion may not cause physical suffering but it is painful for Elsie nonetheless, as it means being exiled from the man from whom she wishes only love: "How to gain her father's love was the constant subject of her thoughts, and she tried in many ways to win his affection," but Elsie's efforts are to no avail, much to her continuous sorrow, expressed through tears (78).

Chloe is a constant presence upstairs, and comforts the child to the best of her ability, encouraging her to put on a happy face: "Be merry, like Miss Enna, and run and jump on Massa Horace's knee, and den I tink he will like you better" (79). Ironically, this advice echoes Aunt Reed's command that Jane Eyre "acquire a more sociable and childlike disposition, a more attractive and sprightly manner" (13). But Elsie is too frightened of her father to make such an attempt, a complex connection suggesting that Finley's heroine may have been in part inspired by Gaskell's life of Charlotte Brontë, who was also painfully shy and was notoriously exploited by her father. Elsie finds solace in reading her Bible, whose authority commands her to obey her parent's commands, but Scripture also causes her great suffering because it suggests that in doing so she is failing to obey the word of God.

Like Ellen Montgomery and Jane Eyre, little Elsie does have a temper, despite her abiding love of Christ, which when she is unfairly treated can result in a confrontation, save of course with her father, whose authority in her mind is absolute, being sanctioned by God. Thus one day, when bullied and hectored by Miss Day, who is feeling out of sorts and as usual takes it out on the helpless little girl, doing everything she can to put her off balance in her recitations, Elsie takes a stand.

Through sobs she rightfully accuses the governess of treating her unfairly: "I did know my lesson, every word of it, if you had asked the questions as usual, or had given me time to answer" (188). What follows is typical of much that takes place in the book, and like comparable passages in *The Professor* and *The Wide, Wide World* it contains parallels with the sado-masochistic literature that had an underground life during the Victorian period:

> "I say that you did *not* know it; that it was a complete failure," replied Miss Day, angrily; "and you shall just sit down and learn it, every word, over."
>
> "I *do* know it, if you will hear me right," said Elsie, indignantly, "and it is very unjust in you to mark it a failure."
>
> "Impudence!" exclaimed Miss Day, furiously; "how *dare* you contradict me? I shall take you to your father."
>
> And seizing her by the arm, she dragged her across the room, and opening the door, pushed her into the passage.
>
> "Oh! don't, Miss Day," pleaded the little girl, turning toward her, pale and tearful, "don't tell papa."
>
> "I will! so just walk along with you," was the angry rejoinder, as she pushed her before her to Mr. Dinsmore's door. It stood open, and he sat at his desk, writing.
>
> "What is the matter?" he asked, looking up as they appeared before the door.
>
> "Elsie has been very impertinent, sir," said Miss Day; "she not only accused me of injustice, but contradicted me flatly."
>
> "Is it *possible!*" said he, frowning angrily. "Come here to me, Elsie, and tell me, is it true that you contradicted your teacher?"
>
> "Yes, papa," sobbed the child.
>
> "Very well, then, I shall certainly punish you, for I will never allow anything of that kind."

As he spoke he picked up a small ruler that lay before him, at the same time taking Elsie's hand as though he meant to use it on her.

"O papa!" she cried, in a tone of agonized entreaty.

But he laid it down again, saying, "No, I shall punish you by depriving you of your play this afternoon, and giving you only bread and water for your dinner. Sit down there," he added, pointing to a stool. Then, with a wave of his hand to the governess, "I think she will not be guilty of the like again, Miss Day."

The governess left the room, and Elsie sat down on her stool, crying and sobbing violently, while her father went on with his writing.

"Elsie," he said presently, "cease that noise; I have had quite enough of it."

She struggled to suppress her sobs, but it was almost impossible, and she felt it a great relief when a moment later the dinner-bell rang, and her father left the room. (189–90)

As in *The Wide, Wide World,* so obviously an influence, the shedding of tears, the natural expression of grief and psychological suffering, are disapproved of by figures of authority in *Elsie Dinsmore:* "You cry quite too easily," Horace tells his daughter: "It is entirely too babyish for a girl of your age; you must quit it" (94). But there seems to be no real purpose in all this misery, no directing of Elsie toward maturity, and when she does on occasion speak out in her defense, it usually results in further misunderstanding followed by more punishment. By contrast, the story of Ellen Montgomery seems a blithe pastoral set in a world of well-intentioned rural folks, given meaning and purpose by the heroine's slow progress toward salvation.

Again, as in the incident above, Mr. Dinsmore never actually resorts to corporal punishment, despite the litany repeated by his own father, that a "good flogging" is the necessary corrective for impudent behavior. By such means, active sadism maintains a constant presence, and always remains a threat: at one juncture, Horace takes Elsie to her room to punish her "severely," and when at the last minute he is informed that she is innocent of the offense of which she has been accused, he is discovered standing over his daughter with "a small riding whip in his hand," obviously about to take his father's advice that Elsie be given "the complete whipping" she seems to deserve (203, 219).

Actually, this is a major turning point in the novel, for having realized that he was about to whip his daughter for an offense masterminded by mean little Arthur (who gets the flogging he hoped Elsie would receive), Horace is consumed by guilt and begs her forgiveness. And when, later on, his command that Elsie remain seated at the piano nearly results in her death, the incident inspires "a depth of tenderness in his love which it had not known before, for he could not forget how nearly he had lost her" (253). From that point on father and daughter become much closer, and during the summer and the governess's prolonged absence they spend delightful days together, but the love they come to share always trembles as it were under the ever-present threat of "punishment," which echoes like a refrain throughout the book.

That is, Martha Finley for whatever purpose provided a story the plot line of which is simply a sequence of repeated episodes in which little Elsie is unfairly punished, only to be forgiven by her father once the truth is discovered, trials that are chiefly designed to emphasize her Christian forebearance. The burden is pious, for the sufferings of Elsie as in all sentimental fiction mirror the sufferings of Christ, but there remains that erotic frame suggested by the heroine's resemblance to her dead mother. Notably, during the Christmas celebration toward the end of the book—a nod both to Dickens and Warner—father and daughter having at last become very affectionate exchange miniature portraits of themselves, thereby bringing the ring full round.

In Swinburne's slyly pornographic novel, *Lesbia Brandon,* the heroine's younger brother is the victim of a sadistic tutor, who, balked in his love for Lesbia, whom the unfortunate child closely resembles, works his sexual frustration out by repeatedly flogging the hapless, howling boy. Elsie is spared the frequently threatened whipping, but the pain she is made to feel is an equivalent agony, inflicted by a proudful, possessive parent whose attitude toward his daughter is perversely conflicted. *Elsie Dinsmore* is not a sophisticated fiction; it is however an extended display of the kinds of child abuse that literature bent to the excuse of piety can produce. An alternative to Mr. Dinsmore is provided by the wealthy and kindly Mr. Travilla, who serves as a contrast to Elsie's father throughout the latter part of the book, and in one of the many sequels the heroine will follow Jane Eyre into the arms of her older man, becoming Mrs. Travilla.

Though she will eventually escape through marriage, the heroine's sufferings as a child lead to no improvement in her character: a perfect Christian at the start of her ordeal, she has nowhere to go, and though her steadfast and forgiving love does eventually draw out her father's affection, it is an imperfect conversion, and he is not at story's end brought to taking Christ as his savior. Though Elsie's painful ordeal may have drawn tears of sympathy from young readers, it hardly would have inspired emulation. The book well deserves the banishment that its miserable little heroine so often experiences, and should not only be sent to a garret room but kept forever locked away.

Little Women, by contrast, is an acknowledged masterpiece, perhaps the only example of domestic fiction to qualify for that distinction. Alcott, following the tradition of Brontë and Warner, uses *Pilgrim's Progress* as a leitmotif throughout the first volume of her novel, which brings the March girls to the threshold of maturity. But Alcott's moves in the opposite direction from Finley's book, mitigating the element of suffering with an abundance of maternal not paternal love. Like Jane Eyre and Ellen Montgomery, moreover, Jo March is transformed by her suffering to a mature young woman.

Rather than being surrounded by a Cinderella-like atmosphere of foster parents, Jo March is immersed in a caring domestic milieu, virtually to the exclusion of other environments. Her father is hardly a bullying tyrant, but is either away from home or up in his study for much of the time, where when consulted he performs a function not much different from that of the elder not the younger Mr. Humphreys, putting into practice the benign pedagogical theories of Bronson Alcott. As with the otherwise unlike *Elsie Dinsmore,* it is difficult to see any obvious similarities with *Jane Eyre,* but we know that Alcott prized Brontë's romance, and if her best-known book is held to a certain slant of light, the defining pattern emerges.

Nina Baym, noting the coincidental date of publication, observes that *Elsie Dinsmore* and *Little Women,* appearing right after *St. Elmo,* signalling "the decline of woman's fiction as we have studied it, because they represent the transformation of woman's fiction into girl's fiction" (296). Yet Baym is quick to admit that Alcott's "is the most technically accomplished work to rise from the genre of woman's fiction," despite its being classed "a children's book" (297). In fact, *Little Women* as a literary phenomenon marks a strategic reversal, for where a number of the novels Baym defines as woman's fiction, including *The Wide, Wide World* and *St. Elmo,* made their way into the hands of girls, so *Little Women* as we know was read by adults, who frequently found themselves like Ellen Montgomery and Jo March bursting into tears.

6

Whispers from the Dark:
Louisa May Alcott and the
Brontëan Connection

Night and silence! Who is here?
—Shakespeare

I

IN 1852, THE YEAR HER FIRST STORY, "THE RIVAL PAINTERS," WAS published, Alcott recorded in her diary her fifteen favorite books, and *Jane Eyre* is in that number, one of a very few works of fiction included on the list, along with *Uncle Tom's Cabin*, that American classic of sentimentality turned to good use just then out in book form (*Journals*, 67–68). Then, in 1857, with eight published stories behind her, Alcott read Gaskell's biography of Charlotte Brontë, whose life she found "interesting" but also "sad," the author having been "so full of talent, and after working long, just as success, love, and happiness come, she dies" (85). Twenty-four years old, leading an independent life in Boston, teaching school, attending the theater and lectures, and beginning to earn enough from writing pseudonymous, sensational stories to support herself and help out at home, Louisa wondered "if I shall ever be famous enough for people to care to read my story and struggles. I can't be a C.B., but I may do a little something yet."

Along with this entry there is the following remark about her sister, Elizabeth, who "was feeble, but seemed to cheer up for a time. The long, cold, lonely winter has been too hard for the frail creature, and we are all anxious about her. I fear she may slip away, for she never seemed to care much for this world beyond home." In less than a year Louisa's fears were realized, and Elizabeth (also called "Lizzie," "Betty," or "Beth") would become immortalized in *Little Women* as a saintly child, "Our Angel in the

House," who like Alcott's sister would "slip away," dying from the prolonged effects of scarlet fever. Beth in effect was a replicated Helen Burns, the saintly child in *Jane Eyre* who was inspired by Charlotte's sister, Maria.

As Louisa noted, she could not be a Charlotte Brontë, at least not in the novels that made her famous. Her penchant for gothic romance, expressed through the stories she wrote for sensational periodicals, would be one of literary America's best-kept literary secrets for a century. Meanwhile, Louisa May Alcott would become known and loved as the author of sentimental, domestic fiction for young readers, much of it derived (with considerable revision) from the life she had known in the turbulent and troubled household of the idealistic but impecunious Bronson Alcott.

"The Pathetic Family" she called it in 1857 (perhaps a play on Ruskin's "pathetic fallacy"), even then thinking that the "trials and triumphs" of the Alcott ménage "would make a capital book," should she "live to do it" (*Journals*, 85). Starting with *Little Women*, and extending through a number of sequels, beginning with *Good Wives*, Louisa Alcott's was a carefully scripted world in which self-sacrifice and self-control would be virtues, hard work redemptive, and grief a gateway to maturity. Thus the death of little Beth would have a transformational effect on Jo March, like that of Alice Humphreys on Ellen Montgomery, despite strategic differences between the two heroines.

The Wide, Wide World is not included in Alcott's list of fifteen "best" books, nor is it mentioned in her diary, but at one point in *Little Women* Jo March is found weeping over Warner's novel. A sentimental counterpart to *Jane Eyre*, it provided an alternative model for Alcott's far greater work, which in its turn was a calculated response to Warner's pious parable. *Little Women* is much more than that, being a radical departure from the conventional domestic novel and an innovative beginning, the source of so much fiction written thereafter for young female readers.

But it is also a reaction to Warner's novel, much as *The Wide, Wide World* was a counterpart to *Jane Eyre*, a genre dialectic that enrolls Jo March in that bright band of sisters (the phrase is Alcott's) stretching from the Yorkshire moors to the heart of the heart of Concord, Massachusetts. If the connections between Alcott's domestic novel and Brontë's gothic romance are tenuous, *Little Women* certainly bears a number of correspondences with Gaskell's account of the Brontë family, most of them coincidental but all acting to cement that empathic connection that Fred Pattee established between the Haworth domicile and the households of New England.

II

In 1862, the young, Virginia-born author Rebecca Harding, following the publication of her first novel, *Margaret Howth,* was invited to Boston by James T. Field, then both a publisher and the editor of the *Atlantic,* in which her sensational short story, "Life in the Iron Mines," had earlier appeared. The lion of the season, Harding was taken to Concord on a ritual visit to the group of savants and celebrities associated with the fast-fading flowering of New England. Harding was most impressed by Hawthorne, who shared with the young author his mischievous skepticism regarding the center of the Concord cosmos, Ralph Waldo Emerson, and the dreamy satellites who gathered around him. She was least impressed by Emerson's favorite satellite, Bronson Alcott, who seemed to her a hot-air balloon rather than a bona fide extraterrestrial phenomenon.

Harding observed that Bronson's oracular pronouncements on the probable course of the Civil War (an easy Union victory) were fueled by ignorance of the facts, which she knew only too well, having just come from Wheeling, then an armed Union camp. "Chanting paens to the war," Bronson was destined to descend from the high-flown skies of his rhetoric to the hard ground of war's reality, which Harding already knew was a brutalizing, corrupting, and demoralizing experience (*Reader,* 445). She was on the other hand to remember favorably Alcott's daughter, Louisa May, whom she met at a subsequent reception in Boston. By that date, Louisa Alcott had given up teaching, having found writing sensational short fiction for popular magazines much more lucrative, and was already at work on two novels, eventually published as *Moods* (1864) and *Work* (1873).

Alcott's book of fairy stories, *Flower Fables,* had appeared in 1854, and two of her short stories had been accepted by the *Atlantic Monthly,* but Bronson's daughter was still an unknown quantity in May, 1862. Still, she made a sufficient impression on Harding so that, though recalling their meeting more than forty years later, the writer had a very clear mental picture of the "tall, thin young woman standing alone in a corner," "plainly dressed" but wearing "that watchful, defiant air with which the woman

whose youth is slipping away is apt to face the world which has offered no place to her."

> Before I met her I had known many women and girls who were fight-
> ing with poverty and loneliness, wondering why God had sent them
> into a life where apparently there was no place for them, but never one
> so big and generous in soul as this one in her poor scant best gown,
> the "claret-colored merino," which she tells of with such triumph in
> her diary [exerpts from which were published after her death, in 1889].
> Amid her grim surroundings, she had the gracious instincts of a
> queen. . . . Years afterward she came to the city where I was living and
> I hurried to meet her. The lean, eager, defiant girl was gone, and in-
> stead, there came to greet me a large, portly, middle-aged woman,
> richly dressed. Everything about her, from her shrewd, calm eyes to
> the rustle of her satin told of assured success. (*Reader,* 447–48)

Rebecca Harding Davis (she had married in 1863) hastened to assure the readers of her aptly titled memoir, *Bits of Gossip* (1904),
that whatever changes success may have brought to Louisa Alcott, "fame and success counted for nothing with her except for
the material aid which they enabled her to give to a few men and
women whom she loved." Her books "were true and fine, but she
never imagined a life as noble as her own."

Yet we can sense in Davis's recollection a clear preference for
that tall, thin, youngish woman who boldly announced that she had
made a forty-mile trip (on foot) from Boston to Concord and back
in order to put on "the only decent gown I have," her tribute to the
honored guest whose new novel she had read and admired. And in
a certain sense "the lean, eager, defiant girl" Miss Harding met in
Boston in 1862 was never really gone, having been preserved for
all time as Jo March in the novel that assured the success of the
"large, portly, middle-aged woman" who still called herself Louisa
Alcott. Moreover, we may doubt that Davis's sketch of that eager
and defiant "girl" of thirty would ever have been written had Alcott
not gained the popularity which brought her fame and wealth. And
that grim alternative was in 1862 more likely than Davis perhaps
realized in 1904, for Bronson Alcott's daughter was soon enough to
experience the horrors of the war to which her father had so
blithely sung a paen, and as a result came close to dying.

Alcott recorded in her journal the meeting with Rebecca Harding, "a handsome, fresh quiet woman, who says she never had any
troubles, though she writes about woes," while, as Lousia told her,
"I had lots of troubles, so I write jolly tales" (*Journals,* 109). Within
six months, she found herself in troubles far more serious than

she had hitherto known: at the start of the Civil War, Louisa had seen the company of Union soldiers from Concord off to Washington, a "sad day" if a dramatic one, "as the brave boys went away perhaps never to come back again" (*Journals*, 105). Having in the past "longed to see a war," she now had her wish, but regretted that as a woman she could not join those boys in battle. Alcott had to content herself with "working for those who can fight," sewing and knitting for "our boys," an experience that suggested "a few energetic women could carry on the war better than the men did it so far." But then, still yearning "for battle like a warhorse when he smells powder," Alcott decided to head for Washington and volunteer her services as a nurse (*Journals*, 110). Help was needed, as she noted, "and I love nursing, and *must* let out my pent-up energy in some new way."

In Georgetown, Alcott discovered that tending wounded and dying soldiers was quite different from her earlier experiences at nursing, which she "loved," having been limited to caring for family members, like Betty and her mother, Abba. Worse, Louisa contracted typhoid fever and was brought home for a lengthy convalescence, but the effects of the disease and the "cure," a mercury compound known as calomel commonly prescribed as a purgative, would be lifelong. *Hospital Sketches*, an account of her experiences, was published in 1863 after being serialized in the *Boston Commonwealth*, and received considerable attention.

That was the "good" that came from the experience, but it was a mixed blessing, for suddenly Alcott found herself in Rebecca Harding's place, being "made a lion of, set up among the great ones, stared at, waited upon, [and] complimented . . . until I was tired of shaking hands & hearing 'Hospital Sketches' uttered in every tone of interest, admiration & respect. . . . I liked it, but think a small dose quite as much as is good for me, for after sitting in a corner, & grubbing a la Cinderella it rather turns one's head to be taken out & treated like a Princess all of a sudden" (*Journals*, 130). Alcott would never get used to this kind of public acclaim, but in 1863 her notoriety was momentary, and she continued her subterranean career of writing lurid pseudonymous stories and novellas for "the weeklies," even while having her "serious" work published under her right name in the *Atlantic*. Then, in 1865 her first novel, *Moods*, appeared.

It was neither sensational melodrama nor what Nina Baym calls "woman's fiction," but something in between, a serious attempt at novel writing in the Brontëan mode, though more in the vein of *Villette* than *Jane Eyre*. Given the book's subject matter, the audience for which it was written was adult and female: it told the story of Sylvia Yule, a teen-age girl who falls in love with an older man, Adam Warwick, a forceful, muscular, hirsute world-wanderer (a Byron with a beard), who writes essays forthright in their criticism of society. At the same time, Sylvia attempts to form an affectionate friendship with Warwick's friend, another older man, a mild-mannered, sensitive poet who occupies the old Manse next door to the Yule home.

The neighbor, Geoffrey Moor, mistakes Sylvia's affection for love, even as his friend, a naturalist-writer like Thoreau, realizes that the young woman's feelings for *him* indicate a much deeper passion, which he is willing to reciprocate until he discovers that Moor is also in love with Sylvia. With that chivalric self-denial typical of sentimental heroes, Warwick departs for distant lands, resuming the restless, Byronic travels in foreign parts he has hitherto pursued, leaving Sylvia to wait for him until she loses hope that he will ever return. Then, yielding to Moor's entreaties she accepts his proposal, in the hope that love will follow.

But on their honeymoon, Warwick suddenly reappears. Having while abroad received a long-delayed letter from Sylvia declaring her love, he reveals his own passion for her, unaware that she has married his friend. At Warwick's urging, Sylvia lets her husband know that her love for the other man will always stand between them, and stung to the depths of his pride, Moor makes plans to leave for Europe. Realizing his mistake, Warwick decides to accompany him, and on shipboard their old friendship is reaffirmed as they leave Sylvia standing on the pier. Torn with conflicting loyalties and passions, Sylvia consults a somewhat older woman she has met through Warwick, Faith Dane—apparently modeled after Margaret Fuller.

Like Mrs. Vawse in *The Wide, Wide World*, Faith lives alone in a cottage near a mountaintop and is also self-reliant and wise through virtue of much personal experience of the world. In response to Sylvia's question, Faith in her characteristically frank and direct manner tells her that she was not sufficiently mature to have accepted either man as her husband. The episode's conclusion recalls the equivalent interview between Ellen and Mrs. Vawse, for Sylvia goes back down the mountain inspired to follow the path of "duty." And duty as defined by Faith, as by Ann Landers, is "to love and live for Geoffrey," because the forever restless Adam Warwick could never be happy as any woman's husband (*Portable Alcott*, 331).

A year goes by, during which the unhappy Sylvia draws very close to her father, but more important, comes to realize that she is not alone in bearing a grievous burden, having "joined that sad sisterhood called disappointed women," who have been emotionally damaged by unfortunate love relationships (337). Alcott compares her to Hester Prynne, who in wearing the scarlet letter became mysteriously aware of how many other sinners lived in Salem. Like Hawthorne's heroine, Alcott's finds maturity through suffering, but where Hester's repentance is a mask only, Sylvia's is a sincere conversion to an acceptance of her lot in life, the lesson Lucy Snowe likewise learns by the end of *Villette*.

Sylvia is sent a book from Moor and Warwick in Switzerland, containing the one's poems and the other's essays, which together contain the qualities of an ideal man: "Warwick's rugged prose gathered grace from Moor's poetry, and Moor's smoothly flowing lines acquired power from Warwick's prose" (342). Sylvia's father dies, leaving the daughter grateful that she had the opportunity to express "her dutiful affection" while he was yet alive. By year's end, "the wayward girl was gone, and in her place a thoughtful woman who could not be satisfied with what had fed her once" (343). Suffering, the constant factor in sentimental fiction, has done its work.

Meanwhile, in his ceaseless travelling about Europe Warwick comes upon a battle in Italy being fought between Garibaldi's revolutionaries and Croatian soldiers, the Italians having taken sanctuary in a convent to which the Croats are laying siege. Manning a cannon by himself, Warwick decimates the Croat army, forcing a withdrawal, and he is hailed as a hero by Garibaldi's men—another link with Byron, who died a martyr to Greek freedom. Having been rejoined by Moor, Warwick and his friend take ship for America, but in a storm the ship sinks, and in assisting his friend to safety, Warwick drowns. It is a death that M. Paul, the older romantic interest in *Villette*, also suffers and which likewise solves Lucy Snowe's dilemma, by removing him from her life forever.

Warwick willingly accepts his fate, for the episode of fighting for Italian freedom, as he has explained, purged him of his lifelong restlessness, and he has gallantly rescued his friend that Moor may resume his life with Sylvia. Moor returns to the Manse and the woman who awaits him there. Sylvia in the meantime has a dream vision of Warwick's apotheotic death, and reconciled to the loss of her lover, she is now prepared to live "a long and happy life, unmarred by the moods that nearly wrecked her youth; for now she had learned to live by principle, not impulse, and this made it both sweet and possible for love and duty to go hand in hand" (358).

So ends the novel as revised in 1882, but the original version of 1865 ends not only with Warwick's heroic death but with Sylvia dying in the arms of her husband, after a long siege with tuberculosis. This is the traditional death of Victorian suffering women, in that it allows leisure for lengthy death-bed pronouncements along the lines of the sermons delivered from her bed by Warner's Alice Humphreys. But Sylvia's death is also an authorial convenience, solving the problem of her divided heart by shutting it down. The 1882 ending is not only the most radical of many revisions Alcott made to her original novel, but one that tells us a great deal about changes in her professional life over the intervening twenty years, as she moved away from sensational to domestic fiction.

Among the many revisions Alcott made to *Moods* was the excision of Otilla, a Cuban beauty with whom Warwick has had an affair, and who seems to have escaped from Alcott's "weekly" fiction into what is supposed to be a serious novel of purpose. The original novel opens with an intense confrontation between Warwick and Otilla, in which he bluntly denounces her for a superficial, scheming woman, but on her promise to reform, he declares himself willing to wait a year for the change to take place. It is this as much as his loyalty to Moor that keeps him from declaring his feelings for Sylvia, who, when she subsequently learns of Otilla's existence, assumes that Warwick still loves the other woman. Indeed, through a misunderstanding Sylvia thinks that during his absence abroad Warwick has married her. It is this that removes the last barrier to her marriage to Moor—though of course she is still in love with the other man.

In part because of its sensational aspects, Alcott's first novel like *Jane Eyre* was instantly popular but was subsequently and unfairly accused of immorality. Unlike Brontë's novel, *Moods* was not able to override the censoriousness of the reading public in Boston, and quickly dropped from sight. This alone gave the author reason enough for subsequently revising out the steamier parts, along with reinforcing the domestic element with a closure that emphasizes Sylvia's "realistic" acceptance of her marriage vows. Moreover, where the original ending certifies the Brontëan tradition in which *Moods* was conceived, the revision may have been a bid for a wider audience, and it certainly was in keeping with the moral tone of *Little Women,* which by 1882 had made her famous.

Alcott's first novel experienced a revival of sorts something more than a century after the revised version appeared, for Sylvia like Jane Eyre and Lucy Snowe has been seen by feminist critics as symbolic of the situation of many women at the time, being trapped as Elizabeth Keyser states in "a rigidly gendered world that allows no scope for her prodigious energy and talent" (*Portable Alcott*, 153). This is the same reading derived by feminists from *Jane Eyre* and *Villette*, but Sylvia is less a prisoner of male-determined social convention than a victim of too much exposure to romantic idealism—the Quixotic theme.

Moreover, as the wise woman on the mountain tells her, Sylvia is too immature to take on the responsibilities of marriage. She needs to grow up, to which in the sentimental tradition (as exemplified by *The Wide, Wide World*) suffering and loss are the necessary adjuncts. Her death in the first version has no such practical function, and is a purely sentimental exercise, being the display of a suffering woman crucified on her crisscrossed loves. In the revised version, by contrast, much is made of the death of her father, which thereby serves as one of the agents of Sylvia's maturation, followed by Warwick's drowning—the final threshold to maturity.

It is certainly a gendered process: Warwick is "cured" of his Manfred-like eternal restlessness by decimating an army with several well-placed cannon balls while Sylvia must undergo a much more gradual process of passive suffering not action. Warwick is hailed a hero by Garibaldi's men; Sylvia's triumph over herself is a lonely victory. The framework is typical of the sentimental novel as defined by Jane Tompkins, in which women are empowered by suffering, not only in terms of maturation but in drawing the reader's sympathy. The passive, sensitive Geoffrey Moor, who has a well-defined "feminine" side, likewise suffers, and it is Warwick who fills the traditional male role, being self-contained and independent, rising above all circumstances, even when sinking to his death in the sea.

It has always been of interest to critics and biographers of Louisa May Alcott that one of the reviewers of *Moods* in 1865 was the very young Henry James, at twenty-one Alcott's junior by a decade. Well aware of who the author was, James wrote a frank but not entirely unfriendly appraisal, and snorted over the accusations of immorality. At the same time he did suggest that the French were better at handling "the old story of the husband, the wife, and the lover," thinking perhaps of Flaubert's *Madame Bovary*, published a few years earlier (Anthony, 176). James likewise took issue with the author's ignorance of the world, for her novel seemed to him largely extrapolated from the familiar formulas of popular fiction, written by and for those women who "appear to delight in the conception of men who shall be insupportable to men" (176). He came down particularly hard on the "lover," Warwick, "who has travelled all over the world, lives on a mysterious patrimony, and spends his time in breaking the hearts and wills of demure little school-girls who answer him with 'Yes, sir' and 'No, sir'" (176, 180).

These passages are quoted by Katharine Anthony, who in 1938 wrote one of the first modern biographies of Alcott, avoiding the sentimental and hagiographic. Yet here she rushed to her author's defense, noting with something of a sneer the youth of the little chap making these worldly remarks, and adding that "when one thinks of Winterbourne, Sir Claude, and Vanderbank, one wonders why Henry James was not more charitable toward Louisa's Warwick." In so doing, Anthony overlooks the main point of James's objection, which was against the sentimental tradition, by 1864 reduced to formulaic constructions: though likewise often supported by a "mysterious patrimony," none of *his* cads serve as the occasion for the shedding by his readers of gratuitous tears.

By James's description, moreover, Adam Warwick sounds a great deal like Brontë's Edward Rochester, but to anyone who has read *Moods* the resemblance is less than slight, even if we include the affair with Otilla. Although Sylvia falls in love with the strong-willed cosmopolite, wise in the ways of the woods as well as the world, she has an independent spirit and lacks the submissive qualities of Brontë's heroines. She is not, in short, a "yes-sir, no-sir" woman. And though James's description emphasizes Warwick's undeniable Byronism, keyed by his restlessness and his sympathy for revolutionary causes, Alcott's allegiance, unlike Brontë's, was perhaps more to Goethe than to Byron, to *The Sorrows of Young Werther* and *The Apprenticeship of Wilhelm Meister* rather than *The Corsair* and *Childe Harold*.

That is, her first novel was very much a product of Concord, Massachusetts, for the daughter of Bronson Alcott took her Transcendentalism seriously. James was certainly more right than he realized in suggesting that the young author was operating under the influence of popular fiction—of which she had been a productive author herself—but she certainly knew the world she was writing about in *Moods*. Thus her journals contain a number of annotations of a later date, and in one of these she noted regarding the reception of her book, that "the relations between Warwick Moor & Sylvia are pronounced impossible, yet a case of the sort exists in Concord & the woman came & asked me how I knew it. I did *not* know or guess, but perhaps felt it without any other guide, & unconsciously put the thing into my book, for I changed the ending about that time. It was meant to show a life affected by *moods*, not a discussion of marriage which I knew little about, except observing that very few were happy ones" (*Journals*, 147).

The specific relationship is not identified, though Thoreau seems to have been overly fond of Lidian, Emerson's wife, which may have suggested to the sharp-eyed adolescent next door an erotic possibility closer to reality than James allowed. The note seems to remove Alcott herself from the triangle, yet despite the differences between her own family life and that of her heroine, the author shared Sylvia's love of nature, her sprightliness and flair for drama, and she was as a young girl attracted to both Thoreau and Emerson, if for quite different reasons.

James felt that the novel in general revealed an ignorance of the matters making up the plot, but his most outspoken objection was to the opening scene, in which Warwick harshly dismisses Otilla for a hypocritical seductress: "He talks to his mistress as no sane man ever talked to a woman. It is not too much to say that he talks like a brute" (Elbert, 1865 edition, 221). There follows a lengthy paragraph quoting Warwick's outspoken denunciation of his lover, whose fault as James observes was merely not proving to be "so excellent a person as he at first supposed her." Likewise, when Warwick returns to find Sylvia married, James finds his behavior reprehensible: "An honest man in Warwick's position would immediately have withdrawn, on seeing that his presence only served seriously to alienate his mistress from her husband. A dishonest man would have remained and made love to his friend's wife. . . . [He] adopts the latter course, and, what is worse, does it like an errant hypocrite" (222).

"Mr. Warwick," concluded James, "is plainly a great favorite with the author. She has for him that affection which writers entertain, not for those figures whom they have well known, but for such as they have much pondered. Miss Alcott has probably mused upon Warwick so long and so lovingly that she has lost all sense of his proportions. . . . There are, thank Heaven, no such men at large in society. We speak thus devoutly, not because Warwick is a vicious person,—on the contrary, he exhibits the sternest integrity; but because, apparently as a natural result of being thoroughly conscientious, he is essentially disagreeable" (220). If we freeze-frame that last sentence, then cut to the familiar photograph of the flint-faced Henry David Thoreau, who was assuredly a person of stern integrity, outspoken in conscientious-

ness, and even to his mentor, Emerson, at times "essentially disagreeable," we will understand that the problem here is one of
communication.

Where Henry James, Jr., was—unlike his father—not on speaking (or any) terms with Thoreau; Louisa May Alcott most certainly
was, and in her portrait of Warwick, impossible as it might seem
to James, she memorialized the sternly outspoken morality of her
dear friend, who had died in 1862. That was the year in which she
began composing both *Moods* and *Work*, otherwise quite different
novels in which a Thoreau-like man serves what would seem to
most the unlikely role of romantic interest—to most but not to
Louisa May Alcott. To anyone who knew Thoreau, that apparently
ridiculous interview with Otilla was quite conceivable, although
pairing the hermit of Walden Pond with a Cuban seductress does
seem a bit of a stretch.

Thoreau had been young Louisa's teacher, and she had a schoolgirl crush on her roughly profiled if not exactly Heathcliffean mentor, accompanying him on his daily hikes through the Concord
woods, a rare privilege as Martha Saxon attests. On Thoreau's
death, she composed a memorial poem, "Thoreau's Flute," in
which the Walden hermit is compared to the pagan nature-god,
Pan, whose pipes continue to produce music after his death. At a
later point Louisa released some girlish gush in letters sent to
Emerson, letters composed in self-conscious imitation of Bettina's adoring correspondence with Goethe. Bettina's book, as
Elaine Showalter tells us, was favorite even required reading in
Concord, and was on Louisa's list of her fifteen best books. (She
may have found the name Otilla there.) Following that model, Alcott addressed her notes to Emerson as "Master," thereby unconsciously imitating Brontë's letters to Heger, which as I have
noted were also in the Bettina mode. But to make Emerson over
to even an approximate Rochester does seem a task beyond anyone's abilities, despite the allusiveness of the name given to his
counterpart in *Moods*—Moor.

Besides, it is the outspoken, nature-loving, politically radical
Warwick with whom Sylvia is passionately in love. A central
episode in the book is an extended, overnight river voyage the
heroine takes with all three of the men in her life—Warwick, Moor,
and her brother, Max (Mark in the original version)—which in effect replicates Thoreau's trip up the Concord and Merrimac, but
with a much larger and heterosexual crew. Sylvia (as her name
suggests) is associated with the world of wild not domesticated
nature, generally figured as a benign, hospitable zone, as opposed

to the sere, gothicized landscape of *Jane Eyre*. Even in the revised version, *Moods* has very few important interior settings, and it is therefore less a domestic than a romantic novel, albeit in the German not the Yorkshire mode.

Again, although Warwick is much travelled, he shares none of Rochester's Byronic world-weariness, his gloomy moods, his ironic turn of phrase. He is perhaps closer to the self-sacrificing Grandison model than to Byron. He does not play word games with Sylvia, for when she asks his frank opinion he gives it, and when she inquires as to his feelings for her, he tells her straight across, a blunt courtship that is a counterpart to his callously frank dismissal of Otilla. And yet as Henry James observes, Warwick is an older man, and is something of a cosmopolite, with a torrid love affair in his past, a combination that presumably triggered James's association with Rochester. Moreover, he has such a strong personality that little Sylvia is soon caught up in his wake— much to her subsquent despair—and to that not very great extent he resembles Rochester and she Jane Eyre.

But Sylvia, for her part, is no timid, pusillanimous orphan turned unhappy governess. Alcott may have felt like a Cinderella after the success of *Hospital Sketches*, but there are precious few Cinderellas in her fiction. Sylvia like so many sentimental heroines lost her mother when she was born—hence the attraction of the motherly Faith Dane—but her father is wealthy and gives her anything she desires, indeed his indulgence is part of her problem. Vivacious, boyish in her athleticism, and with a natural talent for theatrics, except for her wealth Sylvia closely resembles Louisa May Alcott rather than Jane Eyre, but like Brontë's governess she must learn that she can't have everything she desires, because not everything she desires is good for her. Notably, this decision to accept life as it is—including her marriage to Moor— was strengthened by the positive ending that postdates the publication of *Little Women*, with its complex celebration of the marriage bond.

In most other ways, *Moods* is a different novel from the one that made Alcott famous, being a romantic exercise in which domesticity has little place until the closing pages, and this only in the revised version. Nobody is poor, and despite James's sneer concerning Warwick's mysterious patrimony, Sylvia is the only major character in the novel the source of whose income is known. Geoffrey Moor like his friend Warwick does not have to work for a living, and what keeps Faith Dane up on her mountain is not specified. These are all wealthy and privileged folk, the kind of people found in the sensational fiction Alcott was writing in the mid-1860s, who are not only wealthy and privileged but English aristocrats to boot. That is, the characters in *Moods* provide a social frame in which the scheming seductress Otilla is not all that much out of place.

Significantly, in the heavily didactic novel *Work* (1873), which Alcott had begun at the same time as *Moods*—completing six chapters (tentatively called "Success") before abandoning the project for ten years—*Jane Eyre* is dismissed by the autobiographical heroine, Christie Devon, on moral grounds. Admiring Jane, she dislikes Rochester, and doubts that marriage will ever reform his dissolute character—an opinion that suggests Alcott had forgotten the ending of Brontë's novel, which celebrates ten years of wedded bliss between Jane and her beloved Edward. At this point in her episodic career (as housemaid, actress, and now governess), Christie is about to be proposed to by her employer's brother, Philip Fletcher, like Rochester a wealthy older man who has wasted his life by a spendthrift existence, and has reaped the rewards: cynicism and bad health.

The question, which Fletcher puts to Christie, is whether "a man who had only follies to regret might expect a good woman to lend him a hand and make him happy?" (*Work*, 65). Guided by her reaction to *Jane Eyre*, and by the fact that she does not love the wealthy suitor, Christie answers in the negative and refuses his offer, which is (much like Rochester's first proposition to Jane) that she travel with him to Europe with the promise of marriage "by and by." Christie will eventually marry, but it will be to the Thoreau-like and reform-minded nurseryman David Sterling, whose name is a key to his character.

David is killed after enlisting in the Union army, and *Work* ends with Christie forming a "family" consisting of the women she has met during her multifaceted career, another affirmation of the domestic ideal but without the matrimonial element. And "Success" ends after six chapters with Christie alone in her shabby room at Christmas, her misery alleviated by a rose-bush in bloom, a gift from a former prostitute she has befriended. That is, in novels intended for mature as well as juvenile readers, Alcott habitually stressed upbeat, conciliatory, and often Christmastime endings, with heroines who borrow some of Jane Eyre's positive qualities but without having to deal with the kind of sexual passion and gothic melodrama that lend excitement and depth to Brontë's romance.

Again, it is in Alcott's pseudonymously published sensational fiction that elements of the gothicism in *Jane Eyre* appear, even to a madwoman kept locked in an upstairs apartment in "A Whisper in the Dark" (1863). In these stories the heroine's virtue is often threatened by an older man, usually a relative or guardian, a situation in which "domesticity comes dangerously close to incest" with hints that Bronson's domineering personality may have been a subconscious factor (Elbert, 176–78). Whatever the inspiration, whether literary or psychological or both, Alcott casts these sexual predators as profligate villains, a response to *Jane Eyre* similar to that in *Work*.

Thus the evil guardian in "Whisper" as described by the heroine bears a close resemblance to Brontë's Rochester, being "a handsome man, with all the polish of foreign life fresh upon him; yet it was neither comeliness nor graceful ease which most attracted me; for even my inexperienced eye caught glimpses of something stern and somber below these external charms, and my long scrutiny showed me the keenest eye, the hardest mouth, the subtlest smile I ever saw—a face which in repose wore the look that comes to those who have led lives of pleasure and learned their emptiness" (*Portable Alcott*, 25). This "uncle" is old enough to be the heroine's father, yet it is obvious from her description that she is attracted to him by the same stern and secretive manner that draws Jane to Rochester.

In *Moods* as in her subsequent "serious" novels, Alcott is not uneasy about casting her male love interests as older, albeit uniformly virtuous men, whether in the model provided by Bronson, or Thoreau, or Emerson. By such means, the matter of *Jane Eyre* is thoroughly sublimated to Alcott's domestic muse, yet the process does not entirely remove the suggestion of incest or whatever it was that inspired women authors in America to choose fatherly suitors for their young heroines.

One of the most frequently reprinted of Alcott's sensational stories, after having been rescued by Madeline Stern in 1975, is "Behind a Mask; or, A Woman's Power," a tour de force of assumed identity that has been seen as deriving from Alcott's conflicted personality, and which remains a fascinating read. Published in 1866, two years before *Little Women*, it is not only typical of the kinds of stories Jo herself is writing toward the end of that novel—and which she renounces as trash unworthy of her talents—it has a cynical wittiness that is entirely missing from the hyper-serious *Moods*, in which humor takes an arch, mannered quality.

Moreover, as feminist critics have been quick to note, the story empowers a woman not through suffering but through her clever manipulation of the men in her life, for the heroine is a Cleopatra willing to use sex as a lure, rather than a long-suffering Octavia. Perhaps too much has been made of Alcott's alternative "dark" career as a writer of sensational fiction—which was no more a secret than any other aspect of her life—but it is a mistake to read *Little Women* without paying close attention to "Behind a Mask." For more is going on in that deceptively simple parable composed for an audience of young women than immediately meets the eye.

III

Most important for our purposes, "Behind a Mask" most definitely has a Brontëan connection, perhaps coincidental but sufficiently tight to warrant consideration here. For Jean Muir—or "Miss Muir" as she is more often called—is a governess, and at the start of the story seems to find herself in that painful lowly position so carefully defined by both Anne and Charlotte Brontë. That is, her situation is one in which the pay is meagre and humble pie is a regular item of diet, for she must defer always to the whims of her wealthy employers.

As Madeline Stern reminds us in her introduction to *Behind a Mask* (1975), Alcott herself, in one of her many attempts to help put food on the family table, went into service in 1851 as an approximate governess, her charge not being a child but an elderly lady, the spinster sister of the Honorable James Richardson. Louisa's duties were supposed to be chiefly limited to reading to the lady, with some light housekeeping as necessary, but the job did not turn out as described. The housekeeping was heavy, as were the attentions of old Mr. Richardson, being both of a literary and an apparently romantic turn. Whatever his intentions, the relationship involved leaving notes and poems where Louisa would be sure to find them, and when she objected, the housekeeping got even heavier, until she finally quit in disgust.

It is difficult not to read "Behind a Mask" as revenge against the not so Honorable James Richardson, but in terms of genre it is whether intentionally or not a literary deconstruction of the Brontëan trope. In Alcott's novel "a woman's power" does not come from suffering but from a Hester Prynne–like *pose* of suffering, instrumental in the heroine's clever manipulation of an entire household. Jean Muir's role as governess is just that—a role—for in her previous life she has been a professional actress, and proves to be adept at personal transformations.

The Scottish-born Muir is a woman in her early thirties (Alcott's age when she wrote the story), and anticipating that she will soon be too old for ingénue parts, she quits the stage and goes into service as a governess, hoping thereby to bag a wealthy husband. She disguises herself as a much younger woman, with false teeth, added braids of hair, and heavy rouge, and plays the pliant, helpless, long-suffering governess role to the hilt, a "meek, nunlike creature" (*Behind a Mask*, 38). This disguise is revealed to the reader early on, in a Swiftian scene that starts with the *soi-disant* governess in her bedroom taking a snort from a flask, then removing teeth, hair, rouge, resulting in a picture at odds with her initial appearance.

Prior to this shocking disclosure, Jean is interviewed regarding her qualifications by the Coventry family, and fills all conventional expectations of a governess, qualifications clearly derived from the Brontëan type. She informs the lady of the home that she is nineteen years old, and when it is suggested that a somewhat older person had been expected, declares "I wish I was thirty, but, as I am not, I do my best to look and seem old." This of course is the opposite of the truth, yet from the start she inspires sympathy in the family for which she is to work:

> All felt a touch of pity at the sight of the pale-faced girl in her plain black dress, with no ornament but a little silver cross at her throat. Small, thin, and colorless she was, with yellow hair, gray eyes, and sharply cut, irregular but very expressive features. Poverty seemed to have set its bond stamp upon her, and life to have had for her more frost than sunshine. But something in the lines of the mouth betrayed strength, and the clear, low voice had a curious mixture of command and entreaty in its varying tones. Not an attractive woman, yet not an ordinary one; and, as she sat there with her delicate hands lying in her lap, her head bent, and a bitter look on her thin face, she was more interesting than many a blithe and blooming bell. (6)

Meek and mild throughout the interview, as all good governesses in the Brontëan mold should be, as soon as Jean Muir is alone in her room, her "conduct was decidedly peculiar. Her first act was to clench her hands and mutter between her teeth, with passionate force, 'I'll not fail again if there is power in a woman's wit and will!' She stood a moment motionless, with an expression of almost fierce disdain on her face, then shook her clenched hand as if menacing some unseen enemy" (11).

Having expressed the rebellious anger seething beneath her apparently submissive surface, the governess strips off her disguise, and reveals "a haggard, worn, and moody woman of thirty at least." In the privacy of her room, Muir's "mobile features settled into their natural expression, weary, hard, bitter. She had been lovely once, happy, innocent, and tender; but nothing of all this remained to the gloomy appointment which had darkened all her life." The first chapter ends with the governess uncovering her breast to reveal "the scar of a newly healed wound" which she regards "with a terrible glance" (12). It is a gesture recalling the lady Geraldine in Coleridge's *Christabel,* much as the removal of the disguise brings Spenser's Duessa to mind, and Jean Muir will prove to be something of a witch and quite a clever bit of self-handiwork as well.

Both brothers in the Coventry household, the young, impressionable Edward and the older, more worldly and cynical Gerald, are fascinated by the new governess, whose manner is "sweetly submissive," and "expressive of the respect, regard, and confidence which men find pleasantest when women feel and show it" (44). Edward is immediately attracted to Jean Muir, Gerald only gradually and with some intuitive reservations about the woman's sincerity, which endure even after he too falls in love with the bewitching, seductive, and seemingly young woman.

The Coventrys' daughter, little Bella, who is Jean Muir's charge, becomes very fond of the governess, and even the servants like her: "Insead of being, what most governesses are, a forlorn creature hovering between superiors and inferiors, Jean Muir was the life of the house" (25). She is not however liked by Lucia, Gerald Coventry's cousin and his presumed intended. Further complications are introduced by the governess's subtle revelations that she is adored by young Sydney, scion of the family that had previously employed her as a governess, who threatens to kill anyone who attempts to win her affections.

Then Jean Muir lets it "slip" that she is the daughter of Lady Grace Howard and "a poor Scotch minister" with whom the titled young woman had eloped twenty years earlier, only to die "'so obscurely that very little is known of her except that she left an orphan girl at some small French pension'" (47). This information, which like Jane Eyre's inheritance lifts her to the social level of her employers, is relayed through Sir John Coventry, a wealthy uncle of the family, who is the true object of the governess's designs. He is old and therefore likely to die soon after they marry, leaving Muir a wealthy and titled woman. It is here that we overhear echoes of the Honorable James Richardson, whose interest in Louisa May was an expression of elderly infatuation, the very folly that leads Sir John into Muir's web.

Thus though the governess flirts with both of the Coventry brothers, attracting their sympathy by her apparent helplessness and then bewitching them with her seductive wiles, she is actually after Sir John, and her situation suddenly seems hopeless when the truth about the governess is revealed by the youngest son, Ned, who has learned it from young Sydney: "Jean Muir has deceived us all" (96). Over the protests of Gerald, who is now deeply in love with the governess, Ned tells how Jean "tried to charm Sydney as she did us, and nearly succeeded in inducing him to marry her. Rash and wild as he is, he is still a gentleman, and when an incautious word of hers roused his suspicions, he refused to make her his wife. A stormy scene ensued, and, hoping to intimidate him, she feigned to stab herself as if in despair" (97). This last was the cause of the wound that Muir examined while alone in her room.

In substantiation, Ned produces a handful of letters Muir had "written to an accomplice," which reveal the cold-hearted ambition of the aging actress, who as it turns out is also a divorcée, whose claim of an aristocratic family background is spurious. But Jean Muir, catching wind of her approaching disgrace, hurries Sir John into marriage, and the story ends with the former governess now enjoying not only her new-found wealth and position, but immunity from attack from the Coventry family as well. She has already warned her infatuated husband that they will attempt to discredit her from jealous motives.

At a key moment in the story, Gerald Coventry, now in love with the governess, accuses her in jest of being a witch: "Scotland is the home of weird, uncanny creatures, who take lovely shapes for the bedevilment of poor weak souls. Are you one of those fair deceivers?" Playing her game to the point of risk, Jean thanks him for the "compliment," and tells him, laughing, "I am a witch, and one day my disguise will drop away and you will see me as I am, old, ugly, bad and lost. Beware of me in time. I've warned you. Now love me at your peril" (86). Muir is playing a dangerous game, because she is not only older than she seems but is indeed something of a witch, as is the author herself, because as the story develops, the reader increasingly identifies with the admittedly wicked enchantress of the north, so that by the time the novel rushes toward closure, we are hoping that she succeeds in her scheme . . . and she does. This is an unusual twist on the conventional happy ending, and it is a double twist on the governess convention devised by Charlotte and Anne Brontë, with its strictly moral frame, a plot perhaps influenced by the matrimonial schemes of Thackeray's Becky Sharp.

Coincidentally, Jean Muir bears a certain resemblance to Charlotte herself, who because of her diminutive size looked younger than her years, yet close up resembled a much older person, with her missing teeth and thinning hair. There is also a curious coincidence in the circumstances under which Jean was discharged from service with the Sydneys, which resembles the disgrace Branwell brought to the family when his dalliance with Mrs. Robinson was revealed.

But these biographical coincidences aside, there is no doubt that Jean Muir as a character is a clever play on the governess convention, that she is able to win in the end by assuming the role first devised by the Brontë sisters, with a similar if perhaps parodic finale, for unlike Jane Eyre the heroine ends up marrying not only an older but an elderly man.

Moreover, Alcott's ingenious deconstruction of the governess type, demonstrating that these quiet little unassuming nunlike creatures may actually be witches in disguise, plays fast and loose with the gothic coloration of *Jane Eyre* as well. That is, in Jean Muir Alcott seems to be putting the vampirelike Bertha into a Jane Eyre outfit, whose scheme to marry Sir John Coventry is an act of revenge against the world that has pushed her aside. That she succeeds promotes an ending far different from the sacrificial conclusion of *Moods*, Alcott's first attempt to depart from sensational fiction. On the other hand, Jean Muir's strong, rebellious character, combined with her talent for theatrics, looks forward to the heroine of Alcott's first venture into domestic fiction, a book that also plays tricks on the unsuspecting reader.

IV

"There is no reason," James wrote in his review of *Moods*, "why Miss Alcott should not write a very good novel, providing she will be satisfied to describe only that which she has seen. Miss Alcott doubtless knows men and women well enough to deal successfully with their every-day virtues and temptations, but not well enough to handle great dramatic passions. When such a novel comes, as we doubt not it eventually will, we shall be among the first to welcome it" (Elbert, 1865 edition, 224). As Katharine Anthony unnecessarily assured us, such a novel did come, and James's opinion not a little resembles that of Professor Bhaer at a critical juncture in that novel. It also calls to mind George Henry Lewes' letter to Brontë in which he conveyed his response to *Jane Eyre*, warning her "to beware of melodrama," and "to adhere to the real" (Gaskell, 329).

Without realizing Jo's authorship, the professor dismisses as trash the sensational stories she has been writing, regarding them as harmful to young readers into whose hands they might fall. As a result of Bhaer's opinion, Jo—with the encouragement of her mother—turns to more serious and moral fiction, writing a story "that went straight to the hearts of those who read it," which seems from the brief description to have been a novel along the lines of *Moods:* "There is truth in it, Jo," says her mother, "that's the secret; humor and pathos make it alive, and you have found your style at last" (*Little Women,* 436).

In her journal, having "read all I had done to my family," Alcott recorded the reactions of her family to the manuscript of *Moods:* "Mother pronounced it wonderful, and Anna laughed and cried, as she always does, over my works, saying, 'My dear, I'm proud of you'" (104). Later, in correcting the proofs of her novel, the chapters of which now "seemed small, stupid & no more my own," Alcott bolstered her courage by citing Emerson—"'what is true for your own private heart is true for others'"—and by the reflection that "I wrote from my own life & experience & hope it may suit some one & at least do no harm" (*Journals,* 133). These quotations taken together do suggest that *Moods* is the book with which Jo/ Lou turns away from sensational fiction to draw on her own life, though the same of course could be said of *Little Women* itself.

James in his review of *Moods* expressed regret that "Miss Alcott takes [Sylvia] up in her childhood. We are utterly weary of stories about precocious little girls" (Elbert, 1865 edition, 219). The remark suggests that James completely missed the point in Alcott's novel, which is that the heroine at the start of the action is too immature to marry, and though hardly a "child," she is young and needs to grow up, a process that involves some mentoring and considerable suffering and is well within the classic bildungsroman formula. James's remark is a gratuitous slap that Alcott happily chose to ignore, indeed went on to write her most famous novel, which in so many ways followed James's first suggestion while ignoring his other stricture. For like *Moods*, it is about a precocious little girl, perhaps the most precocious little girl in our literature, who is taken up (as James put it) in childhood then carried all the way through to marriage and a family.

We have no record of what James thought about *Little Women*, but when in 1875, with Alcott's popularity at full tide, *Eight Cousins* was published, James wrote a review for the *Nation* indicating that he wasn't at all happy with the direction in which the author had been moving: "Miss Alcott," James announced, "is the novelist of children—the Thackeray, the Trollope, of the nursery and the school-room" (Anthony, 202). It wasn't that James disapproved of literature written for children, but as the specific authors cited might suggest, James disapproved of what Alcott was writing for children, for he regarded satire and smartness as not the proper stuff for "the infant generation." What "youngsters" need are stories filled with all things bright and beautiful, not sharp-edged revelations concerning what adults say about children "when the children are out of the room" (203). Where O where, he lamented, are the Rollo Books of yesteryear?

Well, they were there on the library shelf gathering dust, under "A" for "Abbot, Jacob," while right next to them was a great, wide space, under "A" for "Alcott, Louisa May" because her books were out being read. Having earlier instructed Alcott to write about what she knew, James then took her to task for writing too much about what she knew, far too much for the tender sensibilities of children. Yet the children for whom she was writing loved it, suggesting that Henry James did not know what Maisie knew. As he had to admit, "Miss Alcott seems to have a private understanding with the youngsters she depicts," but it was an understanding the meaning of which escaped a clueless Henry James.

As Katharine Anthony pointed out, what James didn't realize was that the needs of young readers were quite different in 1875 from what they had been when he was growing up. They were not interested in those stiffly didactic stories written for children during the first half of the nineteenth century. Jo herself, after the Professor's lecture on the evil influence on children of sensational fiction, takes a crash course in "Mrs. Sherwood, Miss Edgeworth, and Hannah More," and the story she writes as a result forces "her lively fancy and girlish romance" into "the stiff and cumbrous costume of the last century" (*Little Women*, 356–57). Predictably, it finds no market, for as the publisher of the "Weekly Volcano" has assured her, "morals didn't sell"—to young readers no more than to their parents.

Young women wanted stories with characters who, like Jane Eyre, engaged their emotions, much as their youthful male equivalents sought the adventuresome tales of team Dumas. Alcott's readers had sat along with Jo March weeping their way through *The Wide, Wide World* and Charlotte Yonge's *The Heir of Redclyffe*, and wanted to weep some more. Size was no object, as the heft of Susan Warner's book suggests, which was soon followed by those other elephantine efforts, *Hot Corn* and *The Lamplighter*, all published in the so-called Feminine Fifties, and while not aimed specifically at younger female readers, were undoubtedly the books they read. The lesson was similar to that learned by Charlotte Brontë when publishers rejected *The Professor*, declaring (as she informed Lewes) that what readers wanted were novels filled with "startling incident" and "thrilling excitement" (Gaskell, 329).

Once again, these were all novels close allied to those of Dickens, who was thought a realist in his day, and who certainly provided a long hard look at the dark underside of society, but whose melodramatic plots and sensational elements were precisely what readers (and publishers) wanted. But what Alcott created in *Little Women* was something different, not a tale of crime and passion with the underworld as a backdrop, but a story about young American girls growing up in the suburbs, with young American girls as its intended audience. True, the March sisters are not normal children but ones that resemble the Brontë sisters, less the universal family genius for authorship.

Notably, it is not *Oliver Twist* or *David Copperfield* that is the alternative text to *Pilgrim's Progress* in the March home, but *The Pickwick Papers*, that glorious comic romp through the English countryside, a loose aggregate of miscellaneous adventures that revolve around the bright face of Mr. Pickwick and the celebration of Christmas. As in *The Wide, Wide World*, as well as in its pale child, *Elsie Dinsmore*, Christmas is the most intense of domestic moments, with which the first volume of *Little Women* begins and ends, certifying the tradition in which Alcott's novel belongs. And yet we should not forget her high esteem for *Jane Eyre* and the woman who wrote that book, for both left a mark on an otherwise unlike story.

7

The Mad Girl in the Attic:
Rebellion as a Fine Art in *Little Women*

It is a characteristic of wisdom not to do desperate things.
—Thoreau

I

As HER JOURNAL REVEALS, THE DOMESTIC NOVEL WAS NOT A GENRE that Alcott looked forward to taking on, despite her earlier thoughts of turning the saga of the "Pathetic Family" into fiction, and she did so only with the assurance of her publisher that the market for such books aimed at a juvenile audience was opening up from which money could be made. But she virtually reinvented the genre, setting in motion a whole generation of books aimed at a youthful female audience, many of which were written by herself. Nor was *Little Women* just for children, then or now. In a footnote to *The Rise of the American Novel*, we find Alexander Cowie a half-century ago praising *Little Women*, despite its borrowing from "the tears, the illnesses, the instructive episodes, the domestic detail, and the prevailingly moral and religious atmosphere of scores of contemporary novels" (821).

Alcott's novel, opined Cowie, was "blessedly free from many outworn plot devices, as well as from extremely morbid elements. Moreover it possesses genuine humor. Its characters, if not very complex, are individualized. They could not possibly be interchanged with characters in any other story—a test which few characters in domestic stories could meet successfully." So also Nina Baym, twenty-eight years later, who echoed Cowie when she maintained that to move from "the perplexities, complexities, and absurdities of *St. Elmo* in 1867 to the clarity and control of *Little Women* the following year is an enormous leap in artistry" (297).

Perhaps Alcott took Henry James's advice, but it is more likely that, as Baym suggests, in seeking to write domestic fiction for

162

young readers, she necessarily simplified the traditional woman's novel. True, as James had recommended, Alcott drew upon the best source available, her own youth, with its small struggles and triumphs, all recorded in the diaries she kept. Ironically, as Baym notes, in aiming for a juvenile audience Alcott necessarily compromised both the genre and the facts as she knew them, presenting domesticity as an ideal whereas the norm for women's fiction hitherto was to portray the family as "a source of suffering, conflict, and frustration for the heroine—as indeed it was in fact for Louisa May Alcott" (298).

It was indeed. The facts of the author's miserable childhood bear an uncanny resemblance to the sufferings of Elsie Dinsmore, for Bronson in his austerely gentle way was as domineering as Horace. Convinced of his own moral perfection, he set himself up as a model for his daughters, and where Anna lovingly obliged, little Louisa rebelled. Like Jo March she had a terrible temper, was willful and stubborn, and in Bronson's view needed constant correction in order to become a perfect type of submissive womanhood. If reasoned discourse did not work, these sessions often ended with the same punishment so frequently inflicted on little Elsie: being sent to bed without supper, where like Elsie Louisa could nourish her guilt with grief over having once again disappointed her father by not fulfilling his ideal of female comportment.

None of these torments was preserved in Alcott's fictional version of the Pathetic Family, and Bronson's inadequacies as a provider were likewise expunged, as was his vegetarian regimen and with it Bronson himself, at least as a pervasive if coldly distant presence. In the first part of *Little Women,* Mr. March is away at the front, not as a soldier or nurse but as a chaplain servicing the spiritual needs of Union soldiers; in the second part he is usually upstairs in his study. It is Mrs. March who is in charge of managing her daughters, and though Marmee somewhat resembles Abba Alcott, her methods of coercion are taken from Bronson's educational philosophy. But rather than surrounding her children with a forbidding wall of moral idealism, Marmee is a positive yet a relatively passive presence, a model of female forebearance and motherly love that is there when she is needed but otherwise remains off stage.

In translating the Alcott ménage into the March family, the author made some strategic chronological revisions, for Jo and her sisters are younger than the Alcott equivalents were during the Civil War; but the war is a central fact, giving particular point to the reduced comforts suffered by the March family. As Meg explains at the start of the novel, "the reason mother proposed not having any presents this Christmas, was because it's going to be a hard winter for every one; and she thinks we ought not to spend money for pleasure, when our men are suffering so in the army" (*Little Women*, 1). But their reduced circumstances are chiefly the result of Mr. March's having lost a great deal of money by underwriting a debt for a friend, and perhaps the greatest of their sacrifices to the war effort is the lack of a father for the duration, a familial not a financial impoverishment. Their intensely domestic life, given a strong maternal center by Marmee, is an ideal replication of the homes that the men on the battlefields had left behind and to which (as Alcott well knew) they longed to return.

Whittier's *Snow-Bound*, published two years before *Little Women*, famously commemorated the end of the war and the reestablishment of the Union by celebrating a rural scene and domestic values. The long narrative poem is about an extended farm family trapped for a time by a blizzard, a castaway story in blank verse, and Alcott's novel is a similar exercise. There is no blizzard but the March sisters seldom leave the family compound and when they do bad things often happen. This is in stark contrast to *Moods*, in which good things happen outside, the farther outside the better, a situation derived from the author's childhood, for the tearfully rebellious little girl often found refuge from the grim poverty of the Alcotts' domestic scene in the woods. Then Mr. March returns, and all matters come together once again, with the girls having learned valuable lessons about the proper conduct of life. The first part of the novel ends with everyone celebrating a real Dickens Christmas, this at a time when that holiday had only recently been recognized in New England, having been suppressed for two centuries by the Puritan moral glacier.

Alcott did a clever thing by having the war always in the background, but then *Little Women* is a book filled with clever things. Thus at a central point in the novel Jo and her sisters play croquet with some English children, and one of the British boys is caught cheating, for which he is denounced by Jo with some unpleasant remarks regarding British national character. Puzzling to a modern reader, the episode is another reverberation of the Civil War, during which England remained sympathetic to the Southern cause for the sake of the cotton market. There are other clever things, as we shall see, but we need also to acknowledge that the author was a singular instance, who brought to her novel a rich background of many blessings.

First of all, as she notes in her journal, Alcott had been blessed by a very interesting family, the subject of subsequent books by other authors, some more truthful to the facts, perhaps, but none better than her own. She also had been blessed by a very quick and interesting intelligence, and while reluctantly agreeing to write a domestic, sentimental novel for young readers, she did not completely let go of that other genre, the sensational short romance that had been putting not only bread but butter on the family table. That of course is the kind of stuff Jo is writing upstairs in her attic room, but elements of romance fiction insinuate themselves throughout *Little Women* as well. Moreover, that the Alcott ménage resembled the Brontë family, as portrayed by Gaskell, did no harm.

Henry James was not the only critic who had faulted *Moods* for being unrealistic, inspiring her in 1865 to declare that in her "next book . . . the people shall be as ordinary as possible, then critics will say its all right" (*Journals*, 140). But Alcott did not quite banish her romantic side, and though illicit passions hardly spin the plot, we can find a number of threads salvaged from that earlier exercise in the bildungsroman tradition, not the least of which is a stress on the maturation of a bright but often confused young woman. What is entirely missing, however, is the ideological matrix essential to *Moods*, hardly suitable for a novel intended for young readers. Moreover, by 1868 Transcendentalism like Emerson himself was in slow decline, his "firmament" as he noted in "Terminus" having been reduced to "the compass of a tent," perhaps a wry allusion to his role as a public lecturer as well as to Bronson's ongoing career as a sibylline showman.

II

If Alcott followed in the great tradition of Charlotte Brontë, writing tales of passion before moving into novels with strong moral centers, it must be said that beyond a few superficial characteristics, the *Little Women* we know and love resembles nothing that Charlotte wrote. Both Meg and Jo work for a time as governesses, and Jo eventually finds her older man, but these are incidental if suggestive echoes. There are some similarities as well to *The Wide, Wide World*, as I have already suggested, but anyone who has read Susan Warner's novel must agree that *Little Women* is an entirely different kind of pilgrimage to maturity, in which the Christian burden is a backpack not a millstone. And though the author's life as a child is a wierd prognostication of the sufferings of Elsie Dinsmore, that element is entirely expunged from the auto-biographical basis of the book, which otherwise dictated the way things go in the March household.

First of all, despite the pervasive influence of Dickens, the March sisters are not orphans, although with Mr. March being away serving as an army chaplain, an equivalent situation is es-tablished. They are experiencing hard times, but have a loving mother and equally important they have themselves, where poor Ellen Montgomery like Oliver Twist and David Copperfield is all alone in the world. The lack of material comforts is not extreme— for one thing they keep Hannah the cook and maid of all work— but the deprivation is sufficient to underwrite a lesson Thoreau must have drummed into the head of his little pupil, that we are all better off for having lost the things we thought we owned but which in reality owned us. That the Alcotts, thanks to the improv-ident Bronson, never owned anything that was not bought with Abigail's family money, is not to the point here, although it cer-tainly gave the author plenty of material to work from. The point is that poverty, something short of losing the cook, is good for you, a moral reflecting the example set by Thoreau, who practiced as-ceticism at Walden Pond six days a week and dined with the Emersons on the seventh.

There are no gothic touches to the March family drama, if we except what goes on during the home theatricals or up in Jo's at-tic. Like Aunt Fortune's farm the March's home is very much a re-alistic domestic scene, with a suburban however not a rural set-ting. It is, once again, the kind of milieu that Henry James insisted Alcott should write about, before he went off to Europe where gothic materials could be found in abundance and worked into what he apparently convinced William Dean Howells were realis-tic fictions.

It is, that is to say, a book about the Alcott's home life, but with some strategic changes regarding chronology, character, and, as Baym suggests, the hardships actually suffered by the family thanks to Bronson's sowing his Transcendental wild oats, which provided an insubstantial diet. Again, the Alcott daughters knew about those other sisters in Yorkshire, and the author's emphasis on Jo's creative compulsions most definitely can be seen as re-sembling life in the Haworth Parsonage as described by Gaskell. Yet, inasmuch as Jo is Lou, who undeniably resembled the wildest of the Brontë sisters, the connection is an autobiographical fact rather than a matter of literary influence: perhaps "coincidence" is the best possible word. Though there are some points of resemblance between Patrick Brontë and Bronson Alcott (both men, for example, had radical ideas regarding the education of children), here again we are dealing with matters of chance as well as the pervasive influence of Rousseau on notions of child-rearing.

There were four sisters in the Alcott ménage, but no one even remotely resembling Branwell, although a case might be made for Laurie having been added to the novel in order to make up that deficiency, much as he is admitted to the March sisters' Pickwick Club because a male member is needed. We know that a number of real-life candidates for Laurie's original exist, including the darkly handsome Polish pianist Louisa May met on an extended trip to Europe, a younger man whom she was extremely fond of and called "Laddie." In 1869, Alcott wrote Alfred Whitman, who as a boy had boarded with the family, that "'Laurie' is you & my Polish boy 'jintly.' You are the sober half & my Ladislas . . . is the gay whirligig half" (*Journals,* 148n).

This would seem to settle matters, but there is a third "half" to Laurie, who occasionally acts up in a manner reminiscent of the boy who dwelt on the dark side of the Haworth Parsonage, whereas all the other youths who passed through the Alcott home (sometimes supplementing the family's income by boarding for a year or more) seem to have been (like Alfred) "sober" young men. Even the Polish pianist, though gifted with a mischievous sense of humor, was not the temperamental, moody, at times self-destructive young man that Alcott abstracted from his acquaintance. Again, the common model was Byron, self-consciously selected by Branwell and imposed on Ladislas by Alcott, so all such real-life contingencies are finally coincidental.

Still, if we ask ourselves what *Little Women* would be without the one little man, we can only answer "rather dull," being of less interest to its intended reader than otherwise. Laurie is very much a girl's boy, which does not mean he is effeminate (though he self-consciously masculinizes his name, avoiding "Theodore" lest he be called "Dora"); it does mean that he would be thought sexy by the young women who made up the audience for which the novel was intended. Even more to the point, the relationship that develops between Laurie and Jo would have been regarded by those same young women as an incipient romance, despite Jo's frequent protestations against sentimentality, against growing up, and most pointedly against marriage It is a very clever strategy, a matching of the romantic, temperamental, but thoroughly likeable Laurie with Jo March, who is a prickly, tomboyish, and unromantic young girl.

If the sisters living next door to the Laurence mansion are virtual orphans, Laurie is the real thing, for having lost both his parents he now lives with his often crusty old grandfather. Mr. Laurence has never forgiven his son, Laurie's father, who eloped with an Italian pianist to Italy, where, after Laurie was born, both parents died. This is not a good situation for little Laurie, who on occasion rebels, and when he rebels it is by a display of the fiery temper that Charlotte Brontë in *Jane Eyre* advised against expressing. Jo likewise, although she herself has a temper matching her auburn hair, does what she can to smooth the ruffled feathers of her bantam rooster friend. It is this sympathetic coupling that seems to promise a budding romance between the "unsentimental" Jo and the temperamental boy next door, who is for all intents and purposes a romantic figure.

It is a division that is established early in the novel by a virtual map Alcott provides of the two houses, the humble cottage occupied by the March girls and their mother—the "little nunnery" as old Mr. Laurence calls it—and the exclusively male mansion looming nearby:

> Both stood in a suburb of the city, which was still country-like, with groves and lawns, large gardens, and quiet streets. A low hedge parted the two estates. On one side was an old brown house, looking rather bare and shabby, robbed of the vines that in summer covered its walls, and the flowers which then surrounded it. On the other side was a stately stone mansion, plainly betokening every sort of comfort and luxury, from the big coach-house and well-kept grounds to the conservatory, and the glimpses of lovely things one caught between the rich curtains. Yet it seemed a lonely, lifeless sort of house; for no children frolicked on the lawn, no motherly face ever smiled at the windows, and few people went in and out, except the old gentleman and his grandson. (46–47)

To drive home the implication of the contrast between the Marches' little cottage and the grand mansion next door—an unlikely proximity but a virtual back-lot setting for a fairy tale—we are told that "to Jo's lively fancy this fine house seemed a kind of enchanted palace, full of splendors and delights, which no one enjoyed."

At a later point, having discovered its many wonders, the sisters identify the neighboring mansion with Bunyan's "Palace Beautiful," but the Laurence home however glorious is a home in name only, lacking the necessary maternal element. By contrast, the

Marches' home be it ever so humble is a home in fact, which poor, lonely, and orphaned Laurie regards with envy from his bedroom window. Soon enough, the sad little lad is welcomed into "their cheerful society," and shares the "motherly" warmth of Mrs. March, his romantic spirit in effect absorbed by the domestic spirit that rules "in that humble home of theirs" (60).

In the meantime, old Mr. Laurence begins to dote on little Beth, in whom he sees a resemblance to his dead daughter, and which ties him as well as his grandson to the March family. Though inspired by the generosity of Abba Alcott's brother, the Reverend Sam May, the avuncular Mr. Laurence is also a standard fixture in Dickens's fiction, a personification of benevolence throughout, recalling the kindly old gentlemen who assist Ellen in *The Wide, Wide World.* And we should note that the Christmas banquet of sweets he provides appears as if by a miracle is a Dickensian touch as well, appearing right after the sisters celebrated their family Christmas in a truly Christian spirit by giving away their breakfasts (at their mother's suggestion) to a family more needful than theirs.

While calling immediate attention to the Alcott-family-inspired hence "realistic" goings-on in the March home, thereby obeying the strictures of the very junior Henry James, Alcott quietly establishes in the Laurence mansion precisely the kind of romantic, ultraliterary situation to which James objected. Where Mr. Laurence is a figment of Dickens's imagination, Laurie in temperament bears a remarkable likeness to the heroes in the kinds of romantic melodramas Jo herself is writing in her attic studio. But, most important, the character of Laurie carefully considered reveals that the author has it both ways, and seems to have gotten away with it for a very long time.

Alcott, using the humble March home as a stalking horse, creates in the Laurence mansion with its romantically conceived Laurie and his Dickensian grandsire a highly unlikely alternative house. This is not the only sleight of hand that Alcott was able to pull off in *Little Women,* and we will be considering other, related acts of prestidigitation, but it certainly serves as a signal as to what lies ahead. For having set in motion the relationship between the romantic Laurie and the realistic Jo March, creating in her readers the reasonable expectation that youthful friendship will blossom into mature love, that the poor but admirable girl will marry the poor little rich boy next door, Alcott in the sequel to the first volume of *Little Women, Good Wives,* in effect pulled the magic carpet out from under her readers' feet.

Those readers I think have not been at all pleased with the surprise sprung in the sequel to *Little Women*. It might have been better had Alcott not written *Good Wives*, had followed the lead provided by Susan Warner's novel, which stops short of the promised nuptials of Ellen and her Mr. John. And so, we might ask, why did Louisa Alcott not borrow that last page from a book that was so effectively placed beween her sensibility and *Jane Eyre*, and leave the question of Jo's marriage to Laurie still open? Reader, the answer is simple: she needed the money, which was the reason she wrote the first part of *Little Women*, indeed why she wrote most of what she wrote, which is the same reason that the Brontë and the Warner sisters wrote, indeed is the reason most writers write.

Alcott wrote *Good Wives* in response to the demand of readers who couldn't get enough of the March family, but as we now know she had trouble giving Jo a future, holding her heroine back from her own circumstantial decision to remain single and free to devote her life to writing but refusing to allow the anticipated wedding between Jo and Laurie. The refusal was in part a result of an uneasy relationship with her readers, a rebellious gesture of independence in the face of the universal expectation regarding the union of Jo and Laurie. In effect, she reversed the pattern established by Jane Eyre and its many imitations: Reader, she *didn't* marry him! "Girls write," she groused in her journal, "to ask who the little women marry, as if that was the only end and aim of a woman's life. I *won't* marry Jo to Laurie to please any one" (167). Instead, she gave Laurie to Amy March—who shares his artistic sensibilities—a situation not without its ambiguities as we shall see, and then, to reinforce the domestic center of her novel, she hit upon the idea of Mr. Bhaer.

Nobody was (or is) very happy with her solution, but that seems to have been what Alcott intended. If in *Little Women* she was able to sneak an element of romanticism into her otherwise realistic novel, by taking two steps backward we can see that the Professor Bhaer of *Good Wives*, with his beard and gentle but authoritative manner, is a combination of Warwick and Moor, with his German nationality clinching the Goethean (and Emersonian) connection. As Jo is Lou, so Jo's husband is a combination of the two older men in Lou's life.

Even as she carried out the Brontëan tradition, emphasized in *Moods* and parodied in "Behind a Mask," of marriage to a man superior in years and wisdom, she also domesticated it beyond recall. Despite the Brontëan touch, it should be noted that Catharine Sedgwick in *A New-England Tale* likewise married her heroine to an older man, a wealthy widower who like Bhaer comes with a ready-made family, an attractive alternative to the younger but unreliable suitor to whom she had earlier been engaged. Yet Professor Bhaer is not a rich man, and it is characteristic of Alcott that in adding this realistic touch she soon remedied it with yet another sleight of hand.

III

Thus *Little Women/Good Wives* is both a hybrid and something of a sport. If Warner's book filtered out what were thought to be pagan elements from *Jane Eyre,* so Alcott's book brought forward to the post–Civil War readership those elements found in *The Wide, Wide World* she thought would recommend themselves to readers of a later generation. With Warner she preserved the idea of a mature man as a suitor, though Bhaer bears no more resemblance to Mr. John than to Rochester, a telling difference, because in bringing forward the Christian message of Warner's book, Alcott left out the strident evangelism.

As we have seen, passive not preachy influence is the agent of change, and in *Little Women* Dickensian benevolence plays a much more important role than the submission of self to the rule of stern, moral authority. This is one of several important differences between Alcott's book and Finley's, the both of which were obviously influenced by *The Wide, Wide World.* Self-control remained essential to the agenda, yet Jo March, though brought to realize the folly of surrendering to impulse, is hardly a martyr to Pauline rigor. Notably, she finds salvation in establishing with her husband a school for boys run on humanistic not Calvinistic principles, and the second part of the novel ends with a huge party at Plumfield, very much in the Pickwickian tradition.

At the start of the story, the March sisters are given a lecture by their mother on the beauties of *Pilgrim's Progress,* a story they already dearly love, and are handed for their Christmas presents by Marmee little copies of the New Testament. Okay, the young reader surmises, this is going to be a pious book, in which the sisters like Ellen Montgomery will be brought to Christ. But they of course are not. They are however brought full round at the end of the novel to Christmas once again, an intensely domestic (and Dickensian) moment.

Moreover, like Christian in what Huck Finn politely called an interesting book they are all transformed, first because of the biological process of attaining young womanhood, and second because the experiences they have had, like those of Bunyan's hero, have changed them for the better. In short, *Little Women,* as so many feminist critics have assured us, is like *Moods* a female bildungsroman, and as such was designed specifically to guide young women, not toward salvation but to what in 1875 was Modern Maturity, inevitably equated with marriage.

The daughter of a man who was famous as a pioneering educator, Louisa May Alcott could hardly have ignored an opportunity to address herself to the proper method of raising female children. Bronson was an advocate of a revolutionary way of teaching that set aside rote learning and used instead illustrative examples, the guiding light of instruction through influence, and so Marmee as the mentor of her growing girls lets them (as reformers following the lead of Pestalozzi recommended) learn by their own example. The most memorable instance is the day the girls are given "off," to follow their own inclinations, which ends disastrously for all concerned, with a spoiled dinner and even a dead canary as the result.

Whim, despite the insistence of the Alcotts' close neighbor and family friend, Emerson, is not the motto of a well-run household. Marmee like Bronson Alcott is a careful student of child psychology (ca. 1860) and knows how to motivate her daughters to do right, even if it means allowing them to do wrong. She is hardly a Miss Fortune, who pays no attention to little Ellen except when she is scolding her for making mistakes; even less is she a Mr. Dinsmore, issuing commands that must be obeyed without question. Instead, there is a certain element of play involved in the mechanism of learning, as J. R.Wyss in *The Swiss Family Robinson* (the grand original of the domestic novel of learning by doing) demonstrated a half century before *Little Women* was published.

At the same time, it must be said that Pestalozzi like Wyss and like many other educational reformers of the late eighteenth century was a disciple of Rousseau, himself a pioneer in education theory. It was Rousseau who promoted the idea that children were pure of heart and that it was only the corruptions and pressures of society that perverted their innocent souls. Émile we will remember was to be raised in total isolation from society with *Robinson Crusoe* as his only text. Well, Bronson Alcott may have been a disciple of Pestalozzi, yet the favorite book in the Alcott home was not *Robinson Crusoe* but *Pilgrim's Progress,* and it *was* the New Testament that Marmee placed in the hands of her daughters that Christmas day on which *Little Women* begins.

These pious emphases suggest that the Puritan inheritance of Bronson and Abba Alcott was not entirely forgotten, and that the innate innocence of children, to these parents of four small girls, was a relative matter.

As in her own and her father's diaries, Louisa as Jo is the most troubling and often troubled figure, the rebellious daughter who most needs to mend her ways. It is a process in which Jo's mother plays a defining role, but chiefly (following Bronson's beloved Pestalozzi) as a good example, an ideal toward which her daughter struggles against all adversity, the most of which is provided by Jo herself. She is her own worst enemy, and her temper is the fiercest adversary, as the pivotal chapter entitled "Jo Meets Apollyon" insists. Though the environment is quite different from that in the novels by Brontë, Warner, and Finley, the lesson is pretty much the same: Control thyself . . . or suffer the consequences.

It is, once again, the lesson Sylvia learns in *Moods*, warranting the renewal of her vows with the mild, Emerson-, Bhaer-, and Bronson-like Goeffrey Moor. The irony is that most of us (and we can probably include the author, given the focus of sympathy) prize the wild girl with auburn hair dashing about in a mad quest of self-fulfillment, who weeps over romantic novels and laughs over Dickens then seeks a sanctuary in her attic where she may write her tumultuous dramas and those thrillers that will help sustain the March family in its new-found poverty.

As we know, Lou like Jo had a place in the family attic where she wrote her earliest works, so we perhaps should not make too much of the Brontëan echoes, and see the wild girl in the Alcott attic as an update of the madwoman in Rochester's secret room. Yet it certainly can be said that if Bertha is the counterpart to Jane, a dread alternative to the control of passions, then Jo in the attic is a complex symbol, standing for those creative energies that cannot be separated from the psychological and representing a useful channeling of those energies into works of literature. At the same time, what she writes are those sensational melodramas of which Professor Bhaer disapproves, an equivalent to the fantastic sagas the Brontë sisters wrote as children, and which Charlotte later turned her back upon as dangerous expressions of passion.

However, there is no evidence that Louisa May Alcott ever regarded her earliest work as somehow a dangerous waste of talent, for "rubbish" it may have been but it did put food on the table and clothes on the back. Moreover, Louisa May's departure from that profitable if sensational genre was a mixture of chance and opportunity, rather more drift than a sudden break. Despite Henry James's remarks anent *Moods,* we need to realize that Alcott's first novel was a transitional piece that only temporarily carried her away from purely sensational toward more serious fiction. "Behind the Mask" was written two years later. That the final result happened to be *Little Women* was hardly inevitable, and was in large part attributable to her publisher, Thomas Niles, the person who encouraged her to try her hand at the emerging and profitable genre of children's literature.

But neither can we ignore the looming presence of the Brontë sisters, and although downstairs the March girls play at *Pilgrim's Progress* and the *Pickwick Papers,* upstairs in the attic the young author's imagination carried her into gothic regions, which way not lunacy but lucre lay. And, as I have already stated, in little Teddy (as Jo calls him) Laurence there was established a vital reservoir and residue of turbulent romanticism, suggesting that it was not just a matter of remuneration. Having established that vital alternative, Alcott could then carry Jo on toward maturity, equated as in so much Victorian literature aimed at young women with the suppression of self, including—thanks to Mr. Bhaer's forceful opinion—the writing of sensational fiction.

Notably, Jo's turn toward maturity is rightly or wrongly associated with her refusal of Laurie's proposal. We can also derive from this surprising turn of events the possibility that in having Jo refuse Laurie's proposal Alcott was in effect turning her back not only on her readers but on the spirit of romance, which is to say the element that Jo gives up in deference to Professor Bhaer's opinion of sensational fiction. We find Alcott in her journal exulting in the success of the first part of *Little Women,* which resolved her doubts about the March family, which she now found to be "sober, nice people, and as I can launch into the future, my fancy has more play" (167). This was the same entry in which she resolved not to marry Jo to Laurie, and it attests that *Good Wives* clearly operates in its own dimension, lacking the magic of the first part of *Little Women* and promoting instead a complex, multi–story line that is well within the accepted parameters of Howellsian realism. It is also an example undefiled of domestic fiction, in which everyone finally gets married to the right person, this despite Alcott's grumbling about her readers' expectations.

Alcott may have heeded Henry James's advice, but she also anticipated his use of the European setting, which by 1868 she had experienced as a tourist, meeting Ladislas while staying in

Switzerland with young Anna Weld, an invalid with whom she was traveling as a paid companion. At the time Laurie meets Amy in Nice, they have both matured and suddenly realize how much they have in common, beyond being old friends sharing fond memories of their childhood. Laurie, still carrying a Werthean gloom over having been rejected by Jo, is rapidly maturing, which means he is leaving his impulsive, moody self behind, that romantic element Jo rejects along with Laurie. Amy likewise has learned that she will never succeed in her romantic ambition to become an artist, and has grown from a spoiled, selfish little girl into a vivacious and lovely young woman.

It is a meeting that is highly coincidental hence hyper-literary, with an eventual consummation that becomes increasingly predictable but puts a strain on the reader's credulity. The realization by Laurie and Amy that they are meant for each other takes place after they meet a second time, this time in Vevay, the place where matters for a very brief time became "romantic" between Louisa Alcott and Ladislas. Henry James used the resort across the lake from Calvin's Geneva as a setting ten years later in *Daisy Miller,* but to contrary ends, holding out the promise of a love story but then breaking off a relationship and an expected union that like the one between Jo and Laurie is clearly impossible.

By contrast, the union between Laurie and Amy becomes increasingly inevitable, and "Romance" from this point on takes a much less romantic direction, a bending of the plot that prepares the way for Jo's falling in love with Professor Bhaer. If not entirely realistic, it is a determinedly nonromantic moment that somehow convinces readers of *its* inevitability, even over their objections, and both romances as love stories join forces to carry the novel toward its overwhelmingly domestic conclusion.

Professor Bhaer is hardly a Rochester figure but he bears a remarkable resemblance to the grand original, Professor Heger, remarkable because in 1868 nothing was yet known about the relationship between Charlotte Brontë and her Belgian teacher—though *Villette* had made available an equivalent arrangement that may have contributed its share to *Little Women.* If we accept the possibility that Bhaer is Warwick/Moor redivivus, hence an abstraction of Alcott's mentors, Thoreau/Emerson, then the coincidence becomes much more complex. Again, we must never forget Alcott's fondness for that fabled correspondence between Bettina and Goethe, with which as Elaine Showalter suggests the tradition of teacher/lover begins, predating Charlotte Brontë's several versions.

When Alcott's Professor echoing the two Henrys (James and Lewes) clucks his tongue over Jo's expense of talent in the waste of sensational fiction, it is a logical extension of Marmee's attempts to bring Jo to the realization that the open expression of anger is not only shameful but wasteful. We are witnessing in this opposition that age-old struggle beween the Dionysian and Apollonian categories of creation, and Jo's eventual abandonment of Dionysius for Apollo, her succumbing to maturity in both her social and creative lives is perhaps inevitable. Still, maturity in *Little Women* comes very close to Bronson's notion of repressed rebellion as virtue, accepting the necessity of assuming a traditional female role of submission to male control. It is this emphasis that has provided a barrier between the book and modern readers. Nonetheless, as Alcott arranges things in closing the book that celebrates Jo's new-found control, there is still some hot primal energy bubbling just under the cooling, rigidifying surface.

On that surface, *Little Women* may seem to resemble *The Wide, Wide World,* being a bildungsroman in which a young girl moves steadily toward the conventional notion of maturity, in Victorian terms the abnegation of selfishness, defined as the assertion of self-interestedness. But when viewed internally, Alcott's novel comes much closer to *Jane Eyre,* being a fluid compromise between unkempt wildness and ladylike reserve. Jane never completely gives up her independent spirit, indeed in her marriage to Rochester she seems pretty much in charge; and Jo's decision to join the rest of her sisters in the holy bonds of matrimony falls something short of assuming a domestic yoke. As Nina Baym observes, "Jane's goal in the Bronte [*sic*] novel is dominance while the goal of all the American heroines [in woman's fiction] is independence," and Jo's goal falls somewhere in between (30). Meg becomes an ideal matron, Amy a bestower of her husband's money on worthy causes, while Jo, having undergone a unique metempsychosis, sets aside her literary ambitions to establish with her professor husband a school for boys.

Professor Bhaer like Mr. John may be a stern mentor, but he is not all that stern, and much in the manner of Bronson (and Marmee) he leads Jo to her own conclusions rather than forcing them upon her. Jo may "mature" to the disappointment of her readers but she retains a strong sense of inner purpose, and is one of the most centered characters in our literature. Moreover, when the newly married couple returns home, it is to Jo's home they return, for it is in Plumfield that they establish their school, the great rural estate that is Jo's inheritance. We might even notice the echo between Plumfield and Thornfield, "plummy" being one of Lou/Jo's favorite slang expressions for events that seem to be going very well, but it does not belong to Bhaer, though as a transforming inheritance it resembles Jane Eyre's sudden good fortune.

Jo like Jane comes into her own property at the end, and where Jane's great wealth and recovered family serves to lift her to Rochester's level (an important consideration in a classed society), Jo's much more modest inheritance is sufficient to absorb Mr. Bhaer, his sister's boys and all. Hers is not the trick Jean Muir plays on Sir John Coventry, but it is surely a trick played by the author on her readership, an act of rebellion that keeps Jo from either a romantic or a conventional marriage. Again, in *A New-England Story,* Sedgwick had her heroine marry an older man, but he was a wealthy older man, from whose riches his power derives, whereas Professor Bhaer is a poor man in material terms, although rich in culture and sensibilities.

Whatever may have been Alcott's purpose, and I have suggested several, we never have a sense that Jo's marriage is the point toward which we have been heading, as we do when Jane reunites with Rochester or when Susan Warner's book ends with a promise of nuptials not far off. When the fat lady finally sings for Ellen and Mr. John, we are certain that the song will be "Oh Promise Me" not "O Solo Mio." The real denouement of *Little Women* is still as it were in the future, latent in the promise that Jo and her new husband will start a school for boys, which like *Little Women* will operate on the educational theories of Bronson Alcott. For it is boys that boyish Jo is fondest of, and her "family" already is made up of two adopted sons. With or without *Little Men,* we are assured that the March family cycle will start all over again, only with a radical change of gender emphasis.

Jo's marriage is a ratification of the heroine having attained her maturity, not (as with Meg's marriage) an instrument promoting it. By contrast, the death of little Beth like the death of Alice in Warner's novel is virtually a ritual of passage, by means of which Jo moves on to the next stage of her pilgrimage. Again, Beth is Alcott's sister Elizabeth ("Betty") who did die from the prolonged effects of scarlet fever, an infection brought into the home not by herself but by her mother, Abba, but the responsibility was tactfully removed from the scene of the crime by Louisa May.

Otherwise, the account of Betty's death in Alcott's journal runs a virtual parallel line to that of Beth in the novel, the slow, painful decline, the ever present "shadow" hovering over the little figure on her bed, the family gathering around during the final hours, a prolonged episode of pain then peace at last. Even touches that seem so self-consciously sentimental, as when the March family fix up a special room for Beth, or when the doomed little girl remains busy with her needle, making things which she drops from the window for passing schoolchildren to find, these are all recorded in the journal as fact.

Perhaps the most "literary" event in the journal was Betty's final moment, which came "as Mother and I sat silently watching the shadow fall on the dear little face," for they both "saw a light mist rise from the body, and float up and vanish in the air. . . . Dr. G. said it was the life departing visibly" (*Journals*, 89). It is a phenomenon approximating Little Eva's famous departure heavenward in the stage version of Stowe's novel, and Alcott left this supernatural moment out of the novel, as being one of those facts too strange for fiction.

The others were all matters in which life imitates art, and whether Alcott had absorbed the pieties of her parents or been deeply influenced by the novels of Dickens, she declared herself radically transformed by having witnessed Betty's death: "Dear little saint!" she cries in her journal, "I shall be better all my life for these sad hours with you," and immediately after describing the funeral service, she writes "I know what death means,—a liberator for her, a teacher for us" (88–89). It would be difficult to find a more succinct example of what death as an agent of influence meant to the sentimental age, an emphasis ever present in the works of Dickens, who wrote of the death of Little Nell in *The Old Curiosity Shop* that "of every tear that sorrowing mortals shed on such green graves, some good is born, some gentler nature comes" (659).

A month later Alcott wrote in her journal, "I don't miss her as I expected to do, for she seems nearer and dearer than before, and I am glad to know she is safe from pain and age in some world where her innocent soul must be happy" (89). More grievous to Louisa was her older sister's marriage, which took place in May, Alcott moaning "in private over my great loss, and said I'd never forgive J[ohn] for taking Anna from me, but I shall if he makes her happy, and turn to little May for my comfort"—not that May, who always seemed to have the good luck that forever eluded Louisa, brought her any great joy (89).

Despite her declarations of renewed faith and hope, the twin losses drove Alcott to consider suicide—an episode missing and presumably expunged from the journal. As a gesture, it was a despairing rejection of the burdens of life, from which she paradoxically rescued herself by resolving to get to work—tutoring, sewing, and writing—having learned "that work of head and hand is my salvation when disappointment or weariness burden and darken my soul" (91). Like Jo she felt that the death of her sister had helped her "spiritually. . . . In my sorrow I think I instinctively came nearer to God, and found comfort in the knowledge that he was sure to help when nothing else could. A great grief has taught me *more than any minister,* and when feeling most alone I find refuge in the Almighty Friend" (91–92, italics added).

This last is a virtual redaction of the lesson repeated like a mantra in *The Wide, Wide World,* and it is a refrain typical of so much sentimental fiction, which insists on suffering without the benefit of clergy as the way to salvation. Yet we can hardly credit Alcott's spiritual awakening—if such it was—to the influence of literature. Rather, it was wisdom common to the age, and which, when rendered in fictional form, as in Warner's novel and Alcott's, was part and parcel of those books' instant popularity. "I feel," wrote Alcott in her journal, "that I could write better now,—more truly of things I have felt and therefore *know.* I hope I shall yet do my great book, for that seems to be my work, and I am growing up to it" (92).

This new mood saw her through Anna's marriage, in May the following year, and though she envied the bride when "Mr. Emerson kissed her," thinking "that honor would make even matrimony endurable, for he is the god of my idolatry, and has been for years," she resolved to remain "a free spinster and paddle my own canoe" (99). By August she was hard at work paddling furiously in *Moods,* her "genius burn[ing] so fiercely that for four weeks I wrote all day and planned nearly all night, being quite possessed by my work. I was perfectly happy, and seemed to have no wants" (99). If indeed in that novel she gave her alter ego in marriage to a character modeled after Emerson, the "tender and illustrious man" who had so often proved a "true friend" to the Alcott family, then the mixture of journal notations is suggestive (103).

It must be said that salvation through hard work plays no important part in *The Wide, Wide World,* where Ellen following Alice's death simply moves higher up the social scale even as she moves closer toward heaven. Yet in both novels the experience of loss is seen as a highly influential moment during the heroines' rite of passage, a movement from impulsive, moody youth toward the steadier course of maturity. Once again, it was Dickens who was the master of the mortuary moment, having famously kept Little Nell dying for a very long time—a strategy of suspense, it must be said, not of sentimentality, for the death scene itself was relatively short.

If Dickens was Alcott's competition, then she broke the record with Beth, who almost dies in the first part of *Little Women,* but lingers on to provide that crucial, transforming moment in the second part. Both names resonate with fatality, "Nell" suggesting "Knell" and "Beth" rhyming with . . . well, you get the idea. Which is to say that Alcott in translating the death of her sister into literature filtered it through a Dickensian sieve, thereby gaining control over an event that was truly heartbreaking in real life but a work of art when translated ten years later into literature. And that it is a work of art should put us once again on guard that things are not always as they may seem to be in whatever Alcott wrote.

IV

In the chapter in *The Wide, Wide World* that follows Ellen's mountain meeting with John Humphreys, the reader is allowed to pay a visit "to the room, *the* room," which it is perhaps unnecessary to say is the bedroom of the dead Alice, where Margery, the servant of the parsonage, is found gazing "on the sweet face she loved so dearly" (444). If Dickens institutionalized the death of small boys and virgin girls as essential to the sentimental mode, we may give some credit to Susan Warner for validating the funerary element, which will emerge as critical to the sentimental experience in literature.

There is nothing of this in *Jane Eyre,* where the loss of others is not a liminal experience, and though Helen Burns's death was inspired by that of the author's beloved older sister, Maria, it is an occasion for anger rather than grief, serving to point up the callous and cruel regimen at Lowood. Moreover, Helen's death from consumption cannot be regretted, for it is the consummation she has devoutly desired, and the wisdom she delivers from her death bed has no relevance to Jane's continuing existence: Helen like Little Nell lives literally to die, and for both of them "home" is heaven, but Jane makes the point that her only reality is the present moment, for as yet the notion of home is without meaning, nor will it ever be associated by Jane with the afterlife.

Helen dies an exemplary Christian death, to the very end attempting to convert Jane to her faith, but to the end Jane can only ask questions: "Who is God?" Where is God?" (95). Jane is asleep in her little friend's bed when death comes, but Helen's passing has no lasting effect upon her, nor have her pious instructions influenced her life: "You think too much of the love of human beings," advises Helen, pointing her friend to the love of God, but Jane will never stop yearning for the love of the living rather than for the company of the dead (91).

The one active influence on Jane Eyre during her eight years at Lowood is Maria Temple, the namesake of Charlotte's dead sister, and through her mentor Jane comes to accept her life in the institution, preferring it to life at Gatewood with nasty Aunt Reed and the terrible John. But once Miss Temple becomes Mrs. Nasmyth, that calming presence is removed and Jane becomes restless: the road seen from her window holds out the promise of what lies beyond the hilly horizon. "I desired liberty; for liberty I gasped. . . . For change, stimulus," or that failing at least "a new servitude" (117). What Jane does not desire, nor asks heaven for, is the release provided by death.

The lesson of Helen Burns's martyrdom goes unheeded and her dear, dead friend is forgotten once Jane has entered the precincts of Thornfield. It is not over the grave of Helen Burns that she is at last united with her lover, but over the grave of the unregretted Bertha Mason, and her home is the garden world of Fernwood. Emphases like these convinced Elizabeth Rigby that *Jane Eyre* was an impious book, and though Susan Warner may not have consciously made over Helen Burns into Alice Humphreys, she most certainly made sure that Alice's saintly death would have its contribution to *l'histoire d'*Orphan Ellen.

As I have already pointed out, there is a scene in *Little Women* where Jo is found perched in an apple tree weeping over the pages of *The Wide, Wide World.* The specific passage that has moved her to tears is not revealed, but for our purposes it may well be the account of Ellen's grief over the death of her dearest friend and mentor. Death in Warner's book clears the way to Christ for Ellen—by removing the barriers presented by her mother and Alice—while bringing Mr. John even closer to his intended bride, and is therefore a pivotal episode in the novel. In Alcott's novel Jo protests against sentimentality, but her shedding of tears is so frequent as to suggest that Alcott was putting her boyish heroine's protestations in an ironic framework.

A celebration of domesticity in its several forms, *Little Women* uses death, which at once disrupts and intensifies family relationships, as an instrument promoting Jo's acceptance of her responsibilities as her parent's daughter. There is plenty of evidence that in the sequential death of little Beth, Alcott was reinforcing the domestic center of *Little Women,* increasing the sentimental burden almost to an intolerable level so as to concentrate the March family in an extended drama of mourning. As we will see, the use of this sentimental occasion is another negative response to the romantic tradition, by means of which Alcott is further isolating Laurie from Jo's ongoing story. Laurie and Amy may marry, but they are symbolically shut out of what will prove to be the most formative moment in Jo's development, far more important than her marriage to Professor Bhaer, although that marriage is a culmination of the consequences of Jo's reaction to Beth's death.

The bond of sisterhood was very strong both in Alcott's life and in her novel, for *Little Women* as its title should suggest is a lengthy celebration of sorority, that "bright little band of sisters" as Alcott calls them, "all looking their best, in summer suits, with happy faces," setting out ever and again for a grand and always educational adventure (123). But in *Good Wives,* freed as she declared from fealty to fact, Alcott seems also to have freed herself from the autobiographical necessity. She celebrated that freedom by breaking away from romantic themes and immersing herself in the material of what Baym defines as woman's fiction. Yet, as so often in *Little Women,* what seems to be fealty to convention becomes an act of rebellion.

Once again, we know that Louisa had imperfect sympathies with May, who always seemed to get the breaks that eluded her older sister, and even in the first part of *Little Women,* May's counterpart, Amy, is a spoiled darling, an equivalent to little Enna Dinsmore. In the second part, she matures into a lovely young woman, but even so she is kept out of the episode that brings the rest of the family together in a tight domestic circle. She gets Laurie, but even that is finally a blighted victory, suggesting that the little woman writing in the attic may not have been mad but was, even after the experience of losing two sisters—one to death, the other to marriage—still capable of sustaining covert anger toward the third.

That little Beth is earmarked for an early death is hinted at throughout the first volume of *Little Women,* commencing with the demise and burial of her pet canary. When Mr. Laurence virtually adopts her in the place of his dead daughter, there is an obvious hint of her own early mortality, the sort of thing expressed in Mr. Dinsmore's conjunctive "if she lives." Then, when about half way through the first volume, the March girls go on a play Pilgrim's Progress out into the countryside, to a hill they call "the

'Delectable Mountain,'" Beth expresses an impatience to reach the Celestial City, yearning to "fly away at once, as those swallows fly, and go in at that splendid gate" (141).

This again is a sentimental convention: when Elsie Dinsmore comes close to dying when she falls from the piano bench, she tells her father that she was "ready to go to heaven," loving Jesus as she does and "thinking how glad mamma would have been to see me" (250). This passage was written even as Alcott was composing her own novel, and for all of the differences between the two stories, the echoes reinforce the sentimental necessity, which invests in those earthbound angels a constant threat (or promise) of instant departure for heaven. In dying, Little Eva gains immortality.

And finally, when after her sisters make excuses for not carrying food to the Hummel family, Beth carries out her fatal errand. We are told she "went out into the chilly air with a heavy head, and a grieved look in patient eyes" (177). We have already learned that it is Beth who has been taking the supplies to the Hummels, that her head aches and that she is tired, so we are not surprised when, returning with the news of the Hummel baby's death, Beth is already suffering the symptoms of scarlet fever. Jo is immediately suffused with guilt, having used a head cold as an excuse for not performing the errand, preferring to remain curled up with a favorite book: "Oh, Beth, if you should be sick I never could forgive myself!"

Mrs. March is away in Washington, tending her sick husband, and Meg, who does "not like nursing," allows Jo to take over that duty, which she does willingly, "because it is my fault she is sick; I told mother I'd do the errands, and I haven't" (178). Amy, much against her wishes, is sent to live with the ancient and fussy Aunt March, and "dark days" follow in the little cottage, as "the shadow of death hovered over the once happy home":

Then it was that Margaret, sitting alone with tears dropping often on her work, felt how rich she had been in things more precious than any luxuries money could buy; in love, protection, peace and health, the real blessings of life. Then it was that Jo, living in the darkened room with that suffering little sister always before her eyes, and that pathetic voice sounding in her ears, learned to see the beauty and the sweetness of Beth's nature, to feel how deep and tender a place she filled in all hearts, and to acknowledge the worth of Beth's unselfish ambition, to live for others, and make home happy by the exercise of those simple virtues which all may possess, and which all should love and value more than talent, wealth or beauty. (184)

Amy in quarantine with Aunt March at Plumfield likewise feels guilty, "remembering, with regretful grief, how many neglected tasks those willing hands had done for her," but she remains relatively untouched by the event. Under her aunt's strict regimen, the spoiled little girl realizes "how much she was beloved and petted at home," for the elderly woman—much in the manner of Aunt Fortune—"worried Amy most to death with her rules and orders, her prim ways, and long, prosy talks," and insists that she perform boring chores all day long (191). During her free time, Amy loves to play with the contents of her wealthy relation's jewel box, which she covets, and is overjoyed when she is given a turquoise ring as a reward for good behavior.

She also comes under the influence of her aunt's French maid, a devout Roman Catholic, and they build a little chapel, which brings her closer to Christ. But her greatest moment while in exile is writing her will, so typically a self-centered act, though Laurie, who visits her regularly, reminds her that while Beth has also given away her few possessions (as did Betty Alcott), "she never thought of a will" (198). The chapter ends with Amy praying for Beth "with streaming tears and an aching heart, feeling that a million turquoise rings would not console her for the loss of her gentle little sister," but the emphasis of the episode is on the little girl's superficiality and love of material things, which hardly helps to arouse the reader's sympathy.

It is those gathered around Beth's sick bed who are truly touched by the threat of losing the sweet little girl, and Jo, in tending her sister, like Lou learns "the sweet solace which affection administers to sorrow" (186). At the same time she is grief-stricken over the possibility that Beth might die, for her sister "is my conscience, and I can't give her up; I can't! I can't!," and the "sweet solace" gives way to tears. Laurie, standing by, attempts to comfort her, but first "subdued the choky feeling in his throat, and steadied his lips. It might be unmanly, but he couldn't help it, and I am glad of it. Presently, as Jo's sobs quieted, he said, hopefully, 'I don't think she will die; she's so good, and we all love her so much, I don't believe God will take her away yet,'" to which Jo dolefully responds, "The good and dear people always do die," a truth central to the sentimental idea.

When Laurie runs off to fetch a comforting glass of wine, Jo rests her head "on Beth's little brown hood," which she had worn while on her errands of mercy, and the humble garment "must have possessed some magic, for the submissive spirit of its gentle owner seemed to enter into Jo," an obvious reference to the marvelous properties of Christ's robe. The wine that Laurie brings back has a sacramental function, for with it the boy announces the good news that Mrs. March is on the way back from Washington, and is expected that very evening, restoring the loving center of the family. But as they await their mother's arrival, the sisters lose the momentary thrill of happiness, noticing "the pale shadow which seemed to fall upon the little bed," as the wind howls outside and the falling snow suggests a "winding-sheet" covering the world.

Turning from the window, Jo finds Meg weeping into "their mother's easy chair," and fearing the worst, rushes to Beth's bedside: "To her excited eyes a great change seemed to have taken place. The fever flush, and the look of pain, were gone, and the beloved little face looked so pale and peaceful in its utter repose, that Jo felt no desire to weep or lament. Leaning low over this dearest of her sisters, she kissed the damp forehead with her heart on her lips, and softly whispered, 'Goodby, my Beth; goodby'" (189). With Jo, the reader assumes that Beth has died, but Hannah immediately pronounces that the crisis has passed, and that Beth will live. Meg, who has saved a rose to put into Beth's dead hands, now places it in a vase by the bedside, "so that when the darling wakes, the first thing she sees will be the little rose, and mother's face" (190). The flower chosen is a traditional symbol of love, but also is associated with Mary, the mother of Christ.

While Amy, in her exile, finds comfort in prayer, prayer plays an insignificant role in the March home: we are told that in holding on to Beth, Jo "seemed to lead her nearer to the Divine arm which alone could uphold her in her trouble," but otherwise there are no references to God (185). Instead, Alcott relies on quasi-religious symbols, the mysterious power of the little hood, the glass of wine, the single rose that Meg has saved for Beth's dead hand. Moreover, though it is Amy who prays, there is a mannered frame put around her pious exercises, which are thoroughly mixed in with her desire for her aunt's jewelry and are associated with the pretty little chapel constructed with the help of the Roman Catholic maid, yet another emphasis on artifice.

Amy with her artistic ambitions having been patterned after Alcott's sister May, the problematic relationships between Jo and her youngest sister underline the sibling rivalry in the Alcott home, already alluded to. Amy, in a fit of resentment over having been excluded from an outing, destroys Jo's precious manuscript collection of fairy stories, and as a result Jo is almost the cause of her sister's death by drowning. In the sequel, *Good Wives*, Amy is given the trip to Europe by her Aunt March that Jo had expected but did not receive because of yet another display of her hot temper and pride, where in actual fact Louisa May provided the funds for May's European sojourn, with mixed feelings that seep through the account in her journal. More telling, where Amy decides that her talents are not sufficient for a career as an artist, May remained a painter of modest accomplishment until her relatively early death from the effects of childbirth.

It is while Amy is away in Europe that Beth goes into her final decline, and while Jo is suffering through Beth's lingering death, Amy is falling in love with a reformed Laurie, traveling about Nice in an increasingly joyous mood even as her sister sits disconsolate by Beth's bedside. By the time Amy learns that Beth has died—thanks to a miscarried letter—"the grass was green above her sister," and she is in Vevay eagerly awaiting Laurie's arrival (426).

That Amy and Laurie find themselves in love does not I think fully arouse the reader's sympathy, set as the action is against the devastating effect on Jo of Beth's death. It is a strategy similar to the interlude at Aunt March's during Beth's near-fatal illness, having Amy make out her will and express her grief in her lovely little chapel, gestures presented in terms that distance the reader. For as Laurie and Amy are acting out a pretty love story, a romance in the conventional sense of the word, Jo is being radically transformed by Beth's death. To reinforce her point, Alcott tells us that the union of Laurie and Amy results in a baby girl, also named Beth, which, being a sickly infant, is clearly doomed to an early demise. Thus fate (e.g., Alcott) guarantees that the two persons who have been removed from the immediate pain of witnessing the other Beth's passing will eventually suffer the agony of loss themselves.

Yet we do not witness that scene, which is only anticipated, while we are exposed to the lengthy and intensely sentimental death of Beth March. As in most Victorian mortuary scenes, the setting is carefully prepared with many symbolic and ritualistic touches, rendered in much more detail than in the equivalent passages in Alcott's journal: "The pleasantest room in the house was set apart for Beth, and in it was gathered everything that she most loved—flowers, pictures, her piano, the little work-table, the beloved pussies. Father's best books found their way there, mother's easy chair, Jo's desk, Amy's loveliest sketches; and every day Meg brought her babies on a loving pilgrimage, to make sunshine for Aunty Beth" (414). So much furniture is hauled into Beth's room that it comes to resemble a storage facility, but Alcott is shaping the moment toward an important end, for in the midst of her beloved family, Beth is "cherished like a household saint in its shrine." In effect, the room is made over into a launching platform for the departure of the Angel of the House, action derived from fact but considerably embroidered over Alcott's journal entry.

This relatively happy time soon gives way to "such heavy days, such long, long nights, such aching hearts and imploring prayers," with the dying child's "thin hands stretched out to them beseechingly" (415). Her constant companion is Jo, who never leaves her bedside, but sleeps on a couch, waking to tend to her dying sister's needs. "Precious and helpful hours to Jo, for now her heart received the teaching that it needed; lessons in patience were so sweetly taught her, that she could not fail to learn them; charity for all, the lovely spirit that can forgive and truly forget unkindness, the loyalty to duty that makes the hardest easy, and the sincere faith that fears nothing, but trusts undoubtedly" (416). These are precisely the lessons Jane Eyre was unable to learn from the example of Helen Burns's pious death, and echo the sentiments delivered over Little Nell's grave by Dickens: "When Death strikes down the innocent and young, for every fragile form from which he lets the panting spirit free, a hundred virtues rise, in shapes of mercy, charity, and love, to walk the world and bless it" (659).

That is, Beth's dying serves as a rite of passage for Jo, as Betty's did for Lou, and as Beth prepares to cross over the river, to be greeted by "the Shining Ones," Jo is making a crossing herself, into the maturity that only grief can bring. In Vevay, Amy finds solace for Beth's death in Laurie's arms, but Jo, alone with Beth, promises to carry out her beloved sister's wish that she take her place, "and be everything to father and mother when I'm gone" (418). Beth promises her sister, "you'll be happier in doing that, than writing splendid books, or seeing all the world; for love is the only thing that we can carry with us when we go, and it makes the end so easy" (418). Here, Alcott departs from the record of the journal, obeying the literary necessity that the dying utter words of wisdom and advice for the living, and so Ellen Montgomery agrees to replace the dead Alice Humphreys—with some help from Mr. John.

Alcott makes the point that Beth, unlike dying people "in books," does not "utter memorable words, see visions, or depart with beatified countenances," but quietly slips away, yet her final wish to Jo is obviously an eleventh commandment that cannot be ignored. The family, gathered about the deathbed, sees "with grateful eyes the beautiful serenity that soon replaced the pathetic patience that had wrung their hearts so long, and feels with reverent joy, that to their darling death was a benignant angel—not a phantom full of dread" (419). But Jo's greatest pain awaits her, facing the absence of Beth's loving presence, and she calls upon her dead sister's spirit in an agony of loneliness: "Oh, Beth! come back! come back!" Hers is a cry that curiously echoes Heathcliff in his agony, but where Brontë's hero-villain turns to revenge, Jo discovers that in communing with Beth, her "affliction" becomes "a blessing, which chastened grief and strengthened love" (433).

During this ordeal, Jo's mother is strangely missing, whereas we learn from Alcott's journal that Abba Alcott shared the deathbed vigil with Louisa. It is to her father that Jo turns, and "sitting in Beth's little chair close beside him," she confesses her sorrow, her discouragement, and "the want of faith that made her life look so dark, and the sad bewilderment which we call despair" (433). In time, Jo finds herself assuming Beth's identity, "humming the songs Beth used to hum, imitating Beth's orderly ways, and giving the little touches here and there that kept everything fresh and cosy" (434). Here again, Alcott departs from the record of her journal: Betty's death has strengthened her, and brought her closer to God, but there is no such mystical transference of identity.

Jo does not become a household saint, unlike "the heroine of a moral storybook," for she is "only a struggling human girl," yet she strives toward the beautiful ideal of devoting her life "to father and mother, trying to make home as happy to them as they had to her" (435). This, of course, is precisely where Louisa May Alcott unwillingly found herself after the death of her sister Elizabeth, which was fast followed by Anna's betrothal to John Pratt, but where Lou thought of suicide, Jo gets to work. *Little Women* may not be "a moral storybook," but it is after all a Victorian novel meant for young readers, whereas *Jane Eyre* was not.

Instead, drawing on the spiritual aspects of her own experience, Alcott converted Betty's death to a salutory example of influence from beyond the grave: her psyche transformed by Beth's death, Jo returns to her writing, but it is a very different kind of fiction: "[T]aught by love and sorrow, Jo wrote her little stories, and sent them away to make friends for themselves and her." Jo's thoughts now turn to the Professor who had condemned the kind of sensational stories she had been writing before Beth's death, a hint of the resolution yet to come. But for the moment, she resolves to become "a literary spinster, with a pen for a spouse," providing an occasion for the author to beg of her "dear girls" that they not laugh at spinsters, "for often very tender, tragical romances are hidden away in the hearts that beat so quietly under the sober gowns" (441). But this is as close as Jo will come to paddling her own canoe, for spinsterdom is not to be her destiny, nor will writing occupy her time in sequels to come.

After Amy and Laurie come home, bringing the news that they are married, Jo's turn at the altar is next. Love as Marmee observes of Amy has "done much for our little girl" and grief has likewise sweetened Jo, so that when the knock comes on the door, which when opened reveals "a stout, bearded gentleman, beaming on her from the darkness like a midnight sun," rather much a hirsute Mr. Pickwick or a Santa Claus, she is ready to take him in (448, 450). Unlike Ellen Montgomery, Jo is not united with her lover over a deathbed, but it is made clear that she has been prepared for his coming by the agony of losing Beth and by the maturation process that results from the painful loss.

Beth is gone yet she remains "among them—a peaceful presence—invisible, but dearer than ever; since death could not break the household league that love made indissoluble." Much as Beth's passing serves to solidify the "household league," so it prepares Jo for entering her own domestic phase: "While Laurie and Amy were taking conjugal strolls over velvet carpets, as they set their house in order, and planned a blissful future, Mr. Bhaer and Jo were enjoying promenades of a different sort, along muddy roads and sodden fields" (467). It is in passages like that that we are assured that Professor Bhaer brings forward the spirit of the dead Henry Thoreau, much as Jo is transformed by the spirit of Beth, the two of them looking forward to a life quite different from that of Laurie and Amy, and where Alcott's preference lies seems abundantly clear.

Turning her back on sensational fiction, in *Good Wives* Alcott immersed herself, her characters, and her readers deep in the domestic zone, saturated with the conventions of sentimental literature. The muted Brontëan material in *Little Women* is virtually overwhelmed in its sequel by the Dickensian element, following the lead provided by *The Wide, Wide World*. And yet there remains that connubial perplex, Jo's marriage to Mr. Bhaer, which if we can acknowledge the resemblance of Jo's husband not only to Warwick-Thoreau and Moor-Emerson, but also to Bronson Alcott, then the presumably Dickensian finale reverberates with gothic possibilities, though deeply buried in the bosom of sentimentality. Moreover, in marrying Jo to a replicated Bronson, Alcott may have brought about a figuratively incestuous union, blessed by the Mr. March who is the literal stand-in for Bronson, evoking once again the dark version of the Cinderella story.

It is notable that as soon as Jo falls in love with her Professor, the autobiographical element ceases and the pure fiction begins, for even as Jo marries Mr. Bhaer, Alcott has removed herself from the action. Jo may marry the older man abstracted from the Brontëan convention, but in bringing about the consummation, Lou absented herself from that felicity, paddling her own canoe as fast as possible in the opposite direction. In brief, Alcott's book validated her father's notion of woman's proper role but in doing so she withdrew herself from the incestuous scene, much as Jane Eyre fled from an adulterous union. The marriage is sustained through the sequel, *Little Men,* but without the autobiographical connection, for Lou Alcott broke free of Jo Bhaer to reappear in 1873 as Christie Devon in *Work.* It was quite a different role, one intimate with the struggle for women's rights, and involved a marriage of the heroine with a reasonable facsimile of Thoreau. Like Warwick, Christie's husband dies a hero's death, this time in the war that was virtually invisible in *Little Women,* leaving his widow to struggle on alone, Alcott's own chosen lot.

8

The Glad Boy in the Castle:
Frances Hodgson Burnett and the
Brontëan (Dis)Connection

> It is through art, and through art only, that we can realize our
> perfection.
>
> —Oscar Wilde

I

WHEN CHARLOTTE BRONTË'S LAST, UNFINISHED NOVEL WAS PUBlished as a fragment in *Cornhill Magazine* in 1860, William Makepeace Thackeray provided an introduction entitled "The Last Sketch" in which he avoided any discussion of the fragment entitled "Emma" (which suggests he had not read it) and instead provided a meditation on the destiny of all such work left incomplete. "Is there record kept anywhere of fancies conceived, beautiful, unborn? Some day will they assume form in some yet undeveloped light?" ("Emma: A Fragment," included in Brontë, *The Professor,* 240). Thackeray began his introduction by describing an artist friend's depiction of Shakespeare's Titania, a work left unfinished at the painter's death, and found his head swarming with visions of "fairy elves . . . in laughing clusters." These "gambolling sprites" carried his imagination to a "sphere unknown," a place beyond this mortal world where the "Might Have Been" attains completion: "Some day our spirits may be permitted to walk in galleries of fancies more wondrous and beautiful than any achieved works which at present we see, and our minds to behold and delight in masterpieces which poets' and artists' minds have fathered and conceived only."

Thackeray's is a self-consciously charming conjecture, a transcendent Tate Gallery that lies beyond the bourn, a Louvre from which no tourist returns. It is not at all in keeping with the satiric, even cynical perspective of the man who delighted in disappointing Charlotte Brontë's high-minded notion of the public role that persons of his stature as a writer should fulfil: "She was angry with her favorites," noted Thackeray in his appraisal of the author's personality, "if their conduct or conversation fell below her ideal" (241). Brontë was "an austere little Joan of Arc marching in upon us, and rebuking our easy lives, our easy morals."

> A great and holy reverence of right and truth seemed to be with her always. . . . As one thinks of that life so noble, so lonely—of that passion for truth—of those nights and nights of eager study, swarming fancies, invention, depression, elation, prayer; as one reads the necessarily incomplete, though most touching and admirable history of the heart that throbbed in this one little frame—of this one amongst the myriads of souls that have lived and died on this great earth—this great earth?—this little speck in the infinite universe of God,—with what wonder do we think of to-day, with what awe await to-morrow, when that which is now but darkly seen shall be clear? (241–42)

As the deathbed scenes in *The Wide, Wide World* and the first version of *Moods* bear adequate testimony, Victorians thought of the final words delivered from a person on the point of dying as having a life beyond the grave. Thackeray here regarded unfinished works of art and literature as belonging to the same class of expressions. He told the story of Brontë's reading the opening chapters of "Emma" to her husband, an anecdote credited to Elizabeth Gaskell's biography—"What a story is that of that family of poets in their solitude yonder on the gloomy northern moors!"

He recounted Arthur Nicholls's cautionary remark, and his wife's assurance that she would remedy any hint of "repetition." But, alas! "the trembling little hand was to write no more. The heart, newly awakened to love and happiness, and throbbing with maternal hope, was soon to cease to beat; that intrepid outspeaker and champion of truth, that eager, impetuous redresser of wrong, was to be called out of the world's fight and struggle, to lay down the shining arms, and to be removed to a sphere . . . where truth complete, and right triumphant, no longer need to wage war."

I quote at length from this overdone tribute, because although it was hardly typical of Thackeray or worthy of Charlotte Brontë, it most certainly was in keeping with the mortuary mood of the Victorian sensibility in the United States as well as in England. Moreover, Thackeray's mingling of fairy sprites and the unalloyed happiness to be enjoyed in heaven was in complete syncopation with the lively imagination of a little girl who was born in Manchester, England, in 1849, and who may well have read the fragment entitled "The Last Sketch" in the *Cornhill Magazine* when it was first published in April, 1860. Even at age eleven Frances Hodgson was a prodigious reader of whatever romantic periodic literature reached her hand.

Thackeray toward the end of his lavishly sentimental introduction wondered about the whereabouts of "the rest" of the tiny fragment, and whether "the leaf [might] be turned some day, and the story be told" (242). He of course was thinking about that far, far better place where all unfinished things attain perfection, having as Ben Franklin wryly noted had all their errata corrected, but little Frances Hodgson may have taken it as a double challenge. We know that the precocious young author thought of herself as queen of the fairies, and as such possessing a magic wand with which she might provide Charlotte Brontë's sketch its missing pages.

"We all seek an ideal in life," are the first words in Charlotte Brontë's fragment (243). They could serve as a motto for not only her writings but those of the author best known to us as Frances Hodgson Burnett and most remembered for her books for children, most especially *Little Lord Fauntleroy, The Little Princess,* and *The Secret Garden.* Otherwise there is a world of difference between the two writers, for although in her early middle age Burnett became interested in spiritualism and after the death of her oldest son wrote stories about the presence amongst us of the still-living dead, she was never a writer of books in the gothic mode. Her ghosts always turn out to be friendly apparitions, "White People" as she called them, indistinguishable from regular folks save for their silence.

Like both Brontë and Alcott, Burnett wrote fiction at an early age, but unlike Brontë's fantastic and Alcott's sensational tales, Frances Hodgson's juvenile stories were romantic in the most positive sense of that word, being not about the violent but the tender passions felt by wealthy, high-placed, and noble-intentioned persons. She began her career writing for adults, commencing with the novel that brought her overnight fame, *That Lass o'Lowrie's* (1877); though set in the Lancashire coal mines of England, with a realistic use of dialect and socially disadvantaged characters, the story was irradiated with a positive light.

Hers were happy compositions, the kind that Patrick Brontë preferred, unalloyed by tragic possibilities, a viewpoint that especially qualified her as a writer for young, primarily female, readers. Henry James was numbered among her friends and enthusiasts, and her stories for children fulfilled James's expectations that were disappointed by Alcott's *Eight Cousins.* That is, they were populated by "beautiful specimens" of humanity and lacked any suggestion of the satirical and smart. Which is to say that Burnett's stories for children were intensely sentimental and were domestic only in the sense that the recovery of near relations or a reasonable facsimile was a dominant theme.

Moreover, though like Brontë, Warner, and Alcott, Burnett was influenced by Dickens, the death of children was never her theme, and even the deaths of parents, essential to the orphan idea, always happen off stage. Like Jane Eyre, her heroines ended up happily enthroned in a loving envelope, but unlike Brontë's parable of a long-suffering but finally fortunate young woman, Burnett's fables did not require that females humble themselves before men or that males lose a few operative parts to qualify as husbands. Moreover, none of her Victorian fables for children ends with marriage, her heroic young folks like Horatio Alger's reaching closure well short of (pre-Freudian) sexual awareness. Yet like Brontë and the other writers she influenced, the Cinderella story is essential to her plots.

Burnett's use of the fragment Charlotte Brontë left behind is a revealing register of the great differences between the two writers, both English in origins and education, as well as the similarities between Burnett and Alcott, both of whom are accounted American writers. Alcott is undeniably one of our own, whereas Burnett's assignment is warranted by mutual matters of adoption: she came to the United States at the age of sixteen, had her early work published here, and thought of herself as a transatlantic literary force. In her most famous story for children, *Little Lord Fauntleroy* (1886), Burnett encouraged a rapprochement between her native and adoptive lands that within a decade of the book's publication had become a diplomatic fact. A counterpart to her friend, Henry James, she was a literary amphibian, British by birth, American by self-adoption.

Her friendship with James developed after her emergence as a prominent writer, and aside from the problematic matter of comparative genius (she excelled at writing for the stage where he did not), they in effect complemented one another in sharing this international focus. Her novel *A Fair Barbarian* (1881), written before she met James, was an implicit response to *Daisy Miller* (1878), being an upbeat story for adult readers in which an innocent girl from the American West triumphs over the stiff and stodgy residents of a British provincial town. In that story resides the seed of *Little Lord Fauntleroy*.

Like so many of the authors born in the nineteenth century whose most famous novels deal with the sufferings of orphans,

Burnett lost a parent (her father) at an early age, and as an American writer by adoption, she is something of a foster author. Like Dickens and Brontë in England and Susan Warner and Alcott in America, Burnett experienced poverty and like all the other writers listed above she began writing professionally—as a letter covering the first manuscript sent to an editor stated—with "remuneration" as her "object" (*The One I Knew Best,* 312). She was, like Alcott, chief breadwinner in her family at an early age, sending a stream of short stories out of Knoxville, Tennessee, then a remote village on the southern frontier.

Knoxville was a long way from the centers of publication in the United States, but was even farther from the Manchester mills, where Burnett had grown up with modest but comfortable expectations. Her father, a hardware merchant specializing in decorative materials for homes, had died young, when Frances was only five, and though her mother had managed the business with relative success, the northern blockade of southern ports during the Civil War virtually halted the importation of cotton to Great Britain, creating a general depression in England. The business failed and in 1865 the family joined Mrs. Burnett's brother in Tennessee, traveling south from Canada so that their first introduction to the New World was not a typically immigrant but a wilderness experience.

None of this had an immediate impact on the imagination of the teen-aged young woman, who after an unsuccessful attempt at keeping school à la Brontë, began sending out stories to popular journals, the first of which was accepted by the second magazine to which it was mailed, and all the rest found a ready market. By her own account, Frances Hodgson had been spinning fictions for years, romantic stories akin to fairy tales, and what she wrote in America was virtually insulated from the frontier environment, being so English in character and polished in manner as to cause some concern among editors that the stories mailed from Knoxville might have been plagiarized from British magazines.

Along with Warner and Alcott, although entirely on her own terms, Burnett was responsible for the translation of the Brontëan world into highly sentimental, trans-Atlantic terms, not precisely what Thackeray was talking about, but very close as we shall see. If Alcott was chiefly influenced not so much by *Jane Eyre* as by Elizabeth Gaskell's account of the Brontë family, Burnett was able to abstract the fairy element from Brontë's gothic tale while holding its orphan heroine well back from puberty. There was never a hint of sin in her version of Cinderella, a prepuberty purification process that also eliminated the possibility of marriage.

The author's own married life was irregular. In 1873 she wed a promising young eye specialist from Knoxville, Dr. Swan Burnett, and in 1877 the couple moved to Washington, where the newly famous author was welcomed into high society. Having given Burnett two sons, and published a string of well-received novels, she drifted apart from her husband, spending much of her time in England and Europe. Amicable divorce from Burnett in 1898 was followed by an apparently reluctant union with British-born Stephen Townesend, another doctor but one ambitious to become an actor, who was much younger and considerably weaker in character than his bride.

The arrangement did not endure for long, though it was never legally terminated, presumably because Frances felt no need to repeat her vows a third time. All of her life Burnett (after leaving Townesend she took back her first married and her professional name) had intense relationships with women, but she positively doted (if at times dictatorially) on her two sons. The death of Lionel in 1890 from galloping consumption influenced her subsequent writings, much as the death of Harriet Beecher Stowe's own little boy inspired the leitmotif of lost children in *Uncle Tom's Cabin*.

Where the death of Charlie Stowe contributed to the cause of antislavery, the death of Lionel Burnett increased his mother's commitment to spiritualism. That celebrant of logical thought, Arthur Conan Doyle, was likewise attracted to the notion of life beyond death when his son was killed during the First World War, whom he attempted to reach through spirit mediums, and he was therefore easily taken in by two young girls who claimed to have photographed real fairies. There was never a question of Frances Burnett being taken in—fairies were in the forefront of her imagination from the very beginning—but rather than searching for wee folk in the wildwood, by her own account Frances came even as a child to believe that she herself might be one of them, a bona fide dryad. All this background helps to explain the way in which Burnett brought Brontë's unfinished novel to completion.

II

As Arthur Nicholls remarked to his bride, Charlotte's last, unfinished work is familiar in theme and character: the narrator is a woman, Mrs. Chalfont, who tells the story of a little girl, called

Mathilda Fitzgibbon, who is brought by her father to live at a boarding school for young ladies, run by the two "Misses Wilcox." Obviously inspired by the efforts of Charlotte and Emily to start a similar school, the establishment is a fledgling and not too successful endeavor, with only three young ladies enrolled. Thus the acquisition of Mathilda, who to all appearances is the daughter of a wealthy young aristocrat, is regarded as a blessing by the mistresses of "Fuchsia Lodge." For Mathilda will be a "show pupil," her trunkful of finery a virtual advertisement for the school, and she is to be constant company for Miss Mabel Wilcox, the senior sister in charge: "Miss Fitzgibbon was to be favoured, petted, and screened on all possible occasions" ("Emma," 245).

These attentions, however, "brought their object no real benefit," for the Wilcoxs' favoritism inspired resentment among the other young ladies: "A favourite has no friends" (247). Mathilda's lonely, wretched situation catches the attention and sympathy of a gentleman friend of the Wilcoxes, Mr. Ellin, who realizes that the girl is an exceptional child. She is also a sensitive plant, shrinking from public view, and as the first year of her residence draws to a close she has fainting spells and is found walking about in her sleep. In marked contrast to Mathilda we are given "Diana . . . a daring, brave girl, much loved and a little feared by her comrades," a reminder including her name of how Charlotte viewed her sister Emily, for Diana is the name given to the Rivers sister modelled after her.

Like Emily Brontë, Diana is a rebel, who openly resents the favoritism shown to Mathilda Fitzgibbon. As for Miss Mabel Wilcox, though "not without prettiness," and hence of some interest to Mr. Ellin, the school-mistress is a sharp-nosed, thin-lipped woman with red hair and a "business-like, very practical" turn of mind: "She never in her life knew a refinement of feeling or of thought; she is entirely limited, respectable, and self-satisfied. . . . Miss Wilcox is a very proper and decorous person; but she could not be delicate or modest, because she is naturally destitute of sensitiveness" (252).

When payment for Mathilda's schooling comes due, a note Mabel has sent to the presumed father is returned with the notice that no such person nor any such address exists. Miss Wilcox reacts in predictable, cruel-stepmother fashion ("Her interest had been injured—her pocket wounded—she was vindicating her rights—and she had no eye to see, and no nerve to feel, but for the point in hand"), and the little girl falls instantly from the dubious paradise of Wilcoxian favor to disdain: "I never could really like that child," Mabel tells Mr. Ellin. "She has had every indulgence in this house; and I am sure I made great sacrifice of feeling to principle in showing her much attention; for I could not make any one believe the degree of antipathy I have all along felt towards her" (255).

As Mr. Ellin looks on with apparent indifference, Miss Wilcox summons the little girl and in effect denounces her for a liar, demanding that she tell the truth about herself. The now former Mathilda Fitzgibbon can only tremble in response, regarded as a sure sign of guilt by the hard, unfeeling Mabel Wilcox, and when pressed even harder by the unrelenting schoolmistress, the little girl comes close to fainting. She calls out to Mr. Ellin, who rushes to support her, carries her upstairs to bed, and cautions Miss Wilcox against continuing her harsh treatment of the unfortunate and as yet unknown quantity: "That kind of nature," he opines, "is very different from yours." With Ellin's promise to question the girl in a more kindly fashion the fragment ends.

Thus the story as Arthur Nicholls suggested does have a number of elements familiar to readers of Charlotte Brontë's already published novels, especially *Jane Eyre,* with its use of an orphan turned over to the untender mercies of a boarding school. But the closest parallels are to elements in *The Professor,* which was not published until after the author's death, and had already been parted out for *Villette.* In his mixture of skepticism and a good-natured generosity, Mr. Ellin looks back to Mr. Hunsden, with some hints of Charles Crimsworth, and Mathilda likewise is much closer to Frances Henri (at the start of the novel) than to Jane Eyre. Mabel Wilcox is clearly an updated Mme. Reuter, sharing her red hair and bossy ways, and there are hints of a romantic connection with the young Mr. Ellin, who will turn his attention instead to the wretched girl who serves as the personal football of the schoolmistress.

The stress at the end of the fragment is on the stand-off between Miss Wilcox and the girl, with Ellin interposing himself on behalf of the girl. She we must assume is the Emma of the title, which like "Betty Hodge, Polly Smith, Hannah Jones," the plebeian names suggested in place of the obvious alias "Mathilda Fitzgibbon" by Mr. Ellin, is a signatory of ordinariness not wealth and privilege. But what Charlotte Brontë intended to do with *her* "Emma" remains unknown: the only thing certain we can derive from this suggestive shard is the sharp edge that tells us the author had not yet exhausted her rage regarding Mme. Heger, and yet given Brontë's proclivity for May–December unions, we may assume that the sympathy Ellin feels for little Emma will blossom from what is at the start a positive bedside manner.

But then there remains the forthright Diana, who in her outspoken fealty to righteousness suggests not only Emily but Charlotte Brontë herself, as described by Thackeray, with a hint therefore of the morally rigid Jane Eyre. Perhaps it is to Diana that Mr. Ellin would ultimately be attracted, but then we will never know what the author had in mind—if she did indeed have an ending toward which she was heading—while we do know what Frances Hodgson Burnett did with Brontë's unfinished novel. As long ago as 1950, Marghanita Laski noted the "interesting" similarities between Burnett's *Sara Crewe* and Brontë's fragment, but for our purposes it serves as a key to the essential difference between the two authors, hence to the shift in values as the Brontëan tradition crossed the Atlantic and was inherited by a younger generation of writers. For what Burnett did with the fragment is quite different from any direction toward which Charlotte Brontë could possibly have taken the conflict established in her opening chapters.

In framing her novella, what Burnett borrowed from Brontë is the essential situation and the final contretemps, but there is no sympathetic Mr. Ellin present on the spot to protect the poor young girl, nor is the heroine involved even as an innocent in some kind of con-game or hoax. Like so many suffering children downloaded into Victorian literature from Dickens's novels, Sara Crewe is an orphan. Along with Oliver Twist and Jane Eyre, moreover, she will recover a fortune, which like Jane Eyre's money comes from an exotic place, not the West but the East Indies, and like Oliver she will become a beloved foster-child at the end of the story with no marriage in sight.

In 1886, when Frances Burnett began writing the story of Sara Crewe, Rudyard Kipling was just emerging with *Departmental Ditties* as a prominent new author; by 1888, when Burnett's novella was published, *Plain Tales from the Hills* and *Soldiers Three* were in print; and by 1905, when Burnett enlarged the story as a popular drama and then converted the play into a much thicker novel, renamed *The Little Princess*, Kipling and India were thoroughly implanted in the Anglo-American imagination. We may doubt that Kipling had much influence on Burnett, yet a number of critics have suggested that we cannot separate *Sara Crewe* (1888) or its enlargement in *The Little Princess* (1905) from the pervasive matter of British empire. It is a contingency that was hardly at the forefront of the imagination of either Dickens (for whom transport to Australia was hardly a glorious imperial prospect) or Charlotte Brontë, but the English presence in India serves as background to three of Burnett's novels (including *The Secret Garden*) much as the Civil War provides a significant context for *Little Women*.

The ideological debate that gave way to open conflict is never an explicit issue in Alcott's book, although her family was fiercely abolitionist and during John Brown's trial his daughters found refuge in the Alcott home. Likewise, despite its disastrous effect on the family fortunes, Burnett ignores the Civil War in her fiction, nor does she seem to have been particularly interested in mounting neocolonialist apologetics for the British presence in India. Burnett was a romantic escapist, and for her India served as an exotic because far-off locale, associated in her fiction with great fortunes and fatal tropical fevers. In the expanded version of *Sara Crewe*, the heroine's recovered wealth is associated with diamond mines, and the production of diamonds in India predates any colonial presence. But by the turn of the century diamond mines as a speculative venture were associated with Cecil Rhodes and South Africa, and also with the Boer War, a nasty exhibition of the darker aspects of British colonialism and not a topic of any interest to a "romantick lady"—the title of her son Vivian's biography of Burnett.

All evidence suggests that if India as a land of mystery had a certain impact on Burnett's creative consciousness beyond serving as an exotic region, it was as an empire of the spirit, not of territorial acquisition. By 1883, as Vivian testifies, Burnett had become interested in "some of the new philosophies such as Spiritualism and Theosophy, which had Eastern origins, and this led her to an interest in the new idea of Mind-Healing" (127), an interest Dr. Burnett seems not to have shared. Although his mother never became converted to Mary Baker Eddy's religion, Vivian tells us that she read *Science and Health* and occasionally attended Christian Science services. "Throughout all of her later books," he writes in *The Romantick Lady*, "will be found traces of the faith in that Allness of Good, which is one of the fundamentals of Christian Science" (377). But much as Christian Science owed something to Transcendentalism, so the Concord philosophers had a debt to Eastern thought.

Christian Science was a therapeutic faith to which Burnett was initially attracted because of her own bouts with "nervous" complaints, that signature of the Victorian creative consciousness and (as Freud suggested) the dubious fruit of Victorian sexual repression. But Christian Science was also an optimistic faith that suited her own deep-seated but vague notion that all things work out for the best, in effect a mixture of Ralph Waldo Emerson and peppermint tea. It is notable that when in 1879 the newly famous Frances Burnett was given a banquet by the Papyrus Club in Boston, she was taken on that ritual visit to Concord made by Rebecca Harding twenty years earlier to pay homage to the man Vivian styled "the dear old Sage of Concord," who was by then well into what was politely termed dotage (94).

This is not to say that a reading of Emerson's essays was a formative influence on Burnett, but it does suggest that the vogue for "the Allness of Good" irradiating the Seventies and Eighties was but an updated and strategically simplified version of the Emersonian Oversoul. It was also a spiritual equivalent to the rage for Emerson's ideal of self-reliance that when reduced to a formula found an eager audience among champions of the Protestant Ethic, of which the Horatio Alger hero was an early and Andrew Carnegie a later example. Nor was Burnett herself untouched by the regnant American notion that we all have in us the secret of success, that in dreams are found realities but only after adding hard work to the equation. And yet for her there was a mystical element involved—equated by her with "magic"—a power operating outside the framework of the Protestant Ethic, a hint of which may be found in the closing pages of *Jane Eyre*.

The Far East was the source also of Thoreau's version of Transcendentalism, but it was not the *Bhagavadgita* that was the operating influence on the author of *Sara Crewe* and *The Secret Garden*. The famous if eventually notorious Mme. Helena Petrovna Blavatsky arrived in the United States in 1870, and her lectures on spiritualism had an instant vogue, so much so that Blavatsky became a naturalized citizen, recognizing the financial advantages of her popularity. Nor could the profitability of the interest in spiritualism have escaped Burnett's notice, though we may accept her son's witness that she was a sincere convert.

Certainly spiritualism's emphasis on the divine element in all human beings, needing only contact to release great personal energies, would have appealed to Burnett's mystical streak, behind which there lay a voracious hunger for power. That Blavatsky claimed to be channeling two mahatmas, having spent a critical decade (1848–58) residing in not only Tibet but India itself, adds an occult dimension to the whole matter of British empire. Contrary to neocolonialist readings, this is the most meaningful use of imperialism by the romantic Frances Hodgson Burnett, a passage from India of benevolent spirits not material wealth.

Suffering is the empowering agenda in the novels of Brontë, Warner, Finley, and Alcott, but for Burnett it was spiritualism, implicit at first but explicit by the time she wrote *The Secret Garden.* Modern feminists have testified to the attractions for American women of spiritualism, beginning with the seances held by the Fox sisters a decade before the Civil War. Like early Christianity it was a source of power available to women who were able to harness energy from the infinite Beyond, for spiritualism unlike the organized church provided a conduit of divinity on an egalitarian plan. Again, suffering was to female suffrage closely allied, but as Hawthorne seems to have realized—when in *The Blithedale Romance* he coupled a seance medium and her master with other nutcake reformers—spiritualism had its radical aspect too.

In the post–Civil War enthusiasm for psychic phenomena, however, there was expressed a force for good far beyond what could be obtained by merely attaining the vote. Like Emersonian Transcendentalism, Spiritualism as a faith focussed less on society than on the individual, who could use the power derived from contact with the spirit world to effect social change, perhaps, but it was for many devotees simply a conduit of inner strength, maturity if you will on the highest plane. It is this new-age emphasis that explains the critical difference between *Sara Crewe* and both *Jane Eyre* and *The Professor,* as well as *The Wide, Wide World, Elsie Dinsmore,* and *Little Women:* the maturation process in Burnett's book for children may involve some physical suffering but the submission of self to authoritarian (usually male) rule is not a key element. Her little heroines are all self-directed and self-reliant, which, according to Gillian Avery, is a key to the difference between American and British fiction intended for young female readers (*Behold the Child,* 155–56). Avery therefore classifies the British-born Burnett as an American author, though most of her best known stories are set in England.

Burnett turned to writing *Sara Crewe* immediately after completing *Little Lord Fauntleroy* in 1886; indeed the sudden and unexpected popularity of that story of a happy little boy in a velvet suit not only acted to delay the writing of the subsequent novel but may have contributed to its relatively short plot and hasty denouement. Both were illustrated by Reginald Birch, and both appeared in almost identical embossed covers and format, suggesting either that the publisher was trying to profit from the popularity of the first book or that from the beginning the author thought of the two as somehow sharing a common interface.

I am not sure how far we can push this notion, but much as *Little Lord Fauntleroy* was intended in part to reunite Great Britain with its lost colonies in the New World, so *Sara Crewe* established a mystical connection to the colonies yet remaining. The point being that both of these novels, specifically aimed at a young audience but popular as well with adults, contain ideological subtexts derived from intensely felt cultural movements of the day. These frames of reference help to place the author and her work in the sequence so far established of Jane Eyre's American daughters. Moreover, both stories, taken as one unit, provided inspiration for women writers in the United States who continued to make modifications of the tradition traceable to Charlotte Brontë.

III

Let me say at the start that the Brontë connection in *Little Lord Fauntleroy* is nonexistent, that we are interested here in Burnett's most popular book because it starts us on the way toward understanding the Brontëan aspects of her greatest book, *The Secret Garden*. Not that the story of Cedric Errol is not interesting on its own merits, being unique among books intended for children because of its influence as a fashion statement. We know that Burnett loved finery, which despite her stout build tended toward the frilly and feminine, that a new dress was for her a major dramatic moment, often revealed to friends and family by pulling open sliding pocket-doors to reveal the author draped in her newest acquisition.

And so Burnett fashioned for her youngest son, Vivian, who served as the model for little Cedric, an outfit of elegant design, recorded in a photograph she sent to Reginald Birch to be used in drawing his illustrations. It seems to have been in part derived from the costume worn by Gainsborough's "Blue Boy," but because of the fabric in question—black velvet—Cedric Errol resembles a boy Hamlet, suggesting perpetual mourning for his dead father, and certainly his feelings for his mother doth have a Hamlet-like look.

The boy's long ringlets were an anachronism promoting gender confusion, and the result was imposed by doting mothers on several generations of unhappy American boys. Gillian Avery, who finds *Little Lord Fauntleroy* "curiously compelling" despite its sentimentality, notes that "the odious reputation of the child is founded perhaps partly on the illustrations by Reginald Birch, which represent the boy with fringe and ringlets, always dressed, even when riding out in the country, in [his] black velvet suit and Vandyke collar" (*Nineteenth Century Children,* 178). Avery notes that Burnett mentions it in the novel "only once or twice as a holiday suit," and Birch's repetitious use of it in his illustrations may have been an act of artistic revenge, expressing his resentment over having been directed to use the photograph of Vivian for his model.

Through the agency of Outcault's Buster Brown, the Fauntleroy outfit was given new life, because Buster, despite his androgynous appearance, was like Tom Sawyer and Penrod Schofield the essence of mischief, while Cedric is that nemesis of both Tom and Penrod, a Good Boy. That Fauntleroy on the stage was a role assigned a young woman, though a convention of the day, helped certify the connection. Yet Burnett is at great pains to insist that Cedric is a regular guy, who excels at informal street games like foot races, for he is hard-muscled and very fast, but not because he must distance other little boys eager to do damage to his outfit.

Gillian Avery imagines that "thousands of young readers must have gloried in the noble way the young Lord Fauntleroy bore himself," for he is a manly child, who carries off his fancy dress clothing with the necessary assurance that there is nothing lacking in his virility (177). The kid may we say *tiene cajones.* Indeed, his little manliness is a tribute both to his aristocratic, British blood and to his American upbringing, a mingling of nature and nurture intended in part as a gesture of goodwill to both countries at once.

There is however a second agenda at work in the novel, for Cedric's notorious costume not a little resembles that worn by Oscar Wilde while on tour in the United States in the early 1880s. It likewise resembles the costume worn by Bunthorne in Gilbert and Sullivan's *Patience* (1881), a parody of Wilde and his aesthetic theories. The similarity is probably not coincidental: when Wilde was on tour in America in 1882 he was entertained by Burnett in her home in Washington, D.C., one of a stream of celebrities who were thus honored. Dressed (as Vivian attests) in "a black silk clawhammer coat, fancily flowered dark waistcoat, knee breeches, silk stockings, and patent leather pumps with broad buckles," Wilde wore a flower in his buttonhole (113).

He was likewise buttonholed by his finery-loving hostess: "They sat talking together in a corner for most of the afternoon," and the guest left behind him as her son attested "an increased passion for the 'aesthetic' in the household," of which Vivian was soon a victim. Burnett became a devotee of Wilde's ideas, generally thought of as the Aesthetic Movement and otherwise as the Gospel of Beauty. Notably, one of Wilde's own sons would be named Vivian, without Burnett's excuse (she had intuited—"previsioned"—a daughter, who was to be named Vivien), suggesting a mutual admiration society.

For Wilde, aesthetics were to a spiritual experience close allied, and tasteful interior decoration would not only enhance but improve the lives of those so surrounded with things of beauty. Wilde's theory can be traced back to Ruskin's meditation on the effects of physical surroundings on the development of character, carrying the older man's idea of the beneficial effects of model cottages for working people forward, and transforming the surroundings enjoyed by persons of wealth toward a similar end. Burne-Jones and Rossetti would be associated with the aesthetics movement but it was James McNeill Whistler, the expatriate American painter, who with Wilde enjoyed a certain notoriety while promoting the cause of exquisite interior design.

This involved a bold use of textured wallpapers, including gilt and silver, as well as richly figured textiles, porcelain, fans, and other decorative objects imported from Japan, the source of the "floating world," the patterned woodcuts so influential on Western art of the impressionist period. As the daughter of parents whose family business sold accoutrements used in interior design, and as a woman for whom decor and costuming were an essential adjunct to a life well lived, Frances Hodgson Burnett was open as Wilde's ubiquitous flower to the principles of the Aesthetic Movement. As we shall see, it is not only Lord Fauntleroy's outfit that testifies to the extent to which aestheticism lends its pervading spirit to Burnett's story.

It needs to be said at this point that there are other possible sources for Cedric's famous garment: as Katharine Anthony pointed out in her biography, Louisa May Alcott in 1872 wrote a story about a boy his mother calls "Cupid," because he is a pretty child who loves everyone and who is loved by everyone, and who causes all those around him to love one another, so that he is "a regular little god of love" (261). But the boy goes about in somewhat more substantial clothing than that associated with the pagan god, being "gorgeous . . . in small buckled shoes, purple silk hose, black velvet knickerbockers, and jacket with a lace collar, which, with his yellow hair falling in long, curling love-locks behind, [the which] made him look like an old picture of a young cavalier."

Moreover, in 1950, Marghanita Laski, in one of the first modern studies to take Burnett seriously as an author, noted that the boy

hero of Juliana Horatia Ewing's *A Story of a Short Life,* first published in 1882, wore a costume similar to that in which Fauntleroy
appears (82). As described by Gillian Avery, Ewing's "Leonard is
one of those beautiful boy heroes who were a feature of the last
two decades of the century; brave, incapable of a dishonourable
thought or word, lovely to look upon, and with centuries of noble
blood behind him," a figure which, derived from the British chivalric tradition, certainly suggests the literary pattern to which
Fauntleroy was cut (*Nineteenth Century Children,* 158).

Leonard's "quaint" outfit, likewise, is "a holiday dress of crimson velvet, with collars and ruffles of old lace." On the other hand,
according to Laski, "by 1882 Mrs. Burnett's boys were already
dressed in this fashion," a costume that by then was widely associated with Wilde, giving Oscar and Vivian the priority while not
ruling out a pervasive generational penchant for costume reinforcing the British aristocratic tradition, akin to the revival of interest in the chivalric ideal. In Ewing's book, moreover, the costume is definitely connected to the imperial presence, Leonard
being (in Avery's words) "a boy who passionately longs to be a soldier" like Ewing's husband, a major in the British army.

Laski also notes the Wilde connection, his "visit to Washington
in 1881, when he was entertained by Mrs. Burnett and was wearing a velvet coat with just such velvet knee-breeches, long stockings and buckled shoes" (82). Wilde may have chosen his costume
as a nostalgic gesture, but his main intention was to present himself in what he presumed was elegant beauty. While he was still a
student at Oxford, Wilde's ostentatious displays of couture were
not regarded by his fellow students as either loveable or mannish:
in retaliation they wrecked his room and tossed him into the Cher-
well—Wilde not having the leg power given Lord Fauntleroy.

At what precise date Burnett began dressing her sons in black
velvet and white lace is not ascertainable, but as Laski notes it
seems to have started in the early 1880s, after she and Dr. Burnett
settled in Washington, and the clothes soon became sufficiently
notorious as to earn coverage in the local newspapers. The insin-
uations were such that the mother felt it necessary to communicate to the press a statement declaring that her sons though beautiful and beautifully dressed were regular boys for all of that, an
apologia that would be implicit in the character of the boy Vivian
inspired. Moreover, as he testified, the novel was written at just
the time his mother was in synchronization with the aesthetic
movement. Cedric Errol may share both the costume and the lov-

ing efflatus shed by Alcott's Cupid as well as the noble qualities of little Leonard, but the net effect of the boy on others is inextricable from the gospel promoted by the evangelists of beauty, of whom the foremost in 1884 was Oscar Wilde.

The plot of *Little Lord Fauntleroy* turns on the recovery of the hero's British title and estate, a common theme of the day. In both news stories and fanciful fictions, Americans seek or are suddenly awarded English estates, a genre of which Mark Twain's *The American Claimant* (1883) is a typical example. A counterpart to this romantic theme was provided by less happy stories of Americans seeking aristocratic titles by marrying them, a duplex situation that provided the plot of Burnett's tale but did not supply the spirit that gave it energy and meaning. That was the role of aestheticism combined with the allness of goodness derived from the teachings of spiritualism, a mixture that resulted in a quite novel variation on the idea of influence, no longer a matter of deathbed instructions.

Little Cedric is carefully crafted as a charming, happy, and beautiful child, and it is his physical attractiveness as well as his upbeat attitude that will be the agents bringing about his crusty grandfather's transformation, the conversion on which the story turns. And the velvet suit is essential to the picture, for as Mary, his mother's Irish-American maid, puts it, when Cedric steps outside "ivvery man, woman, and choild looks afther him in his bit of a black velvet skirt made out of the misthress's ould gownd. An' his little head up, an' his curly hair flyin' and shinin'. It's loike a young lord he looks" (*Little Lord Fauntleroy*, 12).

That Dickens likewise used Tiny Tim as a signatory of Scrooge's reformation suggests the ultimate source of this idea, although Bret Harte's "The Luck of Roaring Camp" provided a more recent example of how an innocent child can inspire moral reformation on a large scale. (In a letter to me, Gillian Avery has suggested the priority of the situation in Thackeray's *Vanity Fair*, where old Mr. Osborne undergoes a Scrooge-like transformation because of his love for his grandson.) But where little Tim Cratchit in true Victorian fashion is a cripple hence a sentimental draw, and where the Luck drowns in a virtual flood of tears, Cedric has no physical handicap and succumbs to no natural disaster. Moreover, it is his vitality as much as his beauty and charm that contributes to the plot, where Ewing's Leonard (as the title of the book suggests) dies young, brought down (as Avery tells us) by "one of those mysterious spinal afflictions that decimated the heroes and heroines of Victorian popular literature" (*Nineteenth Century Children*, 158).

Though Cedric is British by paternity, his mother is an American, and he has been brought up in the United States. He shares the get-up-and-go spirit evinced by those American boy heroes, Twain's Tom Sawyer and Aldrich's Tom Bailey, "bad boys" who are actually good at heart. Cedric being a good boy never gets into scrapes, and his friends are adults, like the groceryman, Mr. Hobbs, a relationship perhaps inspired by George Peck's popular "Bad Boy" series. Hobbs is a rabid patriot who hates British aristocrats and who has made a little republican out of Cedric, providing an awkward moment when his young friend becomes little Lord Fauntleroy. And the boy's other confidant in New York is a bootblack named Dick, reminding us of the instant popularity of Horatio Alger's *Ragged Dick* when it was published in 1868, the story of a "bad" boy who made good.

Burnett's New York bootblack has an inexplicable lower-class London accent, but like Alger's Dick he has a heart of gold, and though "he had been a street waif nearly all his life . . . he had never been a bad boy, and he had always had a private yearning for a more respectable kind of existence," the major theme of Alger's book (167). Burnett's ambitious bootblack will serve a critical role in the novel's denouement, much as Mr. Hobbs will set aside his ardently republican principles at the end of the story and join his little friend Cecil in England among the detested aristocracy. All of these details are in the service of Burnett's strategy of rapprochement, and they also indicate the extent to which she was aware of the popular culture of her adopted country.

But these American sources play a minor role in the story, which from the beginning centers on the bond between the beautiful little Cedric and his mother, whom he calls "Dearest," the *nom de coeur* by which Burnett insisted (presumably inspiring Joan Crawford to do likewise) that she be addressed by her children. The relationship between the boy and his mother is especially close because she is a widow, and the book begins with an account of the death of Captain Cedric Errol. He had been sent off to America by his disgruntled father, the Earl of Dorincourt, who is unwilling to accept the fact that his youngest son is far more handsome, intelligent, and likeable than the two oldest—"He had a bright smile and a sweet gay voice . . . was brave and generous, and had the kindest heart in the world, and seemed to have the power to make everyone love him" (7). Because of the system of primogeniture, it is the older sons who are the first in line to inherit the family title and estates, an unhappy situation to which the earl reacts by petulantly sending his youngest and favorite boy into exile. It is a perverse gesture typical of the proud and pampered old man.

While he is in America, Captain Errol meets a lovely American girl, falls in love and marries her, just at the moment when his father, having regretted his action, calls him home. Hating everything American, the earl when notified of the relationship cuts off all communication with his son, who can therefore pass on to his own boy only his "beautiful face and a fine, strong, graceful figure," with an ingratiating personality to match (7). Captain Errol sells his commission, finds work in New York, sires his son and namesake, and is dead by the second page of the novel.

His widow is left with the sole but considerable consolation of little Cedric, who "had so sweet a temper and ways so charming that he was a pleasure to everyone. And . . . he was so beautiful to look at that he was quite a picture" (8). The boy's physical beauty is matched by his physique, for he "had so strong a back and such splendid sturdy legs that at nine months he learned suddenly to walk." Like his father, also, Cedric is a virtual evangelist of friendship: "His greatest charm was his cheerful, fearless, quaint little way of making friends with people" of all walks of life, including Hobbs the groceryman and Dick the bootblack, but his greatest friend is his lovely and charming mother, for whom "he was so much of a companion . . . that she scarcely cared for any other" (10–11).

Then word comes via Mr. Havisham, the earl's attorney, that both of the older sons having prematurely died, Cedric is now Little Lord Fauntleroy, and he is ordered home to take up residence on the family estate. During his visit to the widow Errol, who lives in relative poverty but (like the March family) can still afford a maid with a comic Irish accent, Havisham is impressed by what he sees, not only the gracious and attractive American woman, but the manner in which her home is furnished: "There were no cheap, common ornaments, and no cheap, gaudy pictures. The few adornments on the walls were in good taste, and about the room were many pretty things which a woman's hand might have made" (24). But it is little Cedric who is his mother's best creation, the chief ornament of her home and life: "He is the best-bred-looking and handsomest little fellow I ever saw," is Mr. Havisham's thought (28).

The lawyer is pleasantly surprised, having been led by the old earl to believe that Captain Cedric had married a fortune-and-title-hunting American. She would therefore be of low character and an unworthy because ill-bred mother of the once and future Lord Fauntleroy, who would undoubtedly take his character from her. The earl was wrong, but the lawyer reluctantly carries out his instructions, and informs Mrs. Errol that on orders from Dorincourt she may accompany her son to England but will be separated from him save for occasional visits. She is to occupy a comfortable cottage on the family estate but without the hitherto unbroken association with her son, who will be living with his grandfather in the family castle. As Mr. Havisham admits to himself, the earl is a miserable specimen of humanity, spoiled by a lifelong indulgence of self, which "had only brought him ill health and irritability and a dislike of the world, which certainly disliked him" (43).

The earl is an aristocratic version of Scrooge, whose character was formed by an excess of the commercial spirit not lifelong luxury, but the end result is the same—grumpy old men who hate the world and who are heartily hated in return. We must assume that his son, Captain Cedric, and his grandson, little Ceddie (as his American buddies call him), are genetically traceable to the female end of the line, about which nothing is said, the Mother in the Picture being exclusively Mrs. Errol. Cedric, unlike his grandfather in all ways, uses the money advanced him by Mr. Havisham to do favors for his American associates, including buying out the interest in Dick's bootblack operation owned by his unpopular partner, Jake, and turning the business over to his friend.

On the voyage to England, Cedric continues to work his benign influence on all and sundry, for "there was always laughter in the group of which he was the center," and "among the sailors he had the heartiest friends" (55). Upon Cedric's arrival in England, the modern reader expects that the little boy will be immediately seized up and committed to an asylum for the incurably cheerful, as a danger to himself in this hard, cold world. But Burnett is very serious about all this curative laughter, for happiness in her view is to goodness what cleanliness is to godliness.

The generous Mrs. Errol prepares her son for his first encounter with the wicked old earl by telling him what a wonderful grandfather he has. As the lawyer informs the old man, "The child is prepared to believe you the most amiable and affectionate of grandparents . . . a wonder of generosity," and this expectation will have long-reaching consequences (64). Having been programmed by his beloved Dearest to expect nothing but goodness from his grandfather, that is what little Cedric invariably anticipates, a mind-set that holds the rest of the story in a vicelike if velveteen grip.

Despite Havisham's assurances of Mrs. Errol's good character, the earl remains convinced that she is "a mercenary, sharp-voiced American," even after his lawyer informs him that Cedric's mother will accept the offer of the cottage but refuses the monetary allowance offered in exchange for her son's captivity in the castle (63). Cedric is grief-stricken when his mother tells him they must be separated, but is not told the reason, understanding only that "'Dearest wants me to live with my grandpapa, because, you see, all his children are dead, and that's very mournful'" (53–54). Because of his mother's careful if tear-stained strategy, by the time the boy leaves her behind in the cottage, he is looking forward to meeting his grandfather, and maintains a lively interest in all that he sees on the long drive to the castle.

He is particularly impressed by the great trees on both sides of the roadway and the landscape beyond, feeling "a great, strange pleasure in the beauty of which he caught glimpses under and between the sweeping boughs—the great, beautiful spaces of the park, with still other trees standing sometimes stately and alone, and sometimes in groups" (68). Cedric we are told did not know that "Dorincourt Castle was one of the most beautiful in all England, that its park was one of the broadest and finest, and its trees and avenue almost without rivals. But he did know that it was all beautiful" (67).

This repetitive use of "beauty" and "beautiful," along with the boy's sensitive awareness of that quality, drives home the point that Cedric is not only beautiful in appearance and character but like his mother is sensitive to aesthetic matters, especially when the prospect in view is obviously pleasing: "'It's a beautiful place, isn't it?' he said to Mr. Havisham. 'I never saw such a beautiful place. It's prettier even than Central Park.'" And when the castle itself looms up before them, "stately and beautiful and gray, the last rays of the sun casting dazzling lights on its many windows," Cedric declares it to be "the most beautiful place I ever saw! . . . It reminds anyone of a king's palace. I saw a picture of one in a fairy book" (68). His first sight of the old earl is less reassuring, for "what Cedric saw was a large old man, with a shaggy white hair and eyebrows, and a nose like an eagle's beak between his deep, fierce eyes," while the boy, dressed in that "black velvet suit, with a lace collar, and with lovelocks waving about the handsome, manly face," suggested "a small copy of the fairy prince" who might live in "the palace in a fairy story" (71).

But the author once again hastens to assure us that Cedric is "a sturdy young model of a fairy," being "a strong, beautiful boy" whose appearance immediately sends a "glow of triumph and exultation in the fiery old Earl's heart." The grandfather is equally pleased that the boy shows no fear when approached by his great mastiff, but stands with his hand on the dog's collar (71–72). In the interview that follows between the old man and his grandson, Cedric's emphasis is on the earl's generosity in sending him so much money, and he renders an account of the charitable uses to which it was put, an innocent and honest display of gratitude that shocks the old man's withered soul, in effect bringing it back to life by a spiritual defibrillation.

"He had been so selfish himself that he had missed the pleasure of seeing unselfishness in others, and he had not known how tender and faithful and affectionate a kindhearted little child can be, and how innocent and unconscious are its simple, generous impulses. . . . It seemed almost too good to be true that this should be the boy he had dreaded to see—the child of the woman he so disliked—this little fellow with so much beauty and such a brave, childish grace" (76–77). Confronted by this "picturesque little apparition" of goodness personified, "the Earl's stern composure was quite shaken," and it can be said that he never really recovers from the rude awakening.

For the company of the handsome and gracious little boy continues to work on the old man's heart, and everything he learns about his grandson only acts to endear Cedric further to the earl. The boy is also quite a hit with the castle servants, who soon learn about the barrier placed beween Cedric and his mother, so that their hearts go out to him. To compensate for this maternal loss, Lord Fauntleroy is showered with presents by the earl, the sinister aspect of which the boy fails to realize. Unaware that all this bounty is intended to buy his affections, he regards it as the expression of a kind-hearted grandfather.

The Reverend Mordaunt, who pays his regular visit to the castle in the hope of convincing the earl that he should make a charitable donation for the welfare of his tenants, and who may always count on being bullied and hectored by the gouty old man, is also pleasantly shocked by his first encounter with the heir apparent to the Dorincourt estate. Where his dealings with the grandfather inevitably "cause the Reverend Mr. Mordaunt to wish it were proper and Christian-like to throw something heavy at him," "he liked the little fellow" on first sight, "and it was not the boy's beauty and grace which most appealed to him. It was the simple, natural kindliness in the little lad which made any words he uttered, however quaint and unsuspected, sound pleasant and sincere" (102). When after his interview with the earl and little Cedric, Mr. Mordaunt leaves the castle, he took with him not only a note from the boy interceding on behalf of an impoverished tenant named Higgins, but "a pleasanter feeling and a more hopeful one than he had ever carried home with him down that avenue on any previous visit he had made at Dorincourt Castle" (108).

For Cedric's part, whose good impression of his grandfather is next bolstered by the gift of a pony, he continues to put the best construction on all that the earl has done for him, being ignorant in his innocence of the old man's cynical motives: "You are always doing good, aren't you? And thinking about other people." Coming from another mouth, this praise would be taken as the sharpest kind of irony, but the earl, recognizing the source, is dumbfounded "to see each of his ugly, selfish motives changed into a good and generous one by the simplicity of a child" (108). Once again, little Cedric's insistence on his grandfather's goodness is the result of his mother's work, for whatever she tells him the boy accepts as gospel truth.

The old man and the boy take a ride through the estate so that Cedric may spend a night with Dearest, and while Lord Fauntleroy once again has his heart "filled with pleasure and happiness in the beauty that was on every side," the earl was lost in a review of his "long life, in which there had been neither generous deeds nor kind thoughts. He saw years in which a man who had been young and strong and rich and powerful had used his youth and strength and wealth and power only to please himself and kill time as the days and the years succeeded each other" (110). Now that the earl is old and alone, "without real friends in the midst of all his splendid wealth," he realizes that there is "no one who really cared whether he lived or died, unless they had something to gain or lose by it" (110).

In this passage we can hear the distant strains of Dickens's *Christmas Carol*, but the earl will not be visited by any ghosts. His regeneration will be the work of little Cedric Errol, Lord Fauntleroy, who will continue to praise him as a kind and generous grandfather, leading the earl on to his salvation by believing him "better than he was" (112). In the meantime, Cecil continues to make regular visits to his mother, flying into her arms and "hanging about her neck and covering her sweet young face with kisses," in effect a return to the source of the goodness he personifies and from which he takes nourishment from the milk of human kindness to sustain him further.

Given this twin contingency, the reformation of the worldly old man coupled with the love shared with his mother, Lord Fauntleroy appears at times to be an incarnation of the Christian spirit, and when he visits the church for a Sunday service with his grandfather, the possibility seems even more likely: "Cedric stood with the big psalter open in his hands, singing with all his childish might, his face a little uplifted, happily, and as he sang, a long ray of sunshine crept in and, slanting through a golden pane of a stained-glass window, brightened the falling hair about his young head" (119). By this means Cedric becomes part of the window itself, a haloed figure central to the design.

But this pious icon is only contingent to the chief thrust of Burnett's story, which—despite the approving if brief presence of the Reverend Mordaunt—is a parable operating outside the New Testament. Yes, there is that about Cedric that suggests the boy Christ confounding the Elders, and like Alcott's little Cupid he radiates a spirit of love, but it is not a superior knowledge of holy writ that gives him his strength nor is he a passive figure inspiring feelings of affection merely. Much as the source of his all-abiding and transforming love is piped through a conduit from his mother, Cedric's is the power of positive thinking that works like reverse psychology, thanks to the effect of his personal beauty and charm, but thanks also to his mother's insistence that the old earl is a generous, loving man.

That is, Cedric's flattering interpretation of his tight-fisted grandfather's selfish gestures is self-fulfilling. The old man is used to being reviled; it suits his notion of mankind. He is not used to being loved, however, and each time that Cedric innocently praises him, the earl takes one more step toward regaining his common humanity, until his regeneration is well under way. The situation is succinctly summed up by the earl's sister, Lady Lorridaile, who having heard that "the child has worked miracles," pays a visit to check on the rumor and finds it is true: her brother is actually being converted "'into a human being, through nothing more nor less than his affection for that innocent, affectionate little fellow'" (150, 152).

It is not that the earl is made humble, the ultimate Christian virtue and the lesson of so much Victorian moral fiction. Indeed, as Burnett makes clear, it is the old man's pride that works the necessary magic, that causes him to take a renewed interest in life, for he is proud of the personal qualities of his grandson and proud also of the Dorincourt name: "He wished the child to appreciate his own power and to understand the splendor of his position" (134). That is, the regeneration of the earl is accomplished by an appeal to his worldiness, and the generosity of his grandson inspires him to set aside his selfish ways so that his heir apparent will not learn the truth and be ashamed of his grandfather. He likewise is led to accept Cedric's mother because "she had a beautiful young face and looked as much like a lady as if she had been a duchess" (136). It is always the physical that triggers a response on the part of the earl, and if the physical is handsome or beautiful then the reaction is positive. Taste once again is the operating factor, and the aristocracy may generally be counted upon to have good taste in abundance, at least in the kind of fiction Burnett wrote.

But it is primarily the earl's family pride that is aroused by the positive evidence of Mrs. Errol's good taste. Thus when a rival claimant to the Dorincourt estate shows up, a coarse American woman who fits the earl's original suspicions about Mrs. Errol, bringing with her an unattractive, petulant child of the sort he had feared Cedric would be, it is Dorincourt's pride that is chiefly injured. The woman claims that the boy was sired by the earl's wayward (now gratefully dead) son, Bevis, who in the words of the old man "was always disgrace to us. Always a weak, untruthful, vicious young brute with low tastes," which seem to be validated by the uncouthness of the woman claiming to have been Bevis's mistress (160). Recognizing the irony in the situation, the earl is hardly reconciled to it, and "his rage and hatred and cruel disappointment shook him as a storm shakes a tree" (161). It is only when he notices the beautiful little Cedric asleep in the room, innocently unaware of what is happening, that his anger passes suddenly away, with the sad recognition that the child "would have filled my place better than I have filled it. . . . He would have been an honor to the name" (162).

With help from Cedric's American friends the rival claimant is exposed as an impostor, and the novel rushes on to its inevitable conclusion—"it is astonishing how short a time it takes for very wonderful things to happen"—with Lord Fauntleroy restored to his rightful place, both in the Dorincourt castle and in his grandfather's heart. His mother is likewise accepted by the earl for the honest, generous and lovely person she is: "We have always wanted you, but we were not exactly aware of it" (193, 198). Mrs. Errol has meanwhile not been idle, but has been playing Lady Bountiful among the earl's poorest tenants, and at Cedric's urging the slums on the Dorincourt estate are torn down and replaced by model cottages on the Ruskinian plan, thereby becoming an aesthetic adjunct to the most beautiful castle in England. The grand finale is a huge party thrown to celebrate little Cedric's eighth birthday, to which the tenants, all of whom have come to love little Lord Fauntleroy and his mother, are invited, as are his American friends, and which Cedric Errol compares to a celebration in the United States of the Fourth of July.

One wonders what Elizabeth Rigby would have made of all this, for Cedric unlike Jane Eyre is a supremely grateful little child, a veritable incarnation of every grandparent's dream, and yet he operates outside the framework of conventional Christian doctrine. (The Reverend Mordaunt, having said his piece, silently slips out of the novel, and doesn't even get to attend the party with the tenantry whose cause he has so bravely championed.) Cedric is a type of Christ but without the danger of becoming involved in a cruci-fiction; again, he is equivalent to the child Jesus, hence is held back from any passion beyond his great love for his mother.

Unlike Jane Eyre (and his grandfather), Cedric is never angry, never rages against anyone or anything. Along with being a lovely boy he is a loving boy, the very epitomy once again of the good boy, and it is his lovingness that brings him as close as he can get not only to his beloved and lovely mother, Dearest, but to the Christian ideal. Little Cedric is the very personification of *caritas* in his relations with both his mother and his grandfather, indeed with anyone coming within his charmed circle, but the text, finally, is taken from the Gospel of Beauty and the teachings of Spiritualism, which (in 1884) made up the two testaments of the author's faith.

The modern reader may find the story cloying but the book's popularity suggested that the text vibrated like a harp with a Victorian sensibility, promoting matters more profound than the merely aesthetic. We can hardly fault Burnett for her accomplishment, although we might wonder where all this is heading. Is there not a pagan dimension to the celebration of physical beauty? Is the human body not central to paganism? Is the celebration of beautiful boys not essentially Greek in spirit, or did Housman write in vain? There is certainly no talk of an afterlife in Burnett's book, and all things are focussed on the here and now.

That is, beneath the superficial Christian machinery there seems to be a very subversive force at work, akin to that terrific power set loose in *Jane Eyre* and *Wuthering Heights*. Without betraying itself through the exercise of rage, this subversive power hints at what is meant by the expression and exercise of boy love, in this case not by men but mothers. Cedric is given many male friends and supporters but seems to show no interest in any females beyond the one he calls Dearest. "I never knew any little girls," he tells Dawson his English maid, "but I always like to look at them," another bid for normalcy but as close as Burnett will allow him to get, noticeably expressed in aesthetic terms (92).

Given the difference in gender, we might ask ourselves what would seem to be an obvious question: Why is Cedric a boy in virtual skirts? Why not a girl? The obvious answer, of course, is that Cedric is a boy because Vivian was a boy, for all of the evidence, including the photograph from which Birch took his model, suggests even insists that beyond all other possibilities of influence the story is doubly a testament to mother love. But there are other operative reasons why Fauntleroy is a boy, beginning with the matter of hereditary inheritance, for where women in Great Britain may enjoy titled positions, no or little property comes attached. The American tradition of claimants to British titles inevitably features a male, whereas gaining a title through marriage almost always involves a woman, whose paternal (capitalist) wealth buys her the desired item.

The situation is a reversal of the familiar Cinderella story, in which the ownership of royal titles and castles is always a male prerogative, which falls into female hands only when a prince recognizes the superior qualities of a beautiful but impoverished young girl who herself (in some versions) may be a princess in disguise. The real-life marriage of young American girls to impoverished (and often aging) European aristocracy was regarded as a scandalous situation by many people in the United States and elsewhere, being a purchase rather than an inheritance of a title, therefore sordid rather than romantic. Henry James's *Portrait of a Lady* is an extended demonstration of the unhappiness that such a match can bring, and as we will be seeing, Jane Eyre's American daughters may fall into the pattern established by the story of Cinderella, but always with saving exceptions. It is worth noting that the heroine of Burnett's *A Fair Barbarian*, her response to *Daisy Miller*, rejects the proposal of a snobbish British aristocrat and marries a tanned and handsome American, a Westerner like herself whose wealth was earned not inherited.

Again, Lord Fauntleroy's American energy is admirable, but it is his British physical beauty that opens the way for his other demonstrations of fitness for the earldom, an element entirely missing in Charlotte Brontë's heroine and her American daughters, who are invariably plain Janes. Burnett's story features a boy whose charm and goodness far exceeds the level attained by most immature males—inspiring the necessary correction provided by

Outcault's mischievous kid in a Fauntleroy outfit—but her subsequent story of little Sara Crewe gives us a girl who is hardly goodness personified, and whose physical appearance is far short of the beauty that is so important to the influence Cedric has over others.

Little Lord Fauntleroy is a parable of positive thinking that will leave its mark on a number of subsequent children's books by other authors, but in Burnett's own juvenile fictions Cedric virtually vanishes without a trace. Again, the use of matching bindings and the continuous presence of illustrations by Birch suggests that *Sara Crewe* was intended to be a counterpart novel, and so it seems to be. But in reverting to the Cinderella myth as used by Charlotte Brontë, Burnett was inescapably set along a contrary path, in which a long period of impoverished suffering is the instrument of character improvement. Even if Cedric had been a girl, the child who leads such a charmed and protected life could not have been one of Jane Eyre's daughters, whereas Sara surely qualifies, if in her own peculiar way. For if she at times resembles Brontë's heroine, like Jo March Sara Crewe is cut close to the pattern provided by Charlotte herself, in which salvation is achieved through the exercise of creative powers.

9

The Sad Girl in the Attic:
Bronte's Little Emma Transmigrated as Sara Crewe

Where there is sorrow there is holy ground.
—Oscar Wilde

I

IN NUMBERING THE DIFFERENCES, WHICH ARE MANY, BETWEEN *Sara Crewe* and *Little Lord Fauntleroy*, we need to place at the head of the list the fact that Sara in the first version of her story does not act as an agent of influence, save only in the most indirect way, nor is she particularly attractive. In the expanded version, *The Little Princess*, Sara is charming from the start of the story, suggesting the *post priori* influence of *Fauntleroy*, but her charisma does not work wondrous transformations in others. In the original story, the emphasis is chiefly on the salvation she achieves for herself by using her imaginative powers, identified with creativity, an element entirely missing from *Little Lord Fauntleroy* but central to Jo's identity in *Little Women*.

Jane Eyre, likewise, does not by the power of her example or influence make a new-age man of Rochester—it takes his own physical suffering to accomplish that miracle. Yet Burnett in part seems to be working against the Brontë tradition, for her heroine, unlike the pusillanimous Emma in the fragment that inspired *Sara Crewe*, is a spunky little girl. Like Jo March, she is a rebel at heart and one who draws upon deep personal strengths to survive. Jane Eyre has a creative streak, chiefly evinced in her sketches, but her dominant characteristic is patient endurance, not one of Sara's strongest points. Like Jane, Sara is capable of anger, but unlike Brontë's heroine (or Jo March) she uses it to her advantage—a considerable distinction. The heroine of *Sara Crewe* also differs from earlier prototypes in children's literature in not being an avatar of Christian piety. Nor, even more to the point, does death work as an agent of positive transformation in the book—quite the reverse.

While we are summing up the differences between *Sara Crewe* and the tradition of children's books derived from *Jane Eyre,* we should add the matter of marriage, important in Brontë's romance, as well as in the domestic novels by Warner and Alcott. All of Burnett's children's stories feature little heroes and heroines who are kept well short of puberty, ruling out a marriage as significant closure. We need, however, to establish a parallel between this chaste dimension in the story of Fauntleroy, in which little Cedric is a Burne-Jones Galahad in velvet knickers, and the similar situation in *Sara Crewe.*

There, the orphan who at the start has lost her father ends by finding another, not in the form of an aging lover but simply as a wealthy and loving older man, who assumes a father's role, thereby allowing the heroine to remain a child. This is the variation of the Cinderella story found in *Oliver Twist,* who recovers his family and his fortune but remains a child at the end. Motherhood, even as a benevolent posthumous presence, as in *Jane Eyre,* plays no role in *Sara Crewe,* but the book shares with *Fauntleroy* a faith in the transcendent Allness of Goodness, which if not invested in one charming child nonetheless spins the plot.

If *Little Lord Fauntleroy* is a testament to the power of physical beauty to transform, then *Sara Crewe* like Burnett's subsequent novels for children testifies to the power of deep psychic strength to overcome physical and emotional deprivation. That of course is a not very carefully concealed message in *Jane Eyre.* Derived from Emerson's notion of self-reliance, by 1900 the idea of discovering hidden personal powers will be identified with L. Frank Baum's popular parable of self-discovery, *The Wonderful Wizard of Oz* (1900). And Baum's book was influenced by Burnett's own *Two Little Pilgrims' Progress* (1895), about a couple of little girls who tour the wonders of the Chicago World's Fair of 1893.

In Burnett's invented world, a child properly fortified with a high-level of self-esteem, backed by a vivid imagination, can endure privation and humiliation unscarred, with no help from the clergy or either Testament. We can here recall Alcott in her journals, drawing strength from Emerson's essay on self-reliance and finding salvation through Betty's death, which was far more effective as an agent of salvation "than any minister" could have been. Again, though the Reverend Mordaunt appears briefly in

Little Lord Fauntleroy, like Mr. March in *Little Women* he has no influence on the plot, and in *Sara Crewe* no man of the cloth has even a walk-on role. Susan Warner may have corrected the impieties of *Jane Eyre* by giving Ellen Montgomery Mr. John as a mentor-lover, but the convention (perhaps because of the problems presented by a minister-lover in another American novel published in 1850) seems to have ended with *The Wide, Wide World.*

Recent critical attention devoted to Frances Burnett has focussed on *The Little Princess,* perhaps because as a larger text it provides more material for study, but it should be noted that practically all biographical entries on Burnett until quite recently list only *Sara Crewe* and not the later, expanded version. Over the years, both novels were (and still are) kept in print, suggesting that both remain popular, but my own preference is for the first version, which is not only a shorter but a tighter text. The subsequent expansion, which incorporated changes made in revising the original for the stage, while adding even more material, seems unnecessarily padded and repetitious, overstuffed as it were, as was the author herself by that time.

The essential point being made in *Sara Crewe* is in no way modified or expanded in *The Little Princess.* It is only situations and characters that are enlarged and added, increasing dramatic interest perhaps but only by detracting from the essential fable. In short, *Sara Crewe* is a fine little book while the revision is something of a sequel, and like most sequels it is weaker than the original. Specifying diamond mines as the source of the little princess's fortune may strengthen the imperial connection, but it hardly modifies the Cinderella basis of the story. Even worse, the revisions resulted in some quiet but noticeable changes in the character of the heroine, attempts to make her loveable from the start that to a modern reader are counterproductive, being modifications that not only weaken the process of transformation but add too much treacle to the mix.

Again, where in *Fauntleroy* the beauty and personal warmth of the boy plays an important role, in *Sara Crewe* physical attractiveness is not an issue. It is a distinction that becomes blurred in *The Little Princess,* for Sara seems to have undergone training for pre-teen talent shows in the interval, lessons stressing the importance of personal charm (the Fauntleroy factor) in promoting one's popularity amongst one's peers. Save for her dark hair, olive complexion, and large, grey-green eyes (which she shares with Jane Eyre), the original Sara is in appearance a cipher, is completely without charm and, at the start, lacks any definable positive qualities save an outspoken frankness. She seems, indeed, closer to the spunky Diana of Brontë's fragment than the fragile Emma. As we shall see, the story is another parable of power, exercised not through the display of beauty and innocence but the transforming energy of a creative imagination, which is the force that carries the situation in Charlotte Brontë's unfinished novel to completion.

II

Like Brontë's Emma, Sara Crewe is enrolled by her father in a boarding school—Miss Minchin's Select Seminary for Young Ladies—as a young person of privilege, being the only child of the wealthy widower Captain Ralph Crewe, who serves her Majesty on station in India. As Rudyard Kipling's own boyhood experience attests, the children of British soldiers and bureaucrats in India were routinely sent home for their education so as to remove them from the dangers of infectious tropical diseases. But, as Kipling learned, such an exile could be doubly painful, the removal from beloved parents exacerbated by the treatment received in insensitive even cruel foster homes. And when, as in the case of Sara Crewe, the beloved parent was removed by death, and no other relations were near, then such repatriated children could suffer the torments of hell.

Sara unlike little Emma is not accused of complicity in some hoax, but she *does* suffer. Her privileged position of "favorite pupil" is taken from her the moment it is discovered—during her third year at Miss Minchin's—that Captain Crewe has died penniless: worn out by anxiety over an investment that did not bring the expected returns, indeed brought no returns at all, his weakened constitution succumbed to a tropical fever. Sara's father is not himself a perpetrator of a swindle but seems to have been the victim of one perpetrated by a friend in whom he put his trust, and the outcome is much the same so far as the heroine is concerned.

From a petted favorite Sara overnight becomes the miserable victim of spite, for no sooner has she lost her father than Sara loses her room and is sent up into an attic garret, quarters assigned her by the mean-spirited, miserly Miss Minchin. Like Miss Wilcox in Brontë's unfinished novel, the director of the school takes out her disappointment over the reversal of expectations on its chief victim, whose grief over the loss of her beloved father is both ignored and compounded by her treatment in the hands of

Miss Minchin. There is no Mr. Ellin there to take her side, but then, unlike little Emma, Sara is no nervous wreck but (again like Diana) a resilient figure of righteous inner strength. Not particularly popular among her fellow students, she is a loner, and displays her independence in an interview with Miss Minchin shortly after the news of her father's death is announced. The headmistress informs Sara that she will keep her on as a student, but she will have to earn her keep, running errands, helping in the kitchen, and teaching the youngest students their ABCs as well as instructing them in French, a language as it turns out Sara has learned from her father while on station in India.

In other words, in exchange for a garret room and what prove to be occasional meals, Sara will perform extensive duties, thereby saving the school a great deal of money. Yet Miss Minchin asks in addition that Sara express her gratitude for these favors, the sort of thing that Elizabeth Rigby expected but did not hear from Jane Eyre. If Rigby was still around in 1888, she didn't hear it from Sara either, who stands up to Miss Minchin in a dramatic confrontation that served Reginald Birch as the occasion for one of the strongest illustrations in the book.

The dark-haired Sara in the picture gains power from being dressed like Fauntleroy all in black (in mourning for her father), standing resolute with her beloved doll under her arm before the seated, hard-profiled figure of the headmistress, described earlier as being "tall, with large, cold, fishy eyes, and large cold hands" (*Sara Crewe*, 11). In Birch's, as in all subsequent depictions by illustrators, Sara is a lovely little girl, with delicate features and dainty limbs, which may have increased her attractiveness for her readers but filled in an outline left purposely empty by Burnett.

During this critical interview, Sara remains silent, her "big odd eyes fixed on her teacher," a gaze that makes Miss Minchin nervous and irritable: "The little pale olive face twitched nervously, but the green-gray eyes did not move from Miss Minchin's. . . . 'What are you staring at?' demanded Miss Minchin sharply. 'Are you so stupid you don't understand what I mean? I tell you that you are quite alone in the world, and have no one to do anything for you, unless I choose to keep you here'" (14). And then, having laid down the conditions demanded of Sara, Miss Minchin attempts to break the girl's silence by asking "don't you intend to thank me?"

Sara turned toward her. The nervous twitch was to be seen again in her face, and she seemed to be trying to control it.

"What for?"

"For my kindness to you," replied Miss Minchin. "For my kindness in giving you a home."

Sara went two or three steps nearer to her. Her thin little chest was heaving up and down, and she spoke in a strange, unchildish voice.

"You are not kind," she said. "You are not kind." And she turned again and went out of the room, leaving Miss Minchin staring after her strange, small figure in stony anger. (17–18)

Sara Crewe is obviously a new kind of orphan, an orphan with attitude: neither trembling and nearly fainting away like little Emma, or constantly weeping, like Ellen Montgomery, or exploding in rage like Jane Eyre during a similar confrontation with her Aunt Reed, Burnett's little heroine keeps her emotions under strict control. In the four words addressed to the unbearably callous and conceited Miss Minchin she clearly bests the arrogant, angry woman by keeping her cool.

She was, as Burnett tells us, "a queer child . . . and quite unlike other children. She seldom cried." After her father leaves her at the school, we are told that Sara wept because of the painful separation from her beloved and doting parent, "so much, indeed, that she made herself ill," but she did not cry upon being told of her father's death (11). Instead, after being banished to her shabby attic room, lit by a single skylight in the roof, Sara "laid her doll, Emily, across her knees, and put her face down upon her, and her arms around her, and sat there, her little black head resting on the black crape" (with which the doll has been wrapped in mourning for the dead Captain Crewe), "not saying one word, not making one sound" (19). In the expanded version, it should be noted, Sara locks her door against Miss Minchin, remaining in mute seclusion for a time, a revision typical of the overloading process, which certainly met the requirements of stagecraft but did nothing to improve the effectiveness of the original novel.

Never having been close to the other girls, Sara's increasingly ragged clothes and "her queer little ways" put even further distance between them, so that "they began to look upon her as a being of another world than their own" (19). Like Crimsworth's female students in Brussels, "Miss Minchin's pupils were rather dull, matter-of-fact young women, accustomed to being rich and comfortable; and Sara, with her elvish cleverness, her desolate life, and her odd habit of fixing her eyes upon them and staring them out of countenance, was too much for them" (20). Where Cedric Errol ceaselessly makes friends, Sara has no companion but Emily, whose constant silence at times puts the girl herself out of countenance.

But after each long day of insult and hard work, the sad little girl draws a certain strength from her isolation in the attic, for it provides not only an opportunity but an urgency to create a world of her own imagining. Garrets of course are the traditional places to which suffering females are banished, and an attic, being located in the top of a house, can suggest the mind—thus mad Bertha is kept high in Rochester's mansion. Sara is not mad, but it is in her garret room with its single skylight that she discovers her creative powers, in effect benefitting from adversity and isolation to do so. "Garret," after all, comes from the medieval word for "watchtower," which derives from the Old French word for "defend," an etymology completely in keeping with the dual function of the attic in *Sara Crewe*.

The story has been compared to *Robinson Crusoe* as a parable of survival, but it is quite different in emphasis. There is no guilt to be expiated, no Bible at hand to serve as a guide, no hint that Sara needs to be brought closer to Christ—that is the emphasis of *The Wide, Wide World*. Yet Sara's exile like Crusoe's works to her advantage. Hers is not the attic of Bertha Rochester, but it closely resembles the one to which Jo March goes when she is in one of her writerly spells, for it is a creative space not a cage. Where Jo creates romantic melodramas, Sara creates fairy tales.

Hearing rats in the walls, Sara pretends that her doll, Emily, is a good witch that will protect her, but this is only the start of her defensive retreat into the sanctuary of her imagination. Where Cedric is outgoing, Sara moves in the opposite direction, and where the happy little boy creates a friendly world around him from his effect on people, the sad little girl must create a better world through her creative powers: "Poor little Sara! everything was 'pretend' with her. She had a strong imagination; there was almost more imagination than there was Sara, and her whole forlorn, uncared-for child-life was made up of imaginings. She imagined and pretended things until she almost believed them, and she would scarcely have been surprised at any remarkable thing that could have happened" (21).

It is Cedric's power of positive thinking that converts his grandfather, and it is Sara's imaginative powers that furnishes her refuge in the attic and provides her first line of defense in dealing with Miss Minchin, her sister Miss Amelia, and the other girls in the school, whose insults are met with silence and that terrible, terrifying gaze: "I don't answer very often," she says in one of her soliloquys with Emily. "I never answer when I can help it. When people are insulting you, there is nothing so good for them as not to say a word—just to look at them and think. Miss Minchin turns pale with rage when I do it. Miss Amelia looks frightened, so do the girls. They know you are stronger than they are, because you are strong enough to hold in your rage and they are not, and they say stupid things they wish they hadn't said afterward. There's nothing so strong as rage, except what makes you hold it in—that's stronger'" (21–22).

We are very close here to the central issue in *Jane Eyre*, but where Jane must learn to smother her rage, Sara has already mastered that lesson, and where Jane has no refuge from loneliness, Sara creates a sanctuary in her garret room. Jane stands atop Thornfield's parapet, her soul yearning toward the wide world beyond, but Sara's world in fact is much wider than the physical sphere, being more like that infinite domain of the mind alluded to by Hamlet, but it is a world that grows only by being nourished. When an unhappily "fat and dull pupil" named Ermengarde St. John loans Sara the books her father sends her, the girl in the attic gains the necessary mental diet. I am not sure whether there is any connection between this St. John and the one in *Jane Eyre*, but certainly there is a missionary if not an evangelical function to the books the father sends his daughter.

Mr. St. John, who is something of an intellectual, expects Ermengarde to read and report on the books, and Sara agrees that having read the books she will retell them to the other girl "in a way of her own. She had a gift for making things interesting. Her imagination helped her to make everything rather like a story, and she managed this matter so well that Miss St. John gained more information from her books than she would have gained if she had read them three times over by her poor stupid little self" (27). These are books of history, like those assigned Ellen Montgomery by her Mr. John, but as Ermengarde says of the French Revolution as rendered by Sara, "you make it seem like a story" (28).

"'It is a story,' Sara would answer, who feels a special sympathy for Marie Antoinette, the former queen scorned by the populace: 'They are all stories. Everything is a story—everything in this world. You are a story—I am a story—Miss Minchin is a story. You can make a story out of anything.'" Well, of course Sara's is a story, a story by Frances Hodgson Burnett, who as if to remind us who is in charge steps in at about this time to state, "Yes, it was true; to this imaginative child everything was a story; and the more books she read, the more imaginative she became. One of her chief entertainments was to sit in her garret, or walk about it [another Brontëan connection], and 'suppose' things" (31).

On one cold night, having had not much to eat, like a prisoner in a cell Sara "supposes" a much more delightful space than her garret provides, an ornate grate in the now cold fireplace filled with glowing coals, a thick rug, a soft chair, "and suppose I had a crimson velvet frock on, and a deep lace collar, like a child in a picture [the Fauntleroy connection]; and suppose all the rest of the room was furnished in lovely colors, and there were book-shelves full of books, which changed by magic as soon as you had read them." In this sumptuously redecorated room there would be a table well furnished with linen and silver, holding dishes of hot soup, roasted chicken, even jam-tarts and grapes. Emily would be given the gift of speech, and there would be a comfortable bed instead of her old iron one, on which Sara and her doll could "sleep as long as we liked" (32).

Another and the most important of Sara's suppositions, derived from her sympathy for the disgraced, dethroned, and eventually decapitated Marie Antoinette, is that she was "a princess," a role that inspires her to "go about the house with an expression on her face which was a source of great secret annoyance to Miss Minchin, because it seemed as if the child scarcely heard the spiteful, insulting things said to her, or, if she heard them, did not care for them at all. . . . 'I am a princess in rags and tatters,' she would think, 'but I am a princess, inside. It would be easy to be a princess if I were dressed in cloth-of-gold; it is a great deal more of a triumph to be one all the time when no one knows it'" (32–33).

We should note that Mark Twain's popular *The Prince and the Pauper*, with its story of the future Edward VI, a prince in reality but suffering the indignations of poverty, had been published in 1882. It may be added to Brontë's "Emma" as an inspiration for the situation in Sara Crewe but it hardly matches the impulse behind the fable. Twain's book for children emerged from his psychological identification with twins; Burnett's from her identification with the exercise of psychic powers, a considerable difference. Both writers were concerned with the problematics of power, but in Twain's parable power and powerlessness are dichotomized; in Burnett's, as in so much sentimental literature, they are combined.

III

During one of the "princess's" imaginative "triumphs" of withdrawal which act as invisible armor, Miss Minchin becomes so angry that "she flew at Sara and boxed her ears" (34). Sara, though her dream is rudely interrupted, only laughs aloud, which makes the school-mistress even angrier. When Miss Minchin asks why Sara is laughing, she tells her, after considerable pressure and in front of the rest of the school, that she had been thinking that "you did not know what you were doing. . . . I was thinking what would happen, if I were a princess and you boxed my ears—what I should do to you. . . . And I was thinking how surprised and frightened you would be if you suddenly found out."

Christ's tormentors likewise did not know what they were doing, for which the savior in his agony on the cross asked his father to forgive them, but forgiveness of Miss Minchin is not on Sara's agenda: "She had the imagined picture so clearly before her eyes, that she spoke in a manner which had an effect even on Miss Minchin. It almost seemed for the moment to her narrow, unimaginative mind that there must be some real power behind this candid daring" (34–35). Indeed there is a power, for Sara's imagination has a prophetic quality, which begins to display itself later that same day.

The unhappy little girl, having once again been denied a proper meal, is sent out into a cold, rainy London day to run errands until she is soaked through. She consoles herself by imagining that she has on dry clothes and good shoes instead of the worn-out, wet, and muddy ones she is wearing. She even goes so far as to imagine that in front of a baker's shop she will find a sixpence in the street, when, lo and behold, she looks down and finds a silver fourpence, and there across the street is a baker's shop. But seated in front of the shop is a figure more wretched than she, a homeless waif in rainsoaked rags and with raw, red bare feet, who is obviously close to starvation, so that when Sara buys her buns— the kindly woman baker gives her six instead of four—she hands most of them to the starving girl.

For in her imagination Sara is still a princess and the girl "'is one of the Populace—and she is hungrier than I am'" (38). This is obviously a gesture with a heavy Christian burden, suggesting the parable of the Good Samaritan, but once again Burnett is not interested in promoting the Gospels in any conventional way. It is not Sara's charitableness that will lead to her salvation, nor is her salvation a matter of being jerked like little Eva up off the stage by some machine into heaven. No, it is a matter of her dream-world being realized, not literally, for Sara does not discover that she is truly a princess, but figuratively, in that the story ends with her being elevated to an equivalent status in terms of material comfort and wealth.

I have already cited parallels in Burnett's works with Mark Twain's, and there is something here of *The Adventures of Tom Sawyer*, whose boy hero uses his imagination to embellish the otherwise boring details of life in a small frontier town on the Mississippi. Like Tom, Sara is an imaginative child, who invents roles extrapolated from romances and fairy tales for herself to play, but the stakes are somewhat higher, given the adverse circumstances of her miserable life. Tom though also an orphan is at least warmly dressed, well fed, and loved by his Aunt Polly, while Sara is none of the above. She must make her own world, and it is a world invented in her attic, at once a prison and a kind of sanctuary, but as the story rushes to its conclusion, it becomes much less a prison and much more a sanctuary.

The house next door to Miss Minchin's is occupied by an invalid Sara calls "the Indian Gentleman," for although he is an Englishman, he has spent a great deal of time in the East Indies, and though rich from his colonial connection he has also had his health damaged by tropical fevers, and cannot enjoy his wealth. The gentleman has a "native servant," and because Sara learned "Hindustani" while living with her father, she occasionally holds a brief conversation with the "Lascar" as she calls him, a word from the Hindi *lashkari*, meaning not a servant but a soldier.

Likewise, in the illustration by Birch depicting the first encounter between Sara and the servant, the Indian is dressed in the traditional turban and beard of a Sikh, who were among the most courageous of the native soldiers serving the British. He is likewise tall, and towers over Sara, but unlike later illustrations to the novel in which he is colored black (giving quite incidental evidence to critics seeking colonialist bias in Burnett's book), Birch's Lascar is light complected and handsome. That he is a signature of the east-to-west currents flowing through *Sara Crewes* is suggested not only by the role he will play in the heroine's final triumph but in the name the Hindu is given in *The Little Princess*, "Ram Dass," which by way of the former Richard Alpert gave the story a mystical reach all the way to the twenty-first century. For it is the Hindu who will serve as the agent of the Allness of Goodness, making a reality of Sara's dreams.

Aside from this spiritualist element, the military connection suggested by the "Lascar" designation is an unstated link with Sara's dead father, having presumably been derived by her from the military life she shared with Captain Crewe in India. As it turns out, the "Indian Gentleman" for whom he works is coincidentally the friend who was the cause of Captain Crewe's ruin hence his death, not a swindle but an unintentional accident of high finance. The gentleman had eventually recouped not only his but the Captain's money, and riven with guilt over his mistake, has been searching for little Sara in vain, a situation that exacerbates his declining health. Indeed, he is practically on his death bed when he learns the truth. But before that happens Sara is treated to several more miracles, in which her dreams of comfort and luxury up in her lonely garret come true.

One evening, having passed the Indian Gentleman's house and seen him through a window sitting despondent by a warm fire, Sara returns to Miss Minchin's and another scolding, after which she is sent to bed without supper save for a crust of dry bread. But when she opens the door to her garret the place has been transformed, realizing her game of "suppose," with a real fire in a new, ornate grate, and a table set with dishes filled with food: "On the bed were new, warm coverings, a curious wadded silk robe, and some books. The little, cold, miserable room seemed changed into Fairyland. It was actually warm and glowing. . . . Can you imagine it?" interposes the author, thereby aiding in the suspension of belief by insisting on the unlikeliness of the transformation, "Can you believe it? I find it hard to believe it myself. And Sara found it impossible. . . . 'It is bewitched!' said Sara. 'Or *I* am bewitched. I only think I see it all; but if I can only keep on thinking it, I don't care—I don't care—if I can only keep it up!'" (52–53).

It is of course all very real, but is "like a fairy story come true—it was heavenly," and the only clue to the source of the transformation is an inscription on one of the books left for her to read: "The little girl in the attic." Where the girl in question has never broken down under adversity, this act of kindness breeches her wall of reserve: "Sara put her face down on the queer, foreign-looking quilted robe and burst into tears." What brought tears is the realization that whoever has done this for her is a "friend," the first one (save for the inadequate Ermengarde) she has known since the death of her father, for whom generosity was the signature of his love.

But this is only the first of several mysterious transformations that the garret will undergo, for each evening when Sara climbs to her room it contains still more marvelous things. Thus, the next time she returns she finds

a piece of bright, strange, heavy cloth cover[ing] the battered mantel, and on it some ornaments had been placed. All the bare, ugly things which could be covered with draperies had been concealed and made to look quite pretty. Some odd materials in rich colors had been fastened against the walls with sharp, fine tacks—so sharp that they could be pressed into the wood without hammering. Some brilliant fans were pinned up, and there were several large cushions. A long, old wooden box was covered with a rug, and some cushions lay on it, so that it wore quite the air of a sofa. (56–57)

For Sara these improvements are the realization of her imaginings: where once she "used to pretend, and pretend, and wish there were fairies!" now she is "living in a fairy story! I feel as if I might be a fairy myself, and be able to turn things into anything else" (57). But as the accompanying illustration by Birch suggests, Sara's fairyland world is an approximation of an artist's atelier in Trilby's Paris, for the tasteful use of fabrics and fans is reminiscent of the kind of interior decoration promoted by Wilde and Whistler. But aestheticism is not the main issue here, for the decorations follow and do not trigger the girl's transformation, further reinforcing the difference between *Sara Crewe* and *Little Lord Fauntleroy*.

Again, what has happened is the actualization of Sara's dream, a continuing fairy tale that brings new delights each time the girl opens what has now become her magic door, much as she imagines that the mysterious agent of her happiness is a friendly and generous "Eastern magician, with long robes and a wand." Then parcels arrive at Miss Minchin's, addressed to "the little girl in the attic," and when they are opened are found to contain "pretty and comfortable clothing" with a note promising more of the same. Confronted by this sudden evidence that Sara Crewe may indeed be something more than she had reckoned upon in her meagre and miserly imagination, Miss Minchin begins to treat the orphan with consideration, but it is too late.

A few nights later Sara goes to her room to find it occupied by a monkey she has earlier seen in the Indian Gentleman's house, which had apparently climbed through her open skylight, and when she returns the pet to its owner, the truth begins to come out. Without knowing Sara's true identity, but learning of her miserable quarters through the agency of his light-footed servant (who has spied through her garret window), the Indian Gentleman has ordered all the magical improvements, which were executed in Ariel fashion ("having the silent swiftness and agile movements of many of his race") by the Lascar.

During Sara's interview with the gentleman (whose name is Thomas Carrisford), he questions the girl about her origins and learns that she is the daughter of Captain Ralph Crewe whom he has been searching for. Overcome with emotion and weakened by disease and guilt, Sara's benefactor almost dies, but he recovers to become the girl's adoptive father, her "Uncle Tom." As we will learn, Stowe's sentimental classic took a powerful hold on Frances Hodgson's youthful imagination, and though the connection would seem to be gratuitous here, the illustration by Birch showing Sara resting her head on Carrisford's knee does suggest a connection with the close relationship between Little Eva and the long-suffering black man which proved irresistible as a sentimental subject for graphic artists during the 1850s.

Though it is the Lascar who we are told became "her devoted slave," her Uncle Tom is a rival in that department, and gives Sara a Russian boar-hound with a collar inscribed, "'I am Boris; I serve the Princess Sara.'" It is a gift recalling both "his Highness' dog at Kew" and the mastiff in *Fauntleroy* as well as expressing sentiments emphasizing the male servitude that the self-cast but now *de facto* Princess will enjoy. For Sara is now the child of privilege she has always dreamt of becoming, in terms of material comforts if not a crown, and after one final telling off of Miss Minchin the story ends.

Where *Little Lord Fauntleroy* was about the kinds of regenerative transformations that could be effected by the power of goodness, *Sara Crewe* is a fairy tale in which the heroine discovers the magical uses to which her powerful imagination can be put. Moreover, where nothing really happens to Lord Fauntleroy, who is at the end of the story the same delightful, happy, generous boy he was at the start—it is his grandfather who is changed by his presence—Sara Crewe does undergo a transformation, not only from privileged child to pauper and then on to a very wealthy young lady, but also from a strange little girl with large, unnerving eyes to a virtual elf who discovers she has magical powers of invention. Charlotte Brontë's most famous heroine is also elflike, with large eyes whose gaze can cause consternation, but Sara is no Jane Eyre, who grows up and bears her aging but princely lover a child.

We have already seen the extent to which Cedric is Vivian idealized, his mother an equally idealized self-portrait of the author. But it can also be said that there is a great investment of authorial self in Sara Crewe as well, for it was while suffering the adversity and ignomy of exile to a remote frontier town in the hills of Tennessee—a geographical attic if you will—that Frances Hodgson learned what could be achieved through the exercise of her imagination. By her own account, making up impromptu stories was a gift she used to entertain herself and her friends while the Hodgsons still lived in Manchester, but which was turned to greater good once poverty took the family to the New World.

Lest we forget the Brontëan connection, much the same thing was said of Charlotte, who with her sisters in their unsplendid isolation on the Yorkshire moors learned just what the exercise of powerfully creative imaginations can bring about. Similarly, Jo March writes the plays that she and her sisters put on for their own amusement, creativity not derived from the Brontë story but from Lou Alcott's own experience. Even Elsie Dinsmore is credited with making up fairy tales for the amusement of her friends, suggesting that the creativity of Sara Crewe by 1888 was something of a convention as well as, if we may credit Burnett's autobiography, derived from fact.

As in the examples provided by Alcott's childhood and the fiction they inspired, it is always a problematic matter when fact duplicates literary convention. Thus Frances Hodgson like Sara Crewe lost her father at an early age, and her troubled marital life may have suggested that his idealized match could never be found, that, as many people have suspected, Frances forever remained the little girl her father left behind him. Like Mark Twain (who also lost his father at a critical age) she never grew up, the kind of thing that James Barrie would spin into the most popular myth of the closing nineteenth century, a celebration of eternal immaturity.

Here again we have a connection of sorts with *Little Lord Fauntleroy,* which is about the intense love between a mother and her little boy, for *Sara Crewe* is about the love of a little girl for her father. It can be seen as projecting the author's remembrance of her own protective, wealthy parent into the loving, generous image of Ralph Crewe, whose place is taken by an adoring "Uncle Tom." Together these two novels may be said to provide an incestuous exercise in counterpoint, given energy by a powerful investment of self.

It is *The Tempest* more than *Robinson Crusoe* that was Burnett's model, Mr. Carrisford playing at Prospero, with Sara serving as Miranda—"There was a little joke between them that he was a magician, and so could do anything he liked; and it was one of his pleasures to invent plans to surprise her with enjoyments she had not thought of" (74). It is a contingency that serves to validate Leslie Fiedler's incestuous reading of Shakespeare's play, and helps explain why there is no Ferdinand in sight in Sara's brave new world. Here again we find a pattern suggesting the dark version of the Cinderella story.

In her own imaginings, little Frances was something of the fairy Sara hoped to become, and like most fairies was not a completely dependable item, with a tendency to play tricks on unwary folks, including the readers who chose to believe what she said about herself. And yet if we wish to understand the meaning of Burnett's greatest book for children, *The Secret Garden*—with its detectable debt to both Charlotte and Emily Brontë—we need to familiarize ourselves with what amounts to a third in the series that began with *Little Lord Fauntleroy* and *Sara Crewe*, and not only because it was illustrated by Reginald Birch.

For to grasp the ongoing connection between the two books that went before as well as the revisions that became *The Little Princess* (1905) and the subsequent *The Secret Garden* (1911), we need to consider *The One I Knew the Best of All* (1893) as a venture in autobiography which shows how close Frances Hodgson Burnett came to the surface of her fantasies. The situation recalls nothing so much as the configuration in that popular picture of winged Psyche posed on a rock as she regards her reflection in a pool. She is a female Narcissus fascinated by her self-image and a perfect symbol for the creative aspects of a psychically impowered imagination—or, if you wish, the soul.

10

The Glad Girl in the Garden:
Frances Hodgson's Spirituel Autobiography

Each child has its fairy godmother in its soul.
—Francis Thompson

I

THE NATURAL WORLD PLAYS A VITAL EVEN DEFINITIVE ROLE IN BOTH *Jane Eyre* and *Wuthering Heights* but to far different ends. There is a shared element of the gothic in those landscapes, inspired by the wind-blasted heath around the Brontë parsonage, but where for Emily the Yorkshire landscape gave energy to her villain hero, for Charlotte the wild world of the moors was a somewhat frightening place, out of which rode the spiritlike Rochester and across which she fled to the succor found in her cousins' cottage. As I have already observed, the important interviews between Jane and Rochester take place in a garden inspired by the one maintained by the Hegers.

Susan Warner likewise enrolled the rural landscape of the northeastern United States in her story of Ellen Montgomery, as a region of pastoral beauty but also in a sudden blizzard a territory of nearly fatal adversity. Still, thanks to its association with Alice Humphreys, the world of nature is for the most part a lovely even parklike place, rather Emersonian in its blurry edges and bosky dells. By contrast, Louisa Alcott, despite her own Concord associations, seldom evokes the natural world in *Little Women*, for her scene is primarily the domestic zone, occasionally expanded to include the village which for Thoreau was a place made dead by rural convention. As we have seen, nature plays a vital role in Alcott's first novel, *Moods*, which is thoroughly Transcendentalist in its fix, but in writing her first novel for children, she fell back to the traditional domestic center, and the focus is on the two houses central to the story.

235

Nature is not much seen in *Little Lord Fauntleroy* and *Sara Crewe*, which are mostly, in Melville's famous term, inside narratives, and though the great park that is the Dorincourt estate is described in detail, it is seen from a carriage and never close up. It is in *The Secret Garden* that nature plays a definitively regenerative role, something other than that imagined by Thoreau but sufficiently Emersonian to give added meaning to Frances Hodgson Burnett's pilgrimage to Concord. There is little obvious connection between Burnett's greatest work for children and *Jane Eyre*, but as we shall see little Mary Lenox is yet another descendent of Brontë's famous heroine, albeit several generations removed.

But between *Sara Crewe* and *The Secret Garden* lies Burnett's autobiographical narrative: published in 1893, when the author was barely in her forties, it broke with the usual tradition that memoirs were the prerogative and province of old age. It is in all ways a curious production, and ends at the moment that the author first broke into print, a year short of her twentieth birthday. In effect an immigrant's story, the stress of the first part of the narrative is on the author's childhood and adolescence in the Old World, the prosperous early years followed by the slow descent into relative poverty. But true to her optimistic view of life, Burnett puts a rosey aura around her family's straitened circumstances.

Then comes the consequent removal to Tennessee and Frances's critical decision to try and market the stories she had been writing in England for her own amusement and that of family and friends. Attributing her popularity at school to her creative abilities, which allowed her to construct a highly imaginative if derivative literary world, Burnett's removal to the United States opened yet another world, as if the very air in America is sympathetic to opportunity, and markets for her writing appear at a touch like magic. Rich in descriptive detail, the autobiography is also selective in its treatment of events—no mention is made of Hodgson's brief Brontëan attempt at keeping a school, for example—but it provides much of what we know about that critical period in her life. Vivian's biography of his mother simply includes the same material, often preserving entire sections whole in his account of the years before his mother became famous.

We have no way of course of disproving her account, but we may expect that the woman Vivian called "a romantick lady" might well have refurbished and redecorated the story of her youth, which was recollected nearly thirty years later. It is certainly true that the hardships the family suffered are largely neglected, so that little Frances seems to lead a life almost as charmed—and charming—as that of little Lord Fauntleroy. That is, as an account of the early years of a highly imaginative young girl, the narrative is itself highly imaginative, and though Burnett grew up in the city in England that Thomas Jefferson associated with Satanic mills, in her recollections it was for the most part a pastoral zone.

And finally, we can see the extent to which not only *The Secret Garden* but the expanded version of *A Little Princess* were derived from the autobiography, in the latter instance with what would appear a self-conscious attempt to strengthen the connection between the author and her heroine. And in fattening the opening chapters of the novel in writing her play, Burnett gave further substance to that likelihood, while doing considerable damage to the original story. Thus where the Sara Crewe of the first version is neither charming nor popular among her fellow students at Miss Minchin's, the Sara Crewe of the second version is both. Though Miss Minchin bears a grudge against her from the day she enters school because of a misunderstanding over Sara's knowledge of French, and though one of the other girls is spiteful out of sheer envy, the daughter of the wealthy Captain Crewe is very popular among the younger children because of "her power of telling stories and of making everything she talked about seem like a story, whether it was one or not" (*The Little Princess*, 35).

It is no longer a matter of translating history books into entertaining tales for Ermengarde's benefit, but of inventing from whole cloth one fantastic story after another: "Any one who has been at school with a teller of stories knows what the wonder means—how he or she is followed about and besought in a whisper to relate romances; how groups gather round and hang on the outskirts of the favoured party in the hope of being allowed to join it and listen. Sara not only could tell stories, but she adored telling them. . . . She forgot that she was talking to listening children; she saw and lived with the fairy folk, or the kings and queens and beautiful ladies, whose adventures she was narrating."

This revision, as I have said, acts to vitiate the impact of the marvelous gift that empowers Sara once she is banished to the attic. Because of the expansion, it is chapter 8 (out of nineteen) before she is stripped of her privileged position, and she arrives in the attic already prepared to furnish it with the workings of her fertile imagination. Again, these expansions undoubtedly helped translate *Sara Crewe* to the stage, for establishing at the start that she is a gifted, popular little girl not only evokes echoes of *Little Lord Fauntleroy* (earlier adapted by Burnett as a successful theatrical vehicle) but makes a much more effective dramatic situation than would one little girl sitting in a lonely garret explaining to her doll how she comforts herself through her inventive imagination.

But it weakens the closely compacted parable that is *Sara Crewe,* and moves it far away from Brontë's unfinished story that provided the original inspiration. The revised Sara still suffers, but hardly to the extent of the first Sara, for she is already clothed in the whole armor of creativity and is therefore immune to the privations imposed by the loathsome Miss Minchin. These include exiling her from a suite of rooms to the garret, separating her from the other children at the school, dismissing her French maid and selling her pony (neither of which appear in *Sara Crewe*)—additions designed to up the ante of deprivation but which seem rather silly not sad. How sorry can we be for a girl deprived of a French maid, a luxurious suite of rooms, and a pony?

Moreover, Sara in *The Little Princess* is provided companionship in her exile not only by the faithful Ermengarde and a younger child called Lottie, but by little Becky, a much abused servant girl at the school—borrowed from the "small servant" in *The Old Curiosity Shop*—as well as by a pet rat she calls Melchisedec. The strange name choice may be a subtle reference to Charlotte Brontë, who in a letter to Wordsworth remarked, "It is very edifying and profitable to create a world out of your own brains, and people it with inhabitants, who are so many Melchisedecs, and have no father or mother but your own imagination" (Gaskell, 201). The coincidence is suggestive but Burnett's rodent was inspired we are told by stories of prisoners in the Bastille; it is also second cousin to the pet rat, Scrabble, that Jo March keeps in *her* attic, but where Jo's rat has one son, Melchisedec has a very large family.

This seems a lot of company for the two brief chapters that Sara must remain in her garret before the generous Indian Gentleman and his helpful servant appear, in chapter 10. As a result, the chief burden of the story is not on what happens up in Sara's attic, but what happens before she is sent there, including a demonstration of her genius in handling painfully lonely and in modern terms disturbed small children, like Lottie, for whom she serves as a foster mother. As a result it must be said that Sara II, the Little Princess, is so close in temper and charisma to Lord Fauntleroy that she doesn't really qualify as a daughter of Jane Eyre. She is not only the benefactor but a personification of the Allness of Goodness, and like Cedric Errol undergoes no significant reformation. Where Fauntleroy is little Vivian Burnett, Sara II would appear to be a reasonable facsimile of little Frances Hodgson, at least as re-created by Frances Hodgson Burnett.

II

As a venture in autobiography *The One I Knew Best of All* resembles the *The Education of Henry Adams* in two respects: it is told in the third person and is an egregious exercise in what has been called self-fashioning. But where the Henry Adams of *The Education* is purportedly a man who somehow missed not only his war but his generation, the unnamed "Small Person" of Burnett's book (unlike Dickens's "small servant") is destiny's tot: "What I remember most clearly and feel most serious is one thing above all: it is that I have no memory of any time so early in her life that she was not a distinct little *individual*" (3). She tells the story of how at the age of two she engaged in a debate with a nurse about her right to hold her newborn sister, insisting that merely sharing the precious burden with the older woman was not what was meant by "holding."

She of course lost the argument, and derived from the experience "a perfect realization of the immense fact that people who were grown up could do what they chose, and that there was no appeal against their omnipotence" (9). This momentous insight resulted in a "habit of adjusting . . . silently to the inevitable," an attitude construed by her elders as "indifference," but "which merely evolved itself from private conclusions arrived at through a private realization of the utter uselessness of struggle against the Fixed" (9–10).

The Small Person was also motivated to be "a good child," a quality likewise identified with the acceptance of authority, for loving peace and pleasure was she discovered "not compatible with insubordination. When she was 'naughty,' it was because what seemed to her injustice and outrage roused her to fury. She had occasional furies, but went no further" (15). Clearly the Small Person was at a very young age well on the way toward the wisdom that Jane Eyre, Ellen Montgomery, and Jo March take a relatively long time to obtain but which Sara Crewe likewise possesses as a small child.

Death for the Small Person, even that of "Poor Papa," did not seem to make much of an impression. "The Strange Thing" she called it, and viewed the bodies of little friends and big relations laid out in their coffins with an indifference transcendent in detachment, further evidence of her ability to deal with the inevitable by ignoring it. Like most children of the period, she was early introduced to the Bible, but her favorite text, while resembling the "Brown Testament" from which her grandmother read to her, was a children's alphabet book that used the initial letters of flowers, accompanied by illustrations in color: "It was so beautiful" (24).

There seem to have been moral sentiments attached to each flower, but the specifics had faded, while the once Small Person retained a vivid memory not only of the pictures but the grand adventure of actually buying the book itself. The excursion taken by Ellen Montgomery and her mother to buy a Bible has its equivalent moment in Burnett's autobiography, recalled as "a beautiful and solemn pilgrimage," though the book was hardly holy (27). In time the Small Person's interest in the Flower Book waned and she returned to the old Brown Testament, being especially drawn to the story of Herod and the Slaughter of the Innocents.

The early passion for the Flower Book would later be devoted to the gardens with which the Small Person's home was surrounded. It was "a sort of fairyland" that seemed to resemble "a stately jungle," being "filled with flowering shrubs and trees," along which a child could walk while peering through the branches "and imagine the things which might live among them and be concealed in their shadow. . . . Elephants and tigers might have lurked there, and there might have been fairies or gypsies, though I do not think her mind formulated distinctly anything more than an interesting suggestion of possibilities" (30).

Well, for any child fortunate enough to have a large garden in the grounds behind the family home, such a place soon enough becomes an empire of sorts, though peopled by creatures dictated by contemporary circumstances. For the Small Person it was first and foremost "The Back Garden of Eden," invariably if erroneously in memory "flooded and warmed with sunshine, and filled with the scent of roses and mignonette and new-mown hay and apple-blossoms and strawberries all together" (30–31). This, clearly, is a landscape perhaps derived from nostalgic memories but one that is close to the created world of children's literature.

Thus the counterpart to this marvelous garden was the world of books, invariably associated with the Nursery inside the house and the companionship and instrumentality of a Doll, a simple aggregation of cheap yet durable parts that loaned itself to all manner of roles, from riding a fierce horse (an arm of the Nursery Sofa) to mounting a scaffold as Mary Queen of Scots (the lap of the

Sofa). Starting out with Herod and the Innocents, the imagination of the Small Person seems to have been remarkably ferocious.

While the Doll was invariably the heroine in the action, the Small Person was all the rest—"the hero, the villain, the banditti, the pirates, the executioner, the weeping maids of honor, the touchingly benevolent old gentleman, the courtiers, the explorers, the king" (54). As heroine the Doll was more likely than not the victim, and the Small Person having saturated her sensibility by a reading of *Uncle Tom's Cabin* was found one day by her mother savagely lashing with a little whip a second doll, "a cheerfully hideous black gutta-percha doll who was tied to the candelabra stand and appeared to be enjoying the situation" (56).

The Small Person explained to her horrified mother that she "was 'pretending' something," but only in recollection does she reveal what she was pretending, that the doll was Uncle Tom transmogrified to Topsy and that she was acting the part of Simon Legree. Indeed, the black doll had been "procured" for that very purpose, for her favorite doll was acting the part of Eva, "and was kept actively employed slowly fading away and dying, while she talked about the New Jerusalem, with a hectic flush on her cheeks" (57).

This Nursery moment suggests that the Small Person had missed the point of Stowe's great novel, or rather had read it through the blighted perspective of Manchester, England, whose mills were dependent on cheap cotton and whose citizens therefore might not have been any more sympathetic to Mrs. Stowe's argument than were southern planters who produced the cotton. Thus it would seem that "empire" was not only a matter of tigers and elephants but of maintaining some belated influence over the American colonies so lately lost.

Yet the moral the author drew from this recollection was that "all children possess this right of entry into the fairyland, where anything can be 'pretended,'" a reflection that establishes an immediate ligature with both versions of the book in which the inventive Sara Crewe figures, while admittedly leaving little Lord Fauntleroy and the Allness of Goodness quite out of the picture. If there is an imperial dimension as has been suggested to Burnett's notion of fairyland, then surely we here find it fully displayed, whip in hand, with a blackfella tied to a post.

Along with absorbing the most violent aspects of *Uncle Tom's Cabin*, the Small Person seems to have been attracted to books the subjects of which were meant for Large Persons. These were historical or adventure romances primarily, like the works of G. P. R. James, Harrison Ainsworth, and Captain Mayne Reid, the emphases of which like the story of Herod and the Innocents were on violent matters: "What tragic, historical adventures the Doll passed through in these days; how she was crowned, discrowned, sentenced, and beheaded," the Nursery Sofa serving as "palfrey, scaffold, dungeon, or barge from which she 'stepped to proudly, sadly, pass the Traitors' Gate'" (61). The Doll likewise enjoyed being "rescued from a burning ship," and being pursued by pirates, captured, and then greeted by "the head pirate . . . attired . . . almost wholly in cutlasses and pistols" with the "blood-curdling announcement, 'She shall be mine!'" (63).

What emerges from the opening chapters of this autobiography is a precocious little girl who refrains from questioning adult authority but when by herself indulges in violent, bloodthirsty rites to which her ever-smiling doll submits with apparent pleasure. In these improvised if derivative dramas, the little girl (like Jo March) plays all the male parts, in effect reigning as an "unconquerable being" in the world of the nursery. It does make a kind of frightening sense, yet the similarities between the world of "pretend" created by the Small Person and that which Sara Crewe conjurs up are nil.

In essentialist terms it approximates a boy's world of pretend, and if we can say the same thing about the theater in which Jo March's imagination releases itself, well and good, but where finally do these idiosyncracies bubbling up from Burnett's recollections take us? For this is the same Small Person who while flogging her doll through all kinds of horrible misadventures, when presented by an actual infant child gazes on it not only with "reverence" but "*adoration*," conventional emotions surely and to be expected from a little girl then as now (93).

Where Alcott in *Little Women* borrowed from the Alcotts' painful descent into poverty, Burnett barely alludes to the decrease in the Hodgson family income that resulted in a move to a less desirable neighborhood. There were no back gardens, only a public Square where few flowers grew and where even less fortunate children could be encountered, thought charming because of their exotic verbal inflections. But the most important discovery did not occur outside but in, and was made by opening the doors of an immense "Secrétaire," which required that the Small Person climb laboriously up to a great height. But there she found a brave new world of literature, the stories in the collected volumes of *Blackwood's*

Magazine, which contained reading of a far different kind from the violent pages of Mayne Reid and Ainsworth.

There were other books as well, containing stories written as poetry: "There was a thing about an Ancient Mariner with a glittering eye, another about St. Agnes's Eve, another about a Scotch gentleman called Marmion, others about . . . a Corsair, and a splendid long one about a young man whose name was Don Juan" (125–26). What she had come upon in her explorations was the world of adult romance, which would prove to be an important turning point, moving the Small Person away from historically warranted bloodshed and violence to a marvelous realm of magic in which anything is possible.

Not all of Burnett's recollections consist of literary matters. We hear a great deal about the kinds of concerns that occupy a growing girl, equivalents to what we also find in *Little Women,* including tea-parties, quadrilles, weddings and funerals, and the rest. It is all quite charming, embellished with Birch's illustrations, in which little girls with their hair in long curls are invariably dressed in ruffles and flounces and ribbons with white stockings and slippers of the kind called "mary janes." One half expects to find Lewis Carroll suddenly popping out from behind a bush, camera in hand. Unlike Jo and Meg, the Small Person is privileged to enjoy frequent changes of fancy clothing, and an ever-augmented abundance seems to be on hand.

"Poor Papa" having early removed himself from the scene, the male presence is made up of older brothers, who mostly maintain a constant and healthy distance, while something called "Mamma" occasionally drifts through the Nursery. Noticing her daughter's interest in reading, this friendly apparition suggests that the Small Person "'ought to read something Improving,'" such as "'history and things. . . . History is always improving,'" admirable sentiments that suggest Mamma was not a constant witness to the effect on her daughter's imagination of Ainsworth et al. (179). Moreover, when Mamma entertained the Small Person with recollections of her own youthful reading, Horace Walpole and Mrs. Radcliffe seemed to be the chief authors, sensational stuff that the Small Person yearned to read, but by the time she had access to those books, "somehow their glory had departed" (180). Bloody deeds are fine, but "cloistered ruins" of cardboard and "ghastly victims" that turn out to be made from wax are boring.

At the age of seven, the Small Person was inspired to turn out poetry of her own, the "First One" as Burnett tells us being about church-bells, the day being Sunday, but she was ten before the inspiration again seized her, again on a Sunday, with the weather dark and stormy and no church bells ringing. What resulted was at the start something in a gothic mode, with the constant refrain, "Alone," shrieked by the wind and moaned by the trees, but this dark side of the Small Person's imagination lasted only through the first four lines: "Though a wildly romantic, she was a healthy and cheerful-minded Small Person" (200). Along with *Blackwood* there were volumes of *Punch* in the marvelous secrétaire, and the poem as it grew became correspondingly more cheerful as a result. Indeed, Mamma found it not only funny but "clever," and a career of sorts had been launched.

But poetry was abandoned for prose fiction, as the Small Person began to fill up blank pages in old account books and scraps of paper with fragmentary adventures inspired by the adventures of the Doll. These were not however violent stories but those that involve the tender passions, expressed by young men with names like "Sir Marmaduke Maxwelton" and young ladies with names like "Ethelberta." Her older brothers, not being romantic young men, having come upon evidences of this new activity, found it a constant source of amusement, which offended the Small Person, who was "sensitive and intensely proud" (212).

Even as her fictional characters were protesting their loves for one another, dark thoughts seethed in the imagination of the offended author: "You cannot stop boys unless you Murder them; and though you may feel—for one, wild, rushing moment—that they deserve it, you can't Murder your own brothers" (213). The Small Person, Burnett observes from a distant point in time, "was too young to have reached the Higher Carelessness of Theosophy," and could not at ten "avoid feeling the rage. She was a mild creature when left alone to the Doll and the Story, but she was capable of furies many sizes too large for her" when ridiculed for her creative efforts (213).

This is the familiar dichotomy with which we have been dealing all along, the problem confronting a young girl who aroused to rage must not express it, and the Small Person solved the problem by hiding the evidence of her creative activities from her brothers' eyes, and continued to invent lovely people of both sexes, in fragmentary and never completed fictions. But then came the opportunity not of writing a story but of telling it, the occasion being one of the afternoons in which the female students in her school spent working on embroidery. It came out that the Small Person had written stories, and at the insistence of her friends she obliged by telling one, improvising as she went: "And so began the first chapter of "'Edith Somerville,'" already conceived as a superlatively beautiful young lady, with "'long, thick, heavy curls which fell almost to her knee'" (218, 215).

> The relation lasted for weeks. It began with the heroine's infancy and included her boarding-school days and the adventures of all her companions of both sexes. There was a youthful female villain whose vices were stamped upon her complexion. She had raven hair and an olive skin, and she began her career of iniquity at twelve years old, when she told lies about the nice blond girls at the boarding-school, and through heartless duplicity and fiendish machinations was the cause of Edith Somerville's being put to bed—for nothing. She was always found out in the most humiliating way and covered with ignomy and confusion, besides being put to bed herself and given pages and pages of extra lessons to learn. But this did not discourage her; she always began again. An ordinary boarding-school would have dismissed her and sent her home in charge of a policeman, but this school could not have gone on without her. Edith Somerville would have had no opportunity to shine at all, and her life would have become a flat, stale, and unprofitable affair. (221)

Eager to be thought a Good Girl herself, the Small Person seems to have derived a great deal of vicarious satisfaction in narrating the misadventures of a thoroughly Bad Girl, satisfaction shared by her small friends in equal proportion. If Burnett is accurately recalling the story she narrated as a girl, her perspective does seem considerably removed from the event—a version of romantic irony—and the recollection continues in much the same humorous vein for several pages.

The point of it all is not so much the story as the reception the little improvisatrix herself received, which was not unlike that accorded Mme. de Staël's Corinne as she held forth before the populace in Rome: "And how the audience was enthralled! It would be a pleasing triumph for a story-teller of mature years to see such eyes, such lips, to hear such exclamations of delight or horror as this inchoate Small Person was inspired by" (223).

What we have here is the core situation that would sustain the expansion of *Sara Crewe* into *The Little Princess,* for the Small Person like Sara II has the ability to enthrall her classmates with improvised stories. What the Small Person does not have, however, is the requisite period of isolation and suffering—that is the part of the characters in her story—for nowhere does Burnett indicate that her childhood was anything but a blissful continuity save for occasional interruptions by her rude and unsympathetic big brothers. And they got their comeuppance when her stories began to be published.

Once having discovered her powers, the Small Person continues to use them, with the willing participation of her small audience as well. There was never any thought of profiting from the situation, of "gaining divers school-room advantages.... She simply told the stories and the others listened" (230). When an exercise-book comes her way, the Small Person writes "her first complete story in it," another step toward the point to which the containing narrative is moving (230–31). After the experience of improvising one entire story after another, it would seem to be a fairly simple thing to write one down, and yet subsequent efforts resulted only in unfinished beginnings, each being shoved aside uncompleted to make room for another. What was needed, and was soon provided, was the kind of necessity that is the proverbial mother of invention, conceived as a continuous and completed narrative action, and in Burnett's case the necessary occasion provided a satisfactory closure to her autobiography as well.

III

Reports of the Civil War in America were now heard in the Small Person's home, and factories and stores began to close as the shipments of cotton slowed then ceased. Her brothers brought home reports of economic hard times and repeated news stories as well of the battles being fought abroad, "of the South overwhelmed by armies, of plantations pillaged, magnolia-embowered houses ransacked and burned," as the South she had learned about from *Uncle Tom's Cabin* was destroyed (237). Her heart went out to the plantations, for "how could one help loving a place where there were so many roses." The situation became problematic when she learned that the war was intended to free "the poor slaves," yet "it was so unbearable to think of the plantations being destroyed, the vine-covered verandas disappearing, and the magnolias blooming no more to shade the beautiful planters in Panama hats and snow white linens" (238).

Then came the family's decison to set sail for America, and all the talk was of the terrific advantages to be obtained in a place called New York. Setting sail from Liverpool, the Small Person and her family soon enough landed in the New World, but in the woods of Canada, not New York City. "Dryad Days," is the title of the chapter, and it is an important one in the book, given the direction in which Burnett's writing would take in the years to follow. For as the family made its way south toward Tennessee, the Small Person found herself in an immense version of that Back Garden at home, resembling the romantic terrain discovered in America by Chateaubriand.

On their way to join the Hodgson uncle in Knoxville, the family passed through "forests which seem endlessly deep, mountains covered with their depths of greenness, their pines and laurels, swaying and blooming, vines of wild grape and scarlet trumpet-flower swaying and blooming among them, tangled with the branches of sumach and sassafras, and all things with branches held out to be climbed over and clung to and draped" (251). In this world one did not encounter the "smuts"—tiny particles of soot—that dirtied the Eden at home (the first we have heard of this satanic product of the Manchester mills), for this is a primal Garden, where "one is brought face to face with Dryad haunts, and may live Dryad days" (252).

But the wild garden brought back memories of the gardens at home, one in particular, that was more rumored than real, being hidden by a high wall behind a vacant house. The door in the wall was usually locked, and as she was kept from discovering what lay beyond, the Small Person regarded the situation as "enchanting, because it suggested mystery. So long as one could not cross the threshold, one could imagine all sorts of beautifulness hidden by the walls too high to be looked over the little green door which was never unclosed. It made her wish so that she could get inside" (254). Then one day she heard from friends in the Square that the little green door had been left open, and the Small Person in her turn "passed through the enchanted door and stood within the mysterious precincts looking around her" (255).

Holding before her like a magic glass that glorious expectation of finding something marvelous, the Small Person "saw a Garden," or at least something that "had been a Garden once," and undeterred she walked about the forlorn place, through the power of "pretending" transforming piles of dirt and rubbish into banks of flowers: "The rough, coarse docks were lilies with broad leaves, every poor green thing struggling for life in the hard earth had a lovely name. . . . They *grew*—just as real flowers might have done—in a place which had once been a Garden."

Even though the place was surrounded by bricks and factory smoke, the Small Person had loved all the green and growing things that survived to bloom, however weakly, for hers "were the yearnings of a little Dryad." So she walked about the abandoned, desolate garden "'pretending' with all her power" that there were real flowers blooming here, "and then her dear Angel—the beloved Story—laid its kind, beautiful hand upon her, and as she stood among the docks and thistles . . . light and color came into her child face. 'You *are* roses!' she said. 'You *are* violets—and lilies—and hyacinths and daffodils and snowdrops! You *are!*'" (256).

A number of specific locations have been pointed out as the source of *The Secret Garden,* but if we may depend on Burnett's account, then surely this is it, not however the product of hard work and joint endeavor but as with the transformation of Sara Crewe's attic, the product of the power of the imagination to create a brave new world in the midst of dearth: rambling about the ruined garden, the Small Person continues to embellish it, with a Moat and a Bower and Avenues and banks upon banks of flowers: "'There are fountains and Grottoes—and everything is carpeted with flowers'" (257).

"It was all as abundant," Burnett interjects, "as Edith Somerville's hair," thereby welding one half of the Small Person's world of "pretend" to the other. And what about the Garden? she wonders, was it aware that it had bloomed again? "It would be beautiful to believe that it did, and that some strange, lovely struggle and thrill so moved it, that Nature herself helped it to one last effort to live—expressing itself in a mysterious and wonderful thing. If this was not so, how did a flower grow there," for such a single flower did the Small Person find, "a tiny red speck close to the ground. . . . She took it up as if it had been a holy thing. Only a little Dryad, who had spent her life in the Square looking out at the slates for rain, could have felt as she did . . ." (259).

The garden like the house is doomed, being one of several long-abandoned buildings in the poorer sections of Manchester scheduled for destruction, and there are echoes here of the Small Person's regrets about the loss of the Garden of the South, the roses, the magnolias, the beautiful gentlemen in white suits and panama hats, with the slaves "singing and speaking negro dialect" which was "such a picturesque and lovable feature of the Story" (238). But now the Story has changed, as the Small Person travels through the apparently endless forests of the New World, and it was she who "lived in the Story" (261).

For here was a family of "quiet English people, who, driven by changes of fortune, wandered thousands of miles and lived without servants in a log cabin," and what were they but "a Story themselves." The Small Person was particularly enchanted by the house built from logs in which they lived, for "it was quite like Fenimore Cooper, but that there were no Indians. She yearned inexpressibly for the Indians" (261). Like so many travelers to the American frontier who had been raised on the Leatherstocking Tales, the Small Person quickly realized that whatever this new land of woods and waves was it "was not like Fenimore Cooper."

Here in America there was no longer any need or occasion to "pretend," for the whole world was a garden; moreover, like Wordsworth's boy the Small Person was growing up: "In the Square she had imagined—in the forests she began to feel" (265). Appearances were no longer so important: "She began to deal with emotions." The Doll was set aside after a futile attempt by the Small Person to assume the conventional role of mother, the cold, waxen figure proving so unsatisfactory for that purpose. The Small Person kept on writing, however, with some revisions of setting necessitated by her new surroundings.

Near the simple house in which the Small Person's family set up their home, she found a natural bower, formed of trees over which a thick grapevine grew, and with some help from a masculine hand, an entrance was cut into this private place, in which the Small Person "lived" for two years:

> The walls of the Bower were branches and bushes and lovely brambles, the ceiling was boughs bearing bravely the weight of the matted vine, the carpet of it was grass and pine-needles, and moss. One made one's way to it through a narrow path cleared between blackberry and wild-rose briers, one entered as through a gateway between two slender sentinel sassafras-trees—and the air one breathed inside smelled of things subtly intoxicating—of warm pine and cedar and grape-vines made hot by the sun. (269)

Not only does it attest to the author's love of the green world, but this natural bower in the wilds of Tennessee is one of those nurturing, private places that like Sara's attic leads to a transformation. The Small Person had long felt that she had been "a little Faun or Dryad," a creature mystically transported to the Square in modern Manchester from a time "when there had been fair pagan gods and goddesses who fund the fair earth beautiful enough for deity itself" (265). But here in America she found a real green world hospitable to such pagan creatures as herself.

The bower became a wildwood equivalent to the hidden garden, a sanctuary promoting creative imaginings. It is a liminal zone, surely, where the Small Person goes to write or sew or read or simply rest on the grass looking at the clouds overhead: "It became one of her pleasures to lie or sit and watch a bird light upon a low branch quite near her and sway there, twittering a little to himself and giving an occasional touch to his feathers, as he made remarks about the place" (270). She imagines holding conversations with the little bird, and though the Bower does not appear in *The Secret Garden* as such, the bird will migrate eastward soon enough.

Burnett devotes pages to rendering details of the natural world into which she had been transplanted, no longer a Small Person, but a young woman. She seems to have been reading Emerson, for as she lay on her back in the midst of nature, looking up at the multitudes of the stars at night, there came a feeling of oneness, and the question, "Was she part of it too, as she was part of the growing things and the world they belonged to? She was not sure of that, but there was a link somewhere—she was something to it all—somehow! In some unknown way she counted as something among the myriads in the dark, vast blueness—perhaps for as much as a point of the tiniest star" (277).

But it was not all wildflowers and birds and squirrels and rabbits. The feeling of Allness gave way to practical particulars, and the no-longer Small Person began to consider what she could do to help augment the family income. Inspired by the "Answers to Correspondents" in popular literary periodicals, she began to ask aloud, ignoring the skepticism of her brothers, if she might not succeed in getting paid for a story. And so, after much discussion with her sister Edith about matters of stamps and envelopes and the right kind of paper to use, and after earning the necessary postage by picking wild grapes for "little mulatto girls" to sell in town, "Miss Desborough's Difficulties" was mailed to an editor far away in the East.

On its second submission her story was accepted, and that is, literally, all the lady wrote: "She had crossed the delicate, impalpable dividing line. And after that, Life itself began, and memories of her lose the meaning which attaches itself to the memories of the Mind of a Child" (325). Thus Burnett closed her autobiography at the point where her fame began, and though her recollections were limited to her juvenile writings, she did supply a number of hints as to the direction her mature work would be heading.

For our purposes, once again, the autobiography is chiefly of interest as suggesting the source for what was a radical revision in expanding *Sara Crewe* to *The Little Princess*, and suggesting as well where the idea for *The Secret Garden* came from. Even if there was no such walled-off, dead garden in Manchester, even if Burnett invented it whole, the episode was in effect a dry run for what may be the most memorable garden in our literature, transcending even Thoreau's Transcendental bean patch. In leading us through that little green door, Burnett was leading us through the first of two liminal zones, the first a realm of a little girl's imagination, the second a realm of her own mature creativity.

In *The One I Knew Best of All*, Burnett, in the relative tranquility of wealth and privilege that she enjoyed in 1892, was reformating her past so as to accommodate her future stories about little girls with great creative powers. Still, there are, as I say, some curious things to be found in that book, for the image of a little girl energetically flogging her hapless Topsy doll was unfortunate even if the story was true. And yet it certainly reverses the conventional, Dickensian image of a child as the subject of corporal abuse, never mind the Harriet Beecher Stowe conceit of Little Eva as an Angel of the Plantation.

Unlike Louisa Alcott, little Frances Hodgson was no tomboy, despite her youthful preference for stories of adventure, but she was certainly a complex child, for whom vicarious mayhem was a response to Victorian authority. The Topsy episode is but a whirlpool in the consistent current of violence that characterizes the Small Person's other closet dramas—or nursery plays if you will—with the use of a doll that is quite different from that to which Sara Crewe put her Emily. Indeed, it seems a violation of all the norms we associate with sweet little girls with ruffled skirts and hair in long curls hanging down, seen cradling a dolly as preparation for becoming little mothers themselves.

That is, Hodgson's early acceptance of the necessity of conforming to the rules imposed by adults took under cover of the nursery a subversive direction, including the long improvisation shared with her little friends about the misadventures of a wicked little girl. By her own account, at least, the nursery was a kind of privileged sanctuary, in which her violent imagination could have full sway, and as such was a self-conscious equivalent to Sara Crewe's attic.

This reversal of conventional expectations is I think a healthy thing for the reader, whatever it may have meant to little Frances Hodgson, in that it corrects the myth that little girls are inevitably sweet and pretty and invariably seize up a doll to put it in the nursing position. It is a truth that will like so much else in *The One I Knew Best* be carried forward to Burnett's last and greatest book for children, *The Secret Garden,* to which we will now turn. It brings us back again to the Brontëan matter, which having inspired *Sara Crewe* loans certain gothic touches to Burnett's last (and best) novel for children.

11

The Bad Girl in the Garden:
A Rose Is More than a Rose in
Burnett's Green World

The early Christians strongly disapproved of the employment
of flowers, either at feasts or burials, because they were so
used by the Pagans.

—John Ingram

I

Little Women was twenty-five years out when Burnett sat down to
write her autobiography; so perhaps she was encouraged by Alcott's frankness to record the unconventional aspects of her own
childhood. We know that the two women met in 1879, as Alcott's
career as a writer for children was drawing to a close and as Burnett's was about to begin, equivalent to an apostolic laying on of
hands. But one of the younger woman's earliest efforts in that
genre, *Editha's Burglar,* was more in the Bret Harte than the Alcott vein, being the story of a beautiful little girl who offered to
show a burglar where the family silver could be found if he would
please not awaken her parents, to which the thief gladly assented.

And though she herself grew up in a sizeable family, family as
such was never the subject of Burnett's children's stories, which,
like the fairy tales to which they were so closely related, tended to
concentrate on the fortunes of a single child, whose activities were
often subversive of adult values. Alcott was quite capable of subversiveness in her fiction for young readers, also, but never at the
cost of her moral agenda, much as her own love of fairy tales seldom overrode the influence of literary realism. On the other hand,
Alcott's "secret" literary life as we have seen was distinguished by
fiction for adults that can only be called amoral.

253

Burnett was less interested in morality than—to borrow the operative word from *The Secret Garden*—Magic, and in her children's stories paid little heed to the strictures of realism, despite the grittiness of her first published novel, *That Lass o' Lowrie's* (1877). Again, Burnett's interest in spiritualism and Christian Science added a mystic dimension to her work, so that of the two writers she is the one who comes closest to Charlotte Brontë, sharing a belief in energies and forces that operate beyond the visible wall of being, supernatural phenomena that seem always to work for the good—White Gothic if you will—rather than for the bad. We will remember that when Alcott translated the death of her sister Betty to the death of little Beth, she left out the uncanny vision shared with her mother of the dead child's spirit rising heavenward.

Whatever may have been young Louisa's resentment over having to curb her wildness in order to conform to Bronson's notion of ideal behavior, rebellion in *Little Women* is always counterproductive. Though moral ambiguities may be found in her stories for adults like *Behind the Mask,* in her fiction for children Alcott always draws clear distinctions between bad and good. By contrast, in Burnett's stories, as in Mark Twain's fiction for boys, what may appear to be bad is often actually good, for certainly that is the implication of the rebellious behavior of Sara Crewe.

Despite her olive complexion and dark hair, Sara was not a variation on the wicked little schoolgirl in Hodgson's first attempt at "telling" tales—forever being punished only to return to her mischief. Yet there is in Sara's standing up to Miss Minchin, as well as in her defiant creation of a world of her own, a subversiveness that has no equivalent in Alcott's juvenile fiction. As little Frances Hodgson discovered while embroidering and making up her stories, little girls sitting demure in ruffled white skirts enjoy the hell out of an extended tale of unmitigated viciousness, vicarious revolt against the authoritarian rule that forces conformity on persons too little to rebel.

Again, these were the kinds of stories that Alcott published in secret, but they are not the sort Sara Crewe tells in *The Little Princess*. Instead, she delights her schoolmates with happily sappy tales of fairies and mermaids, in which no one gets anyone in trouble with schoolmistresses. I think had Sara Crewe told the other kind of stories (not likely, of course) that *The Little Princess* would have been a much different and if not a better certainly a more interesting book. Yet we do have that defiant stand before Miss Minchin, consistent in both versions, in which repressed rage is shown to be a powerful agent for good. Burnett's stories for children are never, unlike Alcott's, in the Jane Eyre tradition of equating maturity with exorcising rage: in her world anger often has its uses, though, once again, it seems to be most effective (like steam) when kept under pressure.

Still, anger for its own sake is never approved, but must always be harnessed so as to bring about the triumph of good: whatever lurked in the dark shadows of little Frances Hodgson's psyche, it never made it over into the adult version. Hers as I have said were invariably happy stories, much as Cedric is a happy boy, and when the opportunity came she made over Sara into a much happier girl as well. Perhaps it was the influence of what she called the Carelessness of Theosophy that did it, but when grouped with Charlotte Brontë, Susan Warner, Martha Finley, and Louisa May Alcott, Burnett was the happiest camper by far.

Having been influenced by elements of Spiritualism and Christian Science that resembled aspects of Transcendentalism, her stories often stressed contact with the spirit realm and the integrity of the individual as opposed to the importance of the group. In combination, this was a romantic dimension akin to the emphasis of Brontë's fiction, while lacking the dark shadows of the gothic tradition, and like Charlotte's her most popular stories were by intention modern fairy tales, for which quite a market existed in England and America during the late Victorian age.

Even the stories of Horatio Alger, with their realistic urban and rural settings and characters, all turn on an element of magic, their heroes being lifted out of poverty by the intervention of some equivalent fairy godfather. After all, as Gillian Avery tells us, it was Dickens himself who in 1853 had recommended traditional fairy tales as conduits of virtue to a child's heart, and if Ruskin was the moving force behind the Aesthetic Movement, he was also a champion (and an author, in one instance) of modern fairy tales, so long as they avoided a didactic emphasis (*Nineteenth Century Children*, 43, 55).

Moreover, by making it over into the twentieth century, in person as well as with her writings, Burnett is a bridge into a new kind of children's literature, which will move farther and farther away from the repressive and didactic Victorian spirit. She will be followed in this study by Kate Douglas Wiggin, Eleanor H. Porter, and Jean Webster, all of whom put distance between their heroines and Jane Eyre, even while preserving that essential trope, the young girl who falls in love with an older because wiser and charming man. I am hardly the first person to observe the longevity of the Cinderella myth worked into stories popular among young readers in the nineteenth century, but in the tales featuring the daughters of Jane Eyre, Prince Charming has a definitively avuncular look.

As I have suggested, Sara Crewe's generous, wealthy Mr. Carrington may be a stand-in for the father that Hodgson lost, whose death brought on the family's reverse of fortunes. Perhaps it was inadequate or dead fathers that inspired the Victorian convention of older lovers and wealthy foster fathers, for the pattern is consistent in the lives and works of the writers we have discussed so far. And yet the death of Burnett's "Poor Papa" is barely noticed in her autobiography, of which we may make as much as we wish. Mamma too seems something of a wispy presence, administering doses of literary advice not heeded by her creative little daughter. If childhood is the formative influence on the writer, then Burnett seems not to have taken much note of her parents, and when a mother's ghost takes control of things in her most famous story, it is the ghost of a woman we have never encountered in the flesh.

As Burnett says in the opening pages of her autobiography, the Small Person was characterized from early on as a "distinct little *individual*," and all testimony regarding the Small Person grown Large bears this out as well. When Burnett attained adult status she took full advantage of the truth she early on discovered, that "people who were grown up could do what they chose, and that there was no appeal against the omnipotence." From Small to Large Person Frances Hodgson Burnett seems to have been a formidable piece of work.

Despite the definitive differences between the writings of the Brontës and Burnett, we can sense a shared interest in the uses and abuses of power and control. Little Cedric's power is benign, and he unselfconsciously motivates people by his beauty and his goodness. Sara Crewe in both her manifestations has a terrific power to alter her circumstances by the force of her imagination, a gift that Frances Burnett claimed for her own young self, and in her projection as Dearest she shows how maternal power can be used as well, directing and shaping her little boys toward loving perfection. Indeed, the ghost in the machinery of *The Secret Garden* seems another projection of Burnett's self-fashioned, maternal personality.

It is in that novel that Burnett unleashed a perfect storm of psychic power, and in so doing came very close indeed to that pagan center that radiates out from the novels of Emily and Charlotte Brontë. Those imagined dryad days in the gardens of Manchester and the forests around Knoxville, which Burnett liked to imagine was a conduit back to the days of fauns and satyrs, contributed to *The Secret Garden* a pagan world of energies, not the wild and wicked kind associated with the Yorkshire Heath, but energies nonetheless. Fathers and father figures virtually disappear, and power is associated with little girls and grown women, which in 1909 may be considered a subversive emphasis, and practically everything else in the book substantiates that radical shift.

II

The heroine of *The Secret Garden*, little Mary Lennox, is everything that little girls in the sentimental tradition of children's literature are not, and bears no resemblance to Burnett's two versions of Sara Crewe. She is not only plain, she is unattractive, she lacks creative abilities, and is self-willed to the point where she offends the adults around her. As Burnett puts it politely, "[S]he was not a child who had been trained to ask permission or consult her elders about things" (*The Secret Garden*, 66). Mary's origins are important to the formation of her unpleasant character, and like Sara Crewe she comes to England from India, having lost her parents to an epidemic of cholera, precisely the threat that Captain Crewe (and John Lockwood Kipling) sought to avoid by bringing his child home to England.

Here again neocolonialist theorists have attempted to assert imperial connections, but in *The Secret Garden* even more than in *Sara Crewe* India is a bad place, for it is there that Mary has been spoiled rotten. Unlike Sara, who is adored by her father, Mary is ignored by her parents and is left in the charge of servants who are instructed to obey her every whim. She is also unhealthy because of the tropical climate, to which she loses both her parents. It is hard to see any kind of support here for maintaining a British presence in the East Indies, nor could the book have been read as a recruiting poster encouraging youthful English persons to yearn for service there, whatever the presumed powers and pleasures of the Raj. After all, Queen Victoria had died in 1901, and the zest for imperial adventures was faltering, as suggested by the expression of uncertainty underlying Kipling's famous evocation of empire, "Recessional."

Notably, what Mary brings from India besides her unpleasant attitude is a deep-set bigotry involving persons of color, which after she arrives in England she extends to anyone of the servant class. But what she mostly carries to Misselthwaite Manor, the home of her mother's brother who is to serve unwillingly as Mary's guardian, is a ferocious temper, the product of the indulgence that is attributable to the colonial system. While in India, Mary's anger was intensified by loneliness: her parents avoided her while they were still alive, for her beautiful mother was ashamed of having brought forth such an ugly daughter. She is, as Burnett reminds us, an equivalent to that Mistress Mary in the nursery rhyme who is "quite contrary," and like that other child, she will be identified with a garden, which will be a major factor in her regeneration.

Where the maid at Misselthwaite who is assigned to Mary, Martha Sowerby, sets the little girl straight regarding the proper treatment of servants in England, it is Martha's young brother, Dickon, who serves as Mary's guide into the world of nature, not the domain of wild things but rather nature as tended by human hands. Instrumental in the process also is old Ben Weatherstaff, the gardener at Misselthwaite Manor, a rough-visaged Yorkshireman with a tender heart who is yet another version of Barkis in *David Copperfield*. Mary learns from Martha about the secret garden, secret because the master of Misselthwaite, Archibald Craven, has ordered it locked up after the death of his wife, Lilias, whose walled rose garden it had been, and who tended it with the help of old Ben, who like Archibald adored the beautiful young woman.

No sooner has Mary learned that the garden exists, than the self-willed little girl determines that she must discover a way into the forbidden space, and her efforts are rewarded when a robin, who haunts the hidden garden, points the way to a hidden key that opens a door concealed under the vines covering the garden wall. The situation recalls the story of Bluebeard, but the conclusion couldn't be more different, for Mary is rewarded not punished by persisting in entering the forbidden space. Moreover, it is her stubbornness, essential to her spoiled nature, that actually serves as the necessary impetus of discovery, and with Dickon's help she sets about secretly to restore the secret garden, the tending of which takes her out of herself and into the wonders of the green world. In time, having discovered that she has a cousin living at Misselthwaite, an invalid boy named Colin, Mary enlists him in the effort, with therapeutic effects on her new friend.

Kept hidden away in a sickroom, Colin is an equivalent to the secret garden. But Colin is also Mary's male counterpart, shunned by his father not because he is ugly but because of his sickliness (the senior Craven is himself a hypochondriac, who is absent from

home most of the time in search of a curative climate) and because the boy's birth was associated with the death of his beloved
Lilias. Left alone in his sickbed, with servants only for company,
Colin like Mary has become self-centered and self-pitying, and like
her he is a vessel of tearful wrath, not only because he is spoiled
but because he is certain he will become a hunchback and die
young.

In this respect, Colin is a young version of the old earl of Dorincourt, whose wealth has brought him only unhappiness, and Mary
is a very unlikely Cedric Errol, who will cure the rich little boy of
his soul sickness. She will not do it through the influence of her
beauty and charm, for she too is a reasonable facsimile of the old
earl, having gotten everything she ever desired except what she
needs. And like the old earl, she has that terrible temper, the sort
of thing that all the other daughters of Jane Eyre learn to control,
but as this story works out, it is not only the secret garden that ac-
complishes wonders, it is Mary Lennox's open exercise of fury.

In a curious way, Mary is the daughter not of Jane Eyre but
Bertha Rochester, another victim of self-indulgence in a tropical
clime, but Mary's fury is not an expression of insanity, instead it is
used to rid Colin of his psychosis. "Magic" is the word used to describe what happens within the walls of the secret garden, to
which "magus" is closely related, and little Mary Lennox in her
way is a small version of witch. As we have seen in Alcott's story
Behind a Mask, anger is the force empowering witchcraft, as opposed to the good green maternal Magic that operates as the
transforming force in the garden.

This is not however to establish a dichotomy, in which Magic
and Anger work to opposite ends. No, it is quite consistent with the
idea of the Allness of Goodness to include anger under that umbrella, for rage as well as love has its uses in promoting the larger
Goodness. It is anger that motivates Sara Crewe to stand up to
Miss Minchin, but compared to Sara's dignified and restrained
use of wrath, Mary is violent and savage in her ways, a version of
that outraged, weeping child demanding to be let into Wuthering
Heights, a veritable poltergeist of infantile fury. It is as if the Small
Person has showed up with whip in hand and the whole world was
her Topsy doll.

As in all other instances of infantile anger we have encountered,
Mary's is transformed into useful energies, not by repression,
however, but by cooption. Gardening as modern psychologists
have affirmed is good therapy, and with the gentle but firm assis-
tance of Martha Sowersby and her brother, Dickon, Mary is led

down the garden path of rightful as well as useful behavior. "If you have never had a garden," as Burnett explains, "you cannot understand, and if you have had a garden you will know that it would take a whole book to describe all that came to pass there" (219). Tilling the earth, breathing fresh air, and eating wholesome food work their changes, and Mary begins to leave her old personality behind. Kipling's *Kim* has been cited as an analogous text, but *Captains Courageous* (1896) is closer to the mark, being another story of youthful transformation through hard work and the outdoor life.

In that book for boys, published in 1897, a spoiled rich American boy falls off an ocean liner at night and is hauled aboard a schooner from Gloucester stationed off the Grand Banks during the cod-fishing season. The boy, Harvey Cheyne, demands to be taken into port, but the captain, a hard-handed Yankee named Disko Troop, will have none of it, and when the boy puts up a fuss, he gets a hand across the face that knocks the nonsense out of him and converts him to the viewpoint of the captain. Harvey is put to work with the rest of the crew, hauling in cod and dressing the fish for market, and soon learns the joys of hard physical labor and the kind of pleasure that comes from performing as part of a team. His experience is a baptism of sorts into the Protestant Ethic, as well as a validation of the emphasis on organized sports that was emerging in both Great Britain and the United States in the 1880s. When Harvey is finally returned to his parents' arms, the boy has become a responsible young man, and ends up the owner of a large maritime shipping company.

Mary is not slapped in the face but during her first weeks at Misselthwaite Manor several people suggest that something of that sort might work wonders. And the lesson she learns is equivalent to that learned by Harvey Cheyne, which is that the best therapy for a sickly, spoiled kid is hard work in the out-of-doors, not however as a member of a team but as an individual. For Mary is very much a self-directed child—a reminder that the most salient characteristic of the Small Person was that she was "an odd, determined little person" (87). Despite all warnings to desist from doing so, she not only persists in finding a way into the Secret Garden but tracks down the source of the mysterious sounds coming from one of the many rooms in the great country house. And when she finally discovers Colin Craven, Mary has not yet completely undergone her regeneration, and can on occasion put on a sour little face and stamp her foot in frustration when aroused.

Burnett has saved back Mary's temper for a very good reason. The relationship between the girl and her cousin is rocky at the start, and she is put off by his imperious ways, which she equates with the arbitrary rule of a Rajah, yet another hit at life in India. They quarrel when the invalid becomes jealous over Mary's friendship with Dickon, and when Colin succumbs to one of his tantrums, an extreme expression of his hysteric fear of dying, it is Mary's anger that brings him around. Tired of these tantrums, the servants have long thought that what Colin needed was a good clout, and that in effect is what Mary gives him, not as in *Captains Courageous* a physical but a psychological blow: "'You stop!' she almost shouted. 'You stop! I hate you! Everybody hates you! I wish everybody would run out of the house and let you scream yourself to death! You will scream yourself to death in a minute, and I wish you would!'" (165).

Colin imagines he has detected a lump in his spine, the first sign of a hunched back, and having blown his initial hysteria away, Mary examines his spine "with a solemn savage little face," "sour and old-fashioned" in its lack of pity for the hypochondriac little boy (166). Finding no lump, she dismisses his hysteric fears, "and now that an angry unsympathetic little girl insisted obstinately that he was not as ill as he thought he was he actually felt as if she might be speaking the truth" (166). Mary has hardly been putting on an act: she is outraged over Colin's hysterical behavior, stamping her foot in anger when she is deafened by his screams: "'He ought to be stopped! Somebody ought to make him stop! Somebody ought to beat him!' she cried" (164). But if in her capacity for rage Mary resembles Bertha Mason, so Colin shares something of the mad woman's situation, having been shut away in a secret room. Burnett's most recent biographer, Ann Thwaite, has noted the obvious nod to *Jane Eyre* in *The Secret Garden,* the mysterious sounds of a child weeping that draw Mary Lennox down a maze of corridors in Misselthwaite Manor until, after several tries, thwarted by the household servants, she discovers the ailing heir of the house. Instead of a madwoman in an attic we have a juvenile hysteric concealed behind a curtain, but both are associated with tantrums of terrifying rage. Likewise, the novel is brought to closure when Archibald Craven, wandering through Europe like a sickly Childe Harold, driven by longing for his beloved dead Lilias, receives a message from the spirit of his wife that he is wanted at home.

But there is a debt as well to *Wuthering Heights,* with the emphasis in *The Secret Garden* on the Yorkshire setting with its endless moors, where as Mrs. Medlock the housekeeper at the Manor says nothing grows "'but heather and gorse and broom, and nothing lives . . . but wild ponies and sheep'" (24). Burnett also uses the eerie phenomenon called "wuthering," "a singular, wild, low, rushing sound," which at a key moment merges with the cries coming from the hidden sick room of little Colin, the wind sounding "just like a person lost on the moor and wandering on and on crying," a figure that recalls to mind the child ghost of Cathy Linton (117). Then too, Colin in his whining, self-pitying, yet arrogant manner recalls Heathcliff's misbegotten and weakling son, Earnshaw, and there is something of Heathcliff as well in Colin's father, who when he is not away on lengthy trips, keeps to himself in one wing of his great countryhouse, attended only by a single male servant.

Like the master of Wuthering Heights, moreover, Archibald Craven is eaten up with chronic grief over the death of his lovely wife. His son is tended by a kinsman, Dr. Craven, who expects that the child's early death combined with Archibald's presumably fatal illness will leave the family estate to him. This dark design never really comes to much, for Dr. Craven like all of Burnett's characters is really good at heart, but it is a device that looks back to the matter of estate building central to Emily Brontë's novel. In sum, *The Secret Garden* is the Brontës in a blender, an open response to both *Jane Eyre* and *Wuthering Heights*. There is no interfering pious filter supplied between those gothic texts and Burnett's celebration of the green world; *The Secret Garden* in its way is what Elizabeth Rigby accused *Jane Eyre* and *Wuthering Heights* of being, an intensely pagan parable.

III

At the same time, it needs to be said that the blended Brontë material in *The Secret Garden* was passed through a conduit provided by Louisa May Alcott's *Little Women*. Thus at the start of that novel Laurie like Colin if not to the same degree is an unhealthy boy, a result of the solitary life he leads with his grandfather. He too lives in a large mansion, which is something of a prison because of Mr. Laurence's protectiveness, and the first sight the March girls have of him is "a brown face at an upper window, looking wistfully down into their garden, where Beth and Amy were snow-balling one another" (47). As it turns out, the boy has been sick for a week and shut up in his room, and Jo, realizing that he "'is suffering for society and fun,'" pays him a visit in his sickroom. She learns that he is not only sick but lonely: "The solitary, hungry look in his eyes went straight to Jo's warm heart" (50).

Laurie has no mother, as he tells her wistfully, and has been looking enviously down into the cozy living room of the March home, just to catch a sight of Marmee. By the end of the interview, Jo has got Laurie laughing uproariously, "till the tears ran down his cheeks," and through virtue of their budding friendship, Laurie becomes a new boy: "There was color, light and life in the boy's face now, vivacity in his manner, and genuine merriment in his laugh" (54). Likewise, it is by making Colin laugh that Mary starts the curative process, and like Colin, Laurie is given to throwing tantrums when in conflict with his grandfather, though it is a matter of pride not a fear of dying: "I've been shaken, and I won't bear it!" (211). In such matters, even though she has a terrible temper herself, Jo takes a reasonable stance, talking Laurie out of his tantrum, something quite different from Mary's therapy, but the result is similar.

Still, *Little Women* is about growing up, not about becoming physically healthy: little Beth becomes chronically sick and finally dies, the effect of which is to help Jo toward maturity. Though Burnett may have been in debt to Alcott, she operates very much in her own, quasi-mystical world. For Alcott, as for Charlotte Brontë and Susan Warner, suffering is a necessary adjunct to emotional maturity; for Burnett, suffering is something to be avoided at all costs. As in *Little Lord Fauntleroy,* influence in *Little Women* is a matter of a widening circle of curative love. In *The Secret Garden,* it is a matter of the kind of love called hard.

Likewise, there is plenty of emotion released in *Little Women* but precious little psychic energy. Alcott having grown up in Emerson's neighborhood could not escape the essential optimism of Transcendentalism, which contributes to the opening chapters of *Moods.* But her wisdom finally is that of common sense, the kind of knowledge that is achieved through experience—as Mrs. March points out—not by communion with the Allness of Goodness. Bronson communed with the Over-Soul, it might be said, while Louisa commuted on foot to her job in Boston, so as to save the fare for food. Thus, even if we suggest that Burnett may have borrowed from *Little Women* in framing the relationship between Colin and Mary, we must also admit that it was very much for her own purposes.

Where Burnett's two earlier books for children are variants on the traditional Cinderella story, focussing on the recovery of high social position and great wealth by children who have endured a modest level of poverty, in her greatest children's book she is for the most part constructing a myth of her own. It is one given energy by the author's belief in the power of human will not only to cure illness but to endure beyond the grave—again the mix of Christian Science and Spiritualism. But there is another element at work as well, equating the growth of plants with human vitality, a faith bordering on nature worship—paganism.

Thus, like Wuthering Heights and Thornfield Hall, the great house in *The Secret Garden* has a name, Misselthwaite Manor, which translates "Mistletoefield Manor," a self-conscious evocation of the Druidic religion, associated with ancient mysteries intimate with natural forces. Mistletoe, moreover, was sacred to the Druids because it was believed to be a cure for sterility, not an incidental association where *The Secret Garden* is concerned, and not only because the icon that serves as a secret signal between Mary Lennox and her friends is a "misselthrush" [*sic*] seated on her nest.

Once again, the focus of the novel is the regeneration of both Mary and Colin, a dual, mutually helpful recovery brought about by cleaning up, tending, and setting seeds in the earth of the long-abandoned rose garden, a therapeutic exercise but one with implicit sexuality. Mary, having discovered the buried key to the garden, a phallic object permitting entry to a womblike space, invites Dickon to help her determine whether or not the rosebushes hidden behind the wall are still alive ("wick"), and what follows has a sexual implication, surprisingly so, given the book's intended audience.

Following Mary through the curtain of vines into the wild tangle of her secret garden, which he immediately sees would make a marvelous nesting site, Dickon takes from his pocket "a thick knife . . . and opened one of its blades":

> "There's lots o' dead wood as ought to be cut out," he said. "An' there's a lot o' old wood, but it made some new last year. This here's a new bit," and he touched a shoot which looked brownish green instead of hard, dry gray.
> Mary touched it herself in an eager, reverent way.
> "That one?" she said. "Is that one quite alive—quite?"
> Dickon curved his wide smiling mouth,
> "It's as wick as you or me," he said. . . .
> He knelt and with his knife cut [a] lifeless-looking branch through, not far above the earth.
> "There!" he said exultantly. "I told thee so. There's green in that wood yet. Look at it."

Mary was down on her knees before he spoke, gazing with all her might.

"When it looks a bit greenish an' juicy like that, it's wick," he explained. . . . There's a big root here as all this live wood sprung out of, an' if th' old wood's cut off an' it's dug round, and took care of there'll be . . . a fountain o' roses here this summer." (99–100)

And so Dickon leads Mary about her secret garden, and with "his knife in his hand . . . showed her things which she thought wonderful. . . . She quite panted with eagerness, and Dickon was as eager as she was." I do not wish to press this matter too far, but we have already seen the extent to which Frances Burnett could play games with her reader, and all this matter of shoots and roots, with the little girl kneeling and gazing at the signs of "wickness" does seem suggestive. "Wick," moreover, has its own complex etymology, being both a dialect variation on "quick" (live) and a word that in Anglo-Saxon has variants on a common root. It can mean "pliable," in reference to wickerwork—as in Dickon's use, meaning "alive,"—for one sign of dead wood is its loss of pliability. That "wick" also has a potential phallic association, at least to a modern sensibility, seems obvious, and given Mary's witchlike powers, the common root of "wiccen"—and "wicked"—also applies.

Thanks to the name of Misselthwaite Manor, the story of the secret garden's regeneration, which brings about the restoration of both Mary and her cousin to blooming health, is overhung with that traditional symbol of fertility that has come down from the Druids. The garden therefore is a sacred grove, much like the bower in which Frances Hodgson spent her time in Tennessee, and its sacredness comes also from the presence there of the spirit of dead Lilias, in whose service the robin who dwells there seems enlisted, for he is the one who leads Mary to the buried key and to the garden itself.

It is Lilias's voice that summons her husband back to the garden, signalling the completion of Colin's regeneration, which she has obviously been witnessing from within the garden wall. This once again is the spiritualist dimension, while the psychic will to good health, which Mary first expresses then passes on to Colin, is the part played by Christian Science, but both operate within the much larger framework of paganism, which, as Henry Adams at about this time acknowledged, makes room for a female presence, unlike the overweening patriarchism of the Protestant faith.

Once again, dead or missing parents play important roles in Burnett's fiction, being essential to the orphan theme. It is another of the differences between her stories and those of Louisa May Alcott, for whom the death of parents is not a theme chiefly because during most of her creative life she did not lose one. The death of a child is her Dickensian burden, but no children die in Burnett's stories. In *Sara Crewe* and *The Little Princess* it is the death of Sara's father that causes the crisis, a projection as I have already suggested of Frances Hodgson's loss of her own father at an early age, and the story of Mary Lennox begins with the death of both her parents.

But in *The Secret Garden* it is Colin's dead mother who dominates the text, for in regaining his health Colin regains his resemblance to Lilias, whose portrait hangs in his bedroom, becoming a strong, athletic, handsome therefore thoroughly male facsimile of his mother. Like Lord Fauntleroy, the imperious, princely Colin is every inch his mother's boy, and seems to have inherited nothing from his father save a tendency toward hysteric illness, the very thing that must be expunged, which will send him on the way toward a healthy manhood.

The Secret Garden has enjoyed its own resurrection itself over the past thirty years, a rise in critical favor that may be credited in part to Gillian Avery's influence on students of children's literature: in 1965 she called it Burnett's "one really good book," which in its emphasis on the regenerative effects of loving friendship and gardening "foreshadows modern methods of dealing with delinquent children, believing less in original sin than in lack of security, want of affection" (*Nineteenth-Century Children*, 179). But feminist critics have not been entirely happy with the gendered focus of the book, for it is clear that the regeneration of Mary Lennox takes place so that she may help Colin recover from his illness, a necessary step in reuniting father and son, an event in which Mary is only a witness not a participant.

As we have seen, though Mary in tending her garden has lost much of her contrariness, she does not immediately lose her capacity for impatient rage. It is only after Colin joins Mary and Dickon in the secret garden, gradually assuming leadership of the team, that the little girl becomes true to type, increasingly submissive to the "Rajah's" rule. Indeed, he becomes the "plant" central to her thoughts, and tending him back to health becomes the chief objective of her mission, which implicitly completes her transformation from selfish to selfless little girl. In fact, with Colin now reunited with his father, with the secret garden in bloom and the young robins having hatched and taken flight, there really isn't much left for Mary Lennox to do.

Well, so? It is motherhood after all not sisterhood that is the regnant force in Burnett's book, as in most sentimental stories, and Mary may be seen as from the beginning acting as the agent of Lilias Craven, her destiny directed by the necessity of saving Colin for his father. As in *Little Women,* healing is the operative action, for where Jo cures Laurie of his moodiness, Mary cures Colin of his hypochondria. Jo also labors virtually alone to save Beth from scarlet fever, and stays by her sister's bed attending to her needs in Beth's final illness. Alcott had likewise tended the dying Betty, an experience that convinced her she was qualified to serve as a nurse during the Civil War. Though we may talk of suffering as empowerment perhaps equal space should be given to those who are empowered by mitigating the pain of illness.

"Nursing" has a complex ambiguity, evoking the maternal as well as the restorative function, but from whichever direction we come, the act is one intended to strengthen the family tie, and is therefore essential to the sentimental mode. Most important, perhaps, Mary may serve to restore Colin's health so that he can reunite with his father, but unlike those other daughters of Jane Eyre she does not end in a subservient posture, attending to the needs of some superior male being. Notably, Mary may lose in the footrace with the boy whose health she has restored, but she comes in a very close second.

Again, the true object of all this is to obey the spirit of Lilias, the dead mother whose presence is identified with the secret garden in which she died, which has been kept a secret as a memorial to her by both her husband and Ben Weatherstaff, the old "bachelder" gardener who had adored Lilias from afar. As Dickon's mother, Susan Sowerby, says: "[T]hy own mother's in this 'ere very garden, I do believe. She couldna' keep out of it. Thy father mun come back to thee—he mun!" (260). And to ensure that he does, Susan writes Mr. Craven a letter, urging Archibald to return home, a letter that arrives after Archie has heard the mysterious summons from his dead wife.

Mrs. Sowerby is Burnett's version of Mrs. Vawse, not however a woman with only one daughter who lives alone on a mountaintop, but the mother of many children who occupies a humble peasant cottage. She is a very wise woman, who acts through her daughter, Martha, the servant who tends to the needs of Mary— acting out the gospel dichotomy—and remains off-stage until her final, quite dramatic entry. When she does appear it is very much a theatrical entrance, so as to enhance her importance at a critical moment in the story: the children and Ben are gathered in the

Garden, and have just finished singing the Doxology, giving a pious note (the first we have heard) to the resurrection of both Colin and the Garden itself:

> The door in the ivied wall had been pushed gently open and a woman had entered. She had come in with the last line of their song [*Praise Father, Son, and Holy Ghost*] and she had stood still listening and looking at them. With the ivy behind her, the sunlight drifting through the trees and dappling her long blue cloak, and her nice fresh face smiling across the greenery she was rather like a softly colored illustration in one of Colin's books. She had wonderful affectionate eyes which seemed to take everything in—all of them, even Ben Weatherstaff and the "creatures" and every flower that was in bloom. Unexpectedly as she had appeared, not one of them felt that she was an intruder at all. (255–56)

Not even the reader knows who this woman is when she first appears in the Garden, whose description seems to suggest perhaps the Virgin Mary (the vessel of the Holy Ghost) or even Mother Nature herself, but then Dickon, his "eyes lighted like lamps" cries out, "'It's mother—that's who it is!'" As she stands by the door to the Garden, this woman, Dickon's mother, sees in Colin the features of *his* mother, a reunion of sorts thanks to the joint maternal aegis. As Mary herself has recognized, in comparing Colin with a portrait of Lilias which hangs in his bedroom, "'You are so like her now . . . that at times I think perhaps you are her ghost made into a boy'" (250). And it is Susan Sowerby, once again, who writes Archibald Craven, telling him he needs to come home, thereby bringing together Father and Son, the ultimate maternal presence whose letter preceded the psychic message sent by Colin's dead mother, that Holy Ghost.

IV

Because the central emphasis of the story is on this maternal element, which gives meaning to the discovery and resurrection of the secret garden, it is easy enough to neglect the importance of the Sowerby family, who figure strongly in the plot. Along with the old gardener, Ben, the Sowerbys are representative of the laboring classes, who populate others of Burnett's novels, including the one that brought her fame, *That Lass o' Lowrie's*, and as peasant folk they possess a certain wisdom. Where Martha serves as the patient means by which Mary learns that anger is not an effective emotion when dealing with people other than servants native to India, Dickon is a veritable child of nature, who comes accompanied by a retinue of wild animals, a crow, a fox, sundry squirrels and birds, and instructs Mary in the way of the natural world.

Mary regards the boy as "a sort of wood fairy," and when Dickon is first seen, surrounded by animals and "playing on a rough wooden pipe," the resemblance to Pan seems obvious (106, 92). From her home, by way of Martha, Mrs. Sowerby issues instructions in the proper care and feeding of both Mary and Colin, sending along regular pails of fresh milk and home-baked bread to nourish them. And in all of Susan's pronouncements, as the author declares, "she was quite right, the comfortable wonderful mother creature" (234).

But of equal importance is the broad Yorkshire dialect that is the language of gardener Ben and the Sowerby family and which Mary labors to learn, starting with the all-important "wick." In her conversations with Dickon, she does her best to use "his language," because "in India a native was always pleased if you knew his speech," and the first sentence she uses is a question essential to their relationship: "Does tha' like me?" (105). Her mastery of the dialect improves to the extent that Dickon suggests she "mun talk a bit o' Yorkshire . . . to Meester Colin," which would make the invalid laugh, and "there's nowt as good for ill folk as laughin' is. Mother says she believes as half a hour's good laugh every mornin' 'ud cure a chap as was makin' ready for typhus fever" (174). Mary does so, and healthy laughter is the result.

When later Colin resolves to leave his bed so as to see the marvels taking place in the Secret Garden, it is in the Yorkshire dialect that Mary encourages him to do so, this time not for laughs: "'Aye, that tha' mun,' said Mary quite seriously. 'An' tha' munnot lose no time about it'" (190). Once in the garden, and under the influence of Dickon himself, Colin quickly expresses himself in the other boy's language: "'Does tha' think,' said Colin with dreamy carefulness, 'as happen it was made loike this 'ere all o' purpose for me?' . . . And delight reigned" (201).

Burnett's use of dialect helped promote her first novel, published at a time when vernacular speech was first emerging as a positive aspect of American literature, part of the local color movement that surfaced after the war. Much has been made of Mark Twain's use of southwestern dialect in *The Adventures of Huckleberry Finn,* seen as the language of rural Americans, hence much more honest and true than the ornate, stilted, and artificial language of polite society. For Burnett the whole matter of

Yorkshire has a positive transformational power, and its dialect is associated not only with the pulse and force of nature but with the curative powers of the natural world.

By contrast, for the Brontë sisters the native Yorkshire people are generally seen from afar. They figure hardly at all in *Jane Eyre*, and are represented in *Wuthering Heights* by servants, who prove at times to be an equivocal version of folk, like Joseph the surly old bachelor who serves Heathcliff as the manager of his estate. The story is mostly told by Nellie Dean, who as a servant has the requisite knowledge of Heathcliff's story, but she speaks in a modified vernacular, hardly so broad as that used by Joseph, which is often impenetrable to the general reader.

Again, plain folk are important to the story of Ellen Montgomery, chief of whom are the kindly Van Brunts, mother and son, again taking a leaf from Dickens, but with a democratic emphasis as well, and there is also Mrs. Vawse, a veritable epitome of hard-won rural wisdom. Elsie Dinsmore has her slave mentor, Chloe, a vehicle of piety, but the heroine remains a child of privilege, isolated from plain folk. Likewise, in *Little Women* we see precious little of the common people of the village, and the only lower-class figure prominent in the book is Hannah, the Irish maid-of-all-work and cook.

The important point to be made about the emergence of dialect in serious literature is that it is an aspect of primitivism, which is central to Burnett's use of both nature and the people who live close to nature in *The Secret Garden*. As with Bronson Alcott's theories of education and Thoreau's notion that living at Walden brought him face to face with fundamental facts of life, Burnett's primitivism can be traced back to Rousseau, by way of William Wordsworth, England's most famous celebrant of the language of rural folk as a key to elemental truths. It was Rousseau who regarded the child as a vessel of primal innocence, which could be preserved best by bringing children up untrammeled in the midst of nature, not bending those little twigs into pious shapes with a frequent use of the rod.

The sudden emergence in the last half of the nineteenth century in the United States of what are now classics of children's literature is a related phenomenon, so many of those stories being autobiographical at base. As such they are celebrations of an earlier, simpler, hence better time, put into implicit juxtaposition with the emergence of the modern industrial state, with its complex problems that seemed to threaten the stability of American institutions. This was not necessarily the agenda of the writers of those books, but most critics feel that along with the rise of local color, identified with rural regions, the stories of boy- and girlhood set in antebellum America appealed to readers for the same nostalgic reason. They are essentially parables of innocence preserved, bulkheads against the decline of the Western World.

There was no equivalent literature in Great Britain, where stories for children often broke away from observed reality and were set in either traditional fairyland or invented and fantastic places, and though we may certainly regard fairy tales, in that they originated as folk literature, as having deep roots in the primitive, we can hardly regard the region "Back of the West Wind" as a real place. Like Burnett, George MacDonald wrote serious adult novels celebrating simple folk, who spoke in broad Scots, but when he turned to writing for children, it was by occupying an entirely imaginary dimension. Jack Zipes has written at length on the implication of fantastic utopias in children's literature in both Great Britain and the United States, but that is an entirely different matter, being consciously politicized, whereas fictional children like Huck Finn and Dickon Sowersby are sprung from that same green glory in which Wordsworth saw his own childhood transacted.

This is not, once again, a Brontëan matter. For the Brontë sisters the Yorkshire folk like the moors they inhabited were well beyond the pale of polite letters, and only intrude in *Wuthering Heights* as a negative demonstration of the kind of raw vitality that rural life produces, which can, as in the novels of Hardy, produce violence and tragedy. For Burnett, on the other hand, Yorkshiredom is a place virtually vibrant with positive Magic, a pagan zone in which the Druidical spirit lives on, and where small boys seen from the right angle resemble wood fairies and verdigris replicas of Pan. What she does share with the Brontës, as we have seen at length, is a fascination with anger as the expression of great psychic energy, at once a danger and a source of inner strength.

It is this emotion that is shared in common by so many of the daughters of Jane Eyre, up until now regarded as a forbidden expression of pride. But in Mary Lennox and to a lesser extent Sara Crewe, fury is like fire, being an element that can do great harm but also produce much good. A fire burning in a hearth (the place where fire belongs) is invariably a signal in a story by Burnett that all is well with the world. But by contrast it is fire that nearly destroys Rochester in his bed and finally burns Thornfield to the ground, an element associated with the rampant and destructive fury of the woman in the attic, and released by letting her out. The display of temper is likewise discouraged by Warner and Alcott, as having negative returns, suggesting that with Burnett we are passing a watershed (or firebreak if you will), that the repressive regimen so typical of the Victorian bildungsroman is being left behind for a much more permissive environment.

V

Frances Hodgson Burnett deserves more serious consideration as a writer than she has up until now received, her highly popular stories being vehicles for the transmission of enthusiasms we may identify with the cultural fringes of her day, the aesthetic movement, spiritualism, and Christian Science being chief among them. Only seven years older than Sigmund Freud, Burnett was drawn to movements that were acting to open up late Victorian culture to alternative faiths, aspects of romanticism that stressed the therapeutic benefits of association with the natural world, emphasized the power of the imagination especially when expressed through creativity, and acknowledged that reason does not account for all that happens in this complex world.

The selfish materialism of the earl of Dorincourt, the mean-spirited repressiveness of Miss Minchin, the self-defeating pessimism of Archibald Craven, the hysteric hypochondria of his son, these are the enemy and need to be exorcised. Love—*caritàs*—whether figured by human affection, by benevolence, or by a more transcendent spiritual force, are the expressions of the universal Allness of Good and need to be promoted. These qualities may resemble Christian values but always are found operating outside the organized Church, being related to primal impulses that, as Robert Frost observes, do not like a wall.

We may fault Burnett for her too easy sentimentalism, but the virtues she associates with the exercise of sentimentality are hardly superficial. They are, moreover, virtues associated with what are thought of as feminine characteristics, whether expressed through a sensitive girl like Sara Crewe or a loving boy like Cedric Errol. If motherhood is conceived of as a condition that promotes through its influence the well-being of a young male, then that is part and parcel of the culture of which Burnett was herself an expression, and is no different from Louisa May Alcott's decision to have Jo marry and become the benevolent mistress of a boarding school for boys. It may be a signature of patriarchal values but it most certainly gives the definitively formative power to a matriarchy. As Gillian Avery has pointed out, fathers are absent in most of these works we have studied, being out of the country, upstairs in their studies, or dead (*Behold the Child,* 164–65). One exception is Horace Dinsmore, who is clearly the wrong kind of father.

It is also of interest that Burnett refuses to allow her literary children to grow up, a syndrome associated with Wordsworth's celebration of childhood at one end of the century and James Barrie's at the other—two quite different aspects of romanticism, early and late. Thenceforth, moreover, the literary children we will be identifying as the American daughters of Jane Eyre will not follow the grand model to the extent of marrying the older men in their lives. They will be kept well within the age of innocence, a year short, that is to say, of the age of consent, and while becoming influences for the good, even through the expression of maternal affection—at times figured as tending the sick—they will remain virginal presences. Here again we can attest to the longevity of Ellen Montgomery, whose attractiveness is inextricable from her sexual innocence, lacking only the power of self-expression that increasingly is portrayed as a characteristic defining the American daughters of Jane Eyre.

12

Lighting Aladdin's Lamp:
Kate Douglas Wiggin Adds Laughter
to the Sentimental Continuity

> Thank heaven, for little girls—
> They grow up in the most delightful way.
> —Lerner and Loewe, song made
> popular by Maurice Chevalier

I

As WE HAVE SEEN, FRANCES HODGSON BURNETT STRATEGICALLY modified the sentimental necessity that maturity for young women should involve an extended period of suffering and deprivation, often identified with the death of a loved one. For Burnett, thanks to the influence of Spiritualism, love is a force that is associated with life, even surviving physical death to endure as a psychic phenomenon. And as we shall soon see, the softening of adversity that characterizes the translation of *Sara Crewe* into *The Little Princess* signals an important shift of emphasis on the part of other writers for children that accompany the change of centuries.

There is a detectable moving away from physical suffering and death to much more positive subjects, but the idea of the orphan coupled with sentimental situations endure. I would like therefore, before moving on to a consideration of writers whose works were written in the early years of the twentieth century, to follow up the earlier digression on the nature of sentimental writing with which our consideration of *The Wide, Wide World* opened. That digression was warranted by the use of sentimentalism in Susan Warner's novel and the writers it influenced; now we need by way of preparation for what is yet to come to redefine our terms somewhat.

We begin once again with Jane Tompkins, who has insisted, and as a number of the books we have been discussing verify, that suffering is vital to the sentimentalists' agenda, and it is likewise a major criterion in determining who were and who were not the daughters of Jane Eyre. But suffering is only part of the paradigm, and it is not even imperative to the whole. Thus Jane Eyre suffers mightily, not physical pain for the most part but psychological, but she is brought finally to the supreme bliss of being reunited with the love of her life, after which follows marriage with Rochester and the birth of their child.

Admittedly, we hear very little about their married life, save that she seems to be doing most of the talking now, he the listening, and we may figure the ideal Rochester as a man who has lost all his body parts save his ears. But the major items here are the re-union, the marriage, and the child, for if we can credit Dickens with establishing the dominant sentimental paradigm for the Victorian era, then it is the sanctity of family that is at the core of the sentimental idea. To lose one's family occasions the greatest suffering of all, hence the dominance of orphans in the paradigm; to regain a family, or an operative parent, though not necessarily the original one, brings the greatest bliss.

So Oliver Twist begins his saga of suffering without any family, completely bereft of a comforting, sheltering, supportive network, but by gradual stages—including a prolonged stay with Fagin's horrid parody of family, ruled over by a pederastic sneak-thief— he moves back toward his eventual entry into a family made up of near-relations. It is a family moreover that is affluent, comfortably situated in a rural home, and thoroughly middle-class in station and manners. The boy's sufferings may inspire sympathetic tears on the part of the reader, but his final rescue should bring tears of joy and happiness.

Sentimentalism is the hallmark of much Victorian fiction, the underlying optimism of which is so intense that a later generation of American writers, under the influence of Howellsian realism, dismissed the genre as false in both its premises and plots. Among major writers of the period, O. Henry was a surviving holdout, his sentimental optimism being both widely popular among readers and held in contempt as "cheesy" by such as H. L. Mencken, the sage of literary cynicism during the twenties and thirties. Marghanita Laski we will recall despaired in 1950 of attempting to arouse sympathy for the literature of the Victorian era: "At every turn our deep cynicism stands in the way of our accepting sympathetically their attitudes to life" (12).

Laski doubted that all of her readers had gone completely over to a cynical rejection of Victorian idealism: "[W]e are not wholly

... convinced ... that infant innocence is an outmoded myth; that individual acts of charity are hypocritical palliatives; that the economic regeneration of society is more important than the moral development of the individual; and that religion is the opium of the people." But the result of this "partial doubting conviction" was uncertainty, resulting in an unwillingness on the part of readers to trust literary critics, like Laski, who hoped to inspire a revival of interest in Victorian literature with its essentially sentimental basis.

Well, that was more than fifty years ago, and where are we now? For nearly thirty years, critics like Nina Baym and Elaine Showalter, Ann Douglas and Jane Tompkins, have labored to increase our understanding of the history, rationale, and mechanics of sentimentalism, in large part so as to increase our appreciation of women's work. I doubt if their efforts, however worthy, have acted to convert any cynics, although it surely has resulted in a much better understanding—far exceeding that of the Victorian writers themselves—of the cultural, political, and psychological implications of sentimentality.

We may here make a further distinction. Typically, the radical use of the sentimental mode to promote political reform rules out the reuniting of families: Uncle Tom, who dies a martyr's death for the sake of promoting the antislavery crusade, will never see his wife and children again; the drastically reduced Joad family in *Grapes of Wrath* is left stranded in a flooded boxcar. By contrast, the conventional, conservative use of the sentimental inevitably brings together a family, or at least a reasonable facsimile of one. Sara Crewe finds Mr. Carrington and Oliver Barrett, Junior, in Erich Segal's *Love Story,* having lost his young wife, collapses into the arms of Oliver Barrett, Senior. Of course, nothing in the social sphere is apolitical, and the sentimental novel in both contexts acts to reinforce a bourgeois ideal.

For whether serving radical protest or championing family values, it is the power and comfort of the basic middle-class unit that is central to the sentimental genre, whose loss occasions the suffering of which Jane Tompkins speaks, and whose recovery occasions the joy of which I am speaking now. Indeed, we could say that the suffering is there only to enforce the joy. Cedric is tearfully separated from his mother so he may joyfully rejoin her in the end. Sara is sent to her attic exile and thereby sets in motion the machinery that will restore to her a paternal presence and her wealth. The strategy is akin to the Shakespearean comic convention of separating lovers so as to bring them together at the end.

In theoretical terms, the function of a sentimental novel, depending upon whether it is ideologically motivated or an emotional exercise, provides alternative actions: in the latter instance, someone is removed from the middle-class center out to the margins of society, then returned to the center once again; in the ideological version, the focus is on those already on the margins of society who are drawn toward the center, at least by association. Whether enslaved Africans or dispossessed Okies, these are marginal folks brought to a middle-class center by insisting that they too have families, love one another, enjoy cleanliness and the comforts of the home. Oliver Twist, Jane Eyre, Ellen Montgomery, Sara Crewe, these are little folks who have been torn from the middle-class center and removed to orphanages or the equivalent, in which orderliness without love sets the agenda; thenceforth they strive and are helped by their friends (including God, Magic, Fate, whatever) back toward the center from which they have been removed.

As always, *Little Women* is a special instance, in which the whole matter of margins and motherhood is confused, thanks not only to the dysfunctional confusion in the Alcott home but to a few resulting disjunctions in the thinking of Louisa May herself. Still, the author's agenda is realistic without much social commentary (though it is tending to the needs of the poor that infects Beth with her fatal disease, much as tending sick soldiers brought on Alcott's typhoid fever) and when at last the plot brings Jo to marriage with an older, wiser man, it joins her to that daisy chain of women who share the happy fate of Brontë's most memorable heroine.

Death or the threat of death is an important sentimental occasion in *Little Women,* gathering the family in a tightly knit circle of grief softened by the prospect that they all will be reunited with Beth in the great home up yonder. But the first part ends with the March family reunited for Christmas and the second has a grand finale in which the extended family is brought together at Plumfield. These too are important sentimental moments, akin to the celebration with which *Little Lord Fauntleroy* ends, with all his friends and relations brought together, British aristocrats and American common folks joining hands around.

That of all Jane Eyre's daughters Jo March was the one most influential on other women writing for children may seem strange, given Alcott's dislocations of the norm, but if we reckon in the influence of Susan Warner on Alcott, then the connection becomes much clearer. For in the novels that follow *Little Women,* as keyed by *Sara Crewe,* with its link to Charlotte Brontë's "Emma," there is a return to the orphan convention, suggesting the longevity of the Dickens prototype and the lasting effect of *The Wide, Wide World.* What disappears is the ritualized use of death by Warner and Alcott as a liminal zone, for maturity thenceforth is increasingly identified with the natural process of growth, not the sudden shock of loss. Again, Colin does not die; he recovers both his health and his father, thanks to his mother's lively ghost. Family remains the essential fact, always toward the end of relieving the anxiety of that marginal figure, the orphan.

I hope I have made it abundantly clear by now that sentimentalism in American children's literature bears an enormous debt to the example of Charles Dickens, even when deflected through the novels of Charlotte Brontë. Despite Catharine Sedgwick's priority in America, it was Dickens who popularized the orphan, as well as those other important adjuncts to sentimental literature, the dying child or maiden, the gruff but kindly old man, the reprobate reformed by the influence of a child, and perhaps most important of all, Christmas as a family moment. Given that debt, it is important I think to begin our discussion of Kate Douglas Wiggin's *Rebecca of Sunnybrook Farm* (1903) with a chapter from her autobiography, *My Garden of Memory* (1923), a work that comes close to being a classic of its kind, and suggests in several ways the author's own debt to Dickens.

II

Born plain Kate Smith in Philadelphia in 1856, the author grew up in Hollis, Maine, losing her father and gaining a stepfather along the way, Like virtually all of the authors we have been discussing, Wiggin was for a time an approximate orphan, and experienced a fall from relative prosperity to absolute poverty. Her stepfather, a physician, took his family from Maine to Santa Barbara, California, in the hope of improving his health, but soon afterwards died, and his wealth, having been invested in local real estate at the height of a boom, became largely a matter of debt, leaving his widow and her daughters to survive by their own efforts.

Up to that time Wiggin had spent an idyllic young womanhood in (then) lovely Southern California, but faced by the sudden drop in their expectations, she and her sister, Dora, decided like so many single women of their generation to become schoolteachers (the Brontë priority) and both were pioneers in what was then the new kindergarten movement. After serving a brief apprenticeship with several other women in a school in Los Angeles that enrolled twenty-five scions of the established American middle class, Kate was assigned a kindergarten in downtown San Francisco that enrolled fifty immigrant children of mixed ethnic and religious backgrounds, which she ran by herself for a number of years.

In sum, for a woman who had been an avid reader of Dickens while growing up, this was decidedly an extended Dickensian moment, which she could hardly have anticipated when as a child she quite by chance met the great man himself. Dickens had come to Portland, Maine, in 1867, on his famous second tour of the United States, giving public readings from his works, and although her mother and aunt attended the event, they could not afford a third ticket for little Kate. And so the stepsisters go off to the ball, leaving Cinderella behind. But the next day, as Kate and her family were traveling by train back to Boston, Dickens was discovered riding in the very next car, seated with his publisher, Osgood, and being paid homage by a stream of adoring fans. Here was the Prince himself, thereby providing a Brontëan moment.

The little girl watched the adoring procession pass by for a time, but when Osgood left his seat empty, she quickly replaced him, and what followed was for her (and perhaps for Dickens as well) a very memorable hour. The great author was not only an equivalent (if aging) Prince, he was truly Charming. With the frankness that only childhood enjoys, on being asked by Dickens which of his books was her favorite, little Kate said that it was *David Copperfield*, although she admitted that she had found some parts rather dull. With a burst of laughter, perhaps more of surprise than amusement, Dickens took out a pad and pencil and had the little girl tell him which were the "dull parts" of his great novel, which she in all her innocence obliged, only much later realizing her gaff.

But Dickens, with his abiding love of little girls, obviously enjoyed the interview, and later, when Wiggin became a professional reader of her own stories, the encounter provided the material for a humorous lecture, stressing her own naiveté and its good-natured reception by the great man. It is a highlight in the autobiography, evincing what appears to be total recall, and the self-possession with which the little girl conversed with the great man is delightful in itself, while Dickens's responses suggest what a generous heart the great author had. Wiggin's autobiography has a number of such moments, for she had a sense of humor about herself, and delighted in recounting the embarrassing episodes in her life, as well as more serious stories about her many accomplishments.

It is of some interest that when Louisa Alcott attended one of the readings by Dickens that little Kate Wiggin was forced to miss—presumably at the start of his tour, which began in Boston—her reaction was quite different. "Heard Dickens & was disappointed," Alcott noted in her journal, and inserted at a later time was the disparaging remark, "an old dandy" (*Journals*, 159, 161n). If Alcott's impression of the great man was quite different from that of the little girl from Maine it may be because in 1867 she was no longer a little girl herself, but in any event these sour remarks were from a lemon twice squeezed.

The year before, Alcott had heard Dickens give a reading in London, and noted that his "youth and comeliness were gone, but the foppishness remained, and the red-faced man, with false teeth, and the voice of a worn-out actor, had his scanty grey hair curled" (155). This alum-spiced opinion appeared in a Boston paper two months before Dickens's second trip to America, but did little to dampen the enthusiasm with which the great writer was welcomed. Nor did it seem to change Alcott's high opinion of Dickens's novels, which is reflected most especially in the opening chapters of *Little Women*, the book she would start writing the following year.

The Alcott disconnect continues in Wiggin's account of the summer of 1879, which she spent in residence in Concord, Massachusetts. She had enrolled in the first session of Bronson Alcott's Concord School of Philosophy, at which Emerson was present if not entirely accounted for. Unfortunately, Alcott's famous daughter was then living in Boston, where she did most of her writing, but Wiggin mentions this only in passing. Unlike Rebecca Harding Davis, Wiggin was impressed by Bronson, but it is a pity that she did not meet the author whose *Little Women* was so instrumental in setting in motion a genre with which her own work is associated.

Kate Wiggin's youthful career as a teacher gave way to national work promoting the spread of kindergartens. She and her sister wrote a number of books on the subject, for hers was a lifelong dedication to the movement, out of which as a natural growth came her writings, many aimed at a child audience. One of her early attempts at fiction for children, *The Birds' Christmas Carol* (1887), was privately published to be sold as a fund-raiser for her Silver Street school in San Francisco. Written very much in the Dickensian mode, being about the fading away and death of a beautiful little girl—a connection strengthened by the child's name, which is Carol, she having been born on Christmas Day—

the novella reinforced the sentimental theme by the self-conscious identification of the child's birth with that of Christ.

Despite the missed personal connection, Wiggin's story also suggests Alcott's influence: like Beth's demise, the death of little Carol Bird is long anticipated, and rather than merely prepare a room in which she may fade away, the Birds—a wealthy family with several servants—build a major addition to their house, with many windows to let in the natural sunlight. From these windows the dying girl can see the impoverished Ruggles children at play in the alley below, and her final wish is that they be invited to a great Christmas dinner, a banquet followed by the distribution of presents, including a set of "Miss Alcott's works" which is given to one of the Ruggles girls.

Carol dies that very evening, as her favorite hymns are being sung at her request in the church next door, but as with the Marches, the Bird family is consoled by the thought of the beneficial effects their daughter's death has brought: "I am happy in the child," Mrs. Bird declares, "and I see too clearly what she has done for us and the other children. . . . A quarrel or a hot word is almost unknown in this house, and why? Carol would hear it, and it would distress her, she is so full of love and goodness. . . . And as for me, Donald, I am a better woman every day for Carol's sake" (*The Birds' Christmas Carol*, 11). It would be difficult to find a better example of Alcott's influence on younger writers.

Wiggin's novella was eventually issued by a regular publisher, and her writing career was well launched with what proved to be a very popular book, whose connection with the kindergarten movement was admittedly incidental. By contrast, an earlier tale, also published in pamphlet form, *The Story of Patsy* (1883), is set in the Silver Street school, and Wiggin herself is both narrator and participant. The titular character is a poor crippled boy, the child of Irish immigrants, whose ambition is to attend the kindergarten, and who dies in the arms of "Miss Kate," as she sings his favorite hymn.

"Oh, it is hard to take to heart the lesson that such deaths will teach, but let no man reject it, for it is one that all must learn," the story ends: "Of every tear that sorrowing mortals shed on such green graves, some good is born, some gentler nature comes" (115). Here again we find a moral abstracted from the Alcott/Dickens nexus, for Wiggin's text is taken from *The Old Curiosity Shop*, spoken by the author himself over the grave of Little Nell (Dickens, 659). At the same time, with these early stories Wiggin seems to have discharged her debt to the sentimental occasion, and her best known novel would be planted solidly within the emerging realist tradition.

Kate Douglas's career as a lecturer-reader began informally, but soon became a full-time and lucrative profession, which, along with her writings, brought her into the company of the rich and famous of the day. These were for the most part writers and actors but included titled aristocrats of the Old World as well. Her first marriage ended in the early death of her husband (who left her with her professional name, Wiggin), but a subsequent second marriage endured, and her businessman husband was of sufficient means to ensure that they lived very comfortably in New York and in her summer place in Hollis, Maine, when not traveling about the world. Unfortunately the central chapters of her autobiography are clogged by name-dropping, page-long lists of the famous people she met, many of whom became her friends—including Mark Twain, William Dean Howells, Rudyard Kipling, and Frances Hodgson Burnett (who contributed an introduction to Wiggin's collected works).

Something of a real-life Cinderella, but cut from an American pattern of hard work not the recovery of unearned wealth, Wiggin seems to have never quite accepted her elevation from an unknown and suddenly impoverished young woman to a famous author and a wealthy member of high society. Rendering long lists of the high-and-mighty persons she met seems at first sight an egregious exercise of egotism, but it can also be seen as an expression of wonder, that Wiggin's life after her initial fame had been such a blessed experience. She seems to have been a Cinderella who never got used to living in the Palace. Like Burnett, Wiggin was always interested in matters of costume, interior decoration, and architectural design, and she devotes several chapters of her autobiography to the reconstruction of an old house in Hollis that became "Quillcote," her summer home. Like Burnett also she loved the theater, and discusses in detail the dramatization of her most popular works, including *The Bird's Christmas Carol* and *Rebecca of Sunnybrook Farm.*

On the other hand, Wiggin does not reveal much about the conditions out of which her works of fiction came, and the chapter devoted to that subject is filled with familiar generalities about authorship, though she does tell us that all she needed in order to write was a chair, a table, and an empty room. Fortunately, there is a paragraph devoted to the inspiration for her most famous story for young readers, *Rebecca of Sunnybrook Farm,* which came to her during a spell of illness as a dream about a young girl riding in a stagecoach, reaching through the window so as to poke the driver with her umbrella. Wiggin had no idea of the source of the dream, as it bore no apparent relation to her own childhood, from which as the author said she took the rural backdrop used in *Rebecca* but few of the characters and none of the incidents.

But then the use to which Wiggin put that stagecoach ride in her dream reminds us of similar rides taken by other little heroines, whether Jane Eyre being carried off to Lowood and from there to Thornfield, or Ellen Montgomery in an equivalent stagecoach en route to her Aunt Fortune's. And like Braum Van Brunt, who carries Ellen in an oxcart to her aunt's farm, the driver of Rebecca's coach, old Jerry Cobb, is a Dickensian character, one in a long line derived from Barkis in *David Copperfield.*

The most informative part of Wiggin's autobiography is that devoted to her experiences as a pioneer in kindergarten work, because *Rebecca* marks a shift away from the earlier tradition of home- and boarding-schooled girls to one in which the heroine attends public schools and derives much of her social life and the encouragement of her talents not from parents but from schoolmates and teachers. School stories for boys date back to 1857 and Thomas Hughes's *Tom Brown's Schooldays* and the opening episodes of *The Adventures of Tom Sawyer* (1876) have a school setting, but as Gillian Avery points out, though popular in England, school stories for girls were a "rarity in America" (*Behold the Child*, 169). Morever, it was not until *Rebecca* that public schooling became central to novels written for young female readers in this country.

This difference may be accounted for in part by circumstances: *Jane Eyre* like *The Professor* and *Villette* was influenced by Brontë's own boarding-school years, as both student and teacher, where Louisa Alcott like Jo March was tutored at home, by her parents and most notably by neighbor Thoreau. I think we may assume that Susan Warner during her early years was like most children of wealth educated privately, and Ellen Montgomery is kept from attending school by her aunt. It is only after meeting Alice and Mrs. Vawse that she is able to fulfil her ambition of improving her French.

As a girl in Manchester, Frances Hodgson was privately educated near home, but Sara Crewe is sent away to a boarding school obviously inspired by the one in Brontë's fragment, "Emma," where the emphasis is on the cruelty, amounting to sadism, of a schoolmistress—stand-in for the mean maiden aunts in America.

We should perhaps remember here that a governess eagerly contributes to Elsie Dinsmore's miseries, providing a bridge between Brontë and Burnett.

Moreover, in these novels—and the same holds for stories aimed at boys—we hear virtually nothing about the process of instruction. Jo may be taught at home but by whom and when and what is taught? Little Amy is sent for a brief time to an academy, but after she is humiliated by the (male) teacher for a trifling offense, she is quickly removed by an irate Marmee, and of her further education we hear nothing.

Lord Fauntleroy seems to have acquired his education like his beauty—naturally—and school is not even mentioned in *The Secret Garden,* where learning is chiefly a matter of nurturing the positive development of character, which is the "education" as well of the March sisters—in accordance with the pedagogical theories of Bronson Alcott. But in *Rebecca,* there is a radical shift of emphasis, and the district school provides not only a place of education but a social center for young people of both sexes.

Kate Wiggin, though twice married, never had children, yet her years as a teacher obviously contributed to the creation of Rebecca. Among the first pupils she encountered was a hyperactive little boy named Edgar, who insisted on remaining front-and-center during virtually all of the school activities, an egregious egotism of which Rebecca is not guilty, yet the little girl is a virtual whirlwind of activities that invariably call attention to herself. Wiggin claimed that Rebecca was not an autobiographical projection, but a group portrait of many children she had known, both as a child and as a teacher, and we can certainly take her at her word. Yet we may doubt if her interest in allowing a child the free exercise of creative impulses would have dominated the novel if she herself had not been a creative and precocious child, that self-possessed little girl who does not hesitate to seat herself, Rebecca-like, next to the wizard of Boz. A photograph of her at that time shows a bright, wide-eyed little girl, not difficult to identify with her famous heroine who is about twelve years old as well.

Rebecca as a literary creation may have been in part an autobiographical projection, inspired as well by children Wiggin encountered as a teacher, but she not a little resembles Jo March, virtually an inescapable intertexual fact in 1903. There are also hints of influence on both character and plot in Wiggin's novel by both Warner's *The Wide, Wide World* and Burnett's *The Little Princess.* Published in 1903, *Rebecca of Sunnybrook Farm* preceded the expanded version of *Sara Crewe* by a number of years, yet it followed the London stage production of 1902, and given Wiggin's love of the theater and her frequent stays in England, we cannot doubt that she was aware of the direction in which the original story was being taken.

Certainly Rebecca resembles the revised Sara Crewe in being a highly imaginative and popular little girl, who endears herself to practically everyone she meets, save for Miranda Sawyer, the maiden aunt with whom she comes to stay at the start of the story—a clear debt to Warner's popular novel. Miranda is hardly so mean as Miss Fortune, but she certainly resembles Ellen's aunt in her commonsensical Yankee character and belief in the virtues of hard work and saving ways. As the story progresses, the imaginative if occasionally careless little girl begins to have an influence on Miranda, as well as on other people in the village, and if the transformation of the maiden aunt is not quite so extreme as that of the Earl of Dorincourt, the change is essential to the meaning and the moral of the story.

This is a new development in the evolution of the daughters of Jane Eyre. Brontë's heroine has little influence on anyone in *Jane Eyre*, for it is her transformation that is important, a pattern carried over to the education of Ellen Montgomery, who labors to bring Braum Van Brunt to Christ, chiefly a sign of her increasing piety, but who has no effect whatsoever on her maiden aunt. Jo March most definitely helps Laurie learn to live with his grandfather, but the emphasis once again is on her own maturation, and though Rebecca like Jo most certainly grows up, physically and psychologically, the process has a detectable and positive influence on everyone around her, suggesting the priority of Burnett. Not possessing the physical beauty of Cedric Errol, Rebecca must make do with her abundant flow of optimism, for like Burnett's little boy she characteristically (if not invariably) sees the positive side of things. Like Sara Crewe, she is blessed with creative powers, and is constantly engaged in literary efforts and imaginative projects, most of which are encouraged by her beloved elementary school teacher, Miss Dearborn, a young woman not much older than her students. Like Sara Crewe, Rebecca has a close friend and admirer, Emma Jane Perkins, the daughter of the village blacksmith, who is rather dull and unimaginative, and who like Ermengarde is blindly devoted to the heroine.

As Gillian Avery confirms, Rebecca is surely one of the most likeable children in our literature, and not only because Wiggin tells us how much she is liked (*Behold the Child*, 181). From the moment she pokes the old stage driver with her umbrella, Rebecca engages the interest and sympathies of the reader and quite simply does not let go. Like Cedric Errol she is a vehicle of benevolent influence, but with a tartness that kills the sweet taste of saccharine, and is quite capable of instructing even her teacher, Miss Dearborn, in proper conduct.

Operating in the Dickensian traditon, the novel has its tearful moments, but the emphasis is quite American, bringing forward the sprightly Jo March in a new guise. There is nothing about Rebecca that suggests the tomboy, although she is quite capable of getting into trouble through the overly enthusiastic participation in activities in which schoolgirls are expected to shine. Unlike Jo, moreover, Rebecca does not have a fiery temper she must learn to subdue, and though her forgetfulness drives her obsessively orderly aunt to distraction, it is part and parcel of her creative, generous nature. Finally, it is Rebecca's positive outlook on life, her happy, creative personality, that is the operative force in the novel, working its influence not only on her immediate family but on the community at large, which reshapes itself around her very busy, entirely charming self.

If, as Alexander Cowie notes, Alcott's novel looks forward to *Rebecca*, in which "the best traits of the domestic novel were happily synthesized," it should also be noted that Rebecca like Ellen Montgomery remains single at the end of the story, with an equivalent Mr. John in the offing but not at the altar. That is, as a domestic novel, Wiggin's, like so many other stories of the period intended for a young female readership, looks not only to *Little Women* but to Susan Warner's *The Wide, Wide World*—at least so far as enforcing a terminal celibacy is concerned.

After Alcott, American writers for the juvenile market in the latter years of the nineteenth and the early years of the twentieth centuries tended to keep their heroines not only virginal but well short of the age of consent, leaving a whole plateau to be occupied later on by Judy Blume. The heroines became in fact littler and littler, as in the novels of Francis Hodgson Burnett seldom getting past their tenth birthdays. Even Tom Sawyer, after much talk about marrying Becky Thatcher, is happy to retire to the bachelor fastness of his cave with his all-male bandit gang.

Prepubescence forever! if you will.

III

As we have seen, the dominant role played by Johann Heinrich Pestalozzi in pedagogical reform throughout the nineteenth century spilled over into *Little Women,* by way of Bronson Alcott, whose system (if that is the word) of education was inspired by the Italian reformer. Pestalozzi's influence on Friedrich Froebel led to the kindergarten movement, and in considering the multiple sources of Wiggin's story of Rebecca, it is worth remembering that Pestalozzi was the author of *Leonard and Gertrude* (1781), a novel in which a young woman reforms an entire village through the force of her good example. In a sequel, *How Gertrude Teaches Her Children* (1801), Pestalozzi set forth the principles of his theory of education, texts that Wiggin as a pioneer in the kindergarten movement may well have known.

Certainly, given the schoolhouse setting, the story of Rebecca can be seen as paralleling Pestalozzi's story of Gertrude, with the heroine figuring as a central agent of social reform: for Wiggin as for Pestalozzi it takes a child to educate a village. This is not to say that the plot is overridden by a didactic agenda. If Frances Hodgson Burnett deserves more serious attention because of the ideological freight of her stories for children, we need to recognize Wiggin for the sheer delight that her novels convey. *Rebecca* is wonderfully comic, and if the eponymous heroine is an agent of reform, she is never taken all that seriously by the author: this alone marks a significant advance over even so ebullient a creation as Jo March. Humor is a subject difficult to discuss without losing the risible element, and what follows should not discourage readers unfamiliar with *Rebecca* from reading the novel. It is a book (as Wiggin's contemporaries attested) not aimed exclusively at children, and other adults I have met who are familiar with the book attest to its continuing popularity, beyond considerations of gender.

The novel begins with Rebecca's ride on that stagecoach inspired by the author's dream, and she pokes the driver with her parasol so that she may be taken up next to him in order to have a more comfortable ride (she has been bouncing and sliding around inside the rocking coach) and enjoy the view as well. Her full name as she reveals to the driver is Rebecca Rowena Randall, with a significant debt to Sir Walter Scott, and of the two heroines in *Ivanhoe,* it is the first named that the dark-haired and personable girl resembles. She is traveling to Riverboro, Maine, to live with her aging maiden aunts, Miranda and Jane Sawyer, so as to lend a hand and be supported in turn, her widowed mother being blessed with an overabundance of children and very little income.

The aunts had hoped that an older sister, Hannah, a soberminded, hard-working girl, would be sent, but the overburdened Aurelia Randall needs the services of Hannah herself, so it is Rebecca who arrives, and early on we learn that she is quite an exotic child, thanks in large part to her paternal heritage. Her father, Lorenzo de Medici Randall, twin brother of Marquis de Lafayette Randall, was reputed to have Spanish blood, being dark complected and with a sensitive soul and a love of music—he was a singing master and a violinist. L.D.M. (as he is called) was as impractical as handsome, and having introduced "an element of romance" into Aurelia's life, he invested her inheritance in a sequence of Micawber-like projects, then died, leaving her with no funds and seven children.

Rebecca is very sensitive about her father's failings, and certainly has inherited his creative sensibility, but it is expressed by her in literary terms, including poems and stories of her own composition. Seated with the stagecoach driver, Jeremiah (Jerry) Cobb, she rattles off her interests and capacities, including the romantic literature she prefers, virtually a compendium of the popular books of the day, from *Ivanhoe* to *The Lamplighter*, and reveals as well her willing belief in "elves and fairies and enchanted frogs!" (*Rebecca of Sunnybrook Farm*, 14). The prosaic Yankee driver is quite taken by his young passenger, and though ill-equipped to absorb the information she pours forth, he is virtually mesmerized by the little girl's eyes: "Their glance was eager and full of interest, yet never satisfied; their steadfast gaze was brilliant and mysterious, and had the effect of looking directly through the obvious to something beyond—in the object, in the landscape, in you" (7).

These are the author's reflections, not Jerry Cobb's, and should serve to remind us of both Jane Eyre and Sara Crewe. Rebecca possesses "a small plain face" that is "illuminated by a pair of eyes carrying such messages, such suggestions, such hints of sleeping power and insight, that one never tired of looking into their shining depths, nor of fancying that what one saw there was the reflection of one's own thought" (6). Jane Eyre also had large eyes, a traditional indication of soulfulness, but for Burnett and Wiggin they are signifiers also of abundant creativity, not exactly the talent Rebecca's aunts are in need of, but which proves to be of estimable value in the end. At the start, it is the little girl who is to be the chief beneficiary of the arrangement, receiving her keep and "regular schooling and church privileges, as well as the influence of the Sawyer home" (24). This as we frequently hear throughout the story is to be "the making of Rebecca," but as it turns out it is she who influences the Sawyer home for the better, and the town of Riverboro is a beneficiary as well.

Miranda Sawyer like Aunt Fortune is a prototypical old maid of the Yankee mold, traceable back to Sedgwick's *New-England Tale*, being a stern taskmaster with a sarcastic sense of humor, often exercised at the expense of her niece. Her sister, Jane, is much warmer of heart, having had a grievous hurt in her youth, when her lover went off to fight in the Civil War and was mortally wounded. Jane traveled South to be with him in the hospital, and he died in her arms, a sentimental moment that endows her with a much larger portion of humanity than is exhibited in her sister.

"She was in time . . . to show him for once the heart of a prim New England girl when it is ablaze with love and grief; to put her arms about him so that he could have a home to die in, and that was all—all; but it served" and "sent her home a better woman" (30). Coming early in the novel, this allusion serves notice that attendance on a dying loved one is an experience that widens the heart, an essential aspect of *Little Women*, but one that will not perform a critical service in *Rebecca*. It is as if Aunt Jane was operating under the old dispensation, her niece under the new.

We also learn that Jane like the youngest sister, Aurelia, had attended "a boarding school for young ladies," while Miranda had received only an ordinary "district school" education, which was sufficient for her perceived needs, limited to running the house and the farm after the death of her father, Deacon Israel Sawyer. It is the oldest sister who rules the roost, and Miranda attempts to force Rebecca into the accepted patterns of behavior maintained in the Sawyer home, or "the brick house" as it is called, emphasizing solidarity and rectilinearness, much as Miranda's routines are called "brick house ways." It is for the most part a futile exercise, as the girl's enthusiasms tend to overflow whatever limits her Aunt imposes. "Miss Sawyer," we are told, "shuddered openly at the adjective 'lively' as applied to a child," and lively is the operative if inadequate word for her niece (30).

Much of the book is taken up by the conflict between Miranda and Rebecca, which causes much irritation to the aunt and considerable grief to the niece, whose efforts to please Miranda often have the reverse effect. One day, in secret expiation for her sins, Rebecca throws her favorite pink parasol down the well, but it becomes caught in the bucket chain, drawing down the uncomprehending wrath of Miranda. But the conflicts are often resolved in favor of the niece, with some help from her Aunt Jane, and much of what happens to Rebecca is in a light-hearted vein, nor are the punishments meted out especially rigorous. Rebecca is in some ways a female version of Tom Sawyer (note the family name), being essentially a good-hearted child whose energetic participation in the life of the imagination is often misconstrued as mischief.

"She was a very faulty and passionately human child," as Wiggin explains, "with no aspirations towards being an angel of the house, but she had a sense of duty and a desire to be good—respectably, decently good" (53). There is a detectable shadow here of the young Louisa May Alcott, in whose diaries—published, albeit with deletions, in 1889—her frustrations to live up to the expectations of her parents are vividly expressed. Rebecca feels guilty about accepting the charity of an aunt she cannot possibly love, and "it is needless to say that Rebecca irritated her aunt with every breath she drew" (53). In her often careless, absent-minded way, she is "an everlasting reminder" for Miranda of Rebecca's "foolish, worthless father, whose handsome face and engaging manner had so deceived Aurelia"—and, it is hinted, Miranda as well.

The tension between the two finally explodes when the exasperated aunt scolds Rebecca for her habitual lateness, her apparent disregard for the "brick house routines," and her love for clothes any finer than the drab, brown gingham dresses she has been provided: "I ain't got any patience with your flowers, and frizzled-out hair, and furbelows, an' airs an' graces, for all the world like your Miss-Nancy father" (76). This insult is the final straw, and like Jane Eyre confronting Aunt Reed and Sara Crewe denouncing Miss Minchin, Rebecca who has been apologizing yet once again for her behavior, suddenly flares into anger: "Look here, Aunt Mirandy: I'll be as good as I know how to be. I'll mind quick when I'm spoken to, and never leave the door unlocked again; but I won't have my father called names. He was a p-perfectly l-lovely father, that's what he was; and it's mean to call him Miss Nancy!" (76).

Rebecca is sent off to bed without supper for her impudence, and Jane remonstrates with Miranda for her unnecessary cruelty, but she is unmoved by her sister's "annual burst of courage," and justifies her action by maintaining that Rebecca "will never amount to a hill o' beans till she gets some of her father trounced out of her" (77). The punishment is psychological not physical, but Rebecca's grief is so painful that she runs away from the brick house, finding shelter with "Uncle" Jerry Cobb and his wife, "Aunt Sarah."

Much as Brahm Van Brunt and his mother take Ellen Montgomery to their hearts, the couple adores and sympathizes with the lonely and weeping little girl, who brings to mind their own daughter, who died as an infant. Rebecca tearfully asks Uncle Jerry's help in returning home to Sunnybrook Farm, but the wise old man skillfully works her around so that she sees the wisdom in remaining with her aunts, and with his help she goes back to the brick house without her absence having been discovered. The episode marks a turning point, for Miranda under pressure from her sister realizes that her actions were hasty and ill-considered, and though refusing to admit her fault, becomes for a time more permissive, the first step in her own reform.

But this serious plot-line is spaced out with a great deal of purely comic material, including Rebecca's youthful attempts at poetry, which perfectly capture the clichés that young aspirants for literary fame are heir to, their attempts to maintain high seriousness and pathos inspiring laughter in the reader. (We will remember how Frances Burnett included bits of her own juvenilia in *The One I Knew Best of All,* published more than a decade before Wiggin's novel.) This was a time when Felicia Hemans was considered the proper model for young ladies attempting verse, and Longfellow's birthplace in Portland, Maine was an object of pilgrimage.

Moreover, where the brick house is a place of penitential sorrows the schoolhouse is a scene of frequent triumphs, for Rebecca has a definable talent for "speaking pieces." These classroom rituals provide great fun when parodied in *The Adventures of Tom Sawyer* but are glory days for Wiggin's heroine, whose "advent ... had somehow infused a new spirit into these hitherto terrible afternoons" (68). From the schoolroom her talents flow outward, for "it transpired afterwards at various village entertainments that Rebecca couldn't be kept in the background; it positively refused to hold her."

"Wherever Rebecca stood was the centre of the stage ... and somehow everybody watched her, took note of her gestures, her whole-hearted singing, her irrepressible enthusiasm" (73). There is something here of Kate Wiggin herself, who excelled at public readings, but also of de Stael's Corrine, the byword in the Victorian era for unrepressed, untrammeled natural talent, expressed through public performances. As Aunt Sarah Cobb suggests, "Her gift o' gab is what's goin' to be the makin' o' her. Mebbe she'll lecture, or recite pieces, like that Portland elocutionist that come out here to the harvest supper" (91).

Rebecca possesses other admirable qualities as well. Early on she has a confrontation with "a certain excellently named Minnie Smellie," a girl of her own age but unlike Rebecca "anything but a general favourite," being a "ferret-eyed, blondehaired, spindle legged creature, whose mind was a cross between that of a parrot and a sheep" (64). When enjoying a treat she has brought to school, Minnie always sneaks off so that she doesn't have to share it, and when on one of these occasions Rebecca tricks Minnie into confessing her sin of omission, she later relents and gives the other girl a bit of coral as a peace offering.

But when Rebecca catches Minnie Smellie harassing the Simpson children, the unfortunate progeny of a ne'er-do-well father with a habit of relieving his neighbors of presumably surplus because at the time unattached property, she plants herself in front of Minnie: "With a day of reckoning plainly set forth in her blazing eyes," she threatens to slap the bully if she ever teases the Simpson children again (66). When Minnie is overheard later boasting in the schoolyard that Rebecca's threats meant nothing to her— for she "had spasms of bravery when well surrounded by the machinery of law and order"—she receives the following message on a note from Rebecca:

> Of all the girls that are so mean,
>   There's none like Minnie Smellie.
> I'll take away the gift I gave,
>   And pound her into jelly.
>
> *P.S.—Now do you believe me?* (67)

IV

Despite their joint proclivity for day-dreaming and story-telling, despite their dark hair and deep eyes, Rebecca and Sara Crewe are quite different instances of the sensitive child, and though hardly a tomboy, it is obvious that Rebecca Rowena Randall has a definably muscular sensibility lacking in Sara. As Miranda comes to realize, her niece has as much Sawyer as Randall blood in her veins, meaning considerable Yankee get-up-and-go: Rebecca is an Emersonian compound, being half dreamer, half doer, and while giving her creative powers full exercise, she is always in the forefront planning school activities.

Peddling is intrinsic to the Yankee character, or Bronson Alcott lived in vain, and Rebecca decides that with the help of her great friend Emma Jane, she will sell enough cakes of soap so that the poor Simpson family can enjoy the beauty of a "banquet lamp" offered as a premium by the soap company. Setting off one day with a small wagon loaded with soap, the two girls have very uneven results until they come to a house where a young man sits on the front porch, and though he is shucking corn, he "had an air of the city about him—well-shaven face, well-trimmed moustache, well-fitting clothes" (118). As this is a major turning point in the novel, I quote the initial encounter entire:

> Rebecca was a trifle shy at this unexpected encounter, but there was nothing to be done but explain her presence, so she asked: "Is the lady of the house at home?"
> "I am the lady of the house at present," said the stranger, with a whimsical smile. "What can I do for you?"
> "Have you ever heard of the—would you like, or I mean—do you need any soap?" queried Rebecca.
> "Do I look as if I did?" he responded unexpectedly.
> Rebecca dimpled. "I didn't *mean* that. I have some soap to sell; I mean, I would like to introduce to you a very remarkable soap, the best now on the market. It is called the—"
> "Oh, I must know that soap," said the gentleman genially. "Made out of pure vegetable fats, isn't it?"
> "The very purest,"corroborated Rebecca.
> "No acid in it?"
> "Not a trace."
> "And yet a child could do the Monday washing with it and use no force?"
> "A Babe," corrected Rebecca.
> "Oh, a babe, eh? That child grows younger every year, instead of older—wise child!"
> This was great good fortune, to find a customer who knew all the virtues of the article in advance. (118–19)

What Rebecca doesn't realize is that she is being teased by the citified young man, who is parroting the familiar, hackneyed promotional material for the soap, having been as he later admits something of a "commercial traveler" himself.

In the conversation that follows, this teasing tone continues, the young man drawing the girl out, so that she reveals her family's hardships, and he admits to a childhood of poverty himself. But the handsome young man is obviously quite prosperous now, and when Rebecca reveals the purpose of her errand, to sell enough soap to provide the impoverished Simpsons with the celebrated solid-brass banquet lamp, the young man computes the amount of soap that must be sold for that purpose, and announces that he will "take three hundred cakes, and that will give them [lamp]shade and all."

Rebecca had been seated on a stool very near to the edge of the porch, and at this remark she made a sudden movement, tipped over, and disappeared into a clump of lilac bushes. It was a very short distance, fortunately, and the amused capitalist picked her up, set her on her feet, and brushed her off. "You should never seem surprised when you have taken a large order," said he; "you ought to have replied, "Can't you make it three hundred and fifty?" instead of capsizing in that unbusinesslike way." (121)

The young man is named Adam Ladd, but because of his great generosity associated with a lamp, Rebecca calls him henceforth "Mr. Aladdin," and he will provide a magical presence throughout the rest of the story. He is the most eligible bachelor in the village—"If Ladd was a Mormon," calculates Emma Jane's mother, "I guess he could have every woman in North Riverboro that's a suitable age"—but because of his fondness for the little girl he becomes dedicated to her well-being: "Goodbye, Miss Rebecca Rowena!" he tells her when they part. "Just let me know whenever you have anything to sell, for I'm certain I shall want it" (236, 122). As the name Rebecca gives him suggests, Mr. Aladdin is the Prince Charming of the piece, but he does not take her up into his palace; instead he serves as a benevolent presence in the background, ensuring that she receive whatever is necessary to forward her progress in this world. Though he is more often than not away in Boston, he tends to turn up at critical moments, and uses his wealth to Rebecca's advantage albeit without her knowledge. Absent the motivation of guilt, Mr. Aladdin is an equivalent Mr. Carrisford in *Sara Crewe*, but his interest in the schoolgirl is something other than avuncular. Though almost twice as old as Rebecca, he obviously has more than a charitable interest in her, a subtle eroticism that at times evokes Mr. Rochester's sly playing with Jane Eyre's emotions.

Adam Ladd has none of the Byronism of Rochester, and his motivation (like that of Warner's Mr. John and Brontë's Crimsworth) is more that of Pygmalion than Bluebeard, as his feelings toward the young girl are obviously pure if amorous. Moreover, Adam Ladd is a businessman not a landed aristocrat, who has earned his wealth, and he is also a man of considerable influence, serving as a school trustee of Wareham Academy—which Rebecca attends after graduating from the district school—and on the board of a railroad company as well.

In both of these positions he is able to help Rebecca, and is on friendly terms with Miss Emily Maxwell, Rebecca's English teacher at the Academy, who shares his interest in the talented young woman. Increasingly Mr. Aladdin takes control over Rebecca's life, seldom with her awareness of his influential presence. It is he, not Aunt Miranda, who masterminds "the making of Rebecca." Thus, with Miss Maxwell's connivance, Adam establishes an essay contest, with fifty dollars as the prize, knowing full well that Rebecca is so superior a student that she will win the money, which will go to pay the mortgage installment due on Sunnybrook Farm.

One day Adam pays Rebecca a visit in Miss Maxwell's rooms at Wareham Academy, where she often goes to read her teacher's books—on this particular day it is George Eliot's *Romola*—and what follows is reminiscent of earlier examples of erotic mentoring, albeit with significant differences:

> The light in the room grew softer, the fire crackled cheerily, and they talked of many things, until the old sweet sense of friendliness and familiarity crept back into Rebecca's heart. Adam had not seen her for several months, and there was much to be learned about school matters as viewed from her own standpoint; he had already inquired concerning her progress from Mr. Morrison [the principal of the academy].
>
> "Well, little Miss Rebecca," he said, rousing himself at length, "I must be thinking of my drive to Portland. There is a meeting of railway directors there tomorrow, and I always take this opportunity of visiting the school and giving my valuable advice concerning its affairs educational and financial."
>
> "It seems funny for you to be a school trustee," said Rebecca contemplatively. "I can't seem to make it fit."
>
> "You are a remarkably wise young person, and I quite agree with you," he answered; "the fact is," he adds soberly, "I accepted the trusteeship in memory of my poor little mother, whose last happy years were spent here."
>
> "That was a long time ago!"
>
> "Let me see, I am thirty-two—only thirty-two, despite an occasional grey hair. My mother was married a month after she graduated, and she lived only until I was ten. . . . Would you like to see my mother, Miss Rebecca?"
>
> The girl took the leather case gently and opened it to find an innocent, pink-and-white daisy of a face, so confiding, so sensitive, that it went straight to the heart. It made Rebecca feel old, experienced, and maternal. She longed on the instant to comfort and strengthen such a tender young thing. (198–99)

The portrait of a virginal mother plays an important role in *The Professor*, and in opening the locket to Rebecca, Ladd not only opens his heart but stresses the sentimental, domestic side of his past. His mother had suffered greatly after she married—there are no particulars—and he being only a child could do nothing to help. "Now I have success and money and power, all that would have kept her alive and happy, and it is too late. She died for lack of love and care, nursing and cherishing, and I can never forget it. All that has come to me seems now and then so useless, since I cannot share it with her!"

The conversation comes around to Rebecca's own mother, also suffering from poverty, always "sad and busy," but encouraged and made happy by the success of John Randall, her son: "That's what your mother would have thought about you if she had lived, and perhaps she does as it is" (199). Rising to depart, Adam tells Rebecca that she is "a comforting little person," then suddenly becomes aware that the "little person" is growing up, although as Rebecca reminds him she is not yet fifteen, and is therefore three years short of becoming a "young lady." Adam Ladd tells her that "Mr. Aladdin . . . doesn't like grown-up young ladies in long trains and wonderful fine clothes; they frighten and bore him!" (200).

Adam seems in part inspired by the kindly Dr. John Graham Bretton in *Villette* who falls in love with the sprightly and spiritual girl-child, Paulina Home. Dr. John rejects the proud, vain, and flirtatious Genevra Fanshawe for Paulina, and Genevra has her equivalent in Huldah Meserve, one of Rebecca's schoolmates who overdresses and flirts outrageously with young men: "Don't form yourself on her, Rebecca. Clover blossoms that grow in the fields beside Sunnybrook mustn't be tied in the same bouquet with gaudy sunflowers; they are too sweet and fragrant and wholesome" (201). Looking into Rebecca's eyes, he finds them "as soft, as clear, as unconscious and childlike as they had been when she was ten," and he remembers "the other pair of challenging blue eyes that had darted coquettish glances through half-dropped lids." In a similar passage in *Villette*, Dr. John compares the eyes of Genevra and Paulina, and makes much the same conclusion: both women are beautiful, one boasting "the advantage in material charms, but the latter shone pre-eminent for attractions more subtle than spiritual, for light and eloquence of eye, for grace of mien, for winning variety of expression" (397–98).

The bond established in this intimate conversation is essential to the domestic heart of the sentimental idea, Adam Ladd's mother joined in suffering (and solace) to Rebecca's mother. Clearly Rebecca in her girlish innocence reminds Mr. Ladd of his beloved parent, who in her picture is untouched by the cruel caress of the hard-handed world. In time, Ladd will provide Rebecca's mother a signal service, seeing to it that the railroad on whose board he serves cuts through her property, saving the farm from foreclosure and guaranteeing Aurelia Randall a comfortable income for the rest of her life. That Mr. Aladdin will eventually marry Rebecca is as certain as it is unspoken, although the novel ends with the relationship having progressed not much further than it does in Miss Maxwell's library room at the Academy.

When Rebecca graduates, with plans for taking a position offered her by a boarding school, Adam is in the crowded audience and as always his protégée is the Corinne of the show: "At the end of the programme came her class poem, 'Makers of Tomorrow,' and there, as on many a former occasion, her personality played so great a part that she seemed to be uttering Miltonic sentiments instead of schoolgirl verse. Her voice, her eyes, her body breathed conviction, earnestness, emotion; and when she left the platform the audience felt that they had listened to a masterpiece" (245). At the end of the ceremonies, Mr. Ladd makes his way to the platform, and when the excited girl asks him if he had been satisfied by her performance, he replies: "More than satisfied! Glad I met the child, proud I know the girl, longing to meet the woman," a sequence promising much more to come of their relationship (246).

But the novel does not end with this heavy hint. Instead of being able to accept a teaching position, Rebecca at the graduation ceremony learns from Jerry Cobb that Miranda Sawyer has been paralyzed by a stroke—"She ain't lost her speech; that'll be a comfort to her"—and she returns to the brick house to care for the ailing old lady (249). Miranda's first words to her niece, who enters the room with a bouquet of sweet peas, are typical: "'Come in,' she said; 'I ain't dead yet. Don't mess up the bed with them flowers, will ye?'" (252). Instead of considering the state of her soul, Miranda worries about the state of her farm, which she can no longer manage.

Lacking a "spiritual eye," she is "held fast within the prison walls of her own nature," and Rebecca weeps to think that her aunt, "so grim, so hard, so unchastened and unsweetened," will soon cross over to the "great beyond." But Miranda is not yet ready to go, and with her "unassailable" will, grows stronger each day, until her niece feels that she can make preparations to take a position in a local high school, which will enable her to take over her aunt's care on "nights and Sundays" (254).

But then comes the hope-shattering news that her mother has suffered a bad accident and desperately needs Rebecca's help, for

Hannah is now married with a child of her own. Earlier, in conversation with Adam Ladd, Miss Maxwell declares that "so far I don't regret one burden that Rebecca has borne or one sorrow that she has shared. Necessity has only made her brave; poverty has only made her daring and self-reliant" (217). This sentiment recalls Mrs. Bird's declaration that the death of their daughter Carol has served as a catalyst for change, but death is not the transformational agent in *Rebecca of Sunnybrook Farm:* notably Miranda Sawyer dies off stage, and though her niece regrets her aunt's passing, it otherwise does not much affect her psychologically.

What Miss Maxwell is expressing is the doctrine of adversity that is central to the Brontë tradition, and has a distinctively New England coloration in this instance, the rock-ribbed region with its iron-bound coast being famous for creating the self-reliance of which Emerson was such a champion. Caring for her mother and managing the farm is adversity piled on adversity, however: "No girl of seventeen can pass through such an ordeal and come out unchanged; no girl of Rebecca's temperament could go through it without some inward repining and rebellion" (259). In the meantime, the teaching position in the high school is filled by another, and her future appears bleak indeed.

While at Wareham Academy, Rebecca saw in a locked case a book entitled *The Rose of Joy,* which Miss Maxwell explains is "from Emerson," and expresses an abstract idea perhaps too difficult for a "girl of seventeen." But at Rebecca's insistence the teacher quotes the source of the title: "In the actual—this painful kingdom of time and chance—are Care, Canker, and Sorrow; with thought, with the Ideal, is immortal hilarity—the Rose of Joy; round it all the muses sing" (223). The notion takes a firm hold on Rebecca's imagination, and in caring for her mother she comes to understand its meaning.

Indeed, her role of nurse to Aurelia is an intensely Emersonian experience, illustrating "the law of compensation," for with the cares she must bear, there are corresponding joys, "implanting gaiety in the place of inert resignation to the inevitable" (260). Rebecca finds that she actually enjoys "being mistress of the poor domain of planning, governing, deciding; of bringing order out of chaos," and there is the joy found in the love of her younger brothers and sisters, whom in the manner of Sara Crewe she entertains by telling stories.

Moreover, "in those anxious days mother and daughter found and knew each other as never before," nor was Rebecca's imagination entirely dulled by the experience: "Her physical eye saw the cake she was stirring and the loaf she was kneading . . . but ever and anon her fancy mounted on pinions, rested itself, renewed its strength in the upper air" (260–61). The duality here between material fact and spiritual flight is surely Emersonian, the bread in the pan, the wagon hitched to a star: there was the "fixed fact" of the farmhouse, but within Rebecca's imagination was "many a palace into which she now and then withdrew," and each time "she retired to her citadel of dreams she came forth radiant and refreshed, as one who has seen the evening star, or heard sweet music, or smelled the Rose of Joy." It would seem that Kate Douglas Wiggin is here drawing on that summer spent in Concord, for more and more Rebecca is becoming an Emersonian demonstration, which lends her story a certain depth, a belated product of Transcendentalism.

And yet this concluding section is the weakest in the novel, for Wiggin gives up on dialogue and other dramatic devices, and takes over the narration with a strong, third-person voice, as if in a hurry to bring her story to closure. Perhaps the author's true interest in Rebecca lay in her younger years, that sprightly New England girlhood drawn from her own experience in which were demonstrated the qualities that made her heroine such a popular figure. In a succeeding volume, *The Chronicles of Rebecca*, Wiggin avoided the necessity of a sequel by going back to the beginning, inventing a series of incidents expanding on Rebecca's experiences in Riverboro, taking her to the Warham Academy once again. Along the way the author provided Emma Jane a lover of her own, thereby rescuing her from what had been a certain fate of spinsterhood, even while hinting even more heavily that Adam Ladd was simply waiting until Rebecca was old enough to wed.

In the original story, Rebecca relieves her mother's despondency by exclaiming "it's enough joy just to be here in the world on a day like this—to have the chance of seeing, feeling, doing, becoming!" which suggests that the burden she has been carrying has not entirely subdued her spirit (264). And yet the experience is obviously intended as a rite of passage, equivalent to Jo's caring for little Beth in her final illness. However, it is not Aurelia that dies, but Miranda, who passes away invisibly as it were, and Rebecca returns to Riverboro for the funeral, only to learn (what the reader already knew) that she has been left the brick house by her aunt, much as Jo was left Plumfield. At the same time, news arrives that the railroad will be buying the Randall farm, rescuing it from impending foreclosure, another of Adam Ladd's good deeds.

Putting Rebecca on the train for Riverboro, Adam realizes that "in her sad dignity and gravity," the young woman was "more beautiful than he had ever seen her—all beautiful and all-womanly," yet her eyes were "still those of a child; there was no knowledge of the world in their shining depths, no experience of men or women, no passion nor comprehension of it" (269). Rebecca is both "chastened and glorified" when she emerges from the room in which her aunt lies awaiting burial, but it is not the effect of standing in "the Great Presence" that has brought her to maturity, it is the experience of caring for her mother, her brothers and sisters, and managing the family farm.

Rebecca has been changed for the better, but the practical experience has not blighted her soul, only deepened it, another version of the Emersonian dichotomy. Like Ellen Montgomery, Rebecca's education by adversity has prepared her for marriage to her mentor, but where Warner's heroine has been rendered a pious cypher, Wiggin's has become a wise yet essentially innocent virgin, precisely the bride Adam Ladd desires. Indeed, for Rebecca to remain her mentor's ideal maiden, she cannot marry him, and he will be kept forever waiting just an aisle short of the altar.

Rebecca of Sunnybrook Farm, finally, is a celebration of the Protestant Ethic with a Transcendental dimension, but it is also an intensely domestic fiction, in which sentimentality is diluted by considerable hilarity and all good things come to those who serve and wait. In the closing words of the book, we find Rebecca filled with the awareness that the brick house inherited from Miranda not Sunnybrook Farm is now her home, "her roof, her garden, her green acres, her dear trees," that it would provide shelter for her mother and the children. "And she? Her own future was close-folded still—folded and hidden in beautiful mists; but she leaned her head against the sun-warmed door, and closing her eyes, whispered, just as if she had been a child saying her prayers: 'God bless Aunt Miranda! God bless the brick house that was! God bless the brick house that is to be!'" Whatever her future may bring, Rebecca has at last arrived where all orphans aspire to be—at home.

V

Well, home is also where Ulysses, the prototype of all adventurers, strove to be, albeit on quite different terms. For the man of adventure has his sentimental side, especially during the time of which we are writing, as is shown by a letter sent in 1904 to Kate Wiggin by Jack London, then a correspondent covering the Japanese invasion of Manchuria. It was written to thank the author for a copy of *Rebecca of Sunnybrook Farm*, just published, and is included in Wiggin's autobiography. London like all of the foreign correspondents seeking to send back stories about the war was frustrated by disinformation fed them by Japanese authorities as well as by a policy forbiding access to the front. London said that he had been "whiling away the hours" reading *Penelope's Experiences*, Wiggin's novel about a young American woman traveling abroad, stories that "appealed to my head." But it was *Rebecca* that "won my heart," unique testimony to the book's appeal, given its unlikely source (353).

We generally think of Jack London as one of the hardest hands with a pen, a naturalistic writer who emphasizes the never-ending Darwinian battle for survival set against a Yukon wilderness, yet his reaction to Wiggin's novel was one as he testified of both laughter and tears: "She is real; she lives; she has given me many regrets, but I love her. I would have quested the wide world over to make her mine, only I was born too long ago and she was born but yesterday. Why could she not have been my daughter? Can't I adopt her? and, O, how I envy 'Mr. Aladdin'! Why couldn't it have been I who bought the three hundred cakes of soap? Why, O, why?" London signed himself "Gratefully yours," and gratitude I think has been the expression of all of us who first came to *Rebecca* as older men, and who have followed London's lead by falling in love with a girl who still inspires much more laughter than tears, and those more of happiness than grief.

There is that in Rebecca's Emersonian gaiety that looks forward to Eleanor Porter's Pollyanna and the "Glad Game," yet another testimonial to the power of positive thinking that provides a bridge between *Little Lord Fauntleroy* and the book that made Norman Vincent Peale famous and rich. Pollyanna is yet another orphan who Gertrude-like transforms the household and the community in which she lives, an ultimate exercise in optimism, published on the very verge of World War I, after which the popularity of Pollyannaism virtually turned against itself, and the word became a cynical expression of scorn.

But before moving on to what must be taken as the final stage of an American revolution that began when Susan Warner in effect evangelized *Jane Eyre*, we need to consider a book that in so many ways is a reaction to Rebecca, Jean Webster's *Daddy-Long-*

Legs, another story about a girl in school and an older man who casts a mysterious but highly influential shadow over her life.

Again, in terms of genre we find very little signs of Charlotte Brontë's direct influence, but the key element found in the stories of Jane Eyre's daughters that we have been tracing hitherto, the prevalence of the Pygmalion-Galatea complex, remains consistent.

13

Love Stories:
Jean Webster's Epistolary Experiment
in Education and Eros

In notes with many a winding bout
Of linked sweetness long drawn out.
—Milton

I

THANKS TO THE BIOGRAPHY BY ALAN AND MARY SIMPSON (1984), WE
now know much more about Samuel L. Clemens's grandniece
than can be found in the *Dictionary of American Biography*.
There, we learn that Jean Webster was born in Fredonia, New
York, 1876, the daughter of Annie Moffett, Sam Clemens's niece,
and Charles Webster, the man who was unfortunate enough to
have been for a time Mark Twain's publisher. Her baptismal name
was Alice Jane Chandler Webster, which she changed to plain
Jean because her roommate at the Lady Jane Grey School was
also named Alice, but the shortening, like the bobbed hair she preferred, was typical of her tendency toward a modest modernism.

She was educated at Vassar College (class of '01), where she began her professional career as a journalist and short story writer,
and developed an awareness of contemporary social problems,
thanks to a popular teacher, Professor H. E. Mills. Her college
sketches were gathered and revised as *When Patty Went to College* (1902) and Webster continued to have her short stories and
novels published with generally favorable notices. She was close
friends in college with Adelaide Crapsey, whose poetry she edited
after Crapsey's early death in 1914 and who may have inspired
several of Webster's fictional heroines.

Even before graduating, Webster traveled to Europe, and in
1907 she spent a year circling the globe with four close female

303

friends, all of whom shared what at the time were radical views, including equal rights for women. Though her father, literally harassed to death by Sam Clemens, died in 1891, Jean Webster, unlike most of the other authors we have been discussing, never knew hardship or poverty during her youth. Her interest in disadvantaged children was inspired by her years at Vassar, from its founding a socially conscious institution, as well as by her own wealthy and privileged life, which inspired philanthropic inclinations. As an undergraduate, Webster had visited institutions for orphaned children and became convinced that given a decent break these juveniles, despite their dubious origins, could succeed in life.

But as the Simpsons have demonstrated, Jean Webster's life after 1907 was a post-graduate education in adversity. She fell in love with Glenn Ford McKinney, a wealthy sportsman eleven years her senior and the brother of her close friend Ethelyn McKinney, one of the four women with whom she had traveled around the world. The love affair began shortly after Jean's return but remained a secret for seven years because Glenn was married to Annette (*née* Renaud), daughter of a Creole wine merchant in Martinique. Annette was subject to spells of severe depression, which drove the relatively weak willed Glenn to binge drinking. His sister, by far the stronger of the two, had troubles of her own, including a stepmother a year younger than she and a love relationship with Lena Weinstein, another of the five world travelers, which was at least once interrupted by the prospect of a heterosexual marriage.

Annette McKinney's depression bordered on psychosis and she spent much of her married life in and out of sanitoriums; Glenn likewise needed institutional help to deal with his drinking problems. Jean assisted in this effort, with eventual success, and after Annette finally agreed to a divorce, the two lovers were married, on September 7, 1915, a year after her friend Adelaide's tragic death from tuberculosis. The McKinneys divided the first year of their life together between Glenn's hunting camp in Canada (a near neighbor was ex-president Theodore Roosevelt), their large residence in Dutchess County, and Jean's apartment overlooking Central Park. This idyll was apparently not disturbed by the war in Europe, but by December Jean was suffering from the first stages of a difficult pregnancy. Her daughter was born on Saturday, June 10, and Jean died the following day, a month short of her fortieth birthday.

If Jean's tragic death resembles that of Charlotte Brontë—and Adelaide can serve as a surrogate sister, a poet who like Emily died young—then her husband's troubled first marriage to a mentally disturbed woman of Creole birth cannot but remind us of Rochester's relationship with Bertha, albeit minus the gothic element. Yet Jean Webster's writing both before and during her long secret relationship with Glenn McKinney resembles the upbeat fictions of Alcott, Burnett, and Wiggin. As young Louisa Alcott observed to Rebecca Harding, "who never had any troubles, though she writes about woes," "I had lots of troubles, so I write jolly tales" (*Journals*, 109).

The Simpsons demonstrate that most of Webster's work contains autobiographic elements, derived from her years at boarding school, at Vassar, in Europe, and (as we shall see) her love affair with Glenn. Yet she characteristically stresses the most positive elements of the complex life she led, and was known in her heyday for the sunny optimism of her stories, the most famous of which is *Daddy-Long-Legs* (1912), which Webster successfully adapted for the stage. It became a movie starring Mary Pickford, who also played Rebecca and Sara Crewe, roles that undoubtedly helped earn her the sobriquet, "America's Sweetheart," although Pickford—following the stage tradition of using young women as boy heroes—starred in the first film version of *Little Lord Fauntleroy* as well.

Best known today as the movie vehicle for Leslie Caron and Fred Astaire, *Daddy-Long-Legs* is unfortunately categorized as juvenile fiction, for like *Rebecca* it has much that recommends it to adults. It was first published as a serial in the *Ladies Home Journal* and then as a book by the Century Company, neither of which were venues for children's books. Though framed as a humorous bildungsroman, the novel had a serious purpose, having been written to illustrate Webster's theory that orphans, given a chance, could become productive members of a society that has marginalized them by placing them in institutions.

Though her novel is written in service of a thesis, its ideological function is virtually invisible, thanks to the narrative technique, which is something of a stylistic tour de force, being a first-person exercise that avoids the didactic element. After a brief introduction, the novel takes the form of letters from an orphan, Jerusha Abbot, to her anonymous benefactor, a man who has rescued her at the age of seventeen from an orphan asylum and sent her to college, so as to prepare her for a writing career. The letters are the quid pro quo of the arrangement, for Jerusha is to mail to her patron regular reports on her progress but must not expect replies, for, as she has been told, the man, to be known only as

"John Smith," "detests letter writing" and "does not care for girls" (*Daddy-Long-Legs,* 16, 14).

Jerusha at the start knows only that the benefactor is a trustee of the John Grier Home for orphans, where she has spent all of her seventeen years. Quite by chance she caught a glimpse of him as he left the asylum, "a fleeting impression" that "consisted entirely of tallness," being a shadow cast by the headlights from his automobile, with "grotesquely elongated legs and arms that ran along the floor and up the wall of the corridor. It looked, for all the world, like a huge, wavering daddy-long-legs," hence the name by which she routinely addresses her letters to the man who saved her from an uncertain and unpromising future (13).

We might note the incidental fact that this is the first automobile to make an appearance in the books under discussion, but that is hardly the only innovation that characterizes Webster's novel. It is for example illustrated throughout, simple line drawings that are added to her letters by Jerusha, in contradistinction to the professional pictures provided other children's books by artists not always of the stature or abilities of Reginald Birch. They add a further dimension of humor, and were the work of Webster herself, who displayed considerable artistic talent at Vassar.

Jerusha is at first overcome by her immersion in college life, which seems a miracle of freedom after the lock-step life she has previously led, but all is not perfect: surrounded by young women from privileged backgrounds, she feels like an intruder. Early on, she realizes that the hardest part of being in college is attempting to connect with her classmates, who come from a much different world from the one she has known: "I do want to be like the other girls, and that Dreadful Home looming over my childhood is the one great big difference" (29).

She takes on protective coloration by dropping the unwieldy name given her in the orphanage, reducing it to "Judy," even while admitting that "it belongs to the kind of girl I'm not—a sweet little blue-eyed thing, petted and spoiled by all the family, who romps her way through life without any cares" (27). We never do learn what the narrator does look like, but she is obviously not "a sweet little blue-eyed thing"; since at the start of her college experience she is something of an alien and exile, she may be thought of as having the standard dark coloration of all long-suffering heroines in the *Jane Eyre* tradition.

"Half the time I don't know what the girls are talking about. . . . I'm a foreigner in the world and I don't undestand the language. It's a miserable feeling" (29). But Judy soon takes advantage of the situation to catch up on the reading for which opportunities were decidedly lacking at the John Grier Home: "I never read *Mother Goose* or *David Copperfield* or *Ivanhoe* or *Cinderella* or *Bluebeard* or *Robinson Crusoe* or *Jane Eyre* or *Alice in Wonderland* or a word of Rudyard Kipling. . . . I didn't know that R. L. S. stood for Robert Louis Stevenson or that George Eliot was a lady" (36).

Her hunger for reading is so great that at one time she is reading four books at once, including *Little Women:* "Don't laugh. . . . I find that I am the only girl in college who wasn't brought up on *Little Women.*" Later, Judy reports that she has been reading "*bushels* of poetry" as well as "really necessary novels like *Vanity Fair,* and *Richard Feverel* and *Alice in Wonderland.* Also Emerson's *Essays* and Lockhart's *Life of Scott* and the first volume of Gibbon's *Roman Empire* and half of Benvenuto Cellini's *Life*" (45).

Given our central thesis, it is of particular interest that Judy is quite taken by *Wuthering Heights,* or at least by the circumstances of its composition: "Emily Brontë was quite young when she wrote it, and had never been outside of Haworth churchyard. She had never known any men in her life; how could she imagine a man like Heathcliffe [*sic*]" (51–52). Such youthful accomplishment causes Judy to despair: "Sometimes a dreadful fear comes over me that I'm not a genius. Will you be awfully disappointed, Daddy, if I don't turn out to be a great author?" There is also an interesting citation of a poem by the other Emily, one of those encrypted messages that coyly hint at dark meanings undisclosed:

> I asked no other thing,
> No other was denied.
> I offered Being for it;
> The mighty merchant smiled.
>
> Brazil? He twirled a button
> Without a glance my way:
> But, madam, is there nothing else
> That we can show today?

Judy reports to her patron that the poem appeared on the blackboard in her English class one morning, without identifying the poet, "and we were ordered to comment upon it. When I read the first verse I thought I had an idea—the mighty merchant was a divinity who distributes blessings in return for virtuous deeds—but when I got to the second verse and found him twirling a button, it seemed a blasphemous supposition, and I hastily changed my mind" (53). Judy was not alone, for no one in the class understood the meaning of the poem, and were left "with blank paper and equally blank minds." Nor is the reader enlightened further on the poem or the poet, whose name remains unknown, as is the meaning of the lines.

Within the context of the epistolary situation, in which Judy is writing to an older man who while acting as her benefactor refuses to acknowledge his identity, a mystery she finds increasingly frustrating even painful, the Dickinson poem has a great deal of meaning. The "mighty merchant" is indeed God-like, as is Daddy-Long-Legs, who is the source of Judy's well-being, and as God, he is indifferent to her wishes. By 1912, Charlotte Brontë's anguished, one-sided correspondence with Professor Heger had been revealed, and there are distinct reflections in Judy's unhappy situation. She too asks "no other thing," nothing other that is to say than some response to her letters, and "no other thing" is denied. We are perilously close here to Sylvia Plath's gnomic lines to her own Daddy, and should suspect much more of Webster's book than a designation as juvenile fiction suggests. The relevance of the poem's meaning to the novel will play out as the story comes to closure.

The next novel mentioned is *The Portrait of a Lady*, about a mistaken, tragic marriage, rather heavy stuff for a college girl a century ago, one would think. Later, Judy is reading in class "Marie Bashkirtseff's journal," a once popular book that drew Kate Douglas Wiggin's attention also, for it was purportedly written by a young Russian artist desperate for fame, hence was a text that reached out to women ambitious to succeed in the arts (80; cf. *My Garden*, 205–7). But Judy puts her usual humorous frame around the book, and having quoted the line, "Last night I was seized by a fit of despair that found utterance in moans, and that finally drove me to throw the dining room clock into the sea," she adds: "It makes me almost hope I'm not a genius; they must be very wearing to have about—and awful destructive to the furniture."

At this point in her development, Judy is self-definedly a romantic (Stevenson becomes her favorite author) and, already starting to write her own fiction, she is saturated in sentimental formulae: "Did you ever," she writes her Daddy-Long-Legs, "have a sweet baby girl who was stolen from the cradle in infancy? Maybe I am she! If we were in a novel, that would be the denouement, wouldn't it?" (82). These questions not only hint at Judy's frustration in learning nothing about her benefactor, but bring up the much larger related problem, her own identity: "It's awfully queer not to know what one is—sort of exciting and romantic.

There are such a lot of possibilities. Maybe I'm not American; lots of people aren't. . . . I may be the child of a Russian exile and belong by rights in a Siberian prison, or maybe I'm a Gypsy—I think perhaps I am." At a pivotal point half-way through the novel, Jerusha gets around to the long-deferred *Jane Eyre,* early listed as one of the books she has not read, and her reaction is predictably complex. She sits up half the night reading the romance, but wonders if people ever really did "talk that way?"

> The haughty Lady Blanche says to the footman, "Stop your chattering, knave, and do my bidding." Mr. Rochester talks about the metal welkin when he means the sky; and as for the mad woman who laughs like a hyena and sets fire to bed curtains and tears up wedding veils and *bites*—it's melodrama of the purest, but just the same, you read and read and read. I can't see how any girl could have written such a book, especially any girl who was brought up in a churchyard. There's something about those Brontës that fascinates me. Their books, their lives, their spirit. Where did they get it? When I was reading about little Jane's troubles in the charity school, I got so angry that I had to go out and take a walk. I understood exactly how she felt. Having known Mrs. Lippett, I could see Mr. Brocklehurst. (98–99)

This is the key as it were to the room in Bluebeard's Castle. There are few readers who have not asked Judy's questions about the Brontës, but not every reader has her experience to draw upon. Mrs. Lippett is the stiffly humorless director of the John Grier Home, who while relentlessly exploiting Jerusha tells her how grateful she should be, and who warns the girl that her vivid imagination "would get her into trouble if she didn't take care" (12). She is perhaps more reminiscent of Miss Minchin than Brocklehurst, much as Judy shares Sara Crewe's creativity, but the function of this passage is to draw the reader back to the grand original of these stories about young women who are in the care of older men of mystery. When pressed by a roommate to reveal her mother's maiden name, "I didn't have the courage to say I didn't know, so I just miserably plumped on the first name I could think of, and that was Montgomery" (43).

Jerusha-Judy Abbott is no Ellen Montgomery, however, and rarely weeps. She is older than either Ellen or Sara Crewe, and perceptibly grows up as the novel progresses, the increasing sophistication of her letters to her benefactor revealing the successive stages of her maturity. But one theme that is consistent, hinted at in Judy's desperate response to the question posed by the wealthy and socially conscious girl who "got started on the subject of family, and I *couldn't* switch her off," is not only the matter of her identity, but the void suggested by the word "family" itself.

In her very first letter to her benefactor, filled with gratitude, Jerusha declares that "having someone take an interest in me after all these years, makes me feel as though I had found a sort of family. It seems as though I belonged to somebody now, and it's a very comfortable sensation. . . . I really do love to write to you; it gives me such a respectable feeling of having some family" (21, 145). This feeling, so welcome to an orphan, is the very vortex of the sentimental mode, for during the course of the novel Judy-Jerusha is drawn inward from the outer margins of society toward that family found at the center of middle-class life.

When Daddy-Long-Legs sends her a number of Christmas presents, she pretends to herself that "they came in a box from my family in California," each item from a different member of her imagined kinfolk: "You don't object, do you, to playing the part of a composite family? . . . because you're my whole family rolled into one" (39). When during her sophomore year Judy spends Christmas with a well-to-do classmate, Sallie McBride, it is in just such a house as she used to fantasize about when in the asylum, "a big old-fashioned brick house . . . set back from the street. . . . Everything is so comfortable and restful and homelike. . . . And as for families! I never dreamed they could be so nice" (77).

But when she travels to New York to stay with her wealthy and snobbish roommate, Julia Pendleton—the one who inquired about her mother's family name—Judy begins to have second thoughts: "I know now what people mean when they say they are weighted down by things. The material atmosphere of that house was crushing. I didn't draw a deep breath until I was on an express train coming back" (135). The furniture was "gorgeous," the people "beautifully dressed and low-voiced and well-bred, but it's the truth, Daddy, I never heard one word of real talk from the time we arrived until we left. I don't think an idea ever entered the front door" (135).

Notably, this is a "house" not a home, and revises Judy's ideas about the John Grier Home, which she prefers as a "background" to the Pendleton place: "Whatever the drawbacks of my bringing up, there was at least no pretense about it." Toward the end of the novel, Judy becomes downright grateful for her childhood, and asks her benefactor, the Trustee, to "give the Home my love, please—my *truly* love. I have quite a feeling of tenderness for it as I look back through a haze of four years" (168). The Home with a capital haitch is now truly a home, being a place that "gives me a

sort of vantage point from which to stand aside and look at life."
The sentiments are clearly Thoreauvian: the John Grier Home
has been her Walden, literally an asylum from the burdens of af-
fluence, if not from the dreary confines of routine.

Looking at life from her unique perspective, Judy finds that the
restraints she knew at the orphan asylum, where "[d]uty was the
one quality that was encouraged," can be encountered in the great
world outside as well, as at the Lock Willow Farm where she is
sent by her benefactor for her first summer vacation. Judy finds
that her initial expectation, that living on a farm would encourage
her love of freedom—"I don't have to mind anyone this summer
do I?"—is illusory (61). For eventually life at Lock Willow comes to
resemble the routines at the orphan asylum, "absolutely monoto-
nous and uneventful. . . . It's exactly the same as at the John Grier
Home. Our ideas there were bounded by the four sides of the iron
fence, only I didn't mind it so much because I was younger and was
so awfully busy. . . . But after two years in a conversational college,
I do miss . . . social intercourse . . . and I shall be glad to see somebody who speaks my language" (99, 115–16).

The Semples, the kindly couple who manage the farm, are rock-
ribbed Calvinists, who in Judy's opinion "are better than their god
. . . a narrow, irrational, unjust, mean, revengeful, bigoted person,"
a divinity they "have inherited intact from their remote Puritan
ancestors. Poor Mrs. Semple believes that people who go fishing
on Sundays go afterwards to a sizzling hot hell!" (68, 120). A thor-
oughgoing agnostic, Judy gives thanks that "I don't inherit any
god from anybody! I am free to make mine up as I wish him. He's
kind and sympathetic and imaginative and forgiving and understanding—and he has a sense of humor" (68).

Judy like Rebecca is an Emersonian spirit, who believes "absolutely in my own free will and my own power to accomplish—
and that is the belief that moves mountains" (160). She detests the
apathy that hampers so many people, the easy surrender to necessity: "Humility or resignation or whatever you choose to call it,
it is simply impotent inertia. I'm for a more militant religion!"
(162). The "true secret of happiness . . . is to live in the now. Not to
be forever regretting the past, or anticipating the future; but to get
the most that you can out of this very instant. . . . Most people don't
live; they just race" (136–37). Here again are Emersonian sentiments, perhaps sifted through a Thoreauvian sieve.

Judy (like Webster and her friends) is also something of a feminist, and resents it when during her last year at the college a visiting preacher told the students that being women they should not

"develop [their] intellects at the expense of [their] emotional natures" a doctrine very close to the advice Robert Southey gave to Charlotte Brontë (167; Gaskell, 172–73). "It doesn't matter what part of the United States or Canada they come from, or what denomination they are, we always get the same sermon. Why on earth don't they go to men's colleges and urge the students not to allow their manly natures to be crushed out by too much mental application?" (167).

As her education continues, Judy begins to sound like a potential suffragette: "Don't you think I'd make an admirable voter if I had my rights? I was twenty-one last week. This is an awfully wasteful country to throw away such an honest, educated, conscientious, intelligent citizen as I would be" (130). Class elections at college are intense affairs, filled with intrigue, revealing the political side of women: "Oh, I tell you Daddy, when we women get our rights, you men will have to look alive in order to keep yours" (72). It perhaps needs to be noted that Judy's life at college is not entirely intellectual, for she participates in a number of team sports, including basketball, and excels in the fifty-yard dash. She is a thoroughly modern militant maiden in all respects.

Moreover, Judy finds herself taking what were in 1912 extremely radical positions. Having met Julia Pendleton's uncle Jervis, an older man but "youngish and good-looking," who is a socialist, spending his wealth on worthy causes, she announces to her patron that she thinks she will become a socialist herself: "You wouldn't mind, would you Daddy? They're quite different from anarchists; they don't believe in blowing people up. Probably I am one by rights; I belong to the proletariat" (79, 136). Having spent the following Sunday "looking into the subject," she declares in her next letter that she is "a Fabian. That's a socialist who's willing to wait" (138). It would be "too upsetting" to have a revolution tomorrow; better to put it off until everyone has gotten used to the idea: "In the meantime we must be getting ready, by instituting industrial, educational, and orphan asylum reforms."

Whatever their influence on Webster's readers, her heroine's opinions suggest that a liberal education in 1900 as in 2000 can be equated with a radicalization process, fueling the fears of middle-class parents that letting their little girls go off to college is equivalent to releasing them to picket lines. But as a bildungsroman largely set on a campus patterned after Vassar, what is entirely missing from this novel is any mention by Judy of her teachers. We hear chapter and verse about the subjects she is taking, including plane geometry and chemistry, that being the putative function of her letters to "Daddy," but no mention is made about the people who are responsible for organizing the courses and presenting lectures and leading discussions. Who was the teacher who wrote the poem on the blackboard? We learn as little about her (if it was a she) as we do about the identity of the author of the poem.

Judy is understandably grateful to Daddy-Long-Legs for having provided her with the grand opportunity to improve herself, but none of this gratitude is extended to the presumed instruments of her improvement. This is certainly a humbling experience for those of us who have devoted our lives to college teaching, and a familiar one as well. But it seems untoward to find in a novel presumably devoted to the experience of getting a much needed education not a word about the role played by Judy's instructors. By contrast, Rebecca has close even intimate relations with the Misses Dearborn and Maxwell, and to update the situation, Sylvia Plath had mad crushes on her male teachers at Smith.

In a word . . . Humph!

II

Judy does have a mentor, however, and he is the socialist-minded Jervis Pendleton. She first meets him toward the end of her freshman year, for at Julia's request she agrees to entertain Uncle Jervis while her roommate attended "seventh-hour recitations" that could not be skipped (58). Having earlier formed unfavorable ideas about the wealthy and snobbish Pendleton family, Judy is relieved to find that Jervis is "a real human being—not a Pendleton at all. We had a beautiful time; I've longed for an uncle ever since. . . . Mr. Pendleton reminded me a little of you, Daddy, as you were twenty years ago." It is not giving away a surprise ending to reveal that Mr. Jervis is indeed her "Daddy," and is twenty years younger than Jerusha imagines him to be, for in my experience very few readers do not catch on to that to which Judy remains oblivious.

Despite his radical politics, Jervis Pendleton like Adam Ladd is an updated, thoroughly revised Rochester, for like Rebecca's mentor-lover he seems inspired by Dr. John Bretton, charming even magnetic but without Rochester's shady past and Byronic glooms: "He's tall and thinnish with a dark face all over lines, and the funniest underneath smile that never comes through but just wrinkles up the corners of his mouth. And he has a way of making you feel right off as though you'd known him a long time." It is a long first time that the two spend together, enjoying an afternoon tea and a walk, and when Uncle Jervis departs with barely a word to Julia, it is a clue dropped in plain sight that a meeting with his niece was not the real purpose of his visit. "I wish," she writes her patron, "you'd come and take some tea some day and let me see if I like you." But her Daddy already has, and she does, and increasingly Judy's life is arranged so that opportunities present themselves for encounters with the highly attractive most companionable and definably radical Jervis Pendleton.

Thus Lock Willow Farm turns out to be the place where Jervis grew up and which he once owned before giving it to "Mrs. Semple who was his old nurse. Did you ever hear of such a funny coincidence? She still calls him 'Master Jervie' and talks about what a sweet little boy he used to be" (64). This provides subject matter for intimate conversation when "Julia's desirable uncle" next comes calling at the college: "We had a beautiful gossipy time about the Semples, and the horses and cows and chickens" (79). But then, when the family of her other roommate, Sallie McBride, the Dickensian, fun-loving folks with whom Jerusha had enjoyed her second Christmas at school, invite her to spend the summer with them in their camp in the Adirondacks, she is terribly disappointed when Daddy-Long-Legs insists that she return to Lock Willow Farm.

This comes right after Judy's encounter with *Jane Eyre,* and shortly after she has thanked her benefactor for having given her the life of "freedom and independence" she has been enjoying at college: "My childhood was just a long, sullen stretch of revolt, and now I am so happy every moment of the day that I can't believe it's true. I feel like a made-up heroine in a story-book" (96). This is on May 4th, but by June 5th she is protesting her "Daddy's" orders that she "should not accept Mrs. McBride's invitation, but should return to Lock Willow. . . . Why, why, *why,* Daddy?" (105). In a long letter she lists all the reasons why he should change his mind, chief of which is Sallie McBride's mother, who is by herself "an education. She's the most interesting, entertaining, companionable, charming woman in the world; she knows everything." But when Daddy remains obdurate, the next letter is a terse, formal acknowledgement that "I leave on Friday next to spend the summer at Lock Willow Farm" (107).

No letters follow from Judy for two months, and when she writes in early August, it is to protest her Daddy's dictatorial ways: "It's the impersonality of your commands that hurts my feelings. . . . If there were the slightest hint that you cared, I'd do anything on earth to please you. . . . It is very humiliating to be picked up and moved about by an arbitrary, peremptory, unreasonable, omnipotent, invisible providence" (108–9). There are echoes here of Charlotte Brontë's letters to her Master, and yet Judy has kept her sense of humor through a prolonged spell of hurt feelings, and admits that "when a man has been as kind and generous and thoughtful as you have heretofore been toward me, I suppose he has a right to be an arbitrary, peremptory, unreasonable, invisible providence if he chooses."

It is during this second summer that Judy finds life on the farm so deadly dull, entirely lacking stimulating conversations with intelligent people. Not surprisingly, things improve vastly when "Master Jervie" turns up on the farm, and they have wonderful times together: "He is an awfully companionable sort of man . . . just as simple and unaffected and sweet as he can be—that seems a funny way to describe a man, but it's true. He's extremely nice with the farmers around here; he meets them in a sort of man-to-man fashion that disarms them immediately" (117).

There is that about "Master Jervie" that also brings to mind master Cedric Errol, his sweetness, his personableness, and also his clothes, which had given the farmers an unfavorable impression until they had been treated to Jervis's "man-to-man" discourse: "I will say that his clothes are rather amazing. He wears knickerbockers and pleated jackets and white flannels and riding clothes with puffed trousers." This cut of clothes is quite different from Fauntleroy's velvet costume, but distinctive to say the least, and apparently has a similar effect on innocent bystanders. Jervis's costume, however outlandish down on the farm, is the latest fashion for cosmopolites, and resembles the outfits worn at the turn of the century by Richard Harding Davis, who was the model for the Gibson Man, and the beau ideal of sophisticated masculinity in his day.

During Jervis's extended stay, the two ramble over the countryside, on horseback and on foot, and he teaches Judy how to fish with flies and how to shoot a rifle and a revolver, manly sports that attest to his liberal ways and her modernity. They stay out after dark one night, and Jervis cooks their supper, yet another demonstration of his willingness to counter fixed gender roles, and on the way back supplements the moonlight with the beam from "a flashlight that he had in his pocket," in 1912 a technological innovation (119). "It was such fun! He laughed and joked all the way and talked about interesting things. He's read all the books I've ever read, and a lot of others besides. It's astonishing how many different things he knows."

It is Pygmalion and Galatea all over again, and it is of some interest that Shaw's *Pygmalion* was first produced in the year that Webster's novel was published, a comedy that suggests the best laid plans of mentors seeking absolute control over their students oft gang aglay. Judy's second summer is the last she will spend on the Lock Willow Farm while attending college, thereby asserting her will and innocently frustrating her benefactor's scheme. In the letter describing her good times with Jervie, Judy asserts, "The world is full of happiness, and plenty to go round, if you are only willing to take the kind that comes your way. The whole secret is in being *pliable*" (119).

But "pliable" for Judy means having the freedom to choose her own fate, recalling the complex etymology of "wick." Still, she is willing to solicit Jervis's opinion about her creative work, short stories and poems that she has written during the summer, which were sent out to magazines and returned "with most courteous promptitude" (123). In Jervis's opinion "they were dreadful. They showed that I didn't have the slightest idea of what I was talking about. . . . But the last one I did—just a little sketch laid in college—he said wasn't bad; and he had it typewritten, and I sent it to a magazine." And his advice proves good: by the time Judy is back in school, the story has been accepted, and she is richer by fifty dollars.

During her junior year she begins to declare her independence from Daddy-Long-Legs, accepting a scholarship against his advice, which reduces her dependence on his largesse, and then announcing plans to spend the summer at the seashore with a wealthy woman she met through the McBrides, where she is to "tutor her daughter who is to enter college in the autumn" (147). Daddy to the contrary has arranged to send Judy to Europe for the summer, but she objects to taking his money for travel having refused it while in school.

She has earlier protested against his many gifts, even returning money sent for clothes, and now observes that what one never has had, one never misses: "But it is awfully hard going without things after one has commenced thinking they are his—hers (English language needs another pronoun) by natural right. . . . I have a very strong feeling that the only honest thing for me to do is to teach this summer and begin to support myself" (149). These sentiments are nothing if not admirable (including the sensitivity regarding the desirability of a gender-neutral hence politically correct personal pronoun), and as with her increased interest in "gymnasium," indicate a muscular independence on the part of this modern young woman.

Jervis she discovers is in favor of her benefactor's plan for travel abroad, that being his own destination for the summer: "He said that it was a necessary part of my education and that I mustn't think of refusing. . . . Well, Daddy, it did appeal to me! I almost weakened; if he hadn't been so dictatorial, maybe I would have entirely weakened" (151). The sooner the reader catches on to the joke, the more enjoyable the story becomes, as Judy in her frank and innocent way lets Daddy know that he once again has overplayed his hand.

But then, having heard from Jervis that he plans to see her at Lock Willow when she goes there at summer's end, Judy changes her plans and heads off for the Adirondacks to be with the McBrides, for "I want Master Jervie to arrive at Lock Willow and find me not there. I must show him that he can't dictate to me. No one can dictate to me but you, Daddy—and you can't always. I'm off for the woods." Jervis, being tipped off thereby, sends his regrets to Judy at Lock Willow that he won't after all be able to meet her, having accepted an invitation "to go yachting with some friends" (155).

When not tutoring "a most uncommonly spoiled child," Judy spends her summer at the seashore working on a novel she had started the winter before, and having finished it just before classes began, mailed it off to a publisher. In two months it came back, postage due, with the frank advice that "I put all of my energy into my lessons and wait until I graduated before beginning to write," and along with the letter was the reader's appraisal: "Plot highly improbable. Characterization exaggerated. Conversation unnatural. A good deal of humor but not always in the best of taste. Tell her to keep on trying, and in time she may produce a real book" (157).

Judy burns the manuscript and returns to classes, but during spring vacation she stays with Sallie McBride at Lock Willow, and while visiting the scenes she shared with Jervis, works on another novel: "I've caught the secret. Master Jervie and that editor man were right; you are most convincing when you write about the things you know. And this time it is about something that I do know . . . the John Grier Home! And it's good, Daddy, I actually believe it is—I'm a realist now. I've abandoned romanticism" (170). Well, we are back in Louisa May Alcott territory, are we not? For Jervis's advice added to that of the "editor man" is pretty much what Jo March was told by Professor Bhaer, and Judy like Jo went on to write about what she knew and predictably produced a successful and highly popular book.

Webster's little woman takes the nearly completed manuscript of her new novel to Lock Willow with her after she graduates. She has been assured that Master Jervie is to be there in August, but we hear not much more about him, instead she writes Daddy about how unhappy she has become down on the farm. But then her novel is accepted for publication, and a jubilant Judy is able to send her benefactor a check for one thousand dollars, the first of three, along with the announcement that since "you sort of represented my whole family," he shouldn't mind if "I tell you that I have a very much more special feeling for another man. You can probably guess without much trouble who he is" (180).

It is Jervis's absence from Lock Willow that has made her heart grow fonder: "I miss him, and miss him, and miss him. The whole world seems empty and aching. I hate the moonlight because it's beautiful and he isn't here to see it with me" (181). And yet she admits she has "refused to marry him," for apparently his promise to visit the farm was made good, and the two "got into a dreadful muddle of misunderstanding, and we both hurt each other's feelings" (181). Judy for all her modernity is like a heroine of a sentimental novel in always electing to follow the "right" course of action, however much hurtful it is to herself and others.

Repaying her debt to her benefactor unasked is one thing but refusing the beloved Jervis's proposal is another. "It didn't seem right for a person of my lack of antecedents to marry into any such family as his. . . . Also, I felt sort of bound to you. After having been educated to be a writer, I must at least try to be one." But then with the publication of her novel, and the immediate prospect of paying back the debt, matters have changed, and in any event she regrets her refusal of Jervis's proposal. After two months spent nursing a broken heart, she learns that her lover has been truly sick, that his silence is the result of an extended bout with pneumonia, having been caught out in a storm while on a hunting trip to Canada— the traditional male response in sentimental literature to heartbreak.

"What seems to you the right thing to do?" she asks Daddy-Long-Legs who is Jervis Pendleton. Is there any doubt?

Reader, she marries him.

Naturally, Daddy-Long-Legs commands his sad little correspondent to come to his home, and Jerusha speeds off to New

York, filled with fears over the fate of Jervis and excitement over at last meeting her kindly if authoritative benefactor. She finds that his address on Madison Avenue is a mansion "so big and brown and forbidding" that at first she is frightened to go in, but the butler proves to be a kindly old man, who ushers her into a room and withdraws. Temporarily blinded by having come in from bright daylight, Judy makes out a man "sitting in the big chair propped up by pillows with a rug over his knees" (186). Getting shakily to his feet, he holds out his hand, and says, "Dear little Judy, couldn't you guess that I was Daddy-Long-Legs?" (186). He laughs as he asks the question, for the joke clearly is on Judy, as well as on any reader who hasn't yet caught on, for the scales as they used to say now drop from Judy's eyes, and all things become clear as after a spring shower.

We learn about Judy's sudden shock of recognition in her last letter to the man who is no longer her Daddy but now her darling. This last is also her first bona fide love letter, and is written to Jervis from Lock Willow, where she awaits his recovery and his return by hiking over the bronzed hills of autumn in company with Colin, a dog not the boy from *The Secret Garden*. We need not wonder where Webster found the name, but we may ponder the implications of this peculiar method of (dis)closure. During that brief but "sweet half hour" before Judy was hurried out of the sickroom by Jervis's doctor, did she not have time to tell him what she now tells him in her letter? It is as we shall see a case of literary convention overruling literary convention, for the ending is a virtual whirl of self-conscious contrivances, as a tour de force more force than tour.

III

It became a Hollywood fixture in films of the Thirties for strong-willed, talented, independent, career women to surrender themselves at story's end to strong-willed, talented, independent, career men, and something very like that is happening here. Without at all diminishing the clever charm of this quite exceptional novel, we can ask, it seems to me, a few questions, queries that have become familiar during this consideration of the daughters of Jane Eyre. For if Webster seems to be consciously writing against the sentimental tradition, reversing the Victorian notion that women are empowered not through the exercise of will but by subsuming their personalities to the dominance of the men in their lives—and that is the very clear message during the first three-quarters of the book—then what do we make of the ending?

In the long, soul-searching letter to Daddy-Long-Legs that immediately precedes the revelation of his true identity, in which she spells out the terms of the dilemma presented by Jervis's proposal, Judy observes that a career of writing does not exclude a marriage, that the "two professions are not necessarily exclusive" (182). But it is also in this letter that she admits that her lover "is almost always right; he ought to be, you know, for he has fourteen years' start of me," and though Jervis has presumably learned that he will be dealing with a strong-willed woman, he has proven himself to be an equally strong-willed man (181).

The resonance here of *Jane Eyre* is audible, even to Judy hurrying to be by the side of the man who has been her great benefactor, who turns out to be her lover, and who like Rochester has been weakened by his near fatal illness. And yet, unlike Jane, Judy does not stay by his side to nurse him back to health, but having been sent away by his doctor, departs for the country, there to await his recovery. Of course, her removal is necessary for the letter-writing to continue, so as to bring a decorous closure to the whole. Yet one cannot help but wonder why that last letter was necessary.

Well, to correct the presumed faults of a text nearly a century old, faults that are the perception of a product of a much later system of values, is both presumptuous and futile. The novel has its strengths, and follows closely after the story of Rebecca in reversing the patterns of what we may call reality-challenged sentimental fiction. Wiggin stopped short of letting her heroine marry; Webster stops short only of the marriage ceremony itself. Taken as a whole these two books may be credited with being skillfully crafted and humorous overall, as well as reasonably realistic accounts of two young women who at the beginning of the twentieth century were kicking over the traces of the nineteenth. Education, again, is the common theme, regarded by so many at the time as the necessary elevated threshold if women were to gain social power equivalent to that of men. Vassar College was founded with the purpose of providing single women the education necessary for entering the professions.

Yes, our modern sensibilities may develop a moral heat rash when we read a story about a young woman having her education subsidized by a man fourteen years her senior whose motives are somewhat clouded. Here is yet another lover-mentor who is more

Pygmalion than patron, who is increasingly more interested in procuring a bride than in preparing the young woman he has sponsored to enter the professional world. But at the same time we must admit that this is an advance over the story line in *Jane Eyre*, never mind *The Wide, Wide World*, for Jerusha-Judy has by the end of the novel already successfully commenced the career for which she was prepared, and if she eventually sacrifices that career to her marriage, well, that would be another story.

Dear Enemy, the sequel to *Daddy-Long-Legs*, was that other story.

Published in 1914, it is less a sequel than a tangent to the first, being about the efforts of Sallie McBride, Judy's good friend at college, to bring a new kind of spirit to the John Grier Home, which Jervis Pendleton wishes to make over "into a model institution," presumably at his wife's instigation. Sallie is the young woman from Worcester whose family was a veritable Dickensian swarm of good-natured middle-class folks, a positive alternative to the wealthy and snobbish Pendletons. As Sallie points out in protest, she is hardly qualified to supervise an orphanage of more than a hundred small children, but on the other hand she has no definite career plans nor—at the start of the novel—any immediate marriage prospects. She has, as we know, a good heart, and we soon learn that she has a lively wit, is intelligent and adaptable to swiftly changing circumstances, and these, much more than professional preparation, seem to be qualifications enough for the job.

Webster once again resorted to the epistolary form, less happily in this case, because Sallie's letters, sent mostly to Judy and her bridegroom, although packed with incident, lack that tension that gave such interest to Judy's correspondence with her "Daddy." Sallie's letters, moreover, are clearly designed to illustrate Webster's thesis that disadvantaged children, given the proper attention and care, can be salvaged from the margins and brought toward if not into the middle-class center.

At the start, Sallie, who professes not to like orphans, protests over having thrust upon her the very difficult assignment of bringing a new world order to the John Grier Home, peopled by children from broken homes and other troubled backgrounds and staffed by often incompetent persons inherited from the unimaginative and obsessively orderly Mrs. Lippett. But she becomes involved with her sad little and often bad little charges, and much of the novel is made up of Sallie's reports to Judy regarding their and her progress. By story's end, she rejects the opportunity to leave the Home, having found the career she lacked at the start, hardly a surprising conclusion, a predictability that considerably weakens the book throughout, as we can early on see what is coming.

As for Jervis and Judy, they travel about the world together, following his financial ventures, and although Sallie receives responses to her letters—seldom sufficiently long or timely enough in her opinion—we are not allowed access to that side of the correspondence. She also writes to a young and very handsome politician, Gordon Hallock, to whom she eventually becomes engaged, and who pays occasional visits from Washington to the orphanage. She also sends frequent notes to a physician employed by the Home, Dr. Robin MacRae, a recent import from Scotland, "tall and thinnish, with sandy hair and cold gray eyes" (*Dear Enemy,* 13).

We never learn the doctor's age, but he is presumably somewhat older than Sallie, and has a typical Scottish temperament, being inclined toward the dour and taciturn, being something of a tartar in tartans. Where she had been promised "a man of . . . polish and brilliancy and scholarliness and charm," she finds MacRae "as companionable as a granite tombstone!" (13). The doctor is the "Dear Enemy" of the book's title, in reference to the impudent heading of Sallie's letters to the man whose thoughts regarding the proper care and feeding of orphans are opposed to her own.

Gordon, by contrast, is very charming and agreeable but is mostly absent in Washington, a circumstance the reader may well regard as a hint to the wary. Although he is a generous soul, and bestows toys and the like on the orphans whenever he pays a visit to Sallie, Gordon as a professional politician is chiefly loyal to his congressional seat, and urges his fiancée to give up her orphanage responsibilities and join him in Washington as his wife. But Sallie becomes devoted to the John Grier Home, and is involved in converting it from a dormitory to a cluster of cottages, a conversion that is accelerated when one wing of the Home catches fire and is destroyed. Toward the end of the novel, as she reports to Judy, she has it out with Gordon Hallock and breaks off the engagement, having lost all interest in the man, despite his charm and good looks.

It is finally with the dour Scotchman that Sallie falls in love, as the alert reader will have anticipated, given that he is the "dear enemy" of the title and (like M. Heger) being difficult of intimate access is an obvious object of desire. Robin would seem a most unlikely Rochester, as it is Gordon who has all the personal advantages. But as Sallie learns late on from Robin's truculent and overbearing housekeeper, Mrs. McGurk, the doctor is married to a woman now confined to a mental institution, by whom he has had a little girl, also a borderline psychotic, both of whom are kept off stage. The daughter we are told resembles one of the orphans, a delightful and beautiful child named Allegra, to whom the doctor is drawn and whom he rescues from near death when the orphanage catches fire. The child is untouched but MacRae is badly burned, and his leg is broken when he falls from a ladder down which he is being carried by a fireman.

Over his protests, Sallie visits the injured man and realizes that it is the doctor she truly loves, the two drawn together by their common interest in improving the lot of the poor orphans. She learns that his dour, withdrawn manner (like that of Lucy Snowe's M. Paul Emmanuel) is an expression of his love for her, being as she sees it a typical expression of the Scottish temper—Sallie is of Irish origins, and much more given to displays of various passions. She also learns that MacRae's wife has in the meantime died from that ailment often found in sentimental fictions, authorial convenience, and he is free to marry his new love. Insane wife, nearly fatal fire, severe injuries resulting from a rescue attempt, all of these are familiar elements borrowed from *Jane Eyre* but are recycled through a dissimilar literary vehicle. The obvious shadow of Glenn McKinney hangs over both books, as attenuated as the one cast by "Daddy-Long-Legs," but the debt to *Jane Eyre* overrides the autobiographical element here.

Like all American novels inspired by the example of Charlotte Brontë's fiction, *Dear Enemy* drops the gothic element and promotes the domestic part. Where in *Daddy-Long-Legs,* the emphasis is on Judy's search to find a "real" home, in the sequel it is on Sallie's efforts to make over the John Grier institution into an approximate home—with Ruskinian cottages and other decorative touches that mitigate the institutional look—thereby changing it from the unpleasant environment that Judy came to realize had given her a unique experience of "real" life. Because that realization was central to the development of *Daddy-Long-Legs,* changing the character of the Home would seem to undercut the value of Judy's experience there.

Moreover, Judy's stated hope that she could carry on her career as a writer while married to Jervis Pendleton appears, in the outcome, to have been illusory, as she spends all of her time accompanying her husband in his travels and having their baby while almost literally in motion. Certainly, there are no references in Sallie's letters to any published works by her friend, and their infrequent meetings seem to have been chiefly social occasions. The sequel, moreover, is much less self-consciously "literary" than the original. Sallie does read books when leisure permits—not often—and there are allusions to Marie Bashkirtseff's journal and Thoreau's *Walden,* but the most meaningful references are to the poems of Burns and to Judy's favorite, Robert Louis Stevenson, obvious connections to MacRae's Scottish origins.

Despite the lively prose and the amusing illustrations, drawn in a manner very similar to those in *Daddy-Long-Legs,* the sequel is truly a sequel, being inferior to the original, less complex in many ways and at times not very interesting. The orphans have names and several have well-defined personalities but they remain elusive and not fully present in the story. Sallie brings with her a pet, a Chow dog named Singapore, who is in the foreground early on but then largely forgotten, as is a pet monkey later introduced only to be seldom mentioned. Forgotten also is the McBride family, Sallie's parents and siblings, that Pickwickian ménage that Judy found so warm and friendly, most especially Mrs. McBride, a font of wisdom and information. Not once does Sallie mention her mother, never mind consult her on important matters.

Judy is her sole confidante throughout, and the effect of divorcing Sallie from her real family is of course to emphasize the bonding going on with the adoptive family represented by the orphans at the Home, with which her dismissal of Gordon and her new-found love for Robin, the "enemy" who becomes so "dear," is connected. Sallie not only increasingly identifies with the unfortunate children, who bring with them various personal and familial dysfunctions, but becomes herself a virtual orphan, cut off from contact with a mother who one assumes would be as interested in the painful choices she is making, especially regarding a suitable husband, as is her friend, Judy Pendleton.

With few exceptions, sequels in literature are also-ran affairs, and *Dear Enemy* is not one of those exceptions. I include a brief discussion of the book here because it brings into Webster's extended story a strong Brontëan connection, that terminal fire, injury, and the death of an insane wife that seem out of character with the generally humorous elements of the plot but are clearly a sign of Webster's allegiance to *Jane Eyre.* But the most tragic echo derived from Jean Webster's fascination with the story of Charlotte Brontë is a personal one, for like the lonely genius of Haworth whose source of power so intrigued her, Webster died in childbirth, an ironic fate for a writer whose most successful novels were about children searching for and at long last finding a home.

14

Kissing Cinderella Goodbye: Unfairytale Elements in *Pollyanna* and *Anne of Green Gables*

> Play up! and play the game!
> —Sir Henry Newbolt

I

POLLYANNA WAS FIRST PUBLISHED IN 1913, ONE YEAR AFTER *DADDY-Long-Legs*, but its debt is clearly to *Rebecca of Sunnybrook Farm*, and perhaps even more to *Little Lord Fauntleroy*. Where Burnett's novel inspired mothers to dress their unfortunate boys in black velvet, Eleanor Porter's had a massive impact on American popular culture, for a time lending its name to everything from motor lodges in the White Mountains to a brand of milk bottled in Texas. Naturally, a movie was made of the novel in the 1920s, invariably starring Mary Pickford. Porter wrote a sequel, *Pollyanna Grows Up* (1915), and the profitable formula was perpetuated further by other writers after the author's death.

The Emersonian optimism that motivates Rebecca had its octane rating intensified in Pollyanna, whose "glad game" of seeing something positive in the most discouraging set of circumstances was a version of Mary Baker Eddy's doctrines as formulated in Burnett's fiction. It provided a bridge over the troubled waters of the 1930s in Dale Carnegie's formula for success and survived into the 1950s as Norman Vincent Peale's power of positive thinking. A case could even be made that Ronald Reagan brought a version of Pollyannaism into the White House in the 1980s, for surely the sight of a chief executive smiling happily from a hospital bed after he had been brought down by an assassin's bullet should bring the closing chapters of Porter's book to mind. Which is to say that as a work of children's literature *Pollyanna* has much to recommend it to a student of American popular culture, and to those of you who have not read it, I say it is a far better book than it perhaps deserves to be. I have seen it bring graduate students to sympathetic tears, which may not be thought of as a primary function of literature in general but it most certainly is required of sentimental fiction, of which Eleanor Porter's novel is the essence.

In discussing *Rebecca* I cited the analogous novel by Johann Pestalozzi, *Leonard and Gertrude*, about how a woman reformed an entire village through the display of her innate goodness. That story is even more relevant here; not being an educator Porter may have known nothing about Pestalozzi and his works, but she surely knew *Little Lord Fauntleroy* and *Rebecca*, both cast in the same general shape. There are significant differences, including the scope of the child's influence, and Pollyanna Whittier, daughter of the Reverend John Whittier (hardly a coincidental name), operates without benefit of an influential mother, for she is an orphan complete. Still, the glad game she plays is the sole inheritance left by her impoverished father, a missionary who operated in the far West until he died, and as such was an evangelist of Good News.

Pollyanna has been sent back east by the Ladies Aid Society in the western community where her father preached to live with her mother's sister, Aunt Polly, who is not to be confused with the kindly old lady who takes care of Tom Sawyer and his rotten half-brother, Sid. Polly is typecast in the mold of Rebecca's Aunt Miranda, and like her she has been early disappointed in love. She was not however in love with Pollyanna's father, whom she hates for having married and taken away her sister, Jennie, who had been the intended of a wealthy suitor who resides in their home town.

Unlike Miranda Sawyer, also, Polly Harrington is wealthy and does not have the care of a farm. She has a garden, but that is tended by old Tom, the namesake and likeness of the gardener in *The Secret Garden*, who likewise sees in the little orphan girl the living semblance of her angel-like mother whom he adored. In sum, *Pollyanna* is a clever blend of *Rebecca* and Burnett's *Secret Garden*, but its operating principle, once again, is taken from *Little Lord Fauntleroy*. Thus the emphasis on education that gives dimension to both *Rebecca* and *Daddy-Long-Legs* is entirely missing, and though the little girl eventually enters school, her story like Tom Sawyer's is chiefly a summertime book. As with Cedric Errol, the matter of education is irrelevant, for Pollyanna is a mixture of characteristics inherited from her parents, resembling her mother in appearance and her father in missionary zeal.

Like Fauntleroy, also, Pollyanna is a loving and happy child, who likes beautiful things, and who goes about evangelizing the town, converting everyone she comes in contact with to the glad game. Everyone that is but Aunt Polly, who forbids her niece to mention her missionary father, and thereby does not learn about the game. From the start, Polly treats the little girl like the poor relation she is, assigning her to a blazing hot room in the attic, where the windows must remain shut to keep out flies until screens arrive, and they seem to be on order in a factory located somewhere in Tibet.

It is a barren and unattractive room borrowed from the collective garrets we have been seeing other orphan girls suffering in, but Pollyanna, though grievously disappointed that she has been assigned such miserable quarters by an aunt whose house is filled with beautiful things, puts the doctrine of gladness to work and focusses on the great view obtainable through the window that is never to be opened. Pollyanna does not have the creative resources of Sara Crewe or Rebecca Rowena Randall, but she certainly has a defense mechanism of a high order to see her through hard times.

From the start, Pollyanna like Cedric Errol regards her wealthy relation through rose-colored glasses of intense hue, and insists on bestowing on the unwilling Polly frequent expressions of love, all the while regarding her as the most generous aunt in the world. And as in *Little Lord Fauntleroy* this has a predictable effect, for being put in the position of being generous, Aunt Polly finds herself being a lot more generous than she ever meant to be. Pollyanna is successful in adopting in quick succession a ratty kitten and a scruffy puppy, and is frustrated only when her aunt draws the line on a little orphan boy named Jimmy Bean who with some encouragement follows Pollyanna home.

Though her aunt withholds any sign of affection, Pollyanna finds an ally in Nancy, a maid of all work in Polly Harrington's employ, who provides as well a strong vernacular presence, reminding us of hired help in *The Wide, Wide World, The Little Princess,* and *The Secret Garden,* who among other representatives of the lower classes are habitually sympathetic toward high-born but socially disadvantaged children. We may think of the lowly shepherds gathered in adoration around the haloed figure of the infant Jesus.

As in all examples of sentimental fiction, *Pollyanna* has strong Christian overtones, and the notion of a little girl going about converting everyone to a game devised by her missionary father has evangelical implications as well. But as in so many of the books we have been discussing, representatives of the organized church it-self have no direct impact on the plot. Instead, Pollyanna converts the local minister to her faith, passing on her father's "rejoicing texts" to the Reverend Paul Ford, so that he turns from his habit-ual jeremiads to preaching a message of good cheer. This pious secularism can be seen as having a quietly subversive role, in that, like suffering, it acts to empower the powerless, who more often than not are small orphan girls. And Pollyanna comes in for her share of suffering as well, far more serious than sweating it out in a closed attic room.

Aided and abetted by Nancy, who proves to be an invaluable source of misinformation, the plot becomes a comedy of errors. Pollyanna, operating under the false assumption that a crusty but very wealthy bachelor was once her aunt's secret lover, sets about to break down the barrier of pride that she believes has separated the two. Having found the man lying in the woods, suffering from a broken leg, she summons the local doctor (by telephone), and by visiting the patient frequently during his lengthy confinement she penetrates his cynical reserve, endearing herself to him as to everyone else in town.

As it turns out it was not her Aunt Polly that the wealthy bach-elor was in love with, but her dead mother, Jennie, and once the bachelor realizes the connection, he sees his lost love reproduced in Pollyanna. His name, it should be said, is John Pendleton, and though the echo may be coincidental, he certainly plays a role sim-ilar to that of the anonymous benefactor and demanding lover in *Daddy-Long-Legs*. For John Pendleton becomes an equivalent Rochester (who is helped by Jane Eyre after falling from his horse in the woods), seeking to convince Pollyanna to come live with him, obviously not as his wife or mistress, although his passionate desire for her companionship does seem a trifle too intense.

John Pendleton tells Pollyanna that "[i]t takes a woman's hand and heart, or a child's presence, to make a home," domestic senti-ments that become virtually a litany during the last half of the story (140). What Pendleton seeks, having much earlier been refused "a woman's hand," is a "child's presence," for having Pollyanna with him would make him truly glad: "If ever, ever I am to play the 'glad game,' Pollyanna, you'll have to come and play it with me. . . . And, oh, little girl, little girl, I want you so!" (*Pollyanna*, 146–47).

There is that about a grown man pleading from his bed in such terms to a girl of eleven that makes a modern reader a bit queasy, but "want" in Pendleton's vocabulary is a complexly possessive term. His house is filled with beautiful and valuable things that he has collected in his Byronic wanderings about the world, a restlessness born of his attempt to forget the woman he loved, who has now returned as the girl he desires for his own. As in *Elsie Dinsmore*, where father love is too perverse for modern tastes, the situation in Porter's novel evokes the incestuous version of the Cinderella story, the myth that lies deep beneath the surface of *Jane Eyre*.

However, Pollyanna has no intention of leaving her aunt for Mr. Pendleton, for all his riches and flattering attention. She loves her Aunt Polly and believes that her aunt loves her, but once she discovers that Pendleton was not the man Polly had been in love with, she sets about to find a suitable "child's presence" for him. Happily if not surprisingly, she remembers the orphan, Jimmy Bean, who was rejected by her aunt as well as by the local Ladies Aid Society, which prefers giving its money to orphans in far-off India. Pendleton is reluctant to give up his bid for Pollyanna, but finally accepts the alternative, and thereby makes a true home out of the grey pile of stone that is his house.

As it turns out, the man Aunt Polly once loved is another bachelor, Dr. Chilton, who lives in his two-room office over a store. Because of a misunderstanding, the two went their separate ways, although staying within the limits of Beldingsville, and once again Pollyanna is the agent for their reunion. Struck by a speeding automobile—the second instance of that symbol of modern life playing an instrumental role in these stories—the little girl is paralyzed from the waist down. It is an injury defined as incurable by a specialist that Aunt Polly's physician, Dr. Warren, calls in from out of town, and Pollyanna finds it very hard to find anything about her condition that can be converted to gladness. Even her own favorite formula that persons in her condition should be glad that they, not someone else, is suffering from paralysis does not console her.

But then the townspeople, hearing of her condition, begin to make pilgrimages bearing gifts to the Harrington house, all testifying to the happiness that the girl has brought into their lives, often changing them radically for the better. Aunt Polly is overwhelmed with the evidence of her niece's influence, and finally learns from a triumphant Nancy how the glad game works. And Pollyanna, discovering the extent to which her good work has been successful, becomes reconciled to her condition by realizing what she was able to accomplish when she had her legs.

There is more to *Pollyanna*, for the ending involves one of those massive reconciliations for which sentimental films produced by the Disney studios (including *Pollyanna*, starring Hayley Mills) are famous. Like so many of the novels we have been discussing, the orphan trope in *Pollyanna* is used by way of emphasizing the importance of the domestic core—expanded to include the surrounding community—the essential familial note in sentimental fiction, and in this as in the other books the story ends with the happy heroine looking forward to returning to what is now truly her home.

Pollyanna, glad at last.

Of the heroines we have been considering as Jane Eyre's American daughters, Pollyanna is probably best regarded as a second cousin, for she lacks that requisite personal defect, an abundant fund of anger. It is Nancy who serves as a constant vehicle of indignation, leaving the little orphan girl making a happy face through her fly-specked window, where hang the crystal prisms given to her by John Pendleton, providing the rainbow over which her bluebird flies. The story most certainly works in the way it was intended to work, and I can attest that even on a fifth reading, I was moved to tears, but then I am an easy mark for sentimental stories. Yet the darkly psychic power so evident in *Jane Eyre* and many of the books it influenced is entirely missing here, nor is there any obvious debt to the fairy tale tradition, despite the dependence on miraculous transformations.

In her first sequel, *Pollyanna Grows Up*, Porter made her debt to *Little Lord Fauntleroy* explicit: not only is Burnett's novel mentioned several times, but Pollyanna's perpetual optimism is used to bring a wealthy, lonely woman to think of other people besides herself, chiefly the starving paupers who dwell in a tenement building she owns. In the sequel, also, Porter plays with the plot of *Jane Eyre*, for through another series of amusing misunderstandings Pollyanna (now twenty years old) is brought to think that John Pendleton, who had loved her mother, now loves her mother's daughter—no longer a child but now a young woman— and wants to marry her. Being the kind-hearted person she is, the heroine is prepared to accept his proposal even though she loves another, but as in the earlier mix-up, the confusion is cleared up in time. Her heart is therefore free to be given to the grown-up Jimmy Bean, now Jimmy Pendleton, handsome and brave and thanks to his recently recovered birthright also rich. The conclusion to the sequel brought Pollyanna's story in line with the traditional version of *Cinderella*, a parallelism the original story steadfastly avoided.

II

"Some rewards are great and glorious," writes Rebecca in a school essay on rewards and punishments, "for boys can get to be governor or school trustee or road commissioner or president, while girls can only be wife and mother. But all of us can have the ornament of a meek and lowly spirit, especially girls, who have more use for it than boys" (Wiggin, *The New Chronicles of Rebecca*, 82). In this passage, the schoolgirl with unconscious irony sums up the implication of most of the books we have been discussing, which were written for young women and almost uniformly emphasize the need to control tempers, to curb enthusiasms, to fit however one can into the dominant social pattern. And although we may understand that Rebecca accepts this necessity, we may be sure that Kate Douglas Wiggin did not, being a woman who not only had a well-established career before her first marriage but continued to pursue it through both her marriages. Judging from her letters and autobiography she never wore the Christian ornament of a meek and lowly spirit around her neck.

And yet, much as we admire Rebecca Rowena Randall, it is clear that she fits the general pattern established by *Jane Eyre*, in which maturity for women is equated with controlling one's impulses and sexual love is inextricably tied up with the figure of an older, wiser, wealthier, and authoritarian male. Likewise, for all of her talk about independence and freedom, Judy Abbott ends up hoping she can balance a career with the demands of marriage, but, as the sequel suggests, it is a futile hope. Jervis Pendleton may be willing to cook a romantic meal out in the woods, but will he help raise the children? And Jimmy (Bean) Pendleton may start out as an impoverished orphan, but before he marries Pollyanna he has recovered his birthright and a fortune.

Modern feminists necessarily regard this consistency as deplorable, and regret that even the most liberated of authors, Louisa May Alcott, felt it was necessary to observe the norms of the day, and while in her private life choosing a career and a single life, in her most famous novel she celebrated marriage and service to others. Feminist critics seem for whatever reason to have ignored many of the books discussed here, which being intended for children were designed to inform and shape succeeding generations. Yet it can be said that what happens in those novels that are clearly responses to *Little Women* hardly do much to revise Jo's agenda. That letter from Jack London seems to suggest that Rebecca, for all her sparkle and drive, is essentially a man's woman, not a woman's.

There is no social agenda in *Little Women*, nothing beyond a chronicle, readable as it may be, of the small victories and defeats that made up the life of a well-educated if impoverished middle-class family, ca. 1850–60, and it acts, finally, to reinforce the status quo. *Rebecca* moves the chronology forward, changes the scene from suburban to rural, and focusses on education, but there is no obvious social agenda in that book either. Only *Daddy-Long-Legs*, written to publish the author's notion that delinquent children can be regained to society through education, can be said to have an ideological purpose, but Jerusha-Judy Abbott though an orphan is hardly a delinquent child, hence the need for the sequel, as we have seen.

Placed in that perspective, the books we have been reading are part of a continuity that can only be seen as repressive and conformist, as opposed to, say, the stories of Tom Sawyer and Huckleberry Finn, the first of which celebrates a consistent rebellion against small-town conventions, either through the exercise of the imagination or through an act of bona fide heroism, and the second of which takes an even more radical position regarding contemporary social mores (ca. 1885) by having a boy accept a black man as his equal. But as we maintained at the start of chapter 12, sentimental literature necessarily reinforces middle-class conformity, and is characterized by plots that redeem people on the margins of society to the domestic center.

Serviam once again is the motto for most of these novels with girls and young women as their protagonists, the only exception being those by Frances Hodgson Burnett, which are fairy stories of personal recovery and regeneration. Little Lord Fauntleroy, in his successful efforts to clean up his grandfather's slums, may be seen as illustrating Ruskin's ideals, whereas Sara Crewe and all of the other little women we have been reading about are in search of avenues of self-expression and the recovery of an affluent style of life, often through marriage. Ironically, it is Pollyanna, with her obvious resemblance to Lord Fauntleroy, who does have an agenda, transforming the world through the agency of the glad game, but even that device was her father's invention, and as the sequel suggests, what works in a village does not necessarily work in town.

Let me not end on a negative note. There is yet another of Jane Eyre's American daughters to be discussed, Anne Shirley, heroine of *Anne of Green Gables* (1908). I have saved her for last because L. M. Montgomery was a Canadian writer, and although "American" in the largest sense of that term, not American in the sense used by most Americans—if you get my meaning. That Montgomery's novel is derivative to the point of imitation and at times self-consciously so needs to be said at the start. Yet it enjoys a constant popularity even today, and like *Pollyanna* spawned a number of sequels, which carried Anne on through college and beyond. Such a demand suggests that the readers, most of whom we must assume were female in gender, liked whatever it was that Montgomery was doing, and as we shall see, for all of her dependency on her contemporaries, she hit a note that none of the others were able to reach.

III

Does anyone *not* like *Anne of Green Gables*, the Sara Lee of children's books? Surely, there has never been a more pleasant, positive novel intended for young readers, the heroine of which is a highly imaginative girl, given to dreaming of beautiful worlds inhabited by beautiful people, yet who is alive to the natural loveliness as well of this our real world. "The sweetest creation of child life yet written," said Mark Twain, himself an old softy when around girls with long silken tresses in ruffled white dresses, for they reminded him of his beloved Suzy Clemens, who like a girl in a novel by Dickens died young. This tribute is found in Kunitz and Haycraft under the entry for Montgomery, and they credit Twain with rendering equally high praise for Wiggin's *Rebecca of Sunnybrook Farm* as well: "That beautiful book," he pronounced it, and who in both instances would disagree? Surely not the author of *Anne of Green Gables*, who obviously had Wiggin's book open before her as she sat down to write her novel in 1904.

Like so many heroines of novels intended for young women whom we have called the daughters of Jane Eyre, Anne Shirley has lost her parents, and lives in an orphanage. She leaves at the behest of an aging brother and sister, Matthew and Marilla Cuthbert, who have requested a boy who could help on their farm, but are sent a girl by mistake. Overwhelmed by Anne's passionate entreaties, the elderly couple keeps her, against the better judgment of the sister and with the joyous concurrence of the brother, who was smitten with the girl virtually on first sight. They take Anne Shirley into their home and soon enough the sister also has taken the little orphan into her heart.

In return, Anne falls madly in love with Green Gables, the Cuthbert farm. The highly imaginative girl quickly endows it with fanciful characteristics, changing place names and giving books, ponds, and patches of woods highly evocative associations, most of which are drawn from fairy tales. Anne has survived considerable hardship while growing up because she is able to use the power of pretending to make over what she regards as dreary and mundane facts into marvelous and beautiful inventions. Like Judy Abbott, like Rebecca Randall, like Sara Crewe, like Jo March, and like Charlotte Brontë herself, she is a creative young person with a superior sensibility and skills to match.

Over the next several years, Anne makes many friends, both young and old, in the community of Avonlea on Canada's Prince Edward Island. She attends school, excels in every subject she studies, passes the college entrance examination in a breeze, and is rewarded by a full scholarship at the end of her first year of teachers' college. It all seems so easy, and Anne is hovering on the threshold of a new and exciting phase to her life when Matthew drops dead of a heart attack, having read in his newspaper that the bank in which all his savings are held has failed. Immediately afterwards, Marilla is told by her doctor that she is going blind.

Anne inevitably does the right thing, and like Rebecca abandons plans to attend college so as to take a job teaching in the same local school from which she had a year before graduated, this so that the family farm does not have to be sold and her beloved foster mother put out to board. The novel ends there, not without hope however, for there is, as Anne Shirley realizes, always a bend farther on down the road, beyond which the eye cannot see. She has at the same time come to recognize the strong feelings she has for Gilbert Blythe, a youth of her own age with whom she has competed angrily ever since that day in school when he taunted Anne about her red hair, and the suggestion is that something more may follow from this.

"God's in his heaven, all's right with the world," are the last words whispered by the heroine, to which the reader is apt to respond, "A woman's reach must exceed her grasp, or what is heaven for?" Delightful as it is, there is much too much grasping and much too little reaching in *Anne of Green Gables*. Never has an orphan in English or American literature had such an easy time of it, for although Anne makes a number of very embarrassing and occasionally painful blunders as a young girl, she is seldom punished beyond being sent to her room without supper.

Even then, one or another of the Cuthberts usually relents, often because as it turns out Anne was entirely innocent of the act for which she is being reprimanded—a convention that goes all the way back to *Elsie Dinsmore.*

Although obviously derived from *Little Women, Sara Crewe,* and (especially) *Rebecca of Sunnybrook Farm,* there is in *Anne of Green Gables* none of the adversity that provides those other stories of young women a definable element of tension, even while contributing to their moral development. Anne is after all a very good girl, a likeable girl, even a loveable girl, with few enemies (and those impotent) and foster parents who love her to distraction. She is a bright and intelligent girl, a considerate girl, whose mistakes always result from well-intentioned but badly chosen actions or from becoming lost in the enchanted world of her imagination. She is one of Charles Lamb's Dream Children, come to comfort the Canadian equivalents of Charles and Mary, who are surely the most famous brother and sister act in our literature.

But then Anne Shirley is everyone's dream child, the daughter we all would like to have, a perpetual cause of laughter and good feelings, so much so that readers were willing to follow her further adventures through a number of equally good-hearted, amiable sequels, in which Anne is enabled to go off to college along with Gilbert Blythe, whom she eventually marries. They spend a delightful honeymoon in her dream cottage, but the happy part ends with the death of their baby, Joy; until that loss Anne's is a silken rope without a kink in it.

An orphan of ten when we first meet her, Anne has had a rough time of it in other foster homes and most recently in an orphanage, where as she says the place left "little scope for her imagination" (*Anne of Green Gables,* 12). But once taken into the Cuthbert home she is at last on the sunny side of the street. There is a night and a day of suspense—which the reader is not allowed to share—as to whether or not Anne will be adopted in lieu of the boy the Cuthberts wanted, but this only makes her happiness the greater, and most of her subsequent miseries are not very serious and are soon over. Thenceforth, scope for Anne's imagination is without limits.

Lacking the snarls we have earlier detected in the fabric of novels traceable back to Charlotte Brontë, *Anne of Green Gables* has no obvious subtext: what you read is pretty much what you get. There is sufficient intertextual larding to satisfy the historian of children's literature, but beyond this we are given no dark shadows of implication. Anne at the start resembles Jo March: she displays a fiercely proud temper, matched by and associated with her red hair, but not for very long. Like Rebecca, her creative imagination predictably gets her into trouble but somebody predictably always gets her out, often Anne herself, for she soon develops a handy way with ornate apologies. She deftly uses the fact that she is a poor orphan girl to wring pity from the hard hearts of her adversaries, who wilt like starched collars on a July afternoon. On and on she goes, like a rippling brook, the rocks and pebbles in the channel of which cause music not a discordant sound.

The Japanese people are ardent fans of L. M. Montgomery's books. Carrying the cameras that are the modern equivalent to scrip and scallop shell, they regularly make pilgrimages to the house on Prince Edward Island that is supposedly the one upon which Green Gables was modeled. Souvenirs and like items of association have a high demand in their country, yet another manifestation of the Mysterious Orient (as the old *New Yorker* used to put it). But perhaps in this instance the impulse is not so mysterious, given that the Japanese as a people if not as individuals admire persons who can get along with one another, for theirs is a large, overpopulated country, and Anne Shirley gets along with everybody. She also excels at academic competition, striving ferociously for gold medals and scholarships, goals the Japanese people encourage their children to achieve. Nor are the Japanese alone in their adulation, as the continuing sales of all Anne of Avonlea books in North America testify, but popularity is one thing, cultism is another.

Like so many of the authors we have been discussing, Lucy Maud Montgomery was a virtual orphan, having lost her parents as an infant and been raised by her grandparents, a situation that seems to have inspired the creation of the aging Cuthberts as foster parents. But as Montgomery informed Kunitz and Haycraft, shortly before she died in 1942, her immediate inspiration came from a note she had written for a story but then had forgotten, only to discover once again—"Elderly couple apply to orphan asylum for a boy. By mistake a girl is sent them."

That is the situation at the start of the novel, an amusing and for the girl a painful mixup, which is quickly resolved and never really picked up again, save toward the end. With old Matthew having suffered a series of heart attacks, Marilla belatedly recalls that the chief reason for wanting a boy was to help with the work on the farm. Why Anne Shirley could not have given a hand caring for stock and taking in hay tells us more about the middle-class milieu out of which the book emerged than it does about the realities of farm life in Canada and elsewhere. Farmers have always been equal opportunity employers especially where their own children are concerned.

For our purposes, the most interesting aspect of *Anne of Green Gables* is the extent to which Montgomery assembled a pastiche of every other novel then popular among young female readers. Gillian Avery declares that it "is unashamedly derived from *Rebecca*," but Wiggin's book as we have seen is itself derived from earlier stories (*Behold the Child*, 181). Still, *Rebecca* is the most obvious model, for the story starts with a young chatterbox dazzling her foster father as they head toward home in the Cuthbert buggy, a constant stream of highly imaginative talk that doesn't cease until she learns that she may have to go back to the orphanage, and even then after a suspenseful pause it begins again.

The situation clearly derives from the opening of Wiggin's novel, in which the imaginative little girl charms the whiskers off Jerry Cobb. Even the gender mistake, girl instead of boy, recalls the switch of Rebecca for the much more desirable because stolidly hard-working Hannah Randall. Call it *Rebecca Lite*—or *Sara Crewe Lite Fantastic*, in that much of what Anne Shirley talks about is a kind of imaginative exterior decorating, renaming features of the landscape and endowing them with fanciful characteristics, fairies being alive and well in the far eastern reaches of Canada.

There is the by now ritual explosion of temper, in which Anne tells off an opinionated neighbor who has made a rude evaluation of her physical appearance, and we learn that she is very sensitive about her flaming red hair as well. Like Jane Eyre, Ellen Montgomery, Elsie Dinsmore, and Jo March, Anne needs to curb her temper. Like Rebecca, she needs to rein in her imagination, which takes hold of her attention to such an extent that she often makes mistakes that irritate her foster mother, who like Miranda Sawyer is common sense and sharp Yankee wit personified, but without the edge.

Like Rebecca, Anne is innocent of bad intentions, but like Rebecca she gets into one scrape after another. Like Rebecca she has a powerful effect on all around her and is popular with children her age. Like Rebecca, she temporarily gives up her career to take care of her mother, in this case a foster parent, and although no Mr. Aladdin shows up to rescue Anne, having Gilbert in the neighborhood allows the novel to end on a hopeful romantic note. There is by contrast nothing of *Jane Eyre*'s dark gothic coloration, and if anything even less of *The Wide, Wide World* and *Elsie Dinsmore* with their emphasis on psychological humiliation as the low road to salvation.

As we have already noticed, there is a definable decline in unpleasantness in the novels that follow the lead of *Little Women,* as when we compared for example *Sara Crewe* with Burnett's subsequent revision. *Rebecca of Sunnybrook Farm,* having been published about the time *Sara Crewe* was revised as a play, also marks an improvement in matters of suffering. Judy Abbott in *Daddy-Long-Legs* is in a continuous intellectual ecstasy once she leaves the orphan asylum, and though irritated over her benefactor's dicatorial ways, she hardly suffers greatly from them, and Pollyanna until her terrible accident seems destiny's tot. Moreover, Pollyanna's pain is proof of her philosophical pudding, not something imposed upon her by a discipline- and repression-oriented Victorian society. We are in the process of leaving the world of strict morality behind us, along with the disturbing figure of the suffering female child. Notably, Martha Finley died in 1909, the year after *Anne of Green Gables* was published.

Ding, dong, the wicked witch was dead.

Admittedly, there is suffering and sacrifice in Montgomery's fable, but it is a matter of the heroine having been able to handle that culminating experience because of her essential compassion and sympathy, which in a sense reverses the sentimental process. That is, suffering and sacrifice does not result in maturity; maturity is evincing a capacity for handling sacrifice and suffering. Anne is quite willing to set aside her ambitious plans in order to take care of the woman who was willing to set aside her own plans and take a girl instead of a boy orphan into her home.

Anne of Green Gables is hardly a preachy book, and though a sympathetic minister's wife plays a role in making the heroine's life much better than it was (a situation borrowed from *The Chronicles of Rebecca*), there aren't the references to God the Father that characterize the novels by Susan Warner and Louisa Alcott. In this it is quite in keeping with its model, which regards salvation as chiefly a secular matter, and fits in as well with *Daddy-Long-Legs* which follows Montgomery's book in the chronological sequence.

And yet, there is a Canadian difference, and Montgomery's beloved book is part of it, for if *Anne of Green Gables* is a self-conscious copy of a number of popular books written by citizens of the United States, it is one that transcends them all in its own peculiar way. There is a detectable optimism in this novel, as I have already suggested, and, though like Rebecca, Anne gets into frequent trouble because of her dreamy and forgetful ways, and, though like Sara, she entertains her friends by making up endless stories, and, though like Cedric Errol, she spreads joy like soul-butter wherever she goes, there is neither the rebellious mischief of which Rebecca is capable nor the excessive sweetness associated with Fauntleroy.

Most important, after we add up all the similarities to books by those authors we call American, one great difference remains: no older rich man comes into Anne's young life and captures her heart beyond recall. Hers is not a story that fits the Cinderella pattern. Burnett escapes this necessity by keeping her heroines (and hero) well short of puberty, but Montgomery does not. The first of the Green Gables books ends with the heroine almost eighteen, and beginning to fall in love with her former arch-rival, a handsome young man who like herself (and her dead parents) has chosen schoolteaching as a career. This is a normal adolescent development, and is timed to match Anne's gradual abandonment of her imaginative transformations of the ordinary world around her. That is, the real world is increasingly sufficient, and fairyland is for dreamy little girls. Cinderella in this Canadian fable finds her Prince Charming living next door, not only a boy her own age but one even poorer than she.

There is certainly an element of the marvelous in Anne's effortless pilgrimage through the turbulent passages of life, but it is not so much so as to strain our credulity. It may seem too easy but that is because we expect a certain amount of danger in our popular literature, a sufficient number of disasters to hold our interest, as on the evening news. Here our attention is expected to be held by the story of an attractive and basically happy young woman who is having a good time thanks to the loving generosity of her foster parents, yet is of sufficiently strong character to shoulder responsibilities when they come. If Anne is the daughter we all wanted to have, then isn't she the girl we want our real daughters to imitate, to choose as a role model for themselves?

There is more. L. M. Montgomery, unlike Alcott and others of the American sisterhood, was not so far as I know associated with female suffrage or other reforms during the early years of the past century. Yet of all the books about little girls and young women we have been discussing (including *Daddy-Long-Legs*, with its suffragette leanings), surely hers is the most radical in terms of gender relationships. We find none of the willing abasement before male authority that distinguishes so many of these books, so often expressed by having young women fall in love with men old enough to be their fathers, and accepting corrections of various kinds at their hands. Moreover, Anne Shirley until well into her mid-teens mostly associates with female friends, and carries on a casual, one-on-one relationship with her foster father, Matthew, who obviously adores her but in an avuncular vein.

While maintaining throughout a fierce academic rivalry with Gilbert Blythe, a contest in which they are on entirely equal terms, Anne by the end of the story is falling in love with her opponent, a youth with no family wealth and only his looks and intelligence to recommend him. Short of bonding exclusively with her best friend, Diana, who for whatever reason is kept back from college by a domineering and socially self-conscious mother, it would be hard to posit a more positive profile of modern young womanhood. For all of Montgomery's indebtedness to *Rebecca of Sunnybrook Farm,* her *Anne of Green Gables* breaks free in this critical matter, and the heroine reveals herself not a true daughter of Jane Eyre but a startlingly modern if unmilitant example of maturity.

And there is nothing wrong with that.

Afterword

THIS STUDY WAS INITIALLY INSPIRED BY A RERUN IN THE LATE SEVenties of a television production of *Jane Eyre,* first released in 1971, which starred George C. Scott and Susannah York. Having grown up with the 1944 film version starring Orson Welles and Joan Fontaine, I was not at first happy with the gravel-voiced American actor as Rochester. But by the end of the story my allegiance was won by the power of Scott's performance, carried forward from the famous *Patton* role of the year before. I became even more loyal to the 1971 version after actually reading Brontë's novel, an omission that resulted from my not having taken a course in the Victorian novel as an undergraduate, and because my interest thenceforth—as here—was in American literature.

For it is clear that Rochester is a typical British squire, albeit Byronized, rough-edged and viscerally powerful, a man of horses and dogs, yet with deeply generous even tender impulses. His is a type far more suited to Scott's gruffly masculine manner than to the baby-faced, sensitive Welles, who was matched only by James Dean in his display of on-screen mannerisms associated with severe psychological dislocations.

Moreover, given that the fable underlying *Jane Eyre* is the fairy tale "Beauty and the Beast" (which, as Robert Martin demonstrated in 1977, overrides the familiar Cinderella connection once Jane reaches Thornfield), Scott is sufficiently leonine to carry that part off as well. And yet I was not inspired to read the novel by Scott's performance but by the final scene in the film, in which the badly injured Rochester is cradled in Jane's loving arms, a carefully arranged posture that suggested Michelangelo's *Pièta*—at least to me.

It was about this time I wrote for *New York* magazine an essay about recent books by Gail Sheehy and Joan Didion and the songs by Dory Previn inspired by the loss of her composer husband to Mia Farrow. The controlling thesis of the article had to do with the

341

prevalence of what, at the suggestion of Clay Felker, I called "the suffering woman," the figural counterpart to the "wounded man," personified in the complementary roles of the grieving Mary and her crucified Son. This dichotomy was carried down the centuries to nineteenth-century equivalents, exemplified by Longfellow's Evangeline and Hawthorne's Hester on the one hand and Melville's Ahab and Hawthorne's Dimmesdale on the other. These were powerful archetypes, and where R. W. B. Lewis's *The American Adam* had given early priority to the male side of the arrangement, the emerging interest by feminists in women's fiction soon began to rectify the imbalance.

The suffering woman in sentimental literature has long been regarded as a female Christ. But in the feminist perspective a woman drawing power from the Christian ideal can be seen as sapping strength from the figure of Christ himself. There is something in the arrangement that suggests the vampire and her victim, which Michelangelo's configuration can also be seen as exemplifying, and certainly the image of a woman cradling a wounded man in her arms connotes maternal strength on the one hand and a male regression to infantilism on the other.

In the instance of the final scene in the 1971 movie, which has no literal counterpart in the novel, the implied female dominance is validated by the situation at the end of the book. There Rochester is brought low by his wounds, blinded and crippled in a vain but noble attempt to save his mad wife from death. He is thereby made doubly acceptable as a husband to the long-suffering, self-denying Jane, Rochester now being not only single but impaired, because of a generous, self-sacrificing hence chivalric act.

We are (or at least I was) made to recall Oedipus at Colonus, in which the blind and shattered king is led to his final apotheosis by his loyal daughter Antigone. But the situation also looks forward to a critical episode in Owen Wister's popular *The Virginian* (1902), where the cowboy having been severely injured in an Indian ambush is nursed back to health by his schoolteacher sweetheart. Molly Stark has been packing to leave for the East when she discovers the man whose love she has rejected lying unconscious from his wounds.

In serving as the Virginian's nurse, Molly realizes the depth of her own love, where earlier his powerful and commanding physical presence has convinced her that he would be rejected as uncouth by her New England family. This may not be a healthy message, but it was certainly a popular one, and seems to owe its origins to the resolution of the romantic stalemate in Charlotte Brontë's novel.

Having read *Jane Eyre*, I went on to Brontë's other novels, and read *Wuthering Heights* as well, a literary feeding frenzy. I had never before encountered such ferocious energy in period fiction, such a display of archetypal power, albeit borrowed in part from the erotic energies associated with the Byronic hero, under whose spell both sisters were writing. After reading Elizabeth Gaskell's biography of Charlotte, with its account of the intense bond between the motherless Brontë children, the sere and distant father, the early loss of Maria and Elizabeth, the tragic decline and death of Branwell, I was drawn into the world at Haworth like many readers before me. I started to write a book about Charlotte's novels, which reached over eighty pages before other matters intervened. Parts of that projected study may be found in the first and second chapters of this book.

My original intention was to move on to those American authors contemporary with Charlotte and Emily who were also drawn into the Brontëan vortex, chiefly Hawthorne and Melville but also Emily Dickinson, who seems to have fancied herself the fourth Brontë sister. Hawthorne in his correspondence refers to the lives and works of the Brontës and it seemed to me that *The Scarlet Letter* would not have been written, at least not in the form it took, without the priority of *Jane Eyre* and *Wuthering Heights*. However, I never got that far, and subsequently learned that James Justus in 1960 had written an essay, "Beyond Gothicism," that pretty much sums up what was to be my thesis, at least regarding the influence of *Wuthering Heights* on Hawthorne and Melville.

In 1979 there appeared Sandra M. Gilbert and Susan Gubar's *The Madwoman in the Attic*, with its extended discussion of Emily Dickinson's identification with the Brontës. Moreover, their reading of the meaning of Bertha Mason Rochester (the titular madwoman) echoed even as it contradicted my thesis regarding that problematic figure. Therefore, by 1980 there seemed little sense in going on with what I had so enthusiastically begun. But then in 1985 there appeared Jane Tompkins's *Sensational Designs*, with its argument that a suffering woman in sentimental literature is a figure designed to empower women, where earlier—mostly male—critics had sneered at the mob of weeping ladies as exemplifying the superficiality of sentimentalism.

Though it ranged over a number of authors, including Charles Brockden Brown, Fenimore Cooper, Hawthorne, and Harriet Beecher Stowe, Tompkins's was in effect a book-length argument for the canonization of Susan Warner's *The Wide, Wide World,* a best-seller in 1851, chiefly because it validated her thesis regarding the suffering woman of sentimental fiction as an empowering literary convention. From Tompkins's description it appeared to me as though Warner was another (if neglected) American author operating under the Brontëan influence.

I read Warner's novel, and while appalled by what even Tompkins admits is a situational resemblance to *The Story of O,* I saw that *Wide, Wide World* was in part a response to Charlotte Brontë's novel. This argument was missing from Tompkins's study, which, like so much American criticism of American writers, tends to ignore the transatlantic exchange. Since my unfinished study had argued that *Jane Eyre* was in many ways a response to *Wuthering Heights,* which seemed to Charlotte a much too open display of sexual passion, Warner's intensely pious even evangelical novel provided a third line in an admittedly lopsided triangle.

By 1984, I had arrived at the University of Florida, where a program in children's literature had been started by John Cech, the protégé of my colleague at the University of Connecticut, the late Francilia Butler, a pioneer in introducing the study of children's literature to the college curriculum. Having already taught the subject at Storrs, I began to offer courses in what was the equivalent to young adult fiction in the nineteenth century, including novels originally intended for adults, like Scott's *Ivanhoe* and its American version, Cooper's *Last of the Mohicans,* but also books aimed at younger readers, like *Tom Sawyer* and *Little Women.* It was at Florida, also, that I met Jack Zipes, whose studies of the social and psychological implications of fairy tales have greatly influenced my own readings of the mythic undercurrents in popular literature aimed at juvenile readers.

It seemed to me obvious that Louisa May Alcott's classic had been written under the influence of both Charlotte Brontë's *Jane Eyre* and Gaskell's biography of the author. But it was also a response to *The Wide, Wide World,* which had at mid-century established the agenda for subsequent American novels about the maturation process of young, often orphaned, women. In its turn, *Little Women* provided a model for a number of American novels that followed, including *Rebecca of Sunnybrook Farm* and *The Secret Garden,* all of which responded as well to Warner's novel, with its pious correction of *Jane Eyre.* Unlike Brontë's gothic novel, these books were consciously aimed at a youthful, female readership, but most of them predictably followed the bildungsroman pattern first established in *Jane Eyre,* centered on the Dickensian theme of an orphan's search for a home and family.

I am not sure if authorial anxiety was a necessary characteristic of these books, each of which can be read as a response to the earlier examples, but influence most certainly was. The end result of the process was to move further and further away from the Brontëan model, with an increase in literary realism and a virtual abandonment of gothic elements. And yet one salient characteristic was carried through to the end of the process: most of these heroines on the American side of the ocean found her equivalent Mr. Rochester, an older man who becomes either a loving or at the least a benevolent force in their lives. That is to say, beyond style, beyond matters of plot and characterization, the curious archetype endured.

My early reaction to Brontë's novel had at the time been informed by two important feminist studies that were already available, Ellen Moers's *Literary Women* (1976) and Elaine Showalter's *A Literature of Their Own: British Women Novelists from Brontë to Lessing* (1977), in which references to Charlotte Brontë and her influence appear throughout. I was subsequently helped by a number of essays in *The Voyage In: Fictions of Female Development* (1983), edited by Elizabeth Abel, Marianne Hirsche, and Elizabeth Langland, the last of whom as my colleague at the University of Florida kindly read and constructively commented on that eighty-page draft of my never-completed book on the Brontëan matrix.

Let me also cite as helpful Nina Baym's comprehensive *Woman's Fiction: A Guide to Novels by and about Women in America, 1820–1870* (1978). I am especially indebted to Baym's initial and unqualified statement that "women's fiction developed indigenously in America, and showed itself relatively impermeable to the influence of the major women writers in England during the Victorian age," although "signs of George Eliot and of Charlotte Brontë can be discerned in writing of the 1860s" (30). Thenceforth, not a single reference to the Brontës appears, perhaps because Baym regards the emergence of "girl's fiction" (starting with *Elsie Dinsmore* and *Little Women*) as both a departure and a decline from the tradition of woman's fiction she has been defining.

And yet Baym devoted a number of pages to a discussion of *The Wide, Wide World,* which seems to have been (if Alcott's testimony counts) read by the same audience for which *Little Women* was intended. The same may be said of Mary Kelley's *Private Woman,*

Public Stage: Literary Domesticity in Nineteenth-Century America (1984), which makes frequent reference to Susan Warner and her monstrous novel, but without establishing what we can call the Brontëan connection. Of course, Kelley is interested in the emergence and development of domestic fiction, and Charlotte Brontë has been classed with her sister Emily as a gothic novelist, which as I have suggested is not entirely accurate.

In 1994 there appeared Gillian Avery's *Behold the Child: American Children and Their Books, 1621–1922,* which in several pages anticipated the genesis traced here of American books intended for young female readers, from *The Wide, Wide World* to *Anne of Green Gables.* Avery's stress is on the repeated pattern in those novels of mean maiden aunts and long-suffering orphan girls, which she credits to the influence of Catharine Sedgwick's *A New-England Tale,* while acknowledging the prominence of Susan Warner's popular novel.

My own emphasis, as the reader should know by now, is on the archetype provided by Cinderella, as well as the trope presumably inspired by *Jane Eyre* of a love between a young woman and a handsome, magnetic older man, passed over briefly by Avery. I am pleased however to acknowledge her priority in establishing the continuities in American books aimed at girls and young women and pointing out the British differences, as well as in recognizing the literary value of novels like *Rebecca of Sunnybrook Farm,* which can take adult readers by surprise.

In 1995 I offered a summer seminar at Dartmouth College funded by the National Endowment for the Humanities, entitled "Kids in Bindings: Strategies of Socialization in Children's Literature of the Golden Age." Four of the eight weeks were taken up with a discussion of the texts used here, from *Jane Eyre* to *Secret Garden,* along lines used here as well, and which formed the basis of this book, the writing of which was already under way. It was finished by 2000, when Christine Doyle's *Louisa May Alcott and Charlotte Brontë* appeared, a study in influence that is necessarily much more thorough than mine, in that it considers the impact of all of Brontë's works on Alcott's entire corpus.

Doyle's thesis, despite different points of emphasis, is in essential agreement with my own, for which I am thankful. In considering the "Transatlantic Translations" of Brontë's novels by Alcott, she too finds that the American author was uneasy about the implications of the other writer's works, which she labored to correct. However, Doyle does not consider the intervening influence of *The Wide,Wide World.*, which is essential to my own interpretation of *Little Women.*

Let me conclude by saying that of the writing of books about the Brontës there is no end. Had I set out to read them all I would still be at it. Everything starts, as did I, with Elizabeth Gaskell's *Life,* and back in the Seventies I read as a corrective E. F. Benson's *Charlotte Brontë* (1932). Benson was one of the first to set the record straight regarding Gaskell's stretchers: reacting to her sentimentalized portrait, and operating under the influence of Lytton Strachey, Benson presents a negative view of Charlotte Brontë's character which has offended her admirers. Given the evidence of Brontë's letters and journals, Benson's revision is difficult to gainsay, though perhaps it was overstated in order to overturn Gaskell's hegemony.

When one considers the architecture of modern Brontë biography, Winifred Gerin's 1967 study of "The Evolution of Genius" is the necessary foundation stone, to which Margot Peter's *Unquiet Soul* (1975) provides a more strictly biographical alternative. Of several more recent studies, I cite Rebecca Fraser's *The Brontës* (1988), which turns out to be chiefly about Charlotte, virtually inevitable, given how little we know about Anne and Emily. I found Fraser's book both readable and informative and useful for my purposes, the author having absorbed much recent scholarship about the problematic relationship between Charlotte and Professor Heger and produced a balanced account not only of Patrick Brontë's difficult personality but of Branwell's scandalous last years. Perhaps the most thorough work of revisionism is Juliet Barker's *The Brontës* (1992), a massive instance of investigative scholarship, but it only amplifies and does not modify Fraser's efforts to offset the influence of Elizabeth Gaskell.

In sum, recent biographers have done good work by correcting the errors in Gaskell's popular biography. Their books however arrived a century too late to undo its mischief, if indeed that is what it was, given its role in arousing sympathy for a writer whose public character had suffered from unfair and as Brontë saw it unnecessarily cruel because ignorant reviews. Of those who had been close to Charlotte, it was her husband Arthur Nicholls who was most hurt by Gaskell's book, and modern biographers have relieved him of any condign complicity in her death through callous negligence—the implication of Gaskell's account. Something perhaps should be said here, albeit briefly, about an historical romance lately published which not only accuses Arthur of poisoning his bride but Charlotte of poisoning her sisters, suggesting that the work of correcting Gaskell's imbalance has perhaps gone too far.

This paranoid theory escapes ridicule only because it is posed as fiction, and as such it points back across a century and a half to the way in which Gaskell warped Charlotte into the web of her own fictions, becoming type and symbol of the noble little woman suffering from solitude and for her art, which perhaps more than Brontë's novels worked its influence on so many later and mostly American novelists. Had Gaskell not written the biography when she did, things surely would have turned out differently, and I would not have had this book to write. That in itself might have been just as well, but in adding another to the pile of books about the Brontës, I do so with a clear conscience, this being for the most part not a book about the Brontës.

That voluminous tradition is the subject of a recent study by Lucasta Miller, *The Brontë Myth* (2003), which I have just now this January of 2004 read with considerable satisfaction, because Miller substantiates at length the thesis I arrived at some years ago regarding the intervening influence of Gaskell's biography on the posthumous reception of *Jane Eyre*. She quotes Henry James's complaint in this regard but does not otherwise deal with the impact of the resultant "intellectual muddle" on American fiction, an omission for which I am grateful. Moreover, Miller also validates the ongoing feminist thesis about Jane Eyre's rebelliousness, which I regard as an aspect of her personality that will be corrected by having her eagerly accept the domestic necessity. Finally, Miller's subject is the changing cultural grid imposed on the authors' lives by the Brontës' many biographers, for hers is a book about books about the "wierd sisters" of Haworth (Ted Hughes's epithet), where this is not.

Bibliography

I WOULD LIKE TO BEGIN THIS LIST OF PRIMARY AND SECONDARY SOURCES WITH A citation of two invaluable resources, both edited by Stanley J. Kunitz and Howard Haycraft, *American Authors, 1600–1900* (New York: H. W. Wilson Company, 1938) and *Twentieth Century Authors* (New York: H. W. Wilson Company, 1942). These volumes contain material on writers deemed secondary and tertiary by the academy, and have proved, along with the *Dictionary of American Biography*, edited by Allen Johnson (New York: Charles Scribner's Sons, 1943 edition with supplement volumes), and its necessary update, the *American National Biography*, edited by John A. Garrety and Mark L. Carnes (New York: Oxford University Press, 1999), to be extraordinarily helpful in providing background material.

Primary Texts

In all instances where possible, primary texts cited in this study have been easily available paperback editions.

Alcott, Louisa May. *Behind a Mask: The Unknown Thrillers of Louisa May Alcott*. With an Introduction by Madeline Stern. New York: William Morrow, 1975.

———. *The Journals of Louisa May Alcott*. Edited by Joel Myerson and Daniel Shealy, with an Introduction by Madeline B. Stern. Boston: Little, Brown, 1989.

———. *Little Women*. Edited with an Introduction by Elaine Showalter. New York: Penguin Books, 1989.

———. *Moods*. (Boston, 1864.) Edited with an Introduction by Sarah Elbert. American Women Writers Series. New Brunswick, N.J.: Rutgers University Press, 1991. (For the 1882 edition, see the entry below.)

———. *The Portable Louisa May Alcott*. Edited with an Introduction by Elizabeth Lennox Keyser. (Contains the 1882 version of *Moods*.) New York: Penguin Books, 2000.

———. *Work*. Edited with an Introduction by Joy S. Kasson. New York: Penguin Books, 1994.

Arnim, Bettina von. *Goethe's Correspondence with a Child*. Boston, 1859.

Bashkirtseff, Maria Constantinova. *The Journal of Marie Bashkirtseff*. 2 vols. Translated with an Introduction by Mathilde Blind. London, 1890.

Brontë, Anne. *The Tenant of Wildfell Hall*. Edited with an Introduction and Notes by Stevie Davis. New York: Penguin Books, 1996.

Brontë, Charlotte. "Emma: A Fragment." (See under *The Professor* below.)

————. *Jane Eyre*. Edited with an Introduction and Notes by Michael Mason. New York: Penguin Books, 1996.

————. *The Professor* [and] "Emma" A Fragment." With an introduction by Margaret Lane. New York: Dutton, Everyman's Library, 1975.

————. *Shirley*. Edited by Andrew and Judith Hook. New York: Penguin Books, 1974.

————. *Villette*. Edited by Mark Lilly with an Introduction by Tony Tanner. New York: Penguin Books, 1979.

Brontë, Emily. *Wuthering Heights*. Edited by David Daiches. New York: Penguin Books, 1965.

Burnett, Frances Hodgson. *Little Lord Fauntleroy*. With an Afterword by Phyllis Bixler. New York: Signet Classic, 1992.

————. *The Little Princess*. With an Introduction and Notes by U. C. Knoepflmacher. New York: Penguin Books, 2002.

————. *The One I Knew the Best of All*. New York: Charles Scribner's Sons, 1893.

————. *Sara Crewe, or What Happened at Miss Minchin's*. New York: Charles Scribner's Sons, 1888.

————. *The Secret Garden*. With an Afterword by Faith McNulty. New York: Signet Classics, 1987.

Complete Fortune-Teller and Dream Book. New York: n.p., 1829.

Davis, Rebecca Harding. *A Rebecca Harding Davis Reader*. Edited by Jean Pfaelzer. Pittsburgh, Pa.: University of Pittsburgh Press, 1995.

Dickens, Charles. *The Old Curiosity Shop*. Edited by Angus Easton with an introdction by Malcolm Andrews. New York: Penguin Books, 1972.

Finley, Martha. *Elsie Dinsmore*. New York: Dodd, Mead & Company, 1893.

Montgomery, L. M. *Anne of Green Gables*. New York: Gramercy Books, 1985.

Pestalozzi, Johan Heinrich. *Pestalozzi's Leonard and Gertrude*. Translated and abridged by Eva Channing. Boston: Ginn, Heath, & Co., 1885.

Porter, Eleanor H. *Pollyanna*. With an Afterword by Lois Lowry. New York: Dell, 1986.

————. *Pollyanna Grows Up*. New York: Puffin Books, 1996.

Thackeray, William Makepeace. "The Last Sketch." (Included with "Emma: A Fragment" in Charlotte Brontë, *The Professor*, above, pp. 239–42.)

————. *The Letters and Private Papers of William Makepeace Thackeray*. 4 vol. Edited by Gordon N. Ray. Cambridge: Harvard University Press, 1946.

Tully, James. *The Crimes of Charlotte Brontë. The Secrets of a Mysterious Family: A Novel*. New York: Carroll and Graf, 1999.

Warner, Susan. *The Wide, Wide World*. With an Afterword by Jane Tompkins. New York: City University of New York, Feminist Press, 1987.

Webster, Jean. *Daddy-Long-Legs*. New York: Puffin Books, 1989.

————. *Dear Enemy*. Mattituck, N.Y.: Amereon House, n.d.

Wiggin, Kate Douglas. *The Birds' Christmas Carol, The Story of Patsy, Timothy's Quest, and Other Stories. The Writings of Kate Douglas Wiggin*. Quillcote Edition. Vol. 1. With an Introduction by Frances Hodgson Burnett. Boston: Houghton Mifflin, 1917.

———. *My Garden of Memory: An Autobiography.* Boston: Houghton Mifflin Company, 1923.

———. *The New Chronicles of Rebecca. The Writings of Kate Douglas Wiggin.* Vol. 7.

———. *Rebecca of Sunnybrook Farm.* New York: Puffin Books, 1994.

Secondary Texts

Abel, Elizabeth, Marianne Hirsche, and Elizabeth Langland, eds. *The Voyage In: Fictions of Female Development.* Hanover, N.H.: University of New England Press, 198.

Anthony, Katharine. *Louisa May Alcott.* New York: Alfred A. Knopf, 1938.

Avery, Gillian. *Behold the Child: American Children and Their Books, 1621–1922.* London: The Bodley Head, 1994.

———. *Childhood's Pattern: A Study of the Heroes and Heroines of Children's Fiction, 1770–1950.* London: Hodder and Stoughton, 1975.

———. *Nineteenth Century Children: Heroes and Heroines in English Children's Stories, 1780–1900.* London: Hodder and Stoughton, 1965.

Barker, Juliet. *The Brontës.* New York: St. Martin's, 1992.

Baym, Nina. *Woman's Fiction: A Guide to Novels by and about Women in America, 1820– 1870.* Ithaca: Cornell University Press, 1978.

Benson, E. F. *Charlotte Brontë.* New York: Longmans, Green, 1932.

Bixler, Phillis. *The Secret Garden: Nature's Magic.* New York: Twayne Publishers, 1996.

Branch, E. Douglas. *The Sentimental Years: 1836–1860.* New York: D. Appleton-Century, 1934.

Burnett, Vivian. *The Romantick Lady (Frances Hodgson Burnett): The Life Story of an Imagination.* New York: Charles Scribner's Sons, 1927.

Chase, Richard. "The Brontës, or Myth Domesticated," in *Forms of Modern Fiction.* Edited by William Van O'Connor. Minneapolis: University of Minnesota Press, 1948, pp. 102–13.

Cowie, Alexander. *The Rise of the American Novel.* New York: American Book, 1951.

Douglas, Ann. *The Feminization of American Culture.* New York: Alfred A. Knopf, 1977.

Doyle, Christine. *Louisa May Alcott and Charlotte Brontë: Transatlantic Translations.* Knoxville: University of Tennessee Press, 2000.

Dry, Florence Swinton. *Brontë Sources I. The Sources of "Wuthering Heights."* Cambridge: W. Heffer & Sons, 1937.

———. *Brontë Sources II. The Sources of "Jane Eyre."* Cambridge: W. Heffer & Sons, 1940.

du Maurier, Daphne. *The Infernal World of Branwell Brontë.* Garden City, N.Y.: Doubleday, 1961.

Dundes, Alan, ed. *Cinderella: A Casebook.* New York: Wildman Press, 1983.

Edwards, Mike. *Charlotte Brontë: The Novels.* New York: St. Martin's Press, 1999.

Elbert, Sarah. *A Hunger for Home: Louisa May Alcott's Place in American Culture*. New Brunswick, N.J.: Rutgers University Press, 1987.

Foster, Edward Halsey. *Susan and Anna Warner*. Boston: Twayne Publishers, n.d.

Fraser, Rebecca. *The Brontës: Charlotte Brontë and Her Family*. New York: Crown Publishers, 1988.

Gaskell, Elizabeth. *The Life of Charlotte Brontë*. With an Introduction and Notes by Elizabeth Jay. New York: Penguin Books, 1997.

Gates, Barbara Timm. *Critical Essays on Charlotte Brontë*. Boston: G. K. Hall, 1990.

Gerin, Winifred. *Branwell Brontë*. London: Thomas Nelson and Sons, 1961.

———. *Charlotte Brontë: The Evolution of Genius*. London: Oxford University Press, 1967.

Gilbert, Sandra M., and Susan Gubar. *The Madwoman in the Attic: The Woman Writer and the Nineteenth-Century Literary Imagination*. New Haven: Yale University Press, 1984.

Hoeveler, Diane Long, and Lisa Jadwin. *Charlotte Brontë*. New York: Twayne Publishers, 1997.

Justus, James. "Beyond Gothicism: *Wuthering Heights* and an American Tradition." *Tennessee Studies in Literature* 5 (1960): 25–33.

Kelley, Mary. *Private Woman, Public Stage: Literary Domesticity in Nineteenth-Century America*. New York: Oxford University Press, 1984.

Keyser, Elizabeth Lennox. *Whispers in the Dark: The Fiction of Louisa May Alcott*. Knoxville: University of Tennessee Press, 1993.

Kolbenschlag, Madonna. *Kiss Sleeping Beauty Good-Bye: Breaking the Spell of Feminine Myths and Models*. Garden City, N.Y.: Doubleday, 1975.

Laski, Marghanita. *Mrs. Ewing, Mrs. Molesworth, Mrs. Hodgson Burnett*. London: Arthur Barker, 1950.

Marcus, Steven. *The Other Victorians: A Study of Sexuality and Pornography in Mid-Nineteenth Century England*. New York: Basic Books, 1974.

Martin, Robert K. "Jane Eyre and the World of Faery." *Mosaic, A Journal for the Comparative Study of Literature and Ideas* 10 (Summer): 85–95.

Maynard, John. *Charlotte Brontë and Sexuality*. Cambridge: Cambridge University Press, 1982.

McGillis, Roderick. *A Little Princess: Gender and Empire*. New York: Twayne Publishers, 1996.

Miller, Lucasta. *The Brontë Myth*. New York: Alfred A. Knopf, 2003.

Modleski, Tania. *Loving with a Vengeance: Mass Produced Fantasies for Women*. New York: Methuen, 1984.

Moers, Ellen. *Literary Women*. Garden City, N.Y.: Doubleday, 1976.

Pattee, Fred Lewis. *The Feminine Fifties*. New York: D. Appleton-Century, 1940.

Peters, Margot. *Unquiet Soul; A Biography of Charlotte Brontë*. New York: Doubleday, 1975.

Russ, Joanna. *To Write Like a Woman: Essays in Feminism and Science Fiction*. Bloomington: Indiana University Press, 1995.

Saxon, Martha. *Louisa May: A Modern Biography of Louisa May Alcott*. Boston: Houghton Mifflin, 1977.

Showalter, Elaine, ed. *Alternative Alcott.* New Brunswick, N.J.: Rutgers University Press, 1988.

——. *A Literature of Their Own: British Women Novelists from Brontë to Lessing.* Princeton: Princeton University Press, 1977.

——. *Sister's Choice: Tradition and Change in American Women's Writing.* The Clarendon Lectures, 1989. Oxford: Clarendon Press, 1991.

Simpson, Alan, and Mary Simpson, *with* Ralph Connor. *Jean Webster, Storyteller.* N.p.: Tymor Associates, Stinehour Press, 1984.

Stern, Madeline B. *Louisa May Alcott.* Norman: University of Oklahoma Press, 1950.

Thorslev, Peter, Jr. *The Byronic Hero: Types and Prototypes.* Minneapolis: University of Minnesota Press, 1961.

Thwaite, Ann. *Waiting for the Party: The Life of Frances Hodgson Burnett.* New York, Scribner: 1974.

Tompkins, Jane. *Sensational Designs: The Cultural Work of American Fiction, 1790–1860.* New York: Oxford University Press, 1985.

Wilson, Edmund. "The Ambiguity of Henry James." *Hound and Horn* 7 (1934): 385–406.

Zipes, Jack. *Fairy Tales and the Art of Subversion: The Classical Genre for Children and the Process of Civilization.* New York: Routledge, 1991. (First published in 1983.)

——. *Fairy Tales as Myth / Myth as Fairy Tale.* Lexington: University Press of Kentucky, 1994.

——. *Happily Ever After: Fairy Tales, Children, and the Culture Industry.* New York: Routledge, 1997.

Index